Across Centuries and Cultures

Across Centuries and Cultures

Musicological Studies in Honor of
Joachim Braun

Edited by
Kevin C. Karnes and Levi Sheptovitsky

PETER LANG
Frankfurt am Main · Berlin · Bern · Bruxelles · New York · Oxford · Wien

Bibliographic Information published by the Deutsche Nationalbibliothek
The Deutsche Nationalbibliothek lists this publication in the Deutsche Nationalbibliografie; detailed bibliographic data is available in the internet at http://dnb.d-nb.de.

Cover Design:
Olaf Gloeckler, Atelier Platen, Friedberg

Cover illustration:
Michael Praetorius „Syntagma Musicum II, De Organographia"
Wolfenbüttel 1619
(faksimilie-reprint), edited by Wilibald Gurlitt.
Reproduced by kind permission from
Bärenreiter Verlag / Kassel

The publication of this book was made possible by the financial support of the Bar-Ilan University Research Fund and the University President Fund.

ISBN 978-3-631-59986-0
© Peter Lang GmbH
Internationaler Verlag der Wissenschaften
Frankfurt am Main 2010
All rights reserved.

All parts of this publication are protected by copyright. Any utilisation outside the strict limits of the copyright law, without the permission of the publisher, is forbidden and liable to prosecution. This applies in particular to reproductions, translations, microfilming, and storage and processing in electronic retrieval systems.

www.peterlang.de

Contents

Introduction.. 11

Publications by Joachim Braun: A Partial List................................. 13

Music in Ancient Israel and Jewish Music

Amnon Shiloah
King David and the Devil, Initiators of Two Kinds of Music............ 21

Mira Waner
Ethnic/Religious Distinction Versus Syncretism in the
Musical Culture of Roman and Byzantine Sepphoris:
A Case Study in the Musical Culture of Ancient Israel.................... 29

Jan Stęszewski
Mündliche Musiktradition der Juden in Polen:
Forschungsaufgaben, Ausgangspunkte, Methodik,
Informations- und Quellen-Forschungsstand................................... 51

Alexander Knapp
The Little Goat Meets the Little Chicken: Parallels Between
Two Celebratory Songs in the Jewish and Bukharan Traditions....... 57

Bret Werb
Vu ahin zol ikh geyn? Music of Jewish Displaced Persons............... 75

Rachel Kollender
Jewish Music in the Holocaust as an Assertion of Plural
Identities.. 93

Baltic Musics

Kevin C. Karnes
"Where Space Becomes Time": Music, Landscape, and
Memory in the Latvian Rock Opera *Lāčplēsis*................................ 111

Mikus Čeže
Latvijas Nacionālā Opera und ihre Geburtsdeutungen.
Das Problem von deplazierten Jubiläen.. 139

Dagmāra Beitnere
Musicology and Power in the Discourse of Soviet Latvian
History and Memory... 151

Rūta Stanevičiūtė
Écriture féminine? On Some Intertextual Gestures in
Works by Contemporary Lithuanian Women Composers..................... 169

Vizbulīte Bērziņa
"On a Road to Hell": Jēkabs Graubiņš and the Soviet Regime............... 187

Musical Instruments

Werner Bachmann
Die skythisch-sarmatische Harfe aus Olbia:
Vorbericht zur Rekonstruktion eines unveröffentlichten
und im Kriege verschollenen Musikinstruments................................. 199

Zdravko Blažeković
Perseus, the Harp, and the Scimitar: Iconographic Confusion
as Evidence for Early Terminology for the Harp................................. 213

Myrna Herzog
The Division Viol: An Overview.. 221

Free Historical Subjects

Levon Hakobian
Octoëchos as an Idea: On the Example of Medieval
Armenian Sacred Hymnody... 245

Dagmar Hoffmann-Axthelm
Simone Martini's *Investiture of St. Martin*:
An Iconographical Approach... 253

Fabio Carboni and Agostino Ziino
Una raccolta di mottetti per Leone X: una scoperta e
nuove osservazioni.. 271

Levi Sheptovitsky
Two Chromatic Fantasias by John Dowland: Were They
Composed as a Pair? 291

Wolfgang Ruf
Religiöse Musik und Politik:
Die Aufführung von Händels "Messias" in Berlin 1786..................... 315

Bathia Churgin
Beethoven and the New Development-Theme in Sonata-
Form Movements... 327

Frans C. Lemaire
Dimitri Chostakovitch: Rester et résister... 345

Tatyana Kurysheva
Music Criticism as an Art of Perception.. 359

Notes on Contributors.. 369

Introduction

There is hardly need to open the present volume with a recitation of Joachim Braun's accomplishments as a scholar. In terms of productivity and the scope of his work, the list of publications that follows this introduction speaks for itself. In terms of influence, it is fair to say that Joachim's work has fundamentally altered the scholarly landscape of both of his principal fields: Baltic music and Jewish music. In the 1980s, when serious and critical scholarship on musical life in the Soviet Union was scarce in the English-speaking world, Joachim almost single-handedly opened up what has since become a vital field of musicological research by publishing a series of articles on Latvian music and editing a special, music-related issue of the *Journal of Baltic Studies* (1983)—a volume he presciently described at the time as constituting "formal documentation of the birth of Western Baltic musicology."[1] Although writing from Israel (to which he emigrated in 1972), Joachim's writings on Baltic topics have exerted a powerful influence upon intellectual life in his native Latvia as well. Initially banned, his scholarly essays were widely circulated with the thaw in the cultural climate of the Gorbachev years. And as they were read, they had the effect, as one Latvian scholar recalls, of providing "those remaining in Latvia with a theoretically grounded understanding"—the first non-Marxist-Leninist theoretical understanding —"of Baltic musical languages."[2] Indeed, as another Latvian scholar observes, "Braun's leaving in some way turned into a positive element for Latvian musicology, since, in the West, he had the opportunity to write freely about Latvian and Baltic themes, an activity not possible in Soviet Latvia."[3]

With respect to the primary focus of his research of the past two decades, Jewish music and iconography, Joachim's contributions have been no less monumental. His book *Die Musikkultur Altisraels/Palästinas* (1999)—revised, expanded, and translated as *Music in Ancient Israel/Palestine* (2002)—has been hailed as an exquisite example of "exactly what music archaeology and music

---

See also: *Musik in Geschichte und Gegenwart*, Personenteil. Ed. L. Finscher (Kassel: Baerenreiter, 1999), iii: 774-5; *The New Grove Dictionary of Music and Musicians*. Ed. S. Sadie (London: Macmillan, 2001), iv: 261.

1 Joachim Braun, introduction to *Baltic Musicology*, special issue of the *Journal of Baltic Studies* 14, no. 1 (1983), 3.
2 Dagmāra Beitnere, "Musicology and Power in the Discourse of Soviet Latvian History and Memory," in this volume.
3 Martin Boiko, introduction to Joachim Braun, *Studies: Music in Latvia* (Riga, 2002), liv-lv (I have changed the tense from present to past in the quotation given here). This latter volume, edited by Boiko, anthologizes many of Braun's most important studies of Latvian and Baltic musics, originally published in the 1950s through the 1980s.

iconography aims to achieve."[4] It is a study in which traditional assumptions and methodologies regnant in the field are "turned upside down."[5] Indeed, it is fair to say that the work has become a classic. As yet another reviewer writes, the volume provides "the most comprehensive treatment of its subject that is likely to appear for a very long time."[6] As in the case of his contributions to Baltic musicology, Joachim's impact upon the study of Jewish music and music iconography has been incalculable, and it will surely remain so for many years to come.[7]

For those who have had the privilege of knowing and working with Joachim personally, however, his famous kindness and generosity, his razor-sharp mind, and his seemingly boundless energy have made some of the most lasting impressions. This is certainly true for the editors of the present volume. Upon arriving in Israel from Russia, Levi Sheptovitsky found in Joachim a welcoming, encouraging teacher who helped him not only to become a scholar but to "solve," as he recalls, "the problems of everyday life." For Kevin Karnes, who had known Joachim's scholarship for years before meeting him in person, Joachim's attention and enthusiasm provided invaluable validation at the early stages of a young scholar's career, and Joachim's professional experience opened up numerous opportunities for life-changing collaborative work. Along similar lines, perhaps the greatest tribute to Joachim's legacy is the roster of scholars who have contributed to the present book. The project began modestly, with nine essays and an introduction. Soon, however, it began to grow—first to thirteen, then to sixteen, and ultimately to the twenty-two essays presented here. As word spread of the project's existence, the editors were literally besieged with essays submitted by scholars seeking to contribute. Without a doubt, every contributor to this volume could share fond recollections of personal experiences with Joachim similar to those recounted above. In lieu of doing so, we present to him, on the occasion of his eightieth birthday, this garland of our writings.

Kevin C. Karnes
Levi Sheptovitsky
Atlanta and Jerusalem

---

4   Martin van Schaik, review of *Music in Ancient Israel/Palstine* by Joachim Braun, *Music in Art* 27, nos. 1-2 (2002), 162-63.

5   John Arthur Smith, review of *Music in Ancient Israel/Palstine* by Joachim Braun, *Music and Letters* 85, no. 1 (2004), 95.

6   J.W. Rogerson, review of *Die Musikkultur Altisraels/Palästinas* by Joachim Braun, *Journal for the Study of the Old Testament* 89 (2000), 100.

7   Many of Braun's shorter studies of Jewish topics, originally appearing between 1982 and 2004, are collected in his recent volume *On Jewish Music: Past and Present* (Frankfurt am Main and Berlin, 2006).

Publications by Joachim Braun: A Partial List

Monographs and Other Authored Books

Vijole un alts [The violin and viola; in Latvian] (Riga, 1961).
Vijolmākslas attīstība Latvijā [The development of violin playing in Latvia; in Latvian] (Riga, 1962).
Vijolspēles metodika [Methods of violin playing; in Latvian] (Riga, 1969).
Jews in Soviet Music (Jerusalem, 1977).
A Report Concerning the Authentic Performance of Beethoven's Fourth Symphony (with B. Churgin) (Ramat Gan, 1977).
Jews and Jewish Elements in Soviet Music (Tel Aviv, 1978).
Shostakovich's Jewish Songs "From Jewish Folk Poetry," Op. 79: Introductory Essay with Original Yiddish Folk Text Underlay [in English, Russian, Hebrew, and Yiddish] (Tel Aviv, 1989).
Die Musikkultur Altisraels/Palästinas. Studien zu archaeologischen, schriftlichen und vergleichenden Quellen (Göttingen, 1999).
Music in Ancient Israel/Palestine: Archaeological, Written and Comparative Sources (Grand Rapids, MI, and Cambridge, 2002).
Studies: Music in Latvia [in English, Latvian, and German] (Riga, 2002).
On Jewish Music: Past and Present (Frankfurt am Main, 2006).

Edited Volumes

Latviešu komponistu skaņdarbi vijolei un klavierēm [Works for violin and piano by Latvian composers; score anthology] (with V. Sturesteps) (Riga, 1966).
Kratkaya evreyskaya entsiklopediya [Brief encyclopedia of Judaism; in Russian] (area editor) (Jerusalem, 1976-96).
Baltic Musicology, special issue of the *Journal of Baltic Studies* 14, no. 1 (1983).
Selected Writings on Latvian Music: A Bibliography (with K. Brambats) (Münster, 1985).
Verfemte Musik. Komponisten in den Diktaturen unseres Jahrhunderts (with V. Karbusický and H.T. Hoffman) (Frankfurt am Main, 1995; 2nd ed., 1997).
Socio-Musical Sciences: Congress Report HISM-88 (with U. Sharvit) (Ramat Gan, 1998).
Baltic Musics/Baltic Musics: The Landscape Since 1991 (with K.C. Karnes), special issue of the *Journal of Baltic Studies* 39, no. 3 (2008); reprint, London and New York, 2009.

Post-War Musicology in the Baltic States of Lithuania, Latvia and Estonia: A Reassessment. Papers Read at the 39th World Conference of the ICTM, Vienna, Austria, 2007 (with K.C. Karnes), special issue of *Musikgeschichte in Mittel- und Osteuropa* 12 (2008).

Selected Articles, Chapters, and Shorter Studies

"Čeští hudebníci v Lotyšsku" [Czech musicians in Latvia; in Czech], *Praha-Moskva* (June 1959): 365-69.
"Latvijas Valsts Konservatorijas vijolu klases" [The violin classes of the Latvian State Conservatory; in Latvian], *Karogs* (November 1959): 124-31.
"No latviešu instrumentālas muzikas vēstures" [From the history of Latvian instrumental music; in Latvian], in: *Latviešu mūzika* 2 (1962): 115-31.
"Instrumentālas atskaņotājmākslas attīstība Padomju Latvijā [The development of instrumental performance in Soviet Latvia; in Latvian], *Latviešu mūzika* 4 (1965): 51-73.
"Rihārds Vāgners Rīgā: 1837-1839" [Richard Wagner in Riga, 1837-1839; in Latvian], *Latviešu mūzika* 5 (1966): 287-312.
"Zreyushchïy talant: muzïka Paula Dambisa" [A maturing talent: the music of Pauls Dambis; in Russian], *Sovetskaya muzïka* (March 1970): 38-41.
"Vītola vēstules Ljadovam un Glazunovam: publikācija un komentārijs [Letters by Vītols to Lyadov and Glazunov: publication and commentary; in Latvian], *Karogs* (June 1968): 125-33.
"Rizhskie godi" [Riga years; in Russian], in *Ispolnitel'skoe iskusstvo zarubezhnikh stran: Bruno Walter*, ed. G. Edelshtein (Moscow, 1969), 299-329.
"Die Anfänge des Instrumentenspiels in Lettland," in *Musik des Ostens* 6, ed. Fritz Feldmann (Kassel, 1971), 88-126.
"Evald Berzinsky" [in Russian], in *Muzïkal'noye ispolnitel'stvo* 7, ed. G. Edelman (Moscow, 1972), 142-59.
"Beethoven's Fourth Symphony: A Comparative Analysis of Recorded Performances," *Israel Studies in Musicology* 1 (1978): 54-76.
"The Sound of Beethoven's Orchestra," *Orbis musicae* 6 (1978): 59-90.
"Musical Iconography in Byzantine Manuscripts from Jerusalem and Mount Sinai: A Preliminary Report," *Tatzlil* 18 (1978): 90-95.
"Ha'autobiografia shel Moshe Beregovski" [The autobiography of Moshe Beregovsky; in Hebrew], *Tatzlil* 19 (1979): 159-61.
"Musical Instruments in Byzantine Illuminated Manuscripts," *Early Music* 8, no. 3 (1980): 312-28.
"The Jews and the Jewish Idiom in Soviet Music," in *Bericht über den internationalen musikwissenschaftlchen Kongress Berlin 1974*, ed. H. Kuhn and P. Nitsche (Kassel, 1980), 407-410.

"Der Doppelsinn der jüdischen Elemente in Dmitry Schostakovitschs Musik," in *Garmisch 80: Summaries of Papers at Second World Congress for Soviet and East European Studies* (Garmisch-Partenkirchen, 1980), 92.

"Zur Hermeneutik der sowjetisch-baltischen Musik: Ein Versuch der Deutung von Sinn und Stil," *Zeitschrift für Ostforschung* 1 (1982): 76-93.

"Ein Gerichtsverfahren in Sachen des Königsberger Kaufmanns Schirach Sternberg wider Musikdirektor Richard Wagner, " in *Musik des Ostens* 8, ed. Hubert Unverricht (Kassel, 1982), 113-27.

"Two Unique Baltic Music Collections," in *Musik des Ostens* 8, ed. Hubert Unverricht (Kassel, 1982), 85-88.

"Shostakovich's Song Cycle *From Jewish Folk Poetry*: Aspects of Style and Meaning," in *Russian and Soviet Music: Essays for Boris Schwartz*, ed. Malcolm Hamrick Brown (Ann Arbor, MI, 1984), 259-86.

"The Double Meaning of Jewish Elements in Dmitri Shostakovich's Music," *Musical Quarterly* 71, no. 1 (1985): 68-80; repr. in *Le Musique et le rite sacre et profane*, vol. 2, ed. Marc Honegger and Paul Prevost (Strasbourg, 1986): 737-57.

"Towards a Study of Israeli Musical Culture: The Case of Kiryat Ono" (with T. Bensky and U. Sharvit), *Asian Music* 17, no. 2 (1986): 186-209.

"Moysey Beregovski: Zum Schicksal eines sowjetischen Ethnomusikologen," *Jahrbuch für Volksliedforschung* 33 (1988): 70-80.

"Das jüdische im Werk von Dmitri Schostakovitsch," in *Studien zur Musik des XX. Jahrhunderts in Ost- und Ostmitteleuropa*, ed. D. Gojowy (Berlin, 1990), 103-125.

"Zur nabatäischen und safaitischen Musikkultur in hellenistischer und römischer Zeit," in *Festschrift für Walter Suppan*, ed. B. Habla (Graz, 1993), 167-84.

"Archaeo-Musicology and Some of Its Problems: Considerations on the State of the Art in Israel," in *La pluridisciplinarite en archeologie musicale*, ed. C. Homo-Lechner (Paris, 1994), 139-48.

"Die Musikikonographie des Dionysoskultes im römischen Palästina," in *Imago musicae* 8 (1995): 109-134.

"Jewish Art Music in the Soviet Union: 1917-1950," in *Verfemte Musik: Komponisten in den Diktaturen unseres Jahrhunderts* (ed. J. Braun, V. Karbusický, and H.T. Hoffman) (Frankfurt am Main, 1995), 125-34.

"The Lute and Organ in Ancient Israeli and Jewish Iconography," in, *Festschrift Christoph-Hellmut Mahling*, ed. A. Beer, K. Pfarr, and W. Ruf (Tutzing, 1997), 1:163-88.

"On the Origins of the Harp: The Earliest Depiction of the Triangular Frame Harp," *HARPA* (Spring 1999): 6-11.

Musiques Juives Russes: Chostakovitch, Slonimski, Prokofiev [CD liner notes ; in French, German, and English], Le Chant du Monde CD RUS 288166 (2000).

"The Earliest Depiction of a Harp (Megiddo, late 4th mill. BC)," in *Orient-Archäologie*, vol. 6, *Musikarchäologie*, ed. E. Hickmann and R. Eichmann (Rahden, 2000), 5-10.

"Some Remarks on the Music History of Ancient Israel/Palestine: Written or Archaeological Evidence," in *Orient-Archäologie*, vol. 7, *Musikarchäologie II*, ed. E. Hickmann, I. Laufs, and R. Eichmann (Rahden, 2000), 135-40.

"The Musical Ladscape in Israel/Palestine: 3,000 Years Ago and Today," in *Musikkonzepte – Konzepte der Musikwissenschaft: Bericht über den Internationalen Kongress der Gesellschaft für Musikforschung Halle (Saale) 1998*, ed. K. Eberle and W. Ruf, (Kassel, 2000), 2:52-61.

"Christian and Jewish Religious Elements in Music," in: *Musikgeschichte zwischen Ost- und Westeuropa*, ed. H. Loos and K.P. Koch (Sinzig, 2002), 77-82.

"The Iconography of the Organ: Change in Jewish Thought and Musical Life," in: *Music in Art* 28, nos. 1-2 (2003): 55-69.

"Music as Resistance, Music as Survival," in *Collaboration and Resistance During the Holocaust: Belarus, Estonia, Latvia, Lithuania*, ed. D. Gaunt, P.A. Levine, and L. Palosuo (Bern, 2004), 421-31.

"Music and the Bible: An Archaeological Investigation," in *Analecta Bruxellensia* 12 (2007): 7-19.

"Music in the Ancient Land of Israel," in *Sounds of Ancient Music*, ed. J.G. Westenholz (Jerusalem, 2007), 11-23 [in English] and 9-16 [in Hebrew].

"Reconsidering Musicology in the Baltic States of Lithuania, Latvia and Estonia," *Journal of Baltic Studies* 39, no. 3 (2008): 231-39.

"Baltic Musicology and the Years of Crisis (1940-1991)," *Musikgeschichte in Mittel- und Osteuropa* 12 (2008): 5-14.

"Ancient Israel/Palestine and the New Historiography of Music: Some Unanswered Questions," in *ICONEA 2008: Proceedings of the International Conference of Near Eastern Archaeomusicology, British Museum, December 2008*, ed. I. Finkel and R. Dumbrill (London, 2009) (in press).

Dictionary and Encyclopedia Entries

Latvijas mazā enciklopēdija [The brief encyclopedia of Latvia; in Latvian] (Riga, 1967-70): 16 entries.

Kratkaya evreyskaya entsiklopediya [Brief encyclopedia of Judaism; in Russian] (Jerusalem, 1976-80): 27 entries.

The New Grove Dictionary of Music and Musicians, ed. S. Sadie (London, 1980): 22 entries.

Die Musik in Geschichte und Gegenwart, 2nd ed., ed. L. Finscher (Kassel and Weimar, 1994-2007): "Biblische Musikinstrumente" (*Sachteil*, vol. 1, cols.

1503-37); "Jüdische Musik: I. Einleitung; II. Altisrael; III.1. Mittelalter" (*Sachteil*, vol. 4, cols. 1511-27 and 1557-61).

The Oxford Encyclopedia of Near Eastern Archaeology, ed. E. Meyers (Oxford and New York, 1997): "Musical Instruments" (vol. 4, 70-79).

Eerdmans Dictionary of the Bible, ed. D.N. Freedman, A.C. Myers, and A.B. Beck (Grand Rapids, MI, and Cambridge, 2000): "Music, Musical Instruments" (pp. 927-30).

The New Grove Dictionary of Music and Musicians, 2nd ed., ed. S. Sadie and J. Tyrrell (London, 2001): "Biblical Instruments" (vol. 3, 524-35); "Jewish Music: II. Ancient Israel/Palestine" (vol. 13, 29-37); 18 entries on Baltic musics (partly with A. Klotiņš and U. Lippus).

The New Interpreter's Dictionary of the Bible (Nashville, TN, 2006–): "Musical Instruments" (in press).

Reviews and Varia

Approximately 250 concert reviews and journalistic articles published in newspapers and magazines in Latvian and Russian (1957-71); some reprinted in Braun, *Studies: Music in Latvia* (Riga, 2002).

Music in Ancient Israel and Jewish Music

Amnon Shiloah

KING DAVID AND THE DEVIL, INITIATORS OF TWO KINDS OF MUSIC

The biblical figures of Jubal and David represent two important phases in the history told in the Bible. Jubal's relation to music and its origin is recounted in a brief statement found within the framework of the creation story, where he is identified as "The father of them that play upon the *kinnor* and the *uggav*" (Genesis 4:21).[1] These latter terms are often translated as *harp* (or *lyre*) and the *organ*, but many have read this statement as referring metaphorically to the origin of music itself. King David appears at the time when the tribes of Israel were coalescing into an organized nation, to which a system of law was granted by God at the mount of Sinai. These laws established the basis for which normative religious control and sanctions. This period reached one of its peaks during the reign of David, who is credited with the institutionalization of the Temple's cult, in which music occupied a prominent place. Among other things, David distinguished himself as a poet and musician, to we ascribe the psalms chanted to the glory of God at all Temple rituals. All three of the world's principal monotheist religions regarded David's hymns as an ideal model of religious song and singing across subsequent generations. In the Judaic sources, David is typically called "The sweet psalmist of Israel." The Kabalistic literature includes numerous commentaries on the skillful art of David and its link to divine music. He is described in the *Zohar* (The Book of Splendor) as singing the Glory of God with the angels, as a poet-singer whose hymns were imbued with sacred spirit, and so forth. A famous instance, frequently cited, is the Talmudic *aggadah* that records the following: "a harp was suspended above his David's bed . . . as soon as midnight arrived, a north wind came and blew upon it and it played of itself" (Berakhoth 3b). Among the various kabalistic interpretations, one reads that the *kinnor* sings along antiphonally with David; the *kinnor* says, "Let all people praise thee O God," to which David replies, "The earth has yielded its increase" (Psalms 67:8-7).[2]

In a collection of sermons by Judah Moscato (ca. 1530-90), the most prominent Italian Jewish preacher of the sixteenth century, the first is called *Higgayon be-khinnor* (The melody of the lyre). It is for the feast of *simhat torah* (The joy

---

1   Various translations have been suggested for the instruments mentioned in this verse, ranging from the general categories of string and wind instruments to various members of those families. At the present time, it is widely accepted that the *kinnor* should be identified with the lyre.
2   See Amnon Shiloah, *Music Subjects in the Zohar Texts and Indices* (Jerusalem, 1977), 62.

of the Torah), and is devoted to music. In his introduction, the author claims that "every being and man was created according to musical proportions, God himself is the master of perfect music."[3] This statement is followed by the quotation of the legend of the *kinnor* that was hanging above David's bed. In the body of the main sermon, Moscato refers to *Aqedat Yitzhaq* (The binding of Isaac) by the Rabbi and philosopher Isaac Arama (1420-1494). The cited passage deals with the relationship between the micro- and the macro-cosmos, and compares them to two identically tuned *kinnorot*. This analogy invokes the idea of human music responding to heavenly music, and vice versa. This same concept of resonance between the two spheres is used by Moscato to elucidate the quotation the closed the last paragraph: "David's *kinnor* [= his soul] is tuned identically, and thus in resonance, with the North wind, which makes the *kinnor* play of itself.[4]

A Possible Link Between Jubal and David

A kind of a link between characterizations of Jubal and Daivd is suggested within the context of a Muslim theological tradition, according to which the *'ūd*—a short, fretless lute with major presence in Arabic music—is said to have been invented by Lamekh, Jubal's father,[5] thereafter destroyed by the Flood, and eventually reinvented by David, who hung it in the Temple, where it remained until Nebuchadnezzar's capture of Jerusalem. This tale derives from a work of Askar al-Ḥalabī al-Qādirī, entitled *Wine of the Cup Regarding the Tree of Melodies*.[6] In another Muslim source, *Ḥalbat al-Kumait* by Shams al-dīn al-Nawājī (1382-1455), the the reinvention of the *'ūd* by David is connected with the 4000 Levites, who served as musicians in the Temple of Jerusalem.[7] It seems to me that this idea of the instrument's reinvention may constitute an attempt to counter the insinuation that music was invented by Cain's descendents, among whom Lamekh belonged. It should be noted that these, like most references to David found in Arabic writings, constitute elaborations of post-biblical Jewish rabbinical exegetic sources or *midrash*.[8] According to these sources, Jubal belonged to the descendents of Cain, who used their invention for amusement and those sinful purposes that ultimately caused the Flood. This interpretation has been used by Muslim religious authorities in discourses on the lawfulness of

---

3   Israel Adler, *Hebrew Writings Concerning Music, in Manuscripts and Printed Books from Geonic Times up to 1800* (Munich, 1975), 233.
4   Ibid., 530.
5   Unlike the biblical story which mentions Yuval as the inventor of the music, in all Muslim sources rather Yuval's father Lamekh is accredited with that invention.
6   See Shiloah, *The Theory of Music in Arabic Writings* (Munich: G. Hanle), 240-41. Nothing is known of al-Qādirī's life.
7   Ibid., 294-95.
8   *Midrash* is a particular genre of rabbinic literature, a sort of anthology and compilation of homilies consisting of exegeses and public sermons.

music and its link with depravity and Satanic delusion. The most frequently told version of the story of Lamekh's invention relates that Lamekh has lost only son and grieved sorely for him. To keep his son's form close to his eyes, he made ann *'ūd* from his thigh, leg, foot, and toes, and sung a lament to its accompaniment.[9]

With respect to the fundamental question whether the origin of music is divine or Satanic, two conflicting views are found in sources belonging to the three monotheistic religions. One refers to David as a representative of the divine, and the other refers to Jubal and his descendents as representatives of the Satanic. An example is found in the brief statement of Clement of Alexandria (ca. 160-ca. 220). When considering harmony and harmonious music, Clement said that it should be made "not in accordance with Thracian music, which resembles that of Jubal, but in accordance with the fatherly purpose of God, which David earnestly sought."[10] It is in light of these preliminary remarks that we may situation the central discussion in the present essay.

Variations on the Conflicting Theories of Origin

In Islam, King David (or the prophet Dawūd, as his name is rendered in the Qur'ān and later Arabic writings), was a figure known to the poets of Arabia during the *jāhiliyya*, the heathen period before Muhammad. In their poems, he was considered the inventor of coats of mail, and his connection with the *zabūr* (Psalms) was also acknowledged.[11] Muhammad too mentions that Allah gave the *zabūr* to David,[12] upon whom the Qur'ān bestows the title *Khalīfa fī'l-arḍ*,[13] or "God's delegate on earth."[14] Here and elsewhere in the Qur'ān, David's distinctive virtues are mentioned. One finds, for instance, a passage in which David and 'Īsā (the Arabic name of Jesus) curse the people of Israel because they do not observe the precepts of God.[15] This mention of Mentioning of David together with Jesus may indicate that Muhammad received this tradition from Christians.

There are also numerous references to David and his deeds in the post-Qur'anic literature, and particularly in the *Hadīth*. The *Hadīth*, or Traditions of the Prophet, catalogs sayings by or about the Prophet, which, over the course of

---

9 See Shiloah, *The Dimension of Music in Islamic and Jewish Culture* (London, 1993), chapter 2.
10 Oliver Strunk, *Source Readings in Music History: From Classical Antiquity through the Romantic Era* (New York, 1960), 64-66.
11 In his book *The Perfect Man*, the Muslim mystic 'Abd al-Karīm al-Jīlī (1365-1406) reports that the term *zabūr* is Syrian for Psalter.
12 Koran, *sura* 17:57.
13 Koran, *sura* 38:26.
14 Koran, *sura* 35-38.
15 Koran, *sura* 5:8.

time, acquired the force of law. Many Muslim legalists and theologians refer liberally to this source and draw upon its arguments for the construction of their own theses. Here, one finds a wealth of evidence concerning David, usually concerning also the question of the lawfulness of music.[16] In what follows, however, we shall concentrate upon a favorite theme: David's gifts and excellence as a poet-musician, singing the psalms not only as their creator, but also as a singer endowed with beauty and magical power.

The History of al-Ṭabarī

Al-Ṭabarī, a monumental history in many volumes recorded the historian and commentator on the Qur'ān, Abū Ja'far al-Ṭabarī (830-923), is regarded by many scholars as the most important general history produced in the Islamic world. Certainly, it preserves the greatest array of citations from sources otherwise lost. In his lengthy account of the history of biblical peoples and prophets, al-Ṭabarī included a chapter devoted to David, entitled "Account of David ibn Jesse."[17] There, we learn that David became king after Saul was slain in battle, and that God thereafter made him a prophet. "God gave him the kingdom and the wisdom," meaning prophecy, al-Ṭabarī records. And "When the Israelites gathered around David, God revealed the Psalms to him. . . . He also ordered the mountains and the birds to sing praise with him when he sang."[18] God did not give anyone of His creation a voice like that of David. So when David recited the Psalms, wild beasts would gaze at him with delight until they were lined up, intently listening to his singing. Demons then invented various instruments—*mazāmir, barābiṭ,* and *ṣunūj*[19]—with only David's voice as a model. David was extremely diligent constant in worship, wept much, and displayed great zeal in prayer and especially in fasting. We are also told that David would stay up at night and fast for half the time. And according to al-Ṭabarī's account, 4000 men guarded him day and night.

Other Viewpoints

In his *Book of Diversion and Musical Instruments*, the geographer Ibn Khurradadhbih (830-911) refers to the Prophet David when dealing with the influ-

---

16 For further details, see Shiloah, "Music and Religion in Islam," *Acta Musicologica* 69, no. 2 (1997): 15-28.
17 *The History of al-Ṭabarī*, Vol. 3, *The Children of Israel*, trans. William M. Brinner (Albany, NY, 1991), 140-51.
18 Koran, *sura* 2:251.
19 The term *mizmār* usually designates a double-reed instrument; and according to the *Hadīth*, Muhammad called it *mizmār al-shayṭān* (Satan's *mizmār*). The *barbaṭ* is a short, fretless lute similar to the *'ūd. Sanj* is the Persian name for the harp.

ence of music upon the body and the soul, and with music's therapeutic effect.[20] And the philosopher and music theorist Yaʻqūb ibn Isḥāq al-Kindī (d. after 870), author of thirteen treatises on the art of music (of which only six have come down to us), credits David in one, *Kitāb al-Muṣawwitāt al-watariyya* (Book of sounding string instruments of one to ten strings), with the invention of two biblical instruments: the *sheminit* (an eight-stringed instrument) and the *nebel 'asor* (a ten-string lyre), both of which are mentioned in the book of Psalms.[21] Thus, in addition to exaltations of his voice and its powerful expressiveness, we have references to David's skill as an inventor and skillful player of instruments. It is said, for instance, that David owned a *mi'zafa* (probably a lyre), than that when he wanted to bemoan something, he would play upon it, letting its tones ring out, and thereby making his listeners cry. He also played on a *mizmār* (a double-reed instrument) for the king of the children of Israel—Saul—in order to drive away the evil spirit that had afflicted him. The *kinnor* or lyre replaces the *mizmār* in the original story, which is as follows:

> And Saul's servants said to him, "Behold now, an evil spirit from God is tormenting you. Let our Lord now command your servants, who are before you, to seek out a man who is skillful in playing the lyre; and when the evil spirit from God is upon you, he will play it, and you will be well." So Saul said to his servants, "Provide for me a man who can play well. And bring him to me." One of the young men answered, "Behold, I have seen a son of Jesse the Bethlehemite who is skillful in playing, a man of valor, a man of war, prudent in speech, and a man of good presence; and the Lord with him." (1 Samuel 16:15-18)

Concerning the aforementioned instrument, one anonymous author, in addressing the prohibition of the *mizmār*, wrote: "The instrument *mizmār* is set against *mizmār* [*psalm*, from the Hebrew *mizmor*], which, when performed with a beautiful voice by David, is considered to be the most charming music in existence."[22] (In order to clarify the somewhat bewildering characteristics attributed to this biblical instrument, it is important to note the equivocal meaning of the Arabic term *mizmār*. Typically, it designates an oboe-like double-reed instrument prohibited by Muslim legal scholars. But, in a number of cases, the term seems either related to or derived from the Hebrew *mizmor*, meaning *psalm*. Further complicating the matter, the Hebrew verb from which the noun *mizmor* is derived was at one point used to designate both singing and playing an instrument.[23])

---

20 See Shiloah, *The Theory of Music in Arabic Writings*, 193-94.
21 Ibid., p. 253-55.
22 Ibid., 404.
23 For more details, see Christian Poché, "David and the Ambiguity of the *mizmār* According to Arab Sources," *The World of Music* 25, no. 2 (1983): 58-73.

In the abundant literature dealing with the prohibition of music from a theological standpoint, one finds not only discussions concerning singing and the playing of instruments but also references to dance. An interesting example is found in a treatise attributed to the jurist al-Harawī al-Qāri' (d. 1605).[24] The author quotes the example of King David, who sought divine inspiration in his dance. In particular, al-Qāri' refers to the biblical story of bringing of the Ark of the Lord up to Jerusalem, upon which David expressed his joy by dancing: "And David and all the house of Israel were making merry before the Lord with all their might, with songs, and lyres and harps and tambourines and castanets and cymbals" (2 Samuel 6:5; also 1 Chronicles 13:8).

The Charming and Beautiful Voice of David

In Qur'ān verses, we find David described as endowed with the most beautiful voice that God created. That beautiful voice, which was, of course, associated with the chanting of psalms, has served as an important reference for scholars of religion in supporting their theses. The recurrence of this motif in later interpretations associates the beautiful voice with the overwhelmingly charming power of David's singing or chanting, and with the promise that he will sing on the day of Resurrection. This divinely beautiful music will delight those who abstained from singing on earth. When he raises his voice and sings psalms, birds come to rest on his head and listen, and both domestic animals and wild beasts come together peaceably. They all succumb to its charm.

It is said that King David used to sing psalms once a week in Jerusalem. 'Herat Alī al-Qāri' al-Harawī (d.1605), a fundamentalist jurist who spent most of his life in Mecca, reports an interesting tradition that seemingly combines or mixed up the tradition of extolling David's beautiful voice and singing with another well known story about Archangel *Isrāfīl*. "When he sings," al-Qāri' writes, "all the inhabitants of the heavens stop praying and praising the lord, all the trees bloom, the doors tremble, the birds and *houris* sing; this divine chorale is created to delight those who abstained from musical pleasure on earth, and, in turn, it is overshadowed by the voice of David."[25] *Isrāfīl*, whose origin is probably to be traced to the Hebrew *Saraf* (singular form of *Seraphim*), was appointed by God to announce the Resurrection with a trumpet that he holds continuously to his mouth.

David and the Devil

There is an interesting extension of the story relating the overwhelming magical power of David's singing, which goes as follows. When David raised his voice

---

24 See Shiloah, *The Theory of Music in Arabic Writings*, 248.
25 Ibid., 245.

and sang psalms, birds came to rest on his head and listened, domestic animals and wild beasts were drawn together peaceably. They all succumbed to the charm of his singing. And when he witnessed how everything tamed and everything untamed yielded to the magic of David's voice, Satan summoned his hordes and ordered them to devise something of their own that would be equally powerful. Thus, they invented reed instruments and lutes modeled on David's seventy melodies. It is, therefore, noteworthy that the reed instruments and lutes are subsequently banished by radical religious authorities.

The number of melodies said to constitute the musical corpus established by David varies between thirty and seventy. Some of these melodies derive from David's art of chanting the psalms, while others are related to instrumental invention. It is said, for instance, that David used to chant the psalms (*zabūr*) to thirty tunes or modes that delighted the frantic, and that, by the end of the night, he soul was crying and no animal or beast could resist the urge to cry along with him. In a very different depiction, we meet the Devil as an imitator of David's godly music. There is even one interesting tale that refers to an encounter between David and the Devil, representing two different kinds of music. This latter story combines all of the foregoing elements into a dramatic scene that underscores the mystical and doctrinal approach to discourse on the influence of music. It is included in work of the famous Iranian mystic abū'l-Ḥasan 'Ali al-Hujwīrī, entitled *The Uncovering of the Veiled for People of Heart*.[26] Al-Hujwīrī (d.1072-77) was a strict observer of religious laws, yet he succeeded in reconciling his theology with an advanced form of mysticism. As his English translator, R.A. Nicholson, has observed, al-Hujwīrī's "exposition of Sufi doctrine and practice is distinguished by wide learning and first-hand knowledge, but also by the strongly personal character impressed on everything he writes."

The story of the encounter between David and the Devil is found in al-Hujwīrī's chapter on the principles of audition, which by defining two distinct classes of auditors: "Those who hear the spiritual meaning and those who hear the material sound." Al-Hujwīrī continues with the following account:

> The whole of this topic is illustrated by the story of David, whom God made His vicegerent and gave him a sweet voice and caused his throat to be a melodious *mizmār*, so that wild beasts and birds came from the mountain and plain to hear him, and the water ceased to flow and the birds fell from the air. . . . Then God, wishing to separate those who listened to the voice and followed their temperament from the followers of the truth who listened to the spiritual reality, permitted Iblīs [the Devil] to work his will and display his wiles or trickery. Iblīs fashioned a lute [mandolin, in the translation] and a *mizmār* (flute, in the translation), and took up a station opposite to the place where David was singing. David's audience became divided into two parties: the

---

26 Abū'l-Ḥasan al-Hujwiri, *The kashf al-Mahjub, the Oldest Treatise on Sufism,* trans. R.A. Nicholson (London, 1911; repr., 1970), xvii.

blest and the damned. Those who were destined to damnation lent ear to the music of Iblīs, while those who were destined to felicity remained listening to the voice of David. The spiritualists were conscious of nothing except David's voice, for they saw God alone; if they heard the Devil's music, they regarded it as a temptation proceeding from God, and if they heard David's voice, they recognized it as being a direction of God; wherefore they abandoned all things that are merely subsidiary and saw both right and wrong as they really are. When a man has audition of this kind, whatever he hears is lawful to him.[27]

What is interesting in this heavenly musical contest between David and the Devil is the fact that the Devil makes no effort to imitate David's magical music. Instead, the Devil is the creator of his *own* music, which does not have any link to the divine music transmitted via the David's skill; it is all temptation, and it has an absolutely evil effect. The Devil participates in this by virtue of God's will, and not through any initiative of his own. Thus, a great degree of choice is left to the sincere and true listener, who is knowledgeable of what is good and evil and can see both right and wrong as they really are. The listener makes his choice consciously and with conviction. As the author concludes, "When a man has audition of this kind, whatever he hears is lawful to him." This interpretation harmonizes well with a conviction prevalent among the mystics, which regards music as polyvalent. Music in itself does not have any circumscribed value or effect. Rather, its meaning and influence are determined by the values of listeners.

---

27 Ibid., 402

Mira Waner

ETHNIC/RELIGIOUS DISTINCTION VERSUS SYNCRETISM IN THE MUSICAL CULTURE OF ROMAN AND BYZANTINE SEPPHORIS
A Case Study in The Musical Culture of Ancient Israel

Since the basic and most essential aspect of music—namely sound—has not survived from the period under consideration in this paper, research in the field of musical culture in ancient Israel tends to concentrate upon the material findings of musical instruments, their iconographic descriptions, and their context. These are often complemented by research based upon literary sources, which, together with the study of archaeological objects, provides a more comprehensive picture of the period's musical culture. Since music has always constituted an integral part of culture, it is important to understand that an analysis of the findings throws light not only upon the daily use of music, but also upon the religious life, norms, and values that existed at the time—and, thus, upon the culture as a whole. Therefore, an understanding of musical culture contributes to a more comprehensive reconstruction of the cultural history of the period.

One of the basic assumptions of this study is that the land of Israel during this period provides us with an opportunity to examine the development of musical culture in a region inhabited by people of various *ethnoi*. Utilizing an innovative, multi-disciplinary approach involving archaeology, ethnic studies, and musicology, this study makes use of tools, theories, and methodologies from all of these respective fields. Research in ethnomusicology assumes that in order to examine the musical culture of a region, it is necessary to consider the entire range of social groups who live (or lived) there, and their influences upon the local culture. Material finds, being a primary source for the study of the ethnic affiliation of musical instruments and events, constitute an invaluable tool in this respect. In theory, then, by mapping the regional (or ethnic) distribution of music-related finds, it may be possible to discern various aspects of musical styles based upon religious and/or ethnic variations. Thus combining methods drawn from ethnomusicology and archaeology, I examine the issue of syncretism versus ethnic/religious distinction among the inhabitants of the land of Israel during this period.

For the purpose of my research, archaeological finds of music-related items dating to the period under study were organized in a catalogue according to cri-

---

This essay is based on a chapter in my Ph.D. dissertation, the completion of which was assisted by Professor Joachim Braun. I thank him for his sound advice and assistance.

teria which best enabled me to deduce information pertaining to musical culture. The corpus included some 820 items. Analysis of the findings assessed both local and foreign elements as evidenced in the artifacts of the musical culture. Questions of cultural influence were also considered: The assumption was that the polymorphous culture and multi-ethnic configuration of the local society were absorbed and etched into the music life of the inhabitants of the land. All regions of the country are represented in my findings, and it appears that local elements are characteristic of areas known to have been populated by a particular, specific *ethnos*, such as Jewish, Samaritan, Idomean, or Nabataean. This, however, was not the case in Greek cities and coastal towns, with their dominant pagan component. Furthermore, it appears that artifacts depicting music ensembles, present a varied combination of instruments ranging from those that appear to be foreign or imported to local/Eastern ones, and from those that reflect syncretic tendencies to those that demonstrate ethnic or religious distinction.

In the present paper, discussion is limited to one specific example, to be used as a case study: Roman and Byzantine Sepphoris. It is widely accepted that the Galilee in the Roman and Byzantine periods was a multicultural, poly-ethnic region. Sepphoris at this time was a vibrant political, religious, and cultural capital, which flourished alongside many other cities of the Eastern Roman Empire.[1] For this particular city we have both extensive literary sources as well as many archaeological remains, including a relative abundance of music-related finds. Thus, Sepphoris presents an opportunity to study how people of different religions and cultures coexisted in an urban environment. My challenge was to introduce a different perspective for examining the religion, ethnicity, and identity of the people who lived in the city.

As mentioned above, it is common knowledge that music is a part of culture. Just as culture is directly related to religion, ethnicity, and identity, so is music. The question I set out to answer was: Can we enhance our knowledge regarding the issue of cultural distinction versus syncretism among ethnic/religious groups living in Sepphoris by examining the musical culture of its inhabitants? I started by asking who were the city's inhabitants at this time. During the Roman and Byzantine periods, the Galilee was home to Jews of diverse geographic origins and of varied backgrounds and classes: Christians, Jewish Christians, *minim* ("heretics"), elements of the Graeco-Roman pagan society of the East, and in-

---

1   See Rebecca M. Nagy, Carol L. Meyers, Eric M. Meyers, and Ze'ev Weiss, eds., *Sepphoris in Galilee: Crosscurrents of Culture* (Winona Lake, 1996); Eric M. Meyers, ed., *Galilee through the Centuries: Confluence of Cultures* (Winona Lake, 1999); Ze'ev Weiss and Ehud Netzer, *Promise and Redemption: A Synagogue Mosaic from Sepphoris*, 2nd ed. (Jerusalem, 1998); Rina Talgam and Ze'ev Weiss, *The Mosaics of the House of Dionysos at Sepphoris* (Jerusalem, 2004); and Ze'ev Weiss, *The Sepphoris Synagogue: Deciphering an Ancient Message through its Archaeological and Socio-Historical Contexts* (Jerusalem, 2005).

digenous groups of the Near East who frequently made their way into the Galilee either as itinerant travelers or as residents.[2] All of these attest to the variety of religious expressions that existed within Sepphoris. Like most of the Galilean population, which was predominantly Jewish in the third through the fifth centuries CE, Sepphoris witnessed the gradual growth of Christianity in the early centuries of the Common Era.[3] The city appears to have been a center of Jewish cultural activity. Despite its Hellenistic appearance it was regarded as a Jewish city with a Jewish presence that continued even after the Gallus Revolt and the earthquake of 363.[4]

An intriguing picture of the culture and population of Sepphoris has been revealed in recent years. Inter alia, Jewish ritual baths, seven branched candelabras engraved on vessels, various inscriptions, and the impressive remains of a synagogue attest to Sepphoris as a flourishing Jewish city.[5] This is supported by both Jewish and non-Jewish literary sources, according to which Sepphoris served as an administrative, religious, and cultural center for Jews of both Israel and the Diaspora throughout much of this period.[6] However, excavation finds have also shown that the Christian tradition was firmly implanted there. And at the same time, the findings convey a picture of a Hellenistic-Roman culture, and seem to point to a city with decidedly pagan characteristics. During the Roman and Byzantine periods, Sepphoris did not significantly differ architecturally from the pagan cities of the region, aside from its ritual buildings.[7] Apparently, there was no clear division of the city into neighborhoods or quarters on the basis of economic or social status, or even of religious affiliation.[8] A wealth and variety of mosaics have been found here, many of which depict musical instruments and/or musical events. Their importance lies in the fact that they provide a

---

2 Stuart S. Miller, "Jewish Sepphoris," in Nagy et al, *Sepphoris in Galilee*, 61; Isaiah Gafni, "Daily Life in Galilee and Sepphoris," in Nagy et al, *Sepphoris in Galilee*, 51-57.
3 Jews who lived in the two major cities, Sepphoris and Tiberias, were constantly in contact with the Hellenistic-Roman manifestations of pagan culture and later with Christian practices and beliefs. Hence, the cultural influences that shaped their lives differed from those who lived in the smaller villages.
4 Shmuel Safrai and Menahem Stern, eds. *The Jewish People in the 1st Century: Historical Geography, Political History, Social, Cultural and Religious Life and Institutions* (Assen and Philadelphia, 1976), 410-12; Miller, "Hellenistic and Roman Sepphoris: The Historical Evidence," in Nagy et al, *Sepphoris in Galilee*, 21-24.
5 Hanan Eshel, "The Pools of Sepphoris. Ritual Baths or Bathtubs? They're Not Ritual Baths,"*Biblical Archeology Review* 26, no. 4 (2002): 42-45; Eric M. Meyers, "The Pools of Sepphoris: Ritual Baths or Bathtubs? Yes they are," *Biblical Archeology Review* 26, no. 4 (2002): 46-49; Mark A. Chancey, *The Myth of a Gentile Galilee* (Cambridge, 2002).
6 Miller, "Jewish Sepphoris," 59-65.
7 Weiss and Netzer, *Promise and Redemption*, 10.
8 Weiss and Netzer, "Sepphoris during the Byzantine Period," in Nagy et al, *Sepphoris in Galilee*, 85.

glimpse of this multifaceted world, and they present a clear picture of the nature of Hellenism in one of the most important centers of Jewish settlement at this time.[9]

The Music-Related Finds at Sepphoris

It is reasonable to assume that the musical culture of Sepphoris was influenced by the lifestyle of its inhabitants. Therefore, an examination of the archaeological remains pertaining to music and found at the site may assist in sketching a portrait of the city's musical culture, and thereby add to our understanding of the city's ethnic makeup. The following is a brief description of the musical artifacts discovered in Sepphoris:

1. A small bronze bell (4.3 cm high and 3 cm in diameter), found without its iron clapper (Figure 1). Its shape resembles that of modern church bells, with flared and slightly thickened rims. Two sets of lines are incised on the bell, and its top is designed with two round protuberances at the connection with the perforated handle.

2. A simple bell (4.9 cm high and 3.4 cm in diameter), conical in shape but widening towards the rims (Figure 2). Its body and handle represent a single-cast unit. The clapper is missing.

   Figure 1   Figure 2

3. A small semi-spherical/copula shaped bell with a clapper, depicted in the synagogue mosaic (Figure 3), representing one of the golden apotropaic bells which were sewn into the robe of the High Priest, here ornamenting Aaron's tunic.[10]

---

9   Janine Balty, "La mosaïque antiqe au Proche Orient," in *Aufstieg und Niedergang der römischen Welt. Geschichte und Kultur Roms im Spiegel der neueren Forschung* 2, ed. Wolfgang Haase (Berlin, 1981), 347-429; Ruth Ovadiah and Asher Ovadiah, *Hellenistic, Roman and Early Byzantine Mosaic Pavements in Israel* (Rome, 1987).

10 As described in the book of *Exodus* 28:31-35: "And you shall make a robe... a golden bell and a pomegranate... upon the hem of the robe round about. Aaron shall wear it when he ministers, and its sound shall be heard, so that he may not die."

4. Two pairs of forked cymbals decorate the tip of an oil lamp (Figure 4). They are of the *crotella*/slap-cymbal type.
5. A large pair of cymbals ("tsiltsalim"), linked by a chain, support a wicker basket filled with fruit in the synagogue mosaic floor (Figure 5).

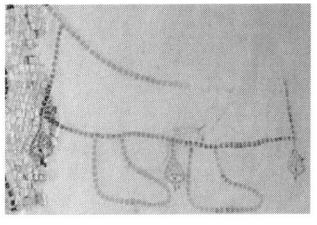 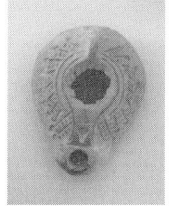 

Figure 3 Figure 4 Figure 5

6-10. Five double *auloi* (Figures 6, 7, 8, 9 and 10.) are part of the depiction on the Dionysian mosaic floor of a *triclinium*. All five wind instruments are similar to one another, and are depicted as a straight double *aulous*/double *tibia*, with long pipes.

Figure 6 Figure 7

Figure 8 Figure 9

33

Figure 10

11. A bronze figurine of Pan or a Satyr holding a syrinx (Figure 11), of which three to five pipes are visible (the small figure represents a seated player absorbed in his music).

12. A large *syrinx* depicted in a medallion on a mosaic floor (Figure 12). The *syrinx* has eleven pipes is of the right-angled variety.[11]

Figure 11   Figure 12

13. Two slightly curved horns, referred to as *hatsotsrot* in the Hebrew inscription on the mosaic (Figure 13). The horns widen gently toward the end and are depicted with rings.

14. Two *shofarot* (ram's horns) appear to the right of the two *menorot* (Figures 14a and 14b). Each is decorated with three coloured rings. In the left panel, the mouthpiece of the *shofar* faces the menorah, while in the right panel it faces away.

Figure 13   Figures 14a & 14b

---

11 In his *Die Syrinx in der Greichischen Bildkunst* (Vienna, 1985), Gerlinde Haas refers to this type of *syrinx* as the "trapezoidal bastard AB form."

15. A *shofar* appears as part of the engraving on a copper seal (Figure 15), in close proximity to a *menorah* (seven-branched candelabra), *mahta* (incense shovel), *lulav* (myrtle), and *etrog* (citron), henceforth referred to as the "symbolic grouping."
16. A *shofar* is depicted on a clay oil lamp near a *menorah* and a *lulav*.
17. A *tympanum* (see Figure 10) is depicted in the Dionysian floor, played by a maenad. It has a single-headed frame and is of a type that is struck directly, hand-beaten with the fingers or knuckles.
18. A three-stringed, symmetrical type of lyre with a rounded base is depicted in the synagogue mosaic (Figure 16).

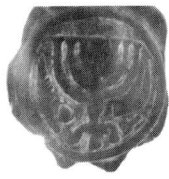   

Figure 15   Figure 16

19. A seven-stringed, square-shaped lyre is held to the left of a seated player (Orpheus. Figure 17). It has no resonator and resembles a Roman *kithara*. Wavy lines above the crossbar and beneath the bottom frame indicate the loose ends of the strings. Many organological details are missing, and hence it appears to be a schematic rendering of the instrument.

Figure 17

This list indicates that there are eleven aerophones (five *auloi*, two *syrinxes*, and four horns), five idiophones (three bells and two cymbals), two chordophones, and one membranophone among the finds. Of these, eight items are from the Roman period and nine are from the Byzantine period, with one of uncertain date.

Of the nineteen music-related items, only two (the bells) are actual instruments. The rest are depictions on mosaics, except for a cymbal inscribed on an oil lamp, *shofarot* on a copper seal and an oil lamp, and a *syrinx* that is part of a bronze figurine. We can therefore conclude that aerophones are the most abundant instruments found at the site (composing more than half—58%—of the total finds), followed by idiophones (26.3%), while chordophones and membranophones are much less common. However, it is important to note that the five *auloi*, accounting for over a quarter of the findings, are all from a single mosaic and depict the same double *tibia*. Eight musical instruments are depicted in Greek mythological scenes and seven within a Jewish setting. We have no direct ethnic association for the two bells found in the city's water system or the cymbals engraved on the oil lamp. We also lack information about the find-location of the oil lamp and the copper seal, both of which bear Jewish symbols.[12]

Discussion

A brief analysis of the cultural context of these instruments is a necessary starting point in any attempt to understand the respective cults and religious beliefs of the city's inhabitants. As will become apparent, the music-related artifacts discovered in Sepphoris indicate first and foremost that the inhabitants were familiar with both Greek mythology and Jewish ritual. It is interesting to note that instruments belonging to all four basic classifications appear in Sepphoris.[13] We assume that the relative abundance of musical instruments depicted in the city's mosaics provides evidence of their importance in the life and culture of the population. In order to understand this phenomenon, the next step is to try and relate the instruments to the settings in which they appear:

Bells: Hundreds of bells dating to the Roman and Byzantine periods have been discovered in Israel.[14] Their relative abundance in tombs demonstrates a

---

12 The discovery of an item found in the city's *decumanus* during the excavations of the Hebrew University's expedition in the summer of 2005 was reported by Weiss in "Sepphoris (Zippori) 2005," *Israel Exploration Journal* 55 (2005): 226-27. A small box (an incense burner?), carved in limestone, bears decorations of various images, among which is a satyr playing a musical instrument and a dancing maenad. There is no description of the instrument, yet mention is made of a bull or ram depicted on another side of the box in a context that is indicative of the Christian rendering of the sacrifice of Isaac. Further details will be useful to our study.
13 This refers to the classification system of Von Hornbostel and Sachs; see Erich M. von Hornbostel and Curt Sachs, "Classification of Musical Instruments" *The Galpin Society* 14 (1961): 3-29.
14 Mira Waner, "Tarbut Hamuzika be'Eretz Israel Batkufot haHelenistit, haRomit ve'haBizazantit – Yihudiyut mul Syncretism Datti/Etni" (Music Culture in Hellenistic, Roman and Byzantine Palestine: Ethnic/Religious Distinction and/or Syncretism) (Ph.D. diss., Bar-Ilan University, 2007), 35.

cultic connotation as well as their apotropaic and prophylactic purpose.[15] Bells were worn as amulets, and their use in ancient Israel in connection with the Dionysian cult is also attested.[16] Their secular use was both decorative and communicative. The two bells found in the Sepphoris water system do not permit us to draw any definite conclusions regarding the religious affiliation of the people who used them. They do not seem to be associated with dancing or with the Dionysian cult. On the other hand, the apotropaic bell depicted on the hem of the High Priest's robe does have an ethnic connotation. The tradition is attested in the Bible, and also appears during the Roman period.[17]

Cymbals: Bronze or copper cymbals appear frequently in the Roman period in Israel as instruments associated with the cult or more artistic musical performances of the established religions.[18] In the Graeco-Roman culture they were associated with orgiastic religious rites in the worship of Dionysos and of Cybele, where they were often beaten to induce ecstasy together with the *tympanum* and the *aulos*.[19] In addition to their use in religious and secular life, cymbals have been accredited with remarkable powers. Their appearance in Sepphoris, both as decorations engraved on a clay lamp and as "wheels" for the basket of first fruits, is of course not within their usual musical context, and thus limits our comments regarding the ethnic affiliation of these particular instruments.

Double *Aulos* (Greek) or *Tibia* (Latin): The *aulos* occupied an important place in Greek civilization. Its use is documented over some ten centuries and its existence is attested in much earlier iconographic records.[20] *Auloi* of varying quality and workmanship were found in numerous settings, including private homes and graves.[21] The musicians who played them were as varied

---

15 Hanoch Avenary, "Magic, Symbolism and Allegory of Old Hebrew Sound Instruments," in *Collectanea Historiae Musicae* (Florence, 1956), 2:21-31; Margaret Schatkin, "Idiophones of the Ancient World," *Jahrbuch für Antike und Christentum* 12, ed. Ernst Dassman and Klaus Thraede (Münster, 1978): 147-72; Waner, "Tarbut Hamuzika," 36-38.
16 Plutarch, *Quaestiones Conviviales*, 4/2:273; Asher Ovadiah, Carla Gomez de Silva, and Sonia Mucznik, "The Mosaic Pavements of Sheikh Zouède in Northern Sinai," in *Tesserae. Festschrift für Joseph Engemann* (Münster, 1991), 181-91.
17 Henri Seyrig, "Antiquité syriennes—La grande statue parthe de Shami et la sculpture palmyrenienne," *Syria* 20 (1939): 177-83; Joachim Braun *Music in Ancient Israel/Palestine: Archaeological, Written, and Comparative Sources*, trans. Douglas W. Stott (Cambridge, 2002), 201. In a Jerusalem grave, small bells were found with scraps of material still attached to them, which could be remnants of a hem (Israel Antiquiry Authority 34.3137).
18 Braun, *Music in Ancient Israel/Palestine*, 238; Waner, "Tarbut Hamuzika," 40-43.
19 James Blades and James Holland, "Cymbals," in *The New Grove Dictionary of Music and Musicians*, ed. Stanley Sadie (London 2001), 6:799.
20 Annie Bélis, "Aulos," in *The New Grove Dictionary*, 2:178-84.
21 Waner, "Tarbut Hamuzika," 53-58.

as the instruments; some were high-ranking professional virtuosos, while others were semi-professional folk musicians.[22]

The *aulos* was a common instrument in ancient Israel, together with a derivative type, the Phrygian *aulos*. Female musicians (*aulterides* or *tibicinae*)—sometimes excellent players and commonly known as "women of easy virtue"—were hired to enliven banquets and all-male parties. Very popular in scenes from the life and cult of Dionysos, *auloi* appear in Sepphoris precisely in this setting. They are depicted in a drinking contest, a triumphal procession (*Pompi*, Πομπη), a presentation of gifts (*Doresoroi*, Δωροφοροι), a procession following a symposium (*Komos*, Κώμος: a festivity in honor of Dionysos and accompanied by the Dionysiac entourage, instrumental music, song, and assorted dancing),[23] and in a scene that probably depicts an offering-procession with an unknown mythological precedent. Dionysian mysteries are known to have been conducted or performed in the private residences of wealthy people in big cities.

It is difficult to determine the ethnic background of the initial owner of the house in which this mosaic was found.[24] But the Dionysian iconography in both the triumphal procession and the presumed sacrificial procession appear to have acquired certain Judaeo-Christian elements, such as the halo around the head of Dionysos, the ass and rider, and the cock offering. It was quite common for artists in the Syro-Palestinain border areas to mix pagan, Jewish, and Christian elements in their iconography, as we see, for example, in the Dura-Europus synagogue, with its David-as-Orpheus mural and Dionysian elements. This fact supports Goodenough's proposal that: although the three main population groups in Roman Palestine all drew from a common inventory of symbols, they interpreted them differently.[25] It also fits in well with the artifacts of Jewish and Christian life that have been uncovered both on the acropolis and in the lower city, indicating that these two segments of the population lived and worked here side by side. This pluralistic blend was complemented by the group of pagans that thrived in Sepphoris throughout late antiquity, though the remains of this latter group are probably the most elusive of all.[26]

An interesting comparison can be drawn between this Dionysian mosaic and the one found in Sheikh Zouède, which dates approximately to the same period. It is important to note that while the Sheikh Zouède scenes evoke an

---

22 Braun, *Music in Ancient Israel/Palestine*, 226-27.
23 Talgam and Weiss, *The Mosaics of the House of Dionysos*, 69; R. DeMarini, "Komos," in *Encyclopedia dell'arte antica classica e orientale* (Rome, 1961), 4:382-84.
24 Weiss, "Ben Paganism leYahadut," *Cathedra* 99 (2001): 15-26.
25 Erwin R. Goodenough, *Jewish Symbols in the Greco-Roman Period* (New York, 1953-68), 10:207-208.
26 Eric M. Meyers, "Conclusions," in Nagy *et al*, *Sepphoris in Galilee*, 150.

orgiastic-pagan atmosphere (enhanced, for example, by the use of a rich variety of regional instruments, including idiophones and a Phrygian *aulos*), those in Sepphoris are considerably calmer and more pastoral (using the classical double *aulos*). Although both mosaics emanate from the Dionysian cult, they present two different social, intellectual, spiritual, and perhaps even musical worlds. Braun has suggested that they may be used to indicate—or at least to symbolize—the point of division between Eastern and Western music, with the Sheikh Zouède mosaic representing the beginning of Eastern music, while the Sepphoris mosaic represents the beginning of Western music in this region.[27]

Syrinx: Also known as a panpipe, being an attribute of the pastoral Graeco-Roman deity Pan, the *syrinx* is another aerophone relating to the Dionysian cult. This instrument has a Mediterranean or oriental origin and is attested some 500 years before its first known appearance in ancient Israel. It became an established symbol on city coins, in terracotta figurines and on mosaics. There is no evidence of this instrument's existence in the region before the middle of the second century CE, when an altar to Dionysos featuring a *syrinx* as a symbol for the diety was erected in Scythopois, a center of Dionysian worship in the region.[28] By that time, the *syrinx* had become accepted as a municipal symbol on the coins of Caesarea Philippi/Paneas. The local organological tradition, however, is not attested graphically until the third century, when it is depicted on a mural from a burial chamber in an Ascalon cave.[29] Its realistic portrayals offer proof of its existence as an actual instrument in Israel during the Roman period.

Bronze statuettes depicting divinities or mythological figures were common items of domestic material culture throughout the Roman Empire. They represent either cultic objects from a household shrine or decorative attachments, often from furniture and thus devoid of explicit religious significance. During this time, the individual deity Pan had become conflated with the satyrs, constituting the retinue of the wine god Bacchus (the Greek Dionysos). Satyr figures therefore symbolized conviviality and were often featured in banqueting contexts, as attachments to banqueting vessels or to furniture. In the absence of a direct monumental prototype, figurines of satyrs such as the

---

27 Braun, *Die Musikkultur Atlisraels/Palästinas* (Freiburg and Göttingen, 1999), 186. See also Christine Kondoleon, *Domestic and Divine: Roman Mosaics in the House of Dionysos* (Ithaca, NY, 1995); Sean Freyne, "Dionysos and Heracles in Galilee: The Sepphoris Mosaic in Context," in Douglas R. Edwards, ed., *Religion and Society in Roman Palestine: Old Questions, New Approaches* (London and New York, 2004), 56-69.

28 Gideon Foerster and Yoram Tsafrir, "The Beth-Shan Excavation Project," *Excavations and Surveys in Israel/Hadashot Arkheologiyot* 6 (1987-88): 7-43.

29 Jacob Ory, 'A Painted Tomb near Ascalon,' *Quarterly of the Department of Antiquities in Palestine* VIII (1939):38-44.

one found in Sepphoris are more likely to represent Roman provincial reinterpretations of a Hellenistic type than a specific copy.[30] The *syrinx* held by the satyr figurine found in Sepphoris supports a banqueting context in a private home. The other *syrinx*, depicted on the mosaic floor of a public building in the center of the city, may also be understood as being loosely associated with this pagan cult, and probably had the same cultural context as the bronze figurine.

Horns (*Hatzotzrot*): Regarded as an "elite" instrument, the trumpet descends from the animal horn and is similar to it.[31] It appears rarely, and in ancient Egypt it exhibits a clear cultic and military affiliation.[32] In Israel, despite its significance in the Old Testament and in the Dead Sea Scrolls,[33] the trumpet appears only in the second and third centuries BCE, on a wall painting in Maresha, possibly associated with hunting and resembling the Roman *tuba*.[34]

In Sepphoris, two horns (*hatzotzrot*) are depicted in the fifth-century synagogue mosaic, and thus in a specifically Jewish context. Although the archaeologists who first described this mosaic referred to them as trumpets, organologically they should not be interpreted as such. They were described as slightly curved tubes that widen gently at one end, decorated with two rings set at regular intervals.[35] Braun claims that trumpets of this period were always straight, or, in the case of metal horns, remarkably curved; that they were clearly wider at the bell; and that they were never decorated, although they sometimes had metal rings for reinforcement.[36] Therefore, it does not seem feasible to accept these trumpets as an accurate rendering of the instruments described in the Old Testament. A possible explanation is that the artist, who was unfamiliar with those trumpets, simply drew horns and took (or rather mistook) them to be the temple trumpets.

---

30 See Sarah H. Cormack's comment in "Catalogue of the Exhibition," in Nagy *et al, Sepphoris in Galilee*, 171-72.
31 Braun, "Musical Instruments," in *The Oxford Encyclopaedia of Archaeology in the Near East*, ed. Eric M. Meyers (Oxford and New York, 1997), 4:25.
32 Hans Hickmann, "Ägypten," in *Musikgeschichte in Bildern*, ed. Heinrich Besseler, Max Schneider, and Werner Bachmann (Leipzig, 1961) 2:74; Subhi Rashid, "Ägypten und Mesopotamien," in *Musikgeschichte in Bildern* 2:143.
33 *The Dead Sea Scrolls Concordance*, vol. 1, *The Non Biblical Texts from Qumran*, ed. Martin G. Abegg with James E. Bowley and Edward M. Cook, in consultation with Emanuel Tov (Leiden and Boston, 2003), ref. 1QM III, 1-10 and VII, 13,15.
34 Amos Kloner and Joachim Braun, "Hellenistic Painted Tombs at Marisa," *Oriental Art* 6 (2000): 47-52.
35 Weiss and Netzer, *Promise and Redemption*, 20-21 and n. 35; In his *The Sepphoris Synagogue*, Weiss describes a horn with an elongated, slightly convex shaft, widening at one end, with rings set at fixed intervals (page 82). See also Curt Sachs, *The History of Musical Instruments* (New York,1940), 120.
36 Braun, *Music in Ancient Israel/Palestine*, 208-209.

Four points are worth mentioning in this regard: (1) the horns do, in fact, differ significantly from the *shofarot* depicted in the second band of the mosaic with regard to their curvature; (2) Braun's argument that trumpets of this period were always either straight or remarkably curved overlooks the fact that the representation here was not intended to be true to the period in which the mosaic was made; (3) although we are unacquainted with an animal whose horns resemble those depicted here, it is noteworthy that the depiction is similar to the one in the "Aaron Panel" of the Dura Europos synagogue;[37] and (4) it is well known that the term *trumpet* was often confused with a single horn or a single pipe, some of which have a very slightly flared bell at the end.[38]

***Shofar* or Ram's Horn**: A sound tool associated with ritual, the *shofar* is a distinct symbol of Jewish faith and of national identity. From the various artifacts found, it appears that the *shofar* did not symbolize simply the idea of atonement or immortality based on Abraham's sacrifice of Isaac, nor did it symbolize merely a certain messianic interpretation.[39] Its eschatological significance has been attested.[40] It was not merely "a decorative convention,"[41] but rather a holistic, national, ethnic symbol that appeared in various artistic forms. Early evidence of the Jewish "symbolic grouping" displayed on the Beth Nattif oil lamps, the Hammat Tiberias mosaic, and the Beth She'an engravings, appeared contemporaneously with the greatest masterpieces of late Roman to Early Byzantine art.

In Sepphoris, the *shofar* engraved on the copper seal and on the oil lamp attest to the presence of Jews in the city. Seals were usually attached to important documents or engraved onto valuable objects. The Jewish traditional motifs found on seals may bear witness to an official consignment of Jewish authority in the city. It is commonly accepted that items engraved on small artifacts such as seals and lamps bear national or religious connotations.[42]

***Tympanum* or Frame Drum**: This type of drum was particularly common in the Near East.[43] Terracotta female figurines from Mesopotamia date to the third millennium BCE, and Egyptian frame drums are also well attested, the

---

37 See Leon Yarden, *The Spoils of Jerusalem on the Arch of Titus* (Stockholm, 1991), 117, fig. III.31.
38 Bélis, "Aulos," 178; also *Mishnah Rosh Hashana*, 3:2. Yarden suggests that the confusion may have arisen on account of the increased use of all kinds of horns in Herod's Temple. See Yarden, *The Spoils of Jerusalem*, 102 n. 7.
39 Cecil Roth, "Messianic Symbolism in Palestinian Archaeology," *Palestine Exploration Fund Quarterly* 86 (1955): 151-64.
40 Goodenough, *Jewish Symbols*, 4:170.
41 Bathia Bayer, *The Material Relics of Music in Ancient Palestine and Its Environs* (Tel Aviv, 1963).
42 Braun, *Music in Ancient Israel/Palestine*, 316
43 James Blades, Janet K. Page, and James Holland, "Drum," in *The New Grove Dictionary*, 7:601.

rectangular shaped drums being popular at banquets and always played by women.[44] Archaeological evidence and ethnographic parallels suggest that the *tuppim* (timbrels or tabrets) mentioned in Genesis 31:27 were probably frame drums without jingles. The *tympanum* appearing in Sepphoris as part of the Dionysian scene is associated with Greek culture, and its appearance together with an *aulos* resembles portrayals of those same instruments found in other Graeco-Roman cities.[45]

Lyre: The symmetrical lyre was popular during the Roman period and used at joyful folk feasts such as Dionysian processions. The lyre with a rounded resonator was a popular folk instrument, often shown in the hands of a centaur (as we see, for example, in the Sheikh Zouède mosaic). It seems reasonable to assume that, in the partly preserved panel depicting a triumphal procession and entitled *Pompi* (Πομπη), the centaur depicted next to his *aulos*-playing companion in front of Dionysos's chariot may have held a lyre in his hands.[46]

The symbolic portrayal of musical instruments became established among the various ethnic, religious and social groups in ancient Israel between the second century BCE and the second century CE. Such portrayals appear on Ptolemaic coins (125-110 BCE) with the portrayal of two types of lyres, the symmetrical and the asymmetrical, and they also appear on Bar Kokhba coins (132-135 CE), presumably as anti-Roman symbols encoding a desire for religious and political freedom.[47] Use of the lyre seems to have dwindled during this period, having been replaced by the smaller, more portable lutes and harps, which were better suited for professional virtuosos and enabled more sophisticated performances. Depictions of lyres soon became more abstract, idealized, and symbolic.

It is interesting to note that the lyres found in Sepphoris are the only instruments that appear in distinctively Jewish as well as Greek mythological settings. These two depictions differ significantly from each other, however. In one case, the lyre is held by Orpheus;[48] in the other, it is part of the zodiac depicted on the synagogue floor. The former constitutes a rare depiction of the instrument. This type of lyre is generally associated with the upper strata of the population, and the inaccurate rendering of the instrument hints at a

---

44 DeMarini, "Komos," 382-84.
45 Waner, "Tarbut Hamuzika," 91-97.
46 During the Roman period, centaurs became part of the Dionysiac *thiasos* and were depicted playing the flute and cithara as contributors to the jubilation. See R.R.R. Smith, *Hellenistic Sculpture: A Handbook* (New York, 1991), 131-32.
47 Ya'akov Meshorer, *Otzar Matbe'ot haYehudim* (Jerusalem, 1997), 135.
48 Orpheus, a Thracian hero, was the son of Oiagros or Apollo and the Muse Kalliope. Known as a gifted singer and kithara player, this divine musician could charm animals, trees and even rocks with his music.

symbolic meaning rather than a relationship to its time and place.[49] Like the Dionysian mosaic, this floor decorated a private *triclinium*, and was found in a residential building situated west of the *cardo* (under the western church), surrounded by panels with scenes from everyday life. Orpheus is depicted sitting and playing (or rather holding) a chordophone, calming the wild animals and birds with his music. The panels of this mosaic were made according to the emblem tradition. They are stylistically similar to those of the Dionysian floor, and have been tentatively dated to the late third or early fourth century CE, by which time lyres had largely been replaced by the smaller chordophones.

Another interesting find relating to music in Sepphoris appears in the zodiac of the synagogue floor. A large, three-stringed, symmetrical lyre is depicted in the sign of Gemini, where it is held by one of the twins. The lyre, considered a symbol of spiritual and physical harmony in both Jewish and Christian thought, was here placed with the twins, a symbol of likeness.[50] The zodiac was considered to be a representative *par excellence* of the cosmos, the symbol of G-d, creator of order and of the universe.[51] The notion of "cosmic music," introduced by Boethius (ca. 480-524), dominated the philosophy of music during the entire Middle Ages,[52] and it is interesting to note that it came into use around the time that the Sepphoris synagogue was built. The zodiac lyre may thus be seen as a symbol of this harmony and order, and the twins with their lyre may have symbolized the orders of *musica mundana* (music of the spheres) and *musica humana* (music of the soul).[53] As such, the depiction of the synagogue mosaic may be seen as a very significant contribution of Judaism to the understanding of the zodiac.[54]

---

49 Waner, "Tarbut Hamuzika," 84-89.
50 Helmut Giesel, *Studien zur Symbolik der Musikinstrumente in Schrifttum der alten und mittelalterlichen Kirche. Von den Anfängen bis zum 13. Jahrhundert* (Regensburg, 1978). The Hebrew word for twins (*te'omim*) derives from the word *te'um/to'em*, meaning coordination, equalization, synchronization, or harmony.
51 Bianca Kühnel, "The Synagogue Floor Mosaic in Sepphoris: Between Paganism and Christianity," in Lee I. Levin and Ze'ev Weiss, eds., *From Dura to Sepphoris: Studies in Jewish Art and Society in Late Antiquity* (Portsmouth, 2000), 37-43.
52 Henry Chadwick, *Boethius: The Consolations of Music, Logic, Theology and Philosophy* (Oxford, 1981).
53 In his *De institutione musica*, Boethius explains that the first term refers to the orderly, mathematical relations observable in the behavior of the stars and planets, and the second to the ways in which such harmonious relations are imprinted on and exemplified in the body and soul of humans.
54 It is important to note that the depiction of Gemini in Sepphoris is based upon a Roman model and is apparently not unique. It appears in a Tunisian mosaic from Bir Chana, and was probably used in Caesarea as well. On this subject, see Margaret Alexander and Aïcha Ben Abed Ben Khader, "Tuburbo Majus," in *Corpus des Mosaiques de Tunisie* (Tunis, 1991), 2:123-27, Plate LXIX, figure 430A; and Weiss, *The Sepphoris Synagogue*, 114.

The lyre depicted in the Sepphoris synagogue is the more popular, folk type of lyre. It is similar to the instrument held by David-as-Orpheus in the Dura Europos synagogue mural (although the resonator of the latter is rounded, whereas here the base is divided into two semi-circles), but it differs significantly from the stylized kitharas that appear on the Orpheus mosaics of the fourth through sixth centuries in Jerusalem and Gaza,[55] and even from the one found in Sepphoris itself, a mere 400-500 meters away from the synagogue.

Thus, the synagogue mosaic is of special importance for our understanding of the city's cultural and ethnic setting. With the zodiac wheel depicted at its center, it comprises part of a deeply rooted tradition in ancient synagogues, first attested at Hammat Tiberias in the fourth century. Frequently compared in significance to the Dura Europos wall murals,[56] the Sepphoris synagogue mosaic is probably the best evidence of the pagan-Judeo-Christian syncretistic culture that blossomed in ancient Israel from the Hellenistic-Roman times to the end of the sixth century.[57] The zodiac itself, a common motif in pagan art, became a popular theme in synagogue floor mosaics. Depiction of the four seasons, the twelve signs, and the sun god Helios was common in pagan and Christian art, but the combination of these three elements appears only in synagogues. This mosaic, which differs stylistically from previously known mosaics, attests, on the one hand, to a high degree of influence exerted by Hellenistic culture upon the Jewish community. Yet, at the same time it also exhibits significant variations upon Hellenistic themes made by members of that same community. Indeed, it might even be regarded as an artistic reflection of the Judeo-Christian discourse regarding the

---

55 Asher Ovadiah and Sonia Mucznik, "Orpheus from Jerusalem—Pagan or Christian Image?" *The Jerusalem Cathedra* 1 (1981): 152-66; Ovadiah, "Excavations in the Area of the Ancient Synagogue at Gaza," *Israel Exploration Journal* 19, no. 4 (1969): 193-98.

56 Carl Hermann Kraeling, *1979 Excavations at Dura Europos: The Synagogue (Final Report)*, vol. 8, pt. 1, *The Synagogue* (New York, 1979), 60-70.

57 Goodenough refers to Zodiac cycles in synagogues as expressions of Hellenistic mysticism made possible by the collapse of rabbinical control. Narkiss provides a cosmological interpretation. Kühnel concludes that the Zodiac's central location in numerous early Byzantine synagogues must be regarded as more than a mere manifestation of Hellenistic beliefs condemned by the rabbis. According to her, Zodiac cycles, though taken from Roman art, constitute one of the most authentic aspects of Jewish art, which were consciously and consistently adapted to fit the beliefs and aspirations of Galilean Jews during the Byzantine period. See Goodenough, *Jewish Symbols*, 2:190-205; Bezalel Narkiss, "Pagan, Christian and Jewish Elements in the Art of the Ancient Synagogue," in Lee I. Levine, ed., *The Synagogue in Late Antiquity* (Philadelphia, 1987), 183-88; Kühnel, "The Synagogue Floor," 31-43.

identity of the chosen people, the rebuilding of the Temple, and Messianic restoration.[58]

To appreciate the complexity of trying to comprehend the ethnic makeup of Sepphoris, we might consider the example of the bronze figurine of Pan (or a satyr) playing the *syrinx*. Ceramic and numismatic evidence suggests that the dwelling under which this figurine was found was occupied by a family of wealth and status. Although the inhabitants' apparent concern for matters of ritual purity could indicate that they were pious Jews, the domicile also yielded examples of Roman decorative art. Thus, it may be assumed that the presence of such artifacts is indicative of aesthetic tastes rather than a pagan inclination of its owner. Although the location of the find indicates a domestic context within a residential area that was probably mostly Jewish, the presence of these artifacts probably reflects the influence of pagan decorative culture rather than the adoption of any set of religious beliefs or practices.

Philip Bohlman maintains that the encounter with forces that challenged Jewish identity and culture—a "cultural and musical Other"—led to a creative response and a conscious mustering of musical symbols and styles to articulate Jewish identity.[59] Referring to Jewish music in nineteenth-century Europe, he writes of a new impetus and a linking of music to Jewish history in profound new ways. Inventing Jewish music during that time became a way of addressing the need for change. We may ask if this was also the case in Roman and Byzantine Sepphoris. So far, apparently, we have no signs of new music in the Jewish population of the city during this period. We could thus conclude that "Jewish" musical instruments—or, rather, sound tools such as horns—were used symbolically, in both a religious context (such as on the synagogue floor) as well as in an ethnic or social context (as evidenced by the copper seal). No other instruments or "ensembles" have survived to demonstrate otherwise, and, based upon the literary sources, we can assume that the Jewish population, rather than striving to demonstrate its own unique identity, chose the syncretic alternative. When Jews visited the local theatre, and thus elicited warnings and objections from sages, they must have encountered mythological scenes, which included musical instruments, all around them. They might have also participated in social events through the city, many of which were not necessarily "Jewish." Enjoying religious autonomy, they were almost certainly powerful and independent enough to make the decisions that governed their own lives. This explains, for example, their decision to depict the sun god in the center of the zodiac mosaic not in the

---

58 Kurt Weitzmann and Herbert Kessler, *The Frescoes of the Dura Synagogue and Christian Art* (Washington, DC, 1990), 178-83; Weiss, *The Sepphoris Synagogue*, 139-40 and 249-56.
59 Philip V. Bohlman, "Inventing Jewish Music," in Eliyahu Schleifer and Edwin Seroussi, eds., *Studies in Honor of Israel Adler* (Jerusalem, 2002), 33-74.

usual manner but as a symbolic representation.[60] Perhaps because they were not, in fact, threatened by "the Other," the Jews of Sepphoris did not find it necessary to invent their own music culture. Rather, they chose only to enhance it through the cultivation and development of its traditional, symbolic aspects.

Bearing in mind that the nature and existence of ethnic groups is widely assumed to depend upon ethnic boundaries defined by manipulations and symbols, and furthermore that these symbols may be either material or behavioral, it seems that the important factor to note in this case is not the sum of all characteristics revealed by the archaeological culture (these may be shared with other groups), but those characteristics that the group has chosen to represent its symbolic identity. The tenacity of the Jews of Sepphoris in upholding their symbolic identity represents, to my mind, their desire to maintain their uniqueness and distinctiveness despite the syncretic tendencies found in other spheres of their daily lives. The musical instruments and sound tools depicted on the "Jewish" mosaic floor found in the city demonstrate this insistence.

The wealth and variety of mosaics found in Sepphoris place the city among the foremost cities of the Roman and Byzantine East.[61] Their importance lies not only in the quantity and richness of style and iconography, but also in the fact that they were found in a city that was mainly populated by Jews. The finds reveal a hitherto unknown facet of urban Jewish life in the Galilee, and present a picture of Jewish society and its relation to the surrounding Hellenistic culture. The level of influence that this latter culture had upon Jewish society is an issue that many scholars have pondered, especially considering that this was a period when paganism was declining and Christianity was on the rise. The musical instruments depicted in these mosaics provide further confirmation of this influence, allowing us to take a closer look at daily life in Sepphoris during the time in which those instruments were constructed and used.

Conclusions

In the first centuries of the Common Era, the ethnic-religious image of Sepphoris began to change. Having been a predominantly Jewish city well into the third century, the city seems to have become more Hellenized toward the fourth century.[62] At that time, still boasting a notable Jewish population, Sepphoris ex-hibited strong syncretic ethnic tendencies, which were reflected in the musical culture of

---

60 Compare the Sepphoris depiction with that of Bet Alpha or the Hammat Tiberias synagogue mosaics. The absence of Helios in the Sepphoris zodiac is a definite and unique "statement," hitherto unknown in synagogue Zodiacs. The complete motif as depicted here has no parallels in the region in any other religious structure, whether pagan or Christian.
61 So far more than forty have been uncovered. Balty, "La mosaïque antique."
62 Mark Chancey and Eric M. Meyers, "How Jewish Was Sepphoris in Jesus' Time?" *Biblical Archeology Review* 28, no. 4 (2000): 19-33.

the city. Along with the Dionysian mosaic and its numerous *auloi* and a *tympanum*, other musical artifacts confirming the popularity of the Dionysian cult have been discovered, among them the bronze figurine, from the second or third century, of a satyr or Pan figure. Yet in the Byzantine period a synagogue was built, demonstrating the existence of a strong Jewish community with its religious aspirations and symbolic use of musical instruments and sound tools depicted in its mosaic floor.

The music-related items, along with other material finds in Sepphoris, demonstrate the flourishing of Judaism in an urban environment during the Roman and Byzantine periods, a time when paganism was still a prominent feature in many cities, and Christianity was beginning to develop. Both the Jewish and the Christian communities apparently found the syncretistic setting of the Hellenistic musical culture a fertile ground and a vibrant catalyst for constructive symbiosis. It should therefore not surprise us to find Dionysian themes on the mosaic floor of a private dwelling, a *syrinx* in a mosaic floor of a public building in the city center, another *syrinx* in the hands of a bronze figurine, and a depiction of Orpheus playing his lyre in yet another private domicile. It seems that although Jews, Christians, and pagans all had their own particular religious beliefs and tenets, daily life linked all elements of Galilean society, rendering the various lifestyles far more similar to one another than the individual groups may have realized.[63] Under such circumstances, we may assume that music, being a part of everyday life and an important component of culture, would present a very similar picture.

However, this study also indicates that even amidst the dynamic cultural syncretism of the period, there probably was, ultimately, divergence rather than fusion in the musical culture of Sepphoris. When the syncretistic inclinations of the local music culture ran counter to Jewish and Christian theology, or when these communities felt a growing threat from "the Other," this conflict assumed, perhaps for the first time, an innovative means of expression—as we saw in the image of a lyre held by the twins in the sign of Gemini on the synagogue mosaic floor in a calm, pastoral setting, and in the Dionysian iconography that subtly included Judaeo-Christian elements. Such artistic expressions served as a response to the prevalent claims made by the Other. Finally, in the music-related finds of Sepphoris we also observe the development of an organised, controlled, and carefully thought-out music culture, despite—or maybe even resulting from—the ethnic conflicts and tensions that must surely have existed in the city.

---

63 Isaiah Gafni, "Daily Life in Galilee and Sepphoris," 51-57.

Table 1: The corpus of musical instruments found in Sepphoris*:

Ref. No.	Musical** Instrument	Classification of Instrument	Material / Art Form	Context & Location of Find	Ethno-Religious Association	Period
1	Bell	Idiophone	Bronze instrument	City's Water system	?	Byzantine (4th-7th C)
2	Bell	Idiophone	Bronze instrument	City's Water system	?	Byzantine (4th-5th C)
3	Bells	Idiophone	Stone tesserae of mosaic floor	Synagogue floor (band 3 – Consecration of Aaron)	Jewish setting	Byzantine (5th C)
4	Cymbals	Idiophone	Oil lamp	?	?	Byzantine
5	Cymbals	Idiophone	Stone tesserae of mosaic floor	Synagogue floor (band 4 – Basket of first fruits)	Jewish setting	Byzantine (5th C)
6	Dbl Aulos	Aerophone	Stone tesserae of mosaic floor	*Triclinium*, private dwelling, acropolis	Gk Mythology	Roman (3rd C)
7	Dbl Aulos	Aerophone	Stone tesserae of mosaic floor	*Triclinium*, private dwelling, acropolis	Gk Mythology	Roman (3rdC)
8	Dbl Aulos	Aerophone	Stone tesserae of mosaic floor	*Triclinium*, private dwelling, acropolis	Gk Mythology	Roman (3rdC)
9	Dbl Aulos	Aerophone	Stone tesserae of mosaic floor	*Triclinium*, private dwelling, acropolis	Gk Mythology	Roman (3rdC)
10	Dbl Aulos	Aerophone	Stone tesserae of mosaic floor	*Triclinium*, private dwelling, acropolis	Gk Mythology	Roman (3rdC)
11	Syrinx	Aerophone	Bronze Figurine	Res. Area W. summit of the acropolis	Gk Mythology	Roman (2ndC)

Table 1 . (continued):

Ref. No.	Musical** Instrument	Classification of Instrument	Material / Art Form	Context & Location of Find	Ethno-Religious Association	Period
12	Syrinx	Aerophone	Stone tesserae of mosaic floor	medallion, public building in 'city centre'	Gk Mythology	Byzantine
13	Horns (ḥaṣoṣrot)	Aerophone	Stone tesserae of mosaic floor	Synagogue floor (band 3 - Consecration of Aaron)	Jewish setting	Byzantine (5th C)
14	Shofarot	Aerophone	Stone tesserae of mosaic floor	Synagogue floor (band 2 – Architectural façade and Jewish symbols)	Jewish setting	Byzantine (5th C)
15	Shofar	Aerophone	Copper seal	?	Jewish	Byzantine
16	Shofar	Aerophone	Oil lamp	?	Jewish	Late Roman (4th C)
17	Tympanum	Membranophone	Stone tesserae of mosaic floor	*Triclinium*, private dwelling, acropolis	Gk Mythology	Roman (3rd-4th C)
18	Lyre	Chordophone	Stone tesserae of mosaic floor	Synagogue floor (band 5 – the zodiac)	Jewish setting	Byzantine (5th C)
19	Lyre	Chordophone	Stone tesserae of mosaic floor	Orpheus, *Triclinium*, private dwelling, 'city center'	Gk Mythology	Roman (3rd-4th C)

* References: 1&2 – Tsuk, 'Aqueducts of Sepphoris', in: Nagy et al., Crosscurrents, 1996: 45-9 [IAA 96-426&7]; 3,5,13,14 & 17 - Weiss & Netzer, *Promise and Redemption: A Synagogue Mosaic from Sepphoris*. 2nd ed, Jerusalem 1998; 4- IAA 99-2789, unpublished; 6,7,8,9,10 & 16 – Talgam & Weiss, 'the Mosaics of the House of Dionysos at Sepphoris', *Qedem* 44, Jerusalem 2004; 15 – on exhibition at the site; 12 – in situ; 18 – Weiss & Netzer, *Qadmoniot* 113/1(1997):3-21; 11&16 Nagy et al, *Crosscurrents*, 1996:171,222.

** Only #1&2 are actual musical instruments.

Jan Stęszewski

MÜNDLICHE MUSIKTRADITION DER JUDEN IN POLEN
Forschungsaufgaben, Ausgangspunkte, Methodik, Informations- Und Quellen-Forschungsstand

Die Komplexität und inhaltliche Weite des hier behandelten Themas, sowie die erforderliche Kürze dieses Artikels bergen in sich das Risiko, dass dessen Wert davon abhängt, ob die Schlüsselproblematik überzeugend auf-gezeigt ist und ob sie mit Hilfe der erforderlichen Beispiele und Verweise mit der bestehende Fachliteratur zu argumentieren ist. Es handelt sich also um die Frage der Methodik und in diesem Zusammenhang um die Frage nach den Chancen einer Rekonstruktion des im Titel bezeichneten Themas.

Die mündliche Tradition, oder genauer, die phonisch-perzeptive Gedächtniskommunikation war und ist auch weiterhin neben der schriftlichen der zweite unverzichtbare Überlieferungsstrang und Wissensquelle über die musikalische Vergangenheit. Nachteil des mündlichen Stranges war und ist die Variabilität der Überlieferung, die Unbeständigkeit der Erinnerung oder gar die Unterbrechung der kontinuierlichen Tradition der Kommunikationsteilnehmer, wie auch die Zeit, die bis zur Erfindung des Walzenphonographen durch A. Edison oder späteren Techniken der Tonaufzeichnung und –konservierung, die das gesellschaftliche Gedächtnis unterstützten oder ersetzten, verging. Zur mündlichen Tradition der jüdischen Musik in Polen gehören religiöse Gesänge (Inkantationen in den Synagogen), weltliche Volkslieder (zum Beispiel, rituelle Volkslieder der Chassidim, Gesänge in den Ghettos) und Instrumentalmusik (Tänze und die so genannte Klezmermusik).

Aus der Geschichte des jüdischen Volks in Polen

Die jüdische Geschichte ist kompliziert und tragisch (ethnische und religiöse Minderheit, zahlreiche Migrationen, isolierte Ghettos, Pogrome, Aufstand im Warschauer Ghetto, durch Philosemitismus, sowie Assimilierung/Polonisierung, kompensierter Antisemitismus, Holocaust). Über Jahrhunderte lebten die Juden innerhalb der sich verschiebenden Grenzen Polens, die seinerseits kein einfaches Schicksal hatten. Die Juden stellten einen erheblichen Anteil der Bevölkerung in Polen dar, bis zu mehreren Millionen.

Die früheste Spur eines jüdisch-polnischen Kontakts, noch vor der Ansiedlung von durch Toleranz und Privilegien angeworbenen Juden in Polen,

---

Übersetzung dieses Essays aus der Polnische von Martin Buscermoehle.

führt zu Ibrahim ibn Jakub aus Tortosa (Spanien), einem jüdischen Kaufmann, Arzt und Reisenden, dessen Reisebeschreibungen europäischer Länder (Deutschland, Böhmen) aus dem 10. Jahrhundert der arabische Chronist Al. Bekri überlieferte, unter anderem, über den polnischen Herrscher Mieszko, sowie wertvolle Informationen über die Kultur der Slawen. Selbst wenn in der damaligen Zeit jegliche ethnischen Identifikationen unsicher sind, so gibt es doch keine besseren.

Die ersten Informationen über die dauerhafte Ansiedlung von Juden in Polen beziehen sich auf die 1. Hälfte des 11. Jahrhunderts. Größere jüdische Ansiedlungen bildeten sich in Lviv (Lemberg) und Kraków (Krakau), später Lodź (Litzmannstadt), kleinere in den Städten und Dörfern der Kresy (Grenzland), also in Südostpolen. Sie pachteten Mühlen, Wirtshäuser, ja sogar Landgüter und besaßen lokale Selbstverwaltungen und eine eigene Gerichtsbarkeit. Sie siedelten auch in Schlesien und Wielkopolska (Großpolen). Über ihre Tradition und musikalische Praktiken ist, außer der Ikonographie,[1] fast nichts bekannt. Ein Hinweis könnte sein, dass sie sowohl dem sefardischen wie aschkenasischen Judentum entstammten und unter der polnischen Landbevölkerung im Ruf standen, gute Musiker zu sein, vor allem die Geiger. Diese Erfahrung und Überzeugung reicht unter den polnischen Dorfmusikanten (z. B. in der Gegend um Sandomierz [Sandomir] bis ins beginnende 21. Jahrhundert). Jüdische Musikanten waren Instrumentallehrer und sowohl Träger der eigenen Tradition, wie auch der polnischen Landbevölkerung.

Das Aufeinandertreffen der Geschichte und der Kulturaustausch zwischen dem jüdischen und dem polnischen Volk ist folglich ein Problem an sich. Damit beschäftigen sich weitsprechende Arbeiten. Es ist jedoch fraglich, ob die in der mündlichen jüdischen Tradition entstehenden und existierenden musikalischen Objekte samt der bestehenden Quellen anderer Art angesichts der vergehenden Zeit, Diaspora und des Versterbens der Teilnehmer der hier besprochenen Tradition, irgend eine Chance haben rekonstruiert zu werden.

Spuren der Tradition und Beispiele interethnischer musikalischer Kontakte

1. Am 15. Juni 1731, in Krotoszyn (Krotoschin) und Wielkopolska (Großpolen), wurde Primas Theodor Potocki bei der Visitation der hiesigen Kirche vom Adel, der Stadt, den Zechen und dem jüdischen *Kahal* (Hebr.: Versammlung) mit Musik begrüßt.[2]
2. In Szafarnia, am 26. August 1825, berichtet in einem Brief der fünfzehnjährige Frederic Chopin in scherzhaftem Ton seinen Eltern von seiner zufälligen Mitwirkung in der Kapelle (des Juden?) Fryc. Die während des

---

1 Jerzy Banach, Die *Musik in den bildenden Künsten Polens*, Kraków, 1965.
2 *Kurier polski* (1731), Nr. 78.

traditionellen Erntedankfestes auftretende Kapelle bestand aus zwei Geigen (davon eine mit nur drei Seiten) und einer Bassgeige (mit nur einer Seite).[3]
3. Am 01. September 1824 schreibt F. Chopin: "die Juden kamen zum Hof in Oborów, um Getreide zu kaufen, ich spielte ihnen den Majufes."[4] Das Spiel von Chopin versetzte die Händler in solche Begeisterung, dass sie alles um sich herum vergaßen und nicht nur fröhlich hüpften und tanzten, sondern den Gutsherren eindringlich baten, er möge dafür sorgen, dass dieser Spieler ihnen in Kürze bei der bevorstehenden Hochzeit aufspiele, "denn er spielte, als wäre er ein gebürtiger Jude."[5]
4. F. Chopins Mazurka a-moll op.17 Nr. 4, genannt *Der kleine Jude*.

Adam Mickiewicz (1798-1855)

Im Nationalepos des polnischen grossen Dichters Mickiewicz "Pan Tadeusz," Buch IV (1832-34), ist der Jude Jankiel eine der Schlüssel- und Symbolfiguren. Jankiel ist ein Wirt, polnischer Patriot und Zymbelspieler, vielleicht geheimer Gesandter des sich formierenden polnischen Heeres, welches Ende des 18. Jahrhunderts an den polnischen Teilungen mitwirkten und dem Befehl zum Aufstand gegen die Russen überbringen sollte. Jankiel spielt auf Zymbeln die Mazurka General Dąbrowskis "Jeszcze Polska nie zginęła, póki my żyjemy" (Noch ist Polen nicht verloren, solange wir leben), die zur polnischen Nationalhymne wurde. Mit seinem Spiel weckte er den Enthusias-mus der Hörer. Juden kommen in der polnischen Literatur sehr häufig vor, sowohl geachtet, wie der jüdische Wirt in "Wesele" (Hochzeit; 1901), einem Drama von Stanisław Wyspiański, wie auch getadelt (z. B. als polnische Bauern zum Trinken verleitende Wirte).

Józef Michał Guzikow (1806-1837)

Józef Michał (Joseph Michael) Guzikow war im 19. Jahrhundert ein weitbekannter jüdischer Musiker, welcher auf einer Strohharmonika (Vorläufer des Xylophons) spielte. Seine Virtuosität mit welcher er eigene Phantasien, Variationen über Opernmelodien und jüdische oder polnische Volksthemen spielte, begeisterten unter anderem Fryderyk Chopin, Felix Mendelssohn-Barholdy, George Sand und Alphonse de Lamartine.

---

3   E. Sydow (Hrsg.), *Korespondencja Fryderyka Chopina*, Warszawa, 1953, S. 54.
4   Ein jüdisches Lied, welches zu bestimmten religiösen Riten und Anlässen gesungen wurde, hier in der Bedeutung *jüdische Melodie*.
5   M. Tomaszewski (Hrsg.), *M. Chopin, człowiek, dzieło, rezonans*, Poznań, 1998, S. 29.

Polnische Schriftsteller

Eliza Orzeszkowa (1841-1910) war Autorin von Erzählungen und Romane, in denen sie die jüdischen Milieus gesellschaftlich analysierte. Julian Stryjkowski (Pesach Stark, 1905-96) aber ist derjenige Schriftsteller, der wohl am ausführlichsten die musikalischen Praktiken, ekstatische Gesänge und Tänze der polnischen Chassidim in der kleinstädtischen Szenerie der zaddikischen Höfe des 20. Jahrhunderts beschreibt, wie zum Beispiel, im Roman "Austeria" (1966), der in 1982 durch J. Kawalerowicz Verfilmt wurde. Die Scriften von Icchok Singer (Isaac Bashevis Singer, 1904-91), Rabinersohn aus der Gegend um Warschau, Nobelpreisträger (1992) stellen die städtisch-jüdische Kultur dar.

Das Sammeln der mündlichen Tradition des 19. Jahrhunderts in Polen

Im Einklang mit der Ideologie der Romantik (J. G. Herder, in Polen–H. Kołłątajs) wurde die mündliche Musiktradition intensiv gesammelt, dabei jedoch die Tradition der jüdischen Minderheit unberücksichtigt gelassen, abgesehen von einzelnen Vokal- und Instrumentalwerken, welche z.b. beim Sternsingen um die Weihnachtszeit jüdische Gesänge und Tänze imitierten, wobei unter den Sternsingern die Figur des Juden unter keinen Umständen fehlen durfte.[6]

Das 20. Jahrhundert, die Zeit der phonographischen Archive

Regionales phonographisches Archiv am musikwissenschaftlichen Institut der Universität Poznań (Posen) (Ł. Kamieński); Zentrales phonographisches Archiv, Warszawa (J. Pulikowski), an der Nationalbilbliothek, später an der Reichsbibliothek Warschau; Staatliches Institut der Kunst, später Institut der Kunst der Polnischen Akademie der Wissenschaften; J. und M. Sobieski-Archivinstitut, Warschau beim Volkskulturzentrum des Polnischen Rundfunks, das eine CD-Serie herausgibt, unter der sich Aufnahmen jüdischer Traditionen befinden. Während des Zweiten Weltkriegs wurden die Archive in Poznań und Warschau völlig zerstört oder gingen spurlos unter.[7] In Warschau sind trotz der Bemühungen Pulikowskis auch von den Aufnahmen jüdischer mündlicher Tradition der Zwischenkriegszeit nur die veröffentlichten Sammlungen von Kipnis und Mordechaj Gebirtig (1877-1942) erhalten.[8]

---

6   Jan Stęszewski, *History of Ethnomusicological Research on Minorities in Poland: Circumstances and Motivations in 1969-75*, in: Hemetek Czekanowska und Naroditskaya Lechleitner (Hrsg.), *Manifold Identities: Studies on Music and Minorities*, London, 2004, S. 68-75.
7   P. Dahlig, *Tradycje muzyczne i ich przemiany. Między kulturą popularną i elitarną Polski międzywojennej*, Warszawa, 1998.
8   Thomas Nussbaumer, *Alfred Quellmalz und seine südtiroler Feldforschungen (1940-42). Eine Studie zur musikalischen Volskunde unter dem Nationalsozialismus*, Innsbruck,

Während eines kurzen Stipendienaufenthaltes in den Fünfzigerjahren des 20. Jahrhunderts in der Bundesrepublik Deutschland im Volksliedarchiv in Freiburg im Breisgau bei Prof. W. Wiora, stieß ich auf Prof. Edith Gerson-Kivi, die mir versicherte, in Israel dokumentiere man die mündliche Tradition der jüdischen Immigranten, darunter mit Sicherheit auch der Immigranten aus Polen. Den Stand dieser Sammlung bezüglich der mündlichen Tradition der polnischen Juden kenne ich jedoch nicht.

Im 20. und 21. Jahrhundert steigert sich in Polen das Interesse an jüdischen Traditionen, darunter an der Musik der Klezmerensembles, die aus dem Ausland importiert werden, oder aber die von polnischen Ensembles, insbesondere anlässlich der Festivale, aufgeführt wird, z. B. in Kraków im jüdischen Stadtteil Kazimierz. Diese Art der Praxis gehört eher in die Kategorie *simulacrum* als zur Kontinuität einer authentischen Tradition.

Die Forschungsprojekte B. Muszkalskas

In den letzten Jahren unternahm Prof. B. Muszkalska einzigartige Anstrengungen, um im In- und Ausland authentische Nachfolger der mündlichen jüdischen Tradition aufzuspüren, infolge derer eine Serie von Artikeln erschienen ist.

Schlussbemerkungen

Wie sich mit Hilfe der dargestellten Informationen leicht zeigen lässt, ist der Stand der Quellen und Untersuchungen unzureichend, auch wenn diese hier nicht vollständig aufgeführt wurden. Deshalb würde es sich lohnen, die Mühe auf sich zu nehmen und die bestehenden Sammlungen sowie die in der Diaspora, z. B. in den USA, Australien, Russland, Belarus, Litauen, Ukraine, in Israel (selbst die dokumentierten musikalischen und tänzerischen Praktiken an der Klagemauer in Jerusalem) und die in Polen anlässlich der Besuche der Rabbiner und Zaddikim (z. B. Lelów, Łańcut) lebenden Informante aufzusuchen, wodurch eine interessante und ergänzende Dokumentation entstehen könnte, die uns einer vollkommeneren Ausarbeitung der im Titel genannten Aufgabe näherbrächte.

Die Idee der allgemeinen Behauptungen, dass die Musik der Juden genetisch bedingt und deren Charakter ein fester Wert, eine Konstante wäre, ist hingegen von vornherein zu verwerfen, denn dabei handelte es sich um eine unhistorische Behauptung von der Art rassistischer Ideen.[9]

Wien, München, 2001; Isachar Fater, *Muzyka żydowska w Polsce w okresie międzywojennym. Przekład z hebrajskiego Ewa Świderska*, Warszawa, 1997.
9 Stęszewski, *Lexikon der Juden in der Musik*.

Ausgewählte Bibliographie

Bobrzymińska, Z. und Żebrowski, R. (Hrsg.) *Słownik Judaistyczny: Dzieje, Kultura, Religia*, Warszawa, 2003.

Buchner, A., *Die fortdauernde Verfemung in Polen*, in: Braun, J., Hoffmann T. und Karbusicky, V. (Hrsg.), *Verfemte Musik. Komponisten in den Diktaturen unseres Jahrhunderts*, Frankfurt am Main, 1995, S. 219-29.

Braun, J. und Sharvit, U. (Hrsg.), *Studies in Socio-Musical Sciences*, Ramat Gan, 1998.

Cała, A., Węgrzynek, H., und Zalewska, G. (Hrsg.), *Historia i kultura Żydów Polskich*, Warszawa, 2000.

Cyz, T., *Klezmerzy: Od skrzypka włóczęgi po prądy alternatywne*, in: *Tsadik Poznań Festiwal, 9-11.08.2007*, Poznań, 2007, S. 43-54.

Fuks, Marian, *Muzyka ocalona. Judaica polskie*, Warszawa, 1983.

Kipnis, Menachem, *6o Folkslider*, Warszawa, 1916.

Kipnis, Menachem, *80 Folkslider*, Warszawa, 1923.

Janion, Maria. *Bohater, spisek, smierc. Wyklady zydowskie*, wydawnictwo WAP, Warszawa, 2009

Muszkalska, Bożena, *Alien Melodies versus Jewish Identity in the Music of Ashkenazim from East-Europe*, in: *Shared Music and Minority Identities*, Croatia, 2006, S. 225-34.

O Problem modusu w aszkenazyjskich śpiewach synagogalnych, in: *Muzyka* 49 (2004), Nr. 3, S. 91-103.

Od rytuału do teatru muzycznego w kulturze wschodnioeuropejskich Żydów, in: *Operomania* (2004-05), Nr. 2, S. 8-9.

Sienkiewicz, W., und Hyciuk, G. (Hrsg.), *Wysiedlenia, wypędzenia i ucieczki, 1939-1959. Atlas ziem Polski, Polacy, Żydzi, Niemcy, Ukraińcy*, Warszawa, 2008.

Statelova, R. (Hrsg), *Freilach, Jazz, and Chopin: The Klezmer-Movement in Contemporary Poland*, in: *The Human World and Musical Diversity*, Sofia, 2008, S. 60-64.

Stęszewski, Jan, *History of Ethnomusicological Research on Minorities in Poland: Circumstances and Motivations in 1969-75*, see in: Czekanowska, H. und Lechleitner, N. (Hrsg.), *Manifold Identities: Studies on Music and Minorities*, London, 2004, S. 68-75.

Teatr żydowski w Polsce do 1939, in: *Kwartalnik Teatralny* 41, Nr. 1-4 (1992).

Uwalnianie iskier bożych - modlitwy w polskich synagogach, in: *Czas kultury* (2002), Nr. 5-6, S. 202-207.

Alexander Knapp

THE LITTLE GOAT MEETS THE LITTLE CHICKEN
Parallels Between Two Celebratory Songs in The Jewish and Bukharan Traditions

> One only kid, one only kid, which my father bought for two *zuzim*. The cat came and ate the kid, which my father bought for two *zuzim*. . . . Then came the dog and bit the cat. . . . Then came the stick and beat the dog. . . . Then came the fire that burned the stick. . . . Then came the water and quenched the fire. . . . Then came the ox and drank the water. . . . Then came the slaughterer and killed the ox. . . . Then came the angel of death and slew the slaughterer. . . . Then came the Most Holy—blessed be He!—and destroyed the angel of death that slew the slaughterer that killed the ox that drank the water that quenched the fire that burned the stick that beat the dog that bit the cat that ate the kid which my father bought for two *zuzim*. Had Gadya, Had Gadya.[1]

And now for something remarkably similar:

> Bravo, chicken, poor chicken. A farmer dammed up the water. Which water did he dam up? The water that put out a fire. Which fire did it put out? The fire that burned a stick. Which stick was burned? The stick that killed a dog. Which dog did it kill? The dog that ate a wolf. Which wolf did it eat? The wolf that ate the chicken. Which chicken did it eat? On top, it was a vividly colored chicken. It gave two eggs at once. The tail was white and it had a comb. My grandfather bought it for 100,000 dinars. He bought it for himself. Bravo, little chicken, poor chicken, bravo. *Murghak*.[2]

This paper opens with warmest thanks to Dr. Rozia Sultanova (formerly of the Music Department of the University of London School of Oriental and African Studies, currently at the University of Cambridge) and her husband, Dr. Hamid Ismailov (of the BBC World Service, Central Asia Section), for so generously sharing with me their invaluable expertise and insights concerning the history, music, cultures, and languages of Central Asia.

1 Translation adapted from George A. Kohut, "Had Gadya," in Isidore Singer, ed., *The Jewish Encyclopedia* (New York and London, 1904), vol. 6, 127.
2 The text is adapted from "Murghak (chicklet)," annotated by Theodore Levin and Otanazar Matykubov, published with the CD *Bukhara: Musical Crossroads of Asia* (Smithsonian/Folkways CD SF 40050, 1991). The original language is Tajik. However, this fact is not indicated in the liner notes to this recording, and the translation of the text into English is incomplete. According to Drs. Sultanova and Ismailov, the second part of the text states that everybody knows *(me do na)* about this chicken: kings, mullahs, doctors, goldsmiths, coppersmiths, carpenters, cooks, tailors, and simple people. It ends with the line, "The chicken belongs to me—it has two legs, two wings, and a crown upon its head" (personal communication).

The first song needs no introduction to those familiar with the *Seder* ritual on the first two nights of *Pesah*, just as the second song may well be familiar to those who have attended or performed in Islamic or Jewish *Toi* celebrations, particularly during weddings, in the Central Asian Bukharan tradition.

Celebratory songs such these two are, on the surface, usually humorous in content and intent, and they exist in folk and nursery-rhyme repertoires throughout the world. However, similarities between individual texts and/or tunes from widely separated regions are sometimes so striking that questions regarding chronology, direction of influence (if any), and the possibilities of a common source must be asked. In this essay, I shall compare *Had Gadya*, one of the most popular of the Jewish *z'mirot* (paraliturgical table songs), with *Murghak,* an equally entertaining Bukharan *mavrigi*—a style of song originating from the oasis city of Merv, now called Mari, in Turkmenistan. First, I shall look at the historical, social, and musical backgrounds of *Had Gadya* and *Murghak*. Then, I will compare their texts and consider the possible significance of their similarities and differences. Finally, I will examine the music itself.

Had Gadya

The theme of the Passover Festival is freedom, and the *Seder* celebration around the meal table at home commemorates and describes the Jewish exodus from Egypt, the redemption from slavery, the victory of light, and justice over darkness, tyranny and suffering. It can last many hours. Attendance is obligatory for all members of the nuclear family, who are often joined by extended family members, friends, and sometimes visitors as well. *Seder* means *order*, referring to the sequence of fifteen parts of the service, the centerpiece of which is the celebratory meal. The text of the celebration is called the *Haggadah*, literally *narrative*, and functions didactically to remind adults and children alike of the central doctrines of Judaism. The oldest parts of the liturgy are said to have developed during the period of the Second Temple. Lofty poetry and prose—partly biblical, partly consisting of later commentary—commingle with light-hearted ditties to suit all tastes. In order to keep even the youngest children awake and attentive deep into the small hours of the morning (the service can last until around 4:00 AM), a set of lively songs, many in the style of cumulative nursery rhymes, are recited towards the end of the service.[3]

Had Gadya is the very last of these songs and, in a sense, forms a kind of musical and social high point in the proceedings. There is some confusion as to its origin and earliest appearance in print. The *Encyclopedia Judaica* cites the 1590 *Haggadah* published in Prague and provides an illustration of the printed text in the original Aramaic (with a translation into Yiddish) in the Italian *Sereni*

---

3   This applies in the Ashkenazi, Provençal, Oriental-Sephardic and Babylonian traditions, but not, apparently, in the Portuguese, Yemenite or Bukharan rites.

Haggadah, which dates from the fifteenth century (Figure 1).[4] However, the song may well have existed in oral tradition for several centuries before it was written down.

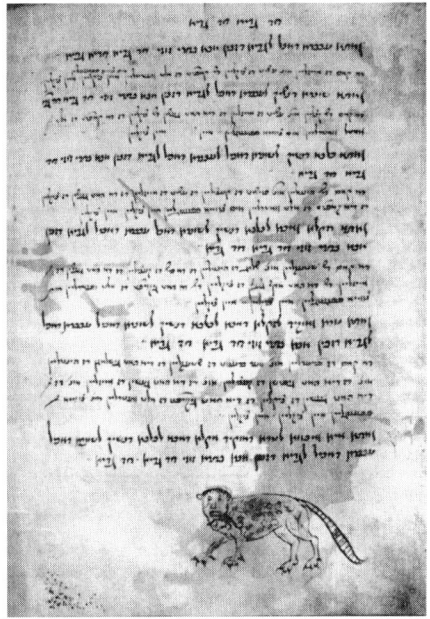

Figure 1. *Sereni Haggadah*

The name of the song is taken from its first two words, which provide the refrain that concludes each of its ten verses. The structure is cumulative, in that new items are added in each successive verse, and all previous items are repeated in reverse order. The content is regarded as an allegory describing the history of the Jews and their relationship with God.

In one interpretation, the Kid represents the Temple.[5] The Father is King David, who collected two *zuzim* from each of the twelve tribes to pay for the Temple expenses.[6] The Cat is Nebuchadnezzar, the King of Babylon who de-

---

4 Cecil Roth, "Had Gadya," in Cecil Roth, ed., *Encyclopedia Judaica* (Jerusalem, 1972), vol. 7, 1049.
5 Abraham Zvi Idelsohn, *Jewish Liturgy and Its Development* (New York, 1932; repr., New York: 1967), 186-87.
6 According to David Brown, a *zuz* was one quarter of a silver shekel, i.e., approximately one day's wages. He adds that, in the Greek New Testament (Matthew 17:24), *zuz* is translated as *drachma*. See AMF International (online; available at http://www.amfi.org).

stroyed the First Temple. The Dog is Cyrus, King of Persia who conquered Babylon. The Stick is Alexander the Great; the Fire represents the Maccabbean victory over the Greeks; the Water is the Roman destruction; and so on.

In another interpretation, the Kid represents the Jewish people; the Father is God; the two *zuzim* are Moses and Aaron, who redeemed the Jews from bondage; the Cat represents the Assyrians; the Dog is Babylonia; the Stick is Persia; the Fire is Macedonia; the Water is Rome; the Ox represents the Saracens; the Slaughterer represents the Crusaders; the Angel of Death represents the Ottomans; and the "Holy One Blessed be He" is God, representing the principal of eternal justice.[7] Other scholars have drawn connections between this song and the Joseph legend or other sources of Jewish mysticism.[8]

Folk texts similar to *Had Gadya,* existing both within and outside of the Jewish tradition, can be found in various languages. For example, there is a fascinating religious nursery rhyme in Judeo-Tat, as sung by the Mountain Jews of Azerbaijan, which is entitled *Raftum e vishe*—"I went to the woods" (Figure 2).[9]

Raflum e vishe	*I went to the woods,*
Chirum banovshe	*I picked a violet*
Dokundum e shishe	*Put it into a can,*
Danorum e kirishe	*Put the can into a sleigh*
Raftum e kale kugooj pargo	*Went to the great Tsar's court,*
Huruz bisto urus ne bisto	*The Russian Tsar was not there, just a rooster.*
Ze vini mere huni soht	*The rooster pecked me on the nose, it bled.*
Hune dorum e zimi	*I gave the blood to the earth,*
Zimi mere gjndum do...	*The earth gave me a grain,*
	I grave the grain to the mill,
	The mill gave me flour,
	I put flour into a jar,
	The jar gave me dough,
	I put the dough into an oven,
	The oven gave me mazzah,
	I gave mazza to the rabbi,
	Rabbi gave me Torah.
	I gave Tora to God,
	God gave long life to my father and uncle.

Figure 2. *Raftum e vishe*

---

7 Kohut, "Had Gadya"; and Roth, *Encyclopedia Judaica*, 1048.
8 Roth, *Encyclopedia Judaica*, 1048.
9 Valery Dimshits, "The Eastern Jewish Communities of the Former USSR," in *Facing West: Oriental Jews of Central Asia and the Caucasus* (Zwolle, Holland, n.d.), 24.

Analogous semi-religious and secular versions occur in English: "The Twelve Days of Christmas," "Old MacDonald had a Farm," and "The House that Jack Built," for example (the last-mentioned dating, probably, from the sixteenth century);[10] and also in German ("Der Herr der schickt den Jokel aus" and, more recently, "Des Knaben Wunderhorn" by Arnim and Brentano), French ("Alouette"), Spanish ("Don Quixote"), Italian, Modern Greek, and Persian; as well as in Indian and Thai languages.[11]

As much as the texts for *Had Gadya* vary among different languages, so too do its melodies. Every Jewish ethnicity, denomination, geographical region, community, and even family within a community will have its own version, which it naturally regards as "authentic," and, therefore, superior to other supposed "corruptions." The Brooklyn-born Abraham A. Schwadron (1925-87), sometime Professor of Music at the University of California at Los Angeles, compiled a "*Had Gadya* Collection" based on twelve years of systematic ethnomusicological research undertaken between 1973 and 1985. This monumental archive, which was donated by his family in September 1988 to the American Folklife Center at the Library of Congress in Washington, DC, includes over 200 versions of *Had Gadya* from all over the world, as well as 160 recordings. In addition to essays written from historical and ethnographic perspectives, lecture transcripts, bibliographies and discographies, newspaper articles, correspondence, transcripts of interviews with individual informants and Jewish communities, fieldwork documentation, and other research materials, the collection contains transcriptions of tunes and texts in Aramaic, Hebrew, Yiddish, German, Russian, English, Italian, Judeo-Spanish, Judeo-Provençal, and Greek. It consists of twenty-eight folders containing manuscripts, twenty-one audio cassettes, twenty-two reel-to-reel tapes, photographs, and the Folkways Recording produced in 1982 (FR 8920), which records both published and unpublished examples from Schwadron's own field work as well as examples taken from other archives.[12]

So, "The Little Goat" has been extensively documented. But what of "The Little Chicken"?

---

10 See *Nursery Rhymes—Lyrics and Origins* (online; available at http://www.rhymes.org.uk/this_is_the_house_that_jack_built.htm) (accessed 8 May 2009).
11 Singer, *Jewish Encyclopedia*, 128.
12 Anthony Palmer, "In Memoriam: Abraham A. Schwadron (1925-1987)," *Ethnomusicology* 32, no.2 (1988): 101-102; and *The Abraham A. Schwadron "Chad Gadya" Collection*, The American Folklife Center, Library of Congress, Washington, DC. A catalog of the collection is available online at http://www.loc.gov/folklife/guides/schwad.html (accessed 8 May 2009).

Murghak

Before taking a detailed look at the song itself, I shall begin with a few background details about Bukhara in the context of Central Asia, and at the *Mavrigi* genre to which *Murghak* belongs. Bukhara is situated near the banks of the Zarafshan River, about 100 miles east of the Amu-Darya, the River Oxus of antiquity (Figure 3).

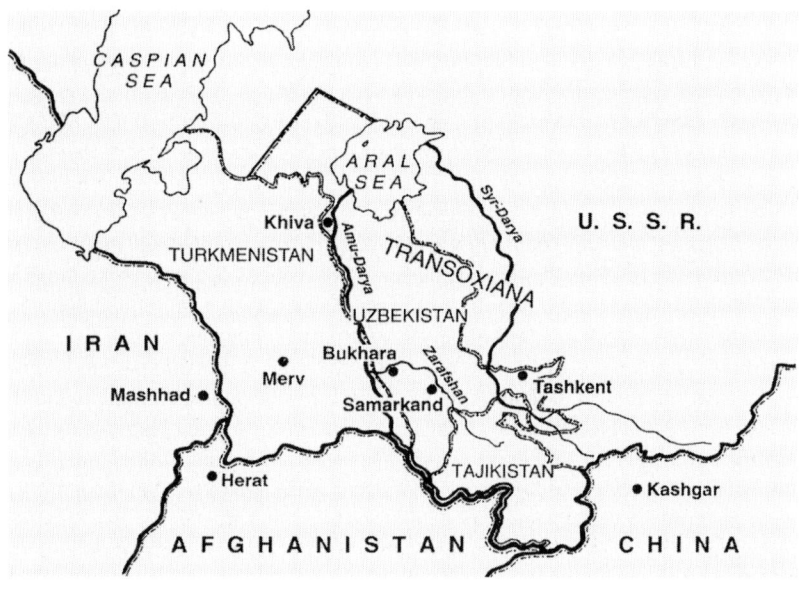

Figure 3. Soviet Map of Central Asia

Bukhara began as an oasis settlement, already well established at the time of the arrival in the region of Alexander the Great (330-329 BCE); its narrow streets and crowded bazaars have long been home to a colorful and urban ethnic melting pot comprising Muslims and Sufis, Buddhists and Hindus, Zoroastrians, Nestorian Christians,[13] and Jews, primarily of Persian and Babylonian provenance. The original inhabitants appear to have been tribes of Iranian and Turko-Mongol stock; and the region around Bukhara in modern Uzbekistan is bilingual—Uzbek being a Turkic language, and Tajik being an eastern relative of

---

13 Named after Nestorius, fifth-century Patriarch of Constantinople, who attributed distinct divine and human characteristics to Jesus.

Persian. Among the many musical genres to be found in the city, three are pre-eminent: (1) *Shashmaqom*; (2) the religious and paraliturgical chants of the mosque and synagogue; and (3) *Sozanda*, with which *Mavrigi* is associated.

Since our investigation will focus upon the third of these genres, I shall offer only a few words about the first two. (1) *Shashmaqom* (literally *Six Modes*) was a Central Asian repertoire of sophisticated and often virtuoso art songs and instrumental suites that flourished in the Emir's courts from the late eighteenth century until the advent of Soviet rule in 1920. Since the collapse of the USSR, it has again become a music of connoisseurs. (2) Religious and paraliturgical chant has developed a distinctive style in Bukhara, which has long been considered a Holy City for Muslims. In the early twentieth century, there were over 200 mosques and nearly 200 religious schools for Shi'ites, Sunnis, and Sufis. Jews have resided in the region since at least the twelfth century—and, according to some sources, as early as the fifth century or perhaps even earlier. Although Jews were subjected to social and professional restrictions, they nevertheless absorbed the cultural identity of their environment (as has so often occurred elsewhere in the diaspora over the past 2000 years). Although the traditions of mosque and synagogue remained distinct, many aspects of social life were shared between Muslims and Jews—not least of which was music, both "classical" and popular.

And this brings us to our third genre: (3) *Sozanda* and the *Mavrigi*. The most important occasion in the everyday life of Bukhara was and remains the *Toi*—literally, *celebration*. This can pertain to any joyful event, usually connected to cycle of life: birth, male circumcision, a boy's first haircut, a child's first day at school, and especially a wedding. At large and small gatherings, family and friends enjoy food, drink, and live musical entertainment. Sunnis invite Shi'ites; Shi'ites invite Sunnis. Muslims invite Jews; and Jews invite Muslims. In earlier times, male musicians would sing and play music for the men, and female musicians for would sing and play for the women. In more recent times, there has been a tendency for the sexes to celebrate together. The most popular ensembles are known as *Sozanda* (Tajik for *musician*), typically comprising between three and seven female singers and instrumentalists. Traditionally, these ensembles were almost exclusively Jewish. Nowadays, some *Sozanda* may include Muslim men.

Mavrigi is a complementary genre associated specifically with Muslim men. It is a Tajik version of a style of singing, playing, and dancing founded by the illustrious Central Asian musician Borbad in the sixth or seventh century. There are now two kinds of *Mavrigi*: one associated with Bukhara, and another found in the Ghissar Valley in Tajikistan. Here we are concerned only with the former. It is usually performed by a *Mavrigikhon,* a male singer, who is accompanied by the *dayra (doyra, doira,* etc.) or frame-drum (Figure 4). Historically, however, a larger ensemble would have provided the accompaniment.

Figure 4. *Dayra*

The Tajik word *Mavrigi* means *sweet*. But, as noted earlier, it may also be derived from the Turkmen city of Merv, which was, for centuries, one of the principal centers of Khorasan, the borderland region linking Central Asia with Iran and Afghanistan, also one of the principal slave markets in the area. In Bukhara, a typical *Mavrigikhon* would be identified as a distant descendant of Iranian or Farsi slaves, who had been captured either in Iran by Turkmen tribesmen or in Khorasan by Uzbek invaders, and in either case taken to Bukhara via Merv. A large influx of Iranian immigrants to Bukhara took place during the second half of the eighteenth century. They preserved their Shi'a heritage, despite—or perhaps because of—their status as a marginalized group in comparison with Bukhara's majority Sunni population. As was the case with the Jews, the Shi'a found themselves undertaking work considered unsuitable for Sunnis, and this included entertainment—an essential ingredient in the life of the community as a whole, but not a respectable profession. Thus, both the female, Jewish *Sozanda* and the male, Muslim *Mavrigi* represent musics of an underclass in Bukharan society. Indeed, there are musical similarities between the two repertoires.

Nowadays, although the *Mavrigikhon* tends to be replaced by entertainers who are experts in contemporary Western styles, there are still some who sing, dance, and tell humorous stories during the *Bazm* (a feast organized by men for men during a *Toi*). *Mavrigi* has been described as a kind of Bukharan "soul-music" that includes laments by the early slaves for their lost homeland.[14] For

---

14 Stephen Blum, "Central Asia," §3, "Structure and Genre," in Stanley Sadie, ed., *The New Grove Dictionary of Music and Musicians*, 2d ed. (London, 2001), vol. 5, 368; and Theo-

this reason, the genre is also known as *gharibi* ("homeless stranger, wanderer").[15] However, upbeat elements are also found in this genre.

The musical structure of *Mavrigi* can be likened to a vocal suite of consisting of several movements, typically lasting between thirty and forty minutes. Unlike the *Shashmaqom*, the sequence of the movements of the *Mavrigi* is not fixed, with one important exception: the first movement, entitled *Shahd*, is always melismatic and non-metrical, comprising phrases of varying length, in *parlando* and *rubato* style, highly ornamented, and sung in a high register. It cannot stand alone. *Shahd* has been translated, variously, as *honey*, or, from the Tajik word *Shohid*, as *witness*. This introductory movement is followed by a number of dance-like movements in a livelier tempo, some comprising several sections. These movements consist of phrases of more or less equal length. They are rhythmical (a rapid compound duple or 6/8 being the favored meter) and are performed without a break. Though the mood shifts gradually from introspection to *bonhomie*, the *Mavrigikhon* can choose from several possibilities in his selection and ordering of the metrical songs.

Murghak ("Chicklet") comes from the *Mavrigi* repertoire. But, unlike the hundreds of melodies for *Had Gadya* mentioned earlier, I have been able to find only one musical rendering of this song.

Comparison of Had Gadya and Murghak

Before comparing the musical characteristics of these two songs, we may enumerate their extra-musical similarities and differences as follows:

I. Extra-Musical Similarities

1. One may respond to both songs on a number of different levels. They both exhibit elements of humor and simplicity and thus can be appreciated by children. However, both can also be understood metaphorically by more sophisticated listeners, as poignant or even pungent commentaries on the human condition.
2. Both songs are self-standing, but are also comprise part of a much larger repertoire.
3. Both can be designated paraliturgical, i.e. displaying links with both sacred and secular contexts and philosophies.
4. Traditionally, both songs would be sung by men. However, in certain situations they may be sung by both men and women.

---

dore Levin, "Uzbekistan," §1, "Urban Traditions," part iv, "Mavrigi," in Sadie, *The New Grove Dictionary*, vol. 26, 183.
15 Levin, liner notes to *Bukhara, Musical Crossroads of Asia*.

5. Neither song would be performed at the beginning of a festivity; both are performed when both participants and audience are fully "warmed up."
6. The content of the texts are, in some ways, remarkably similar:
    (a) Both focus upon a defenseless animal, and both are expressive of the power of the stronger over the weaker.
    (b) Both narratives include water, fire, the stick, and the dog, in this order.
    (c) In both cases, a senior family figure—the father in *Had Gadya*, the grandfather in *Murghak*—purchases an animal for a fixed sum, two *zuzim* for the kid, and 100,000 dinars for the chicken. (It would be interesting to translate these numismatic units into modern coinage.)

II. Extra-Musical Differences

1. Had Gadya is a Jewish song, whereas Murghak is essentially of Shi'a Muslim origin.
2. Had Gadya is specific to a single Jewish festival, and is sung only twice a year—on successive evenings (or just once, where Jews choose to celebrate only one Seder evening). Murghak, however, can be sung at any Toi celebration.
3. Although Had Gadya is always sung at a "communal Seder" in the synagogue, it may be better suited to an intimate home environment, where the assembled company sings together while seated. Murghak finds its natural milieu in a large-scale celebration, such as a wedding party, involving dozens or hundreds of people listening and/or dancing in a sizeable venue.
4. The symbolism behind Had Gadya is generally considered to reflect religious values and a historical perspective, whereas that behind Murghak might be seen to explore social relationships and hierarchies.
5. Had Gadya is cumulative, whereas the chain-reaction of question and answer in Murghak is more akin to the structure of songs like "There's a hole in my bucket, dear Liza."[16]
6. The text of Had Gadya is slightly macaronic, insofar as the basic Aramaic is occasionally interspersed with Hebrew words. The text of Murghak, in contrast, is in Tajik throughout.
7. The content of the texts differs in the following respects:
    (a) The farmer and the wolf, as well as the description of the little animal of the title in Murghak, are all absent from Had Gadya.

---

16 http://parentingteens.about.com/library/sp/gs/blsongs30.htm

(b) The cat, the ox, the slaughterer, the angel of death, and the "Holy One, blessed be He" (a poetic appellation for God) are all absent from Murghak.

Now we may turn to the music itself. I have chosen a version of *Had Gadya* that, in my opinion, comes closest (in certain respects, at least) to the style and performance practice of *Murghak*—namely, the idiosyncratic and compelling interpretation of the text by Cantor Moishe Oysher (Figure 5).

Figure 5. Cantor Moishe Oysher (record sleeve)

On this recording, Cantor Oysher is accompanied by a mixed choir (a common procedure in the early twentieth century, but unknown in a twenty-first century Orthodox religious context) with the addition of an organ and a cymbal at the end.[17] In this version and rendering, *Chazen* Oysher is unambiguously the soloist. The main musical materials of *Had Gadya* are shown in Figure 6.

Had Gadya - Musical Materials (1)

---

17 Moishe Oysher with the Abraham Nadel Chorus, *The Moishe Oysher Seder* (Leisure Time Music, CD LTM-158CD-1, 1994), end of track 9.

Had Gadya - Musical Materials (2)

Figure 6. *Had Gadya*: musical materials

The rendering of *Murghak* is sung by *Mavrigikhon* Mahdi Ibadov (Figure 7), who, according to his own testimony, is a Farsi Shi'ite rather than a Tajik.[18]

---

18 Levin, *The Hundred Thousand Fools of God: Musical Travels in Central Asia (and Queens, New York)* (Bloomington and Indianapolis, 1996), 122.

Figure 7. Mahdi Ibadov

Ibadov is essentially the soloist. However, he is often joined in a responsorial fashion by Tofakhon, a Bukharan *Sozanda* celebrity, and members of her ensemble (Figure 8). Throughout, the *dayra* (see Figure 4 above) provides a pulsating accompaniment.

Figure 8. Tofakhon and her ensemble

The primary musical materials in *Murghak* are shown in Figure 9.

Figure 9. *Murghak*: musical materials

We may now enumerate their musical similarities and differences:

I. Musical Similarities

1. The performance of Murghak lasts three minutes, that of Had Gadya about three and a half minutes.
2. Both are fast, lively, and intentionally amusing.
3. Both are sung by celebrated solo singers within their respective genres and cultures; Ibadov represents Bukharan performance practice and voice production, and Oysher the florid East-European Ashkenazi cantorial tradition.
4. Both artists indulge in what might be termed non-semantic vocal techniques: Ibadov introduces a few farmyard expostulations towards the end of his song, whereas Oysher laces his text with expressive syllables that are part and parcel of the East-European Hassidic style.
5. Both melodies fall clearly into smaller sections, all of which are repeated according to a fixed pattern.
6. Both melodies are supported by strong rhythmic accompaniments: Murghak in a rapid 6/8, and Had Gadya in a relentless 4/4, especially in the solo sections (quarter-eighth-eighth and eighth-eighth-quarter on the repeated words "Had Gadya, Had Gadya."
7. The Sozanda ensemble decorates Ibadov's melody with occasional, gentle, high-pitched vocal "squeaks," whereas the chorus brings Had Gadya to a close with a rousing, Mormon-Tabernacle-style cadence.

II. Musical Differences

1. The rendering of Murghak is solo or unisonal, whereas the accompaniment to Had Gadya follows the principles of Western four-part harmony.
2. The modality of Murghak seems to follow the notes of the Western major scale, without adhering to any specific maqam, whereas Had Gadya falls squarely into the Adonoy (Hashem, Adoshem) Moloch Shtayger, which resembles, in some respects, the Gregorian Mixolydian mode. The lowered seventh degree, in comparison to the Western major scale, is a prominent feature of certain sections of this version, as are occasional flirtations with the Mi Shebeirach/Av Horachamim mode, known in Eastern Europe as "Ukrainian Dorian"—a mode whose most prominent feature is the interval of an augmented second between the mediant and subdominant (third and fourth) scale degrees.
3. The melodic range covered by Had Gadya is wide, and the melody includes several leaps, whereas the contour of Murghak moves generally stepwise, and its range is narrower.

4. The rhythm of the solo line in Murghak is wedded to that of the dayra, whereas the rhythm of Had Gadya is sometimes related metrically to the chorus and sometimes completely independent of it, especially in quasi-improvised recitative passages.

5. The performance of Murghak, though possibly abbreviated for the purposes of inclusion on the CD, is close to a rendering that might be given during an actual Toi celebration in situ. As to the performance of Had Gadya, it is unlikely that a family would accommodate a four-part mixed choir plus organ and cymbal around the Seder table, especially in an Orthodox Jewish context, where there are strict prohibitions against the use of instruments on Sabbaths and such major festivals such as Pesach, and where there are also restrictions with respect to men listening to the female voice.[19]

Conclusions

I have attempted to compare the salient elements of two paraliturgical songs from different parts of the world, from different religious traditions and cultural backgrounds, expressed through the medium of different languages and musical styles. Following descriptions of and commentaries on, their respective provenance, religious significance, symbolism, social context, structure, and meaning, we have enumerated their musical and extra-musical similarities and differences. We may now return to the questions posed at the beginning of this essay—namely, questions of chronology, influence, and the possibility of a common source.

To date traditional melodies is much more hazardous than to date traditional texts, for the latter are often written down, whereas folk music is often transmitted orally—though there are, of course, scattered examples of musical transcriptions in Western and other notations that reach back several centuries. The musical origins of *Had Gadya* and *Murghak* may be attributed in part to tradition and folk memory, and in part to the creativity of their respective performers, who have stamped their individuality upon their own renderings. Despite similarities between texts and performance practices, there is little likelihood of a sufficiently close connection to suggest either mutual or directional influence between the two songs or a specific, determinable common source. However, future research may reveal hitherto undreamt-of relationships between the little goat and the little chicken.

---

19 Although this performance is designed for concert hall and recording studio, I have heard this version sung by the master of the house at the end of a *Seder* service—unaccompanied, yet joined by the voices of other male participants where the melodic line is not too demanding technically.

Bret Werb

VU AHIN ZOL IKH GEYN? MUSIC OF JEWISH DISPLACED PERSONS

The cultural life of the Displaced Persons camps established in Germany and elsewhere in Europe at the end of the Second World War was as diverse as the backgrounds and life experiences that their inhabitants brought with them, and as varied as the zones and localities to which the survivors were drawn or sent. Such cultural activity in the wake of the immediately preceding catastrophe was often noted, sometimes as a manifestation of Jewish cultural renewal, by visitors to the camps and by camp inhabitants themselves. That no full study of the subject has yet been undertaken might owe to the daunting nature of an enterprise needing to account for upwards of 700 camps scattered across postwar Europe.[1] A detailed inventory of musical performances within German Displaced Persons (DP) Camps, a project of the Arbeitsgruppe Exilmusik at Hamburg University, remains an impressive work in progress.[2] With the present paper, my more modest goals are to examine some sources of DP music and to describe the varieties of music that characterize the repertoire.

My first serious engagement with DP music began when, as music curator at the Holocaust Memorial Museum, I helped to program two concerts for an international gathering of former DPs. Scores of survivors and their families planned to convene in Washington, DC, in January 2000, to commemorate the crucial period of transition marked by life in the camps, and the programs would need to showcase music genuinely evoking or reflecting that time.[3] I sought

---

Recordings of some works mentioned in this article are available for online listening via the United States Holocaust Memorial Museum's online exhibition, *Music of the Holocaust* (http://www.ushmm.org/museum/exhibit/online/music) (accessed 9 May 2009).

1 The Internet resource "Displaced Persons' Camps" (http://www.dpcamps.org) lists over 700 Jewish and non-Jewish DP camps in Germany and Austria alone (accessed 2 February 2009). Of specifically Jewish camps, Kurt Grossman writes "At its peak the number of Jewish camps ran as high as 80 in all DP areas." See *The Jewish DP Problem: Its Origin, Scope, and Liquidation* (New York, 1951), 29.
2 See "Musik in den DP-Camps der Britischen Zone 1945-1950," at www.sophie.fetthauer.de/projekte.htm; and "Musik in norddeutschen DP-Lagern," at www1.uni-hamburg.de/musik/exil/ueberuns.html#anker_2 (accessed 2 February 2009).
3 "Life Reborn: Jewish Displaced Persons 1945-1951," international conference sponsored by the U.S. Holocaust Memorial Museum Second Generation Advisory Group in association with the American Jewish Joint Distribution Committee, Washington, DC, 14-17 January 2000.

such music in archives, DP Camp periodicals, published and manuscript writings, and period recordings. I also learned much from former DPs, who shared recollections of their musical experiences, and from musicians who had toured the DP camps as performers. Sorting through these sources—the memoirs, interviews, recordings, handbills, broadsides, and other performance ephemera—I came to distinguish three broad categories of DP music.

"Nostalgia music"—repertoire remembered from before the war—makes up the first big grouping. To this category would belong familiar Yiddish standards such as "Belz," "Eli Eli," and "Bay mir bist du sheyn"; songs by the Yiddish troubador Mordechai Gebirtig, whose folk creations were recalled by many DPs; Russian and gypsy-styled folk songs; and Russian, Polish, Italian, and American popular tunes. Orchestral and chamber works also formed part of this repertoire: operetta potpourris, Palestinian dances, and light classics by the likes of Suppé, Liszt, and Chopin.

Less prevalent than nostalgia music among DPs was the "imported repertoire" introduced soon after the war's end by American Jewish entertainers on goodwill tours of the camps. One of the first such visitors, in 1946, was the Detroit-based operatic soprano Emma Schaver, who later published an account of her experiences and recorded an album of songs she had performed for—and, in turn, learned from—DPs.[4] Another was the Yiddish stage actor Herman Yablokoff, who, in his autobiography *Der Payatz* (named for his stage persona, "The Clown") recalled a typical performance:

> I began my program with "Lost Mich Lebn"—Let Me Live. In song and recitation I depicted a meeting at the United Nations, where a Jew is beseeching the representatives of the world to "Let Me Live" . . . thereby recounting how the Jew had given the world some of the greatest personalities who had enriched mankind in every phase of life . . . science, art, music, literature, medicine, as well as the Ten Commandments and, for many people in the world, their Son of God, Jesus Christ! After all that we have contributed to the world, we Jews demand—"Let us Live!!!" This intensely dramatic composition was met by a storm of applause.[5]

Yablokoff's three-hour show also included folk songs, theater songs, excerpts from plays, and anecdotes and monologues by Sholem Aleichem and others. In his memoir, he notes his sometimes-awkward efforts to connect with his

---

4 Emma Schaver, *Mir zaynen do! Eyndrukn un batrakhtungen fun a bazukh bay der sheyres-hapleyte* (New York, 1948). See also *Songs of the Concentration Camps from the Repertoire of Emma Schaver* (New York, 1948); and *I Believe* (sound recording; Vox, 1947).

5 Herman Yablokoff, *Der Payatz: Around the World With Yiddish Theater*, trans. Bella Mysell Yablokoff (Silver Spring, MD, 1995), 357 (ellipses in original). "Lost Mich Lebn" was written ca. 1945 by American Yiddish stage performer Hymie Jacobson.

audience in the face of the profound divide separating his experience from theirs. As befitted his role as emissary from America, he settled on an optimistic approach, telling the crowd: "To lift your morale I have brought you the token gift of a lively little song called 'Nisht Gezorgt'—don't worry . . . don't despair. I will sing it for you. Now then, my friends, what is the gift the Clown has brought to you from America? Let me hear it from the men, women and children!' With sparkling eyes and great gusto, the entire crowd roared, 'Nisht Gezorgt!' "[6]

Imported music such as this commingled in the camps with the repertoire that most concerned me as curator and programmer: music by and for the Displaced Persons themselves. Some works falling into this broad category were, in fact, newly created by survivors. Others, such as certain well-remembered prewar and ghetto songs, had clearly gained fresh currency in the camps. Among these are "lamentation songs" that reflect the survivors' need to recall and mourn the past (evident in many texts about destroyed families and *shtetlekh*, ghetto life, and the death camp Treblinka); and "topical songs": humorous and stinging satires on the UNRRA (United Nations Relief and Rehabilitation Administration), the "Joint" (Joint Distribution Committee, another welfare agency), and camp conditions in general.

There were also "songs of protest," in which DPs commented on or railed against their plight as stateless individuals. The frequently heard Yiddish phrase *"Vu ahin zol ikh geyn?"* (Where shall I go?), which became a byword among the *shayris hapliteh*, the "surviving remnant" of European Jewry, had been drawn from a song that would serve as an anthem for Europe's displaced Jews. It might be appropriate to discuss this piece in the context of the protest song. The text originated during the war, written by I. Korntayer, a popular Warsaw librettist and lyricist before the war.[7] In the Warsaw ghetto, Korntayer carried on writing songs, and "Vu ahin zol ikh geyn" ranked among his most popular creations. According to theater historian Jonas Turkow, "Vu ahin" struck an especially responsive chord among Jews who had converted to Christianity, a particularly wretched element of the ghetto population.[8] Korntayer did not survive the war, but his words continued to resonate among Displaced Persons whose fate was to remain, as one former DP reported, "stranded, belonging nowhere, unwanted everywhere."[9]

---

6 Yablokoff, *Der Payatz*, 357 (ellipses in original). The song referred to is likely "Nisht gezorgt" (ca. 1945) by Moshe Konstantinowski and Samuel Kelemer.
7 I. Korntayer (also known professionally as I.M. Korentajer and S. Korn-Teuer) was the pseudonym of a figure whose identity remains elusive.
8 Jonas Turkow, *Farloshene shtern* (Buenos Aires, 1953), 1:105. Turkow refers to the song by its probable original title, "Vuhin zol ikh geyn" (wither shall I go?).
9 Interview with Gita Baigelman, New York, 23 January 1999.

Vu ahin zol ikh geyn,	Tell me, where shall I go?
ver kon entfern mir?	Who can answer me?
Vu ahin zol ikh geyn,	Tell me, where shall I go?
az farshlosn z'yede tir?	Every door is closed to me.
S'iz di veld groys genug,	Though the world seems large enough,
nor far mir iz eng un kleyn—	For me, it's crowded, small.
Vu a blik kh'muz tsurik,	What I see is not for me,
s'iz tseshtert yede brik:	Every path is closed to me.
Vu ahin zol ikh geyn?	Tell me, where shall I go?[10]

The melody to "Vu ahin zol ikh geyn," like that to many ghetto songs, predates the war. As "Golubiya glaza" ("Sky-Blue Eyes," in Russian), it was one of a string of international hits for its composer, Oskar Strok (1892-1975), the Latvian "Tango King." Born to a family of Jewish musicians in Daugavpils and educated in St. Petersburg, Strok made his reputation in the Latvian capital, Riga. It was Strok's fate, too, to join Europe's Jewish displaced, although he was never interned in a DP camp. With the German invasion of Latvia in 1941, he fled east, living out the war years in Kazakhstan. However, soon after returning home to Riga, now the capital of Soviet Latvia, in 1945, he found himself cast into personal and professional disrepute.[11] Accusations of "formalist tendencies" and "bourgeois influences" hung over him and his music in the wake of Stalin's dissolution of the Jewish Anti-Fascist Committee and the subsequent crackdown on so-called "cosmopolitan culture." In such a charged climate, Strok's worldwide fame was viewed with suspicion. So, too, was his specialty, the tango. The style scarcely seemed homegrown; it was, rather, looked on as a relic of the decadent West. Yet, while Strok's works were neither officially performed nor published in the USSR during the 1950s, it was rumored that his old melodies could still be heard, woven into movie soundtracks, where they signaled the appearance on-screen of foreigners, degenerates, or anti-Soviet conspirators. And film—improbably and late in life—ultimately played a role in Strok's rehabilitation. The underground success of Bernardo Bertolucci's motion picture *Last Tango in Paris* (1972) revived interest in tango music within the Soviet Union, and the aging, almost forgotten composer found himself a celebrity again.[12]

The process of folklorization, accelerated in the hothouse setting of the ghettos and camps, acted to obliterate the true authorship of Strok and Korntayer's song. By the time of its publication, in Paris in 1948, credit for both the words

---

10 Translation adapted from Eleanor Mlotek and Malke Gottlieb, eds., *We Are Here: Songs of the Holocaust* (New York, 1983), 16.

11 First absorbed into the Soviet Union in August, 1940, Latvia was again proclaimed a Soviet Republic in 1944, following nearly three years of German occupation.

12 Details on Strok's life related by Strok family acquaintance Dmitri Goldgaber (personal communication, August 1998). See also Marina Mihailets, "Estrādes postlūdija," in *Savā krāsā varavīksnē* (Riga, 1997) 57.

and music of "Vu ahin zol ikh geyn" had been claimed by the pianist-composer-impressario Sigmunt Berland (1908-1956), who might have first encountered it in the Warsaw ghetto. Berland's edition updates the ghetto text, perhaps reflecting a DP tendency to answer the title question, "*Vu ahin?*" (Where to?), with "*Keyn tsion!*" (To the Jewish homeland!). And Berland's score provides the musical equivalent to this response, when, in the coda, beneath the vocalist's sustained final note, the piano right-hand pounds out the Zionist anthem, "Hatikvah" (Example 1).[13]

Example 1.   Sigmunt Berland, "Vi Ahyn Sol Ich Guen?" (Paris: Éditions Musicales Nuances, 1948), final two measures and coda.

Earlier, I referred to "lamentation songs." Many such songs, written in the aftermath of the German occupation, were remembered and sung by ingathered *landsmen* at the DP camps. An anonymous song set in a nameless camp might serve to represent this genre:

Dort in dem lager, in a vinkele bay nakht,	There in the camp, in a corner at night,
shteyt zikh a yidele, farsinkn, fartrakht.	Stands a Jew, sunken in thought.
Er trakht vegn takhles,	He thinks thing over
un er zingt zikh azoy tsi:	And sings quietly:
a shod yeder arbayt, a shod yeder mi.	What a waste, all this labor, all this misery.
Tatenyu in himl, vi lang nokh erdoyert?	Father in heaven, how much can I bear?
Ale mitlen hob ikh shoyn probir,	I've endured every torment,
ikh hob shoyn mir keyn koyekh.	I've no strength to bear.
Un yetst bin ikh aleyn do,	And now I'm here all alone,
un trakht vegn mayn umgliklikhe sho—	Dwelling on my misfortune.
Hob shoyn rakhmones, tatenyu.	Have mercy soon, Father.[14]

---

13 I am grateful to Peter Nahon, Paris, for biographical information about Berland.
14 Tradate Camp, 1946; informant: Shmuel Edelshtayn. Source: USHMM Archives RG-50.472 (Songs of Tradate/David P. Boder Collection). Text transcribed from recording.

Given the diverse backgrounds and personal experiences of Jewish DPs, this song's lack of specificity may account for its resonance: the unidentified *lager*, after all, can stand for any number of concentration or Displaced Persons camps. Recorded at the northern Italian camp at Tradate on 1 September 1946, "Dort in dem lager" is one of several songs that might have been forgotten but for the efforts of Dr. David Boder, a psychologist affiliated with the Illinois Institute of Technology.

Born, like Strok, in Russian Latvia, schooled in Germany and Imperial Russia, Boder reached the United States via Mexico in 1926, at the age of forty. His specialty was comparative psychic trauma, and as the war drew to a close he grew keenly interested in documenting—for historical and psychological reasons, as he put it—the fate of concentration camp survivors. Boder wanted the survivors to relate their stories while these were still fresh in their memories. Furthermore, and perhaps uniquely for his time, he wanted these stories told in the survivors' own voices. With this objective, and after about a year of stubborn petitioning and delays, Boder obtained a small grant and a wire recorder, and set off for liberated Europe (Figure 1).

Figure 1.   David Boder, with wire recorder, preparing to record a survivor interview, 1946 (David Boder Collection/US Holocaust Memorial Museum).

Boder arrived in Europe in the summer of 1946, and from July through October of that year conducted 109 interviews with Displaced Persons in France, Germany, Switzerland, and Italy. He then returned to the United States, eager to report his findings. Yet the book he soon published, *I Did Not Interview the Dead* (1949), garnered little attention from either the academy or the general public. Boder later moved to California, where he continued his work in growing obscurity at the University of California, Los Angeles. After his death in 1961, his sound recordings, among the most immediate and compelling of Holocaust eyewitness testimonials—predating by ten years the first oral history project attempted by Yad Vashem—were neglected and eventually forgotten. It was only in the mid-1990s, thanks to efforts by the Library of Congress in Washington, DC, that Boder's 180 spools of wire, representing over 120 hours of survivor interviews, were at last uncoiled and transferred to magnetic tape.[15] Boder, of course, was not engaged in ethnomusicological fieldwork. But it might be noted that he frequently asked his informants to sing. For him, singing might have been a way of establishing a human connection. And it was also a practical means of summoning up associative memories.[16]

Among the Displaced Persons themselves, there were also some who were passionately concerned with documenting the recent Jewish catastrophe and the continuing tribulations of the surviving remnant of that community. A special issue of the DP organ *Undzer shtime* (Our Voice), published at Bergen-Belsen in January 1946, was devoted to poetry and songs collected from survivors at the camp. Edited by Zami Feder, director of the camp theater, this *Zamlung fun katset un geto lider* (Anthology of Songs and Poems from the Ghettos and Concentration Camps) is among the earliest printed collections of its kind.[17] The leading DP periodical *Fun letstn khurbn* (From the Recent Destruction) also regularly solicited, from its readership, historical documentation in the form of songs (Figure 2).

אין צ. ה. ק. װערן צוגעגרײט צום דרוקן געטאָ־
און קאָצעט־לידער מיט נאָטן.
עס איז דער חוב פון יעדן לעבנגעבליבענעם ייד צו
פֿאראײביקן די לידער, װאָס זײנען געזונגען געװאָרן
אין זײן געטאָ אָדער ק. צ. שטעלט זיך מיט אונדז
אין פֿארבינדונג!   אונדזער אדרעס:

Central Historical Commission at the Central Committee of Liberated Jews in the American Zone of Occupation in Germany, Munich, Möhlstr. 12a

Figure 2. "The Central Historical Committee is preparing to publish ghetto and concentration camp songs, with music notation. It is the duty of every surviving Jew to perpetuate these songs that had been sung in the ghettos or concentration camps. Get in touch with us!" *Fun letstn khurbn* (March 1947): 41.

---

15 Illinois Institute of Technology Psychology Laboratory Project MH 156: David P. Boder Oral History Interviews with Displaced Persons, 1946 (USHMM Archives). For Boder's rationale for undertaking the interview project, see *Topical Autobiographies of Displaced People Recorded Verbatim in Displaced Persons Camps, with a Psychological and Anthropological Analysis* (n.p., n.d.), vol. 16, 3161. See also David P. Boder, *I Did Not Interview the Dead* (Urbana, 1949).

16 On singing as memory aid, see Leah Wolfson, *A path through the abyss: reinventing testimony through post-Holocaust survivor poetry, memoir, and video oral histories* (Ph.D. Dissertation, Emory University, 2008).

17 Zami Feder, ed., *Zamlung fun katset un geto lider* (Bergen-Belsen, 1946).

One announcement, published in the paper in September 1946, called upon readers to "Record the songs that were sung during the Nazi period in the ghettos, camps, and partisan hideouts, etc. Record the jokes, proverbs, legends, anecdotes, and prophecies that circulated during those times. When possible, also make known the name of the author, locale, and source information. Send this material to the Historical Committee, which will safeguard it and make it available in print." Another appeal, from October 1947, read: "Come to the Central Historical Committee and record onto 'Pathéphone' disk the ghetto and concentration camp songs you know. These disks can record up to 7 minutes. They have been demonstrated around the globe. The YIVO exhibition in New York awaits them. This, more than anything, serves to honor the memory of your ghetto! Come, don't make us beg you!"

The author of these advertisements may well have been *Fun letstn khurbn* editor Israel Kaplan, a Kovno ghetto survivor and one of the directors of the Munich-based organization known formally as the Central Historical Committee of Liberated Jews in the American Zone of Occupation in Germany. The sound recordings so fervently sought can be identified with a collection of disks now housed at Yad Vashem, Jerusalem.[18] While most of the songs the Committee collected and recorded chronicle the period from occupation to liberation, several items recorded were postwar creations. One such song was "S'vet geshen" (It will happen), a tango with a topical edge made explicit by its author's dedication: "To the martyrs of the ship Exodus." The theme of illegal immigration was often compounded (as it is here) with another serious motif of DP songs: the determination of stateless Jews to make a new beginning in a land of their own.[19]

Gebroyst hot der yam dan fun tsorn,	The sea surged and raged with fury,
mit farpaynikte fun veg,	The ship filled with weary exiles,
do zaynen mir yunger gevorn,	But our youth and our vigor returned
ven mir hobn derzen dem breg.	When we spied the longed-for shore.
Un khotsh bin geven dan farmartert,	Exhausted, I raised high our banner,
hob ir dikh vi a fon tseflatert.	Lifted our fluttering flag;
shalom mir rufn, nor plutsim krigshifn,	"Shalom!" we cried; then, with a surprise,
bafaln oys krik, men firt undz tsurik . . .	Warships attacked, forcing us back . . .
S'vet geshen, s'MUZ geshen,	It will happen, it MUST occur,

---

18 Yad Vashem Archive, cat. M.1 PF.
19 Two further DP "Exodus" songs are "Dos yid fun eksodus" (The Jew from the Exodus; Papenheim, 1947), with text by Yitzkhak Perlov and music by Lola Folman, printed in Perlov, *Eksodus 1947 poeme un andere lider* (Munich, 1948), endpage; and "Eksodus—1947" (Munich, 1947), with music and text by Reuven Lipshits, printed in Lipshits, *Tsu zingen un tsu zogn* (Munich, 1949), 37-39.

un mir veln ale vider zayn tsuzamen,	We will all dwell together again;
ir vet zen, ir vet zen,	You will see, you will see,
oykh undzer shif vet shvimen fray oyf ale yamen.	Our ships sailing free upon the waters.
Undzer heyliker farlang	Our greatest desire
umtsukern zikh in land fun di neviim,	Is to go back to the land of the prophets;
vet mekuyim vern kh'her shoyn di gezangn,	I can hear their song of greeting already:
vi men bentsht undz brokhim habaim.	"May their homecoming be blessed."[20]

Shmerke Kaczerginski, the lyricist of "S'vet geshen," had begun collecting Shoah-related songs and poems before the end of the war.[21] He conducted important fieldwork among DPs while on a lecture tour of the American Zone in 1947, during which time he also stopped by the office of Central Historical Committee to record a series of his original songs, "S'vet geshen" among them. For a topical song, "S'vet geshen" had unusual staying power: toward the end of the DP period it was commercially recorded in France, the "B" side to a lavishly decorated "picture disc" release of the evergreen "Vu ahin zol ikh geyn" (Figure 3).[22]

Another significant DP music resource is the Ben Stonehill Collection of over 1,000 songs, recorded, often by fresh immigrants, in New York City in 1948. Like David Boder, the Polish-born Stonehill (1906-64) relied on a wire-recorder, but his motives were quite different from those of the trauma psychologist. A small businessman by day (he owned a flooring shop), Stonehill was otherwise a dedicated *zamler* (folklore collector), who desired above all to preserve the Yiddish songs he believed were in danger of disappearing forever. Determined to pursue his mission, he applied for a sales position at a wire-recorder dealership and emerged from the showroom with a salesman's demonstration model. Nearly every weekend that summer, Stonehill hauled this machine by subway to the Hotel Marseilles in Manhattan, a major gathering point for refugees, in order to record songs and stories from hundreds of survivors he encountered in the hotel lobby. By the end of the season, he had documented an

---

20 "S'vet geshen" (also titled "Eksodus 47"), third verse and refrain. Text by Shmerke Kaczerginski, music by Sigmunt Berland. Transcribed from Central Historical Committee recording; translation by Herman Taube.
21 Kaczergsinski published his findings in the anthology *Lider fun di getos un lagern* (New York, 1948). For more on Kaczerginski's collecting activities, see Bret Werb, "Shmerke Kaczerginski, the Partisan Troubadour," *Polin* 20 (2008), 392-412.
22 Another recording appeared in the U.S. at about the same time: Columbia 8268. Variants were recorded by Ben Stonehill in New York and noted by Miriam Hoffman at Hindenburg-Kaserne (see below).

unparalleled cross section of repertoire current among the *shayris hapliteh*, from dynastic-Hasidic *nigunim* and prewar folk and popular songs in Polish, Yiddish, and Russianto songs of the Yishuv; from songs recalled from the ghettos and camps to topical items about the DP experience. Toward the end of his life, Stonehill bequeathed his collection, by then copied to magnetic tape, to the YIVO Institute for Jewish Research in New York, and to the Library of Congress. Yet this evocative mosaic of sounds, so fortunately preserved, has, to this day, been scarcely examined.[23]

Figure 3. "Wie Ahin Soll Ich Gehn"; Saturne S-205 (1950); illustrator unknown. The artwork on this picture disc is an unambiguous response to the question of the eternal refugee. (Image courtesy Julian Futter and Mike Aylward.)

The YIVO archive in New York also houses a large collection of DP performance ephemera, much of it relating to cultural events sponsored by the Central Committee of Liberated Jews in Berlin. Of particular interest are three items of sheet music on the DP theme, published by the Culture Section of the Central

---

23 Ben Stonehill Collection of postwar recordings of European Jewish folksongs from prewar, wartime, and post-war Europe (USHMM Archives 2005.458).

Committee and representing the work of two DP performers with ties to the Latvian Jewish community, Gregor Shelkan and Lev Aronson (Figure 4).[24]

Figure 4.   "Der durchgematerter Weg" (The Arduous Path) (Berlin: Kultur Sektor beim Central Committee fun die bafrajte Idn in Berlin, n.d.). Dedicated to the memory of the songwriters' parents (YIVO/ USHMM).

Another item deposited at YIVO is a songbook-journal kept by Miriam Shmulevich Hoffman, then a precocious preteen living at the DP camp Hindenburg-Kaserne near Ulm. According to Hoffman, the children in the camp, who often had no common language, would amuse themselves by teaching each other songs. Over a three-year period beginning in 1946, Hoffman jotted down words to sixty-three songs she had learned at the camp. These were in a variety of languages—Polish, Russian, Hebrew, and Yiddish—and of varied purport, with ideological songs (Zionist, communist) nestling alongside popular classics such as "Besame mucho" (with Yiddish text) and "There is a Tavern in This Town" (in Russian). Among the topical materials Hoffman transcribed is the humorous

---

24 In the U.S., Shelkan (1915-99) served as longtime cantor to Congregation Mishkan Tefila, Boston, while Aronson (1912-88) became a cellist with the Dallas Symphony and a highly respected pedagogue. Also among YIVO's sheet music holdings are two settings of H. Leivick's poem "Dos lid fun yidishn DP" (The song of the Jewish DP), by Meshulam (Sylvain) Lewin (Paris, 1947), and A. Yones (Berlin, n.d.).

counting song "Tsen vagonen unrra" (Ten Wagons from UNRRA), about the serial disappearance of care packages from America. Given below are the last five verses, excerpted from Hoffman's songbook:

Finf vagonen "unrra"	Five wagons from UNRRA,
mit vayn on a shir;	With boundless wine in store;
gevesn a katastrofie	But there was an accident—
iz nor geblibn fir.	What remained were four.
Fir vagonen "unrra"	Four wagons from UNRRA,
mit pushkes alerlay;	With canned foods in variety;
baym oysmaydn a tunel	But they had to avoid a tunnel—
iz nor geblibn dray.	What remained were three.
Dray vagonen "unrra"	Three wagons from UNRRA,
far pleytim zayer fayn;	For the survivors, very nice;
farndik durkh a berze change—	But they went through a stock exchange—
iz nor geblibn tsvey.	What remained were two.
Tsvey vagonen "unrra"	Two wagons from UNRRA,
der tsutayl blaybt a kleyner;	To divide into small portions;
genekhtikt oyf a rampe	But they spent the night out on a ramp—
tsu morgns geshtanen eyner.	In the morning remained but one.
Eyn vagon fun "unrra"	One wagon from UNRRA,
mentshn lustik, freydik;	The people were overjoyed;
ven men gehot der vagon geefnt	But when that wagon was opened—
iz er nebekh gevesn leydik.	Nothing remained inside.[25]

Keeping to the theme of music by and for DPs, I will now touch on a final manifestation of the musical culture of the camps: touring ensembles comprised of professional musicians who were themselves Displaced Persons. Among these performers were the Yiddish actor Yitskhok Perlov; his wife, the actress, singer, and songwriter Lola Folman; the theater director and historian Jonas Turkow; and Turkow's wife, the actress and singer Diana Blumenfeld. Turkow and Blumenfeld, together with a third DP performer, Dydjo Epstein, played many venues in Germany and Austria; arriving in the United States in 1948, they continued to concertize, sometimes billed as the "DP Trio" (Figure 5).

---

25 Miriam Shmulevich Hoffman Collection, YIVO, New York. Dr. Hoffman kindly recorded portions of her songbook for the archives of the USHMM, thus preserving several melodies (interview with Miriam Hoffman, New York, 5 October 1999). Variants of "Tsen vagonen unrra" were also recorded by Ben Stonehill in 1948.

> **Veranstaltung**
> **des Internationalen Komitees für jüd. KZ-ler**
> **und Flüchtlinge**
> Wien XVIII, Währingergürtel 97-99
>
> ## Lieder- u. Rezitationsabend
> Konzerthaus, Kleiner Saal   Dienstag, 13. November 1945   Beginn 18.30 Uhr
>
> *I. TEIL*
>
> 1. „Kol Nidrej im Ghetto"
> 2. „Un a Heim"   Worte: Kacyzne, Muſik: Szajewicz
>   Dydio Epftein
>
> 1. „Un Jibn"   Worte von Heller
> 2. „Weltgewiſſen"   Worte von Kacyzne
> 3. „Morgenappell im KZ" Verſe von Willy Krell
>   Jonas Turkow
>
> 1. „Klejnczyker Sznejderl"   Worte von Manie Lajba, Muſik von Rozental
> 2. „Gehat hob ich a Heim"   Worte von M. Gebirtig, Muſik von A. Komaromi
> 3. „Majn Mame fyn Pojln"   Worte von Sz. Szigl, Muſik von A. Komaromi
> 4. „A hajm znaczy do domu"   Worte und Muſik von Pauline Braun
> 5. „Joyeze Chaſene"   Volkslied
>   Diana Blumenfeld
>
> *II. TEIL*
>
> 1. „Der Balagule"   Volkslied
> 2. „Rozynkes myt mandlen" Goldfaden
>   Dydio Epftein
>
> 1. „Szlch"   Dr. Berkowicz
>   Jonas Turkow
>
> 1. „Awrejmo der marawicher"   M. Gebirtig
> 2. „S' brent"   M. Gebirtig
> 3. „Ich wil ahejm"   Ch. Rozental
> 4. „Male fzmugler"   Worte von Lazowert, Muſik von Tom
> 5. „Ejceler"   Worte von M. Broderfon, Muſik Bajgelmann
>   Diana Blumenfeld
>
> Am Klavier: Ioo Weoby   Preis des Programmes 50 Groſchen

Figure 5.   Turkow, Blumenfeld, and Epstein concert program, Vienna, 13 November 1945 (YIVO/Diana Blumenfeld Collection). The presence of pieces such as "Kol Nidrej im Ghetto" and "Morgenappell in KZ" indicate that the performers were not averse to recreating aspects of their and their audiences' shared narrative.

Yet another husband-and-wife team consisted of the Dutch-born singer and dancer Lin Jaldati, a camp survivor, and the pianist and dance historian Eberhard Rebling, a refugee from Nazi Germany. In the main, Jaldati and Rebling performed Jewish-styled classical music. However, the couple also confronted contemporary events with recent works such as "Am Yisroel Chaj 1947" (The Jewish People Live 1947) and the celebrated "Partisan Hymn" by the Vilnius ghetto poet Hirsh Glik.[26]

Lastly, I would like to consider two larger DP touring ensembles. The first of these was the St. Ottilien Orchestra, named for the monastery-turned-sanatorium near Landsberg, Bavaria. U.S. Army journalist Robert E. Hilliard witnessed this group's debut in May 1945, and later wrote:

---

26 See "Ein Abend Jüddischer Kunst," concert program, Berlin, 11 May 1948, in the collection *Displaced Persons Camps in Germany* (YIVO record group 294.2). Authorship of "Am Yisroel Chaj 1947" is credited to "Maeke Li."

87

Onto the stage men and women carried fiddles, horns, bass, viols. Through the years in the camps many of these instruments were smuggled, hidden, cared for, held on to as a link to what was remembered of a rational civilization. One of the musicians walked to the front of the stage. "This is our liberation concert," he announced. A liberation concert at which most of the liberated were too weak to stand. A liberation concert at which most of the people still could not believe they were free. I walked to a chair and sat among the people. The musicians played. Mahler and Mendelssohn and others who had been forbidden for years. . . . The movements and faces of the musicians alternated between the euphoria of artistic interpretation and the cramped, tight fear of not fully believing that there was room to move a bow, or air in which to blow a note, as if they momentarily expected guns and clubs to tear away what, after so many years, must have seemed like only a dream. When the concert ended most people were crying, few more openly than I.[27]

The St. Ottilien Orchestra later changed its name to the Ex-Concentration Camp Orchestra, and was known in its final incarnation as the Representative Orchestra of the Shearith HaPleitah. Conducted by Mikhail Hofmekler, the former director of the Kovno ghetto orchestra, and sponsored by the Joint Distribution Committee, the orchestra toured Bavaria from 1945 to 1949 and programmed classical works by composers such as Weber, Bizet, Grieg, and Tchaikovsky. Yet ghetto songs, Hebrew songs, and arrangements of Jewish folk music were also important components of the Shearith HaPleitah Orchestra repertoire. These were often performed by the group's vocalist, Henny Durmashkin, who, along with her pianist-sister Fanny, had survived the Vilnius ghetto and several labor camps. In a memoir, Durmashkin recalled a concert at the Nuremberg Opera House, where, attired (like the rest of the orchestra) in a newly fashioned striped uniform, she performed a set of ghetto songs for members of the International War Crimes Tribunal and representatives of the world press.[28] Guest artists sometimes appeared with the orchestra, as in May 1948, when Leonard Bernstein conducted *Rhapsody in Blue* from the piano in concerts at two Bavarian DP camps. Bernstein also accompanied Durmashkin in a set of Hebrew songs (Figure 6); according to Durmashkin, he declined to perform reper-

---

27 Robert L. Hilliard, "The Liberation Concert, a Memoir of St. Ottilien, Germany, 1945," *Boston Jewish Times* (October 1989): 13-15. See also Hilliard's *Surviving the Americans: The Continued Struggle of the Jews After Liberation* (New York, 1997), 9-10; and two documentary films by John Michalczyk inspired by Hilliard's writings: *Displaced! A Miracle at St. Ottilien* (2002) and *Creating Harmony: The Displaced Persons' Orchestra from St. Ottilien* (2008).
28 Henny Durmashkin-Gurko, "Songs to Remember," in Isaac Kowalski, ed., *Anthology of Jewish Resistance* (Brooklyn, 1986), 3:630.

toirein Yiddish, commonly dismissed at that time as the language of diaspora; Figure 6).[29]

Figure 6. Left: members of the Jewish Ex-Concentration Camp orchestra perform on stage in Nuremberg, Germany, ca. 1946 (USHMM Collections: 1998.017.002). Right: Shearith HaPleitah Orchestra program, 10 May 1948, with guest conductor Leonard Bernstein (courtesy Sonia Pauline Beker).

A second Jewish touring DP troupe, sponsored by UNRRA, was a small jazz band much like those that flourished in Polish nightspots before the war. Also recalling youthful fashions and bygone, better days, this group took an American-sounding name, the Happy Boys (Figure 7). Featuring eight survivor-musicians from Łódź, the troupe toured the American Zone for four years, programming a variety of popular instrumental and vocal music, from operetta overtures to Duke Ellington arrangements to Jewish folksongs. But, like the Shearith HaPleitah Orchestra, the Happy Boys also offered their audience fare related to their recent shared history, including original topical songs about the plight of the displaced population. One such song, by bandleader Chaim (later Henry) Baigelman, was named for the DP Camp Feldafing. Another bore the title "Es bengt sich nukh a hajm" (I Long For a Home; Figure 8).

---

29 Ibid.; and personal communication with Henny Durmashkin-Gurko, May 1999. The Durmashkin sisters came to the U.S. in 1949, and in 1962 they recorded an album, *Songs to Remember*, that included some of their Shearith HaPleitah Orchestra repertoire. See also *Symphony on Fire* (New Milford, NJ, 2007), a family memoir by Fanny Durmashkin's daughter, Sonia Pauline Beker.

Figure 7. The Happy Boys, ca. 1947 (Henry Baigelman Collection/United States Holocaust Memorial Museum). Bandleader Henry Baigelman is standing fourth from the left.

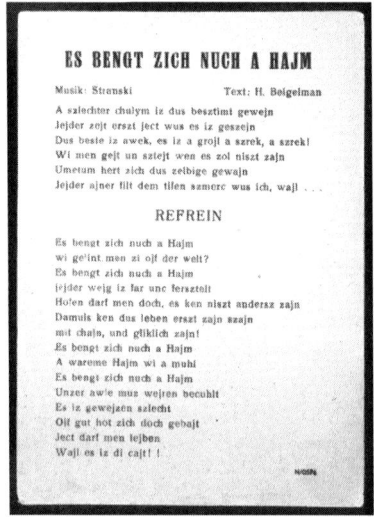

Figure 8. "We Long for a Home" song sheet, handed out at Happy Boys concerts (Henry Baigelman Collection/United States Holocaust Memorial Museum).

In 1947, during a concert at the DP camp Fürstenfeldbruck, the Happy Boys introduced an original composition for piano and jazz ensemble, *Rhapsody 1939-1945*, by Lazar Szpilman. Written over a two-year period at Fürstenfeldbruck, where Szpilman played piano at the Officers' Club, the piece is a remarkable evocation of the fateful years commemorated in its title. As described by the composer, the *Rhapsody*'s linked sections depict, in succession, the invasion of Poland, Jewish misery, flying bullets, birdsong overheard in a basement hideaway, the longing for rescue growing to urgent expectancy, and, finally, liberation, heralded by the laden melody of "Hatikvah" (Example 2).[30]

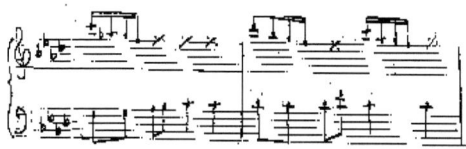

Example 2. Lazar Szpilman (Leo Spellman), *Rhapsody 1939-1945*, piano part, mm. 8-7 from end (unpublished manuscript, composer's collection).

For two or more hundred thousand stateless Jews adrift in postwar Europe, the question "Vu ahin zol ikh geyn?" was of course far from rhetorical. Reference to the emblematic "Hatikvah" was cue enough for many, and by the time the last camp in Germany was shuttered in 1953, Palestine, then Israel, had taken in almost half of the refugee population. To judge from speakers and attendees overheard at the Washington gathering, this period of transition was not a pleasant time, an exciting time, or even, necessarily, a time to "return to life" following wartime traumas. Most Jewish DPs simply wanted to get out of Europe and did so at the nearest opportunity. Within this climate, music—whether an "escapist" Palestinian dance or a nakedly polemical ballad, certainly helped to push a political agenda.

Among the Displaced Persons, there were also many who saw in music yet another utility, and who exercised the art as a much-needed diversion from the uncertainties of daily life and (as with the satirical topical songs) as a time-honored way for the historically powerless to channel pent-up tension and hostility. Finally, it was among the DPs that pioneer cultural historians and folklorists such as Shmerke Kaczerginski, Israel Kaplan, David Boder, and (although at a remove in New York City) Ben Stonehill recognized a unique community, and first began urging survivors to *fareybik*—perpetuate—their stories and their songs.

---

30 A first cousin of Władysław Szpilman (of *The Pianist* movie fame), Lazar Szpilman (now Leo Spellman; b.1915) survived the Ostrowiec ghetto and became a popular pianist and bandleader in Toronto. For further biographical information, see www.ushmm.org/ museum/exhibit/focus/pianist/spellman.htm (accessed 9 May 2009). The description of *Rhapsody 1939-1945* is provided by the composer (personal communication, June 1999).

Rachel Kollender

JEWISH MUSIC IN THE HOLOCAUST
An Announcement of Plural Identities

Music is an expression of time, spirit, and history for all human beings. Therefore, it is also both evidence and testimony of Jewish existence. Singing and playing music has been an integral part of daily life across the history of the Jewish Diaspora, throughout the cycles of years and lives. The present paper analyzes Jewish music that was performed in the Holocaust. The repertoire includes popular songs created before and during the Second World War. Some of these songs are still performed today.[1] There are four common features that unite this repertoire:[2]

1. The texts of these songs express the struggle of millions of victims. The language of the texts is mostly Yiddish or Ladino.[3] Only a small number of the songs are in Hebrew[4] or in the predominant local language (Polish, Hungarian, German, etc.).

2. The content of all of these songs reflects upon the events of the Holocaust, upon dreadful and devastating conditions and deep feelings. The songs document despair and fear, and they describe the miseries of ghetto life, killings, hard labor, and hunger. But laments were not the only type of popular songs sung during these times of overwhelming disaster. We also find humoristic and satirical songs, full of hatred for the tormentors, side by side with songs of hope, calls for revenge, and proclamations of enduring faith.

3. Most of these songs were written (the texts as well as the music), by anonymous poets and composers, most of whom were probably amateur artists. Only a few of these poets and composers were well-known professional artists.

---

1 The research presented in this essay is based on a group of songs in my private archival collection, which includes interviews and recordings of performances.
2 A similar categorization appears in Joachim Braun, *On Jewish Music* (Frankfurt am Main, 2006), 331-39. Braun deals with East-European ghettos, but this categorization seems relevant to the situation in all ghettos and camps under the Nazi regime.
3 Ladino is a Jewish-Spanish language, based on a Castilian jargon. During the Holocaust, Ladino was a "secret language" of Jews from the Balkans and elsewhere.
4 Hebrew songs were brought to Jewish congregations in the Diaspora by members of the Zionist movements.

4. The songs of the ghettos and concentration camps spread orally. They were not written down, and they may therefore be considered part of an oral tradition.

There were three types of songs sung during the period of the Holocaust:

1. Old and well known songs, that were popular before the war. These songs - some of them are excerpts from the Jewish liturgy—included song-setting of prewar texts that later came to be viewed as prophetic. A famous example is "Our Little Village is a Flame," written in 1938 by M. Gebirtig, who perished in Krakow four years later. Another is "Ghetto," with a text by Abraham Reisen and music composed by Arie Ben Erez Abrahamson in Bratislava in 1932:

A gezunt zalber acht	Healthy eight persons,
Und bettn nur zwei	And beds only two . . .
Und kumt un di nacht	And the night draws near;
Wu schlufen zei?	Where shall they all sleep?
Dan heibt un di mame	Then mother begins
Dem toit oif sich beitn	To wish she be dead.
Zi meint mit an emess	She means it in truth;
S' is nit kein wunder	No wonder -
Eng is der keiver	For narrow is the grave
Doch liegt men dort bazunder.	But one lies there by oneself.[5]

2. New texts adapted to familiar old melodies. These songs provide us with insight into daily life in the ghettos and concentration camps. Reusing pre-war popular Jewish tunes, they reflect the efforts of camp inhabitants to preserve the Jewish heritage and to hold on to traces and symbols of their traditions. Here we may mention the song "Oifn Pripichuk," – "On the Stove," a folk tune composed by M. Varshavsky:

Oifn Prijpetschik	On the stove
Brent a Faierl	A fire burns
Un in Schtub is hejss	And the room is warm
Un der Rebbe lernt	And the Rabbie teaches
Klejne Kinderlech	Little kids
Komez Alefbejss...[6]	A and B and C...

---

[5] The song was written in Yiddish. The text here is quoted from program notes of a concert of Art Songs by Arie Ben Erez Abrahamson, presented at the Tel Aviv Music Center on 25 March 2007. The translation is as published in the program notes, prepared by Eliyahu Schleifer, Naftali Stern, and Anat Aderet.

[6] E. Janda and M. Sprecher, *Lieder aus dem Ghetto* (Munchen, 1962), 140-43. See also I. Fatter, Musika Yehudith be Polin bein Shtei Milchamot Olam – Jewish Music in Poland

This song was recast as "Back from Labor" – "Zurick fun der Arbet," the text by Visnetzesky:

Baym geto-toyerl	Near the ghetto gate
Brent a fayerl	A fire burns
Di kontrol iz groys;	The control is fierce,
Es geyen yidelekh,	Jews are coming
Fun di brigadelekh,	From the Brigades
Fun yedn gist zikh shveis…[7]	Sweat pouring from each face…

Another example is the song "Papirosn," – "Cigarettes," a Yiddish song derived from a Bulgarian folk tune. The words by H. Yablokoff:

A kalte nacht a nebeldike	A cold night, foggy
Finster umetum	And darkness everywhere
Shtet a yingele fartroiert	A boy stands sadly
Un kukt zich arum	And looks around.
Fun regn shtitst im nor a vant	Only a wall protects him from the rain
A koshikl halt er in hant	He holds a basket in his hand
Un zaine oigen betn yedn shtum…	And his eyes beg silently…
Kupitye koiftzhe koiftzhe papirosn	Buy my cigarettes!
Trukne fun regn nit fargosn	Dry ones, not wet from the rain
Koiftzhe bilik b'nemones	Buy real cheap
Koift un hot oif mir rachmones	Buy and have pity on me
Ratevet fun hunger mich atsind…[8]	Save me from hunger now…[9]

This song was remade as "S'iz Geven a Zumer Tog" – "It Was A Summer Day," with the text by Rivka Glaser:

Un izt iz frilling shoin	And now it's sunnily beautiful once more
Un frachtful als arum	Everything around here smells splendid.
Un mir in zich, farsholtene	And we are tortured ones
Mir muzn leidn shtum	And all suffer without a word.
Farshtelt far unz di groisse velt	Cut off from the world
Mit hoich moiern farshtelt	Hidden behind high walls
A shtral fun hofenung dergreicht iz koim	A ray of hope barely stirs.
Of Ponar dort ligen of di veign	At Ponar one now sees on the roads
Zachn, hitlech durchgewiklt fun regn	Things, hats, soaked through with rain
Das zeien zachen fun korbunes	These are things of those who died sacrificial deaths

---

between the World Wars (Tel Aviv, 1992); R. Rubin, *The Yiddish Folksong* (New York, 1974).
7 A. Vinkovetzky and others, *Anthology of Yiddish Folksongs*, Vol. IV (Jerusalem, 1987), 133-35.
8 V. Pasternak, *The International Jewish Song Book*, (New York, 1994), 88-9.
9 The English translation appears in www.fishtankensemble.com/lyrics.html

> Fun umshuldike korbunes
> Der soine hot dergreicht of zei zein gzar.[10]
>
> Of holy souls
> The enemy has reached his great goal.[11]

3. New songs composed in the ghettos and in the concentration camps. Most of these songs resulted from collaborations between amateur poets and composers. The composer received from the poet an outline of the general idea of a song; he wrote music and returned it to the poet, who then completed the poem-song according to the melodic pattern. Thus, text and the music were created almost simultaneously. Such songs became popular among the inhabitants of the ghettos and camps immediately. The following analysis, including the musical examples, deals mainly with the songs of this category.

Forcibly confining the Jewish population to separate quarters –ghettos - was the first stage of the Jews' liquidation. The entire Jewish population of Europe, was forced into the ghetto, separated from the gentile population, and subjected to an ongoing process of mass murder. The ghettos of Poland and the Soviet Union had the same system of administration. Yet, despite the brutal conditions and constant threat of death, every ghetto had its own local character and system of survival, which were reflected in its unique brand of cultural and musical creativity. Therefore, in spite of commonalities of language and population, every ghetto had its own pattern of musical activities. The remainder of this paper will consider several examples, drawn from some of the "leading" ghettos and camps.

The musical activities of the Warsaw ghetto present us with a mixture of artistic and popular music. Testimonies reveal that until April 1942, members of the ghetto participated in concerts in which cantorial pieces, symphonies, and chamber music were performed. This shows how the Jewish citizens of the occupied capital of Poland tried to continue their spiritual lives, in spite of the impossible physical conditions in which they were forced to live. Some even wrote critical articles for the ghetto's own local newspaper.[12]

On the other hand, the hardships of the daily life of the ghetto are expressed in the songs composed and sung by the inhabitants. A song that provides a revealing picture of ghetto life is "Arois iz Gegangen a Ijd" – "One Morning a Jew

---

10 E. Horowitz and others, *In Distress – Min Hamezar* (Tel Aviv, 1987), 148-49.
11 The English translation was taken from the notes of the CD *Partisans of Vilna* (Flying Fish records, 1989).
12 See M. Hoch, "The Musical Life in the Ghettos" – "Hachaim Hamuzikalim Bagetaot" *Machanaim* 8-9 (1995): 108-111.

Went Out into the Street," with a text by I. Katsenelson and music by I. Gladshtein (Example 1).[13]

Arois iz gegangen a ijd oif der gass	One morning a Jew went out into the street
Oh, zugt, gute menschen,	O tell me what happened, my brethren,
Far was zenen schteiner un zemdalech nass	Just why is it wet on the sand at our feet
Oifn weg zu Okentsche?...	On the road that leads out to Okentshe?...
Togteglich an umglik–a zeitung was dorsht	Each day and its mishap–a paper that thirsts
Nach jidische blunt	For blood of the Jews, it incites them –
Der Jude der Jude dergangen, derporscht	Der Jude! Der Jude! He's exiled and cursed,
Die Juden! Die Juden! ...	To harass the Jews it invites them...[14]

The poem has the pattern of a ballade. It contains eight stanzas and includes a great deal of information about daily life in the ghetto: humiliations, "yellow strip," torture, hard labor, hunger, and death. The song, like most, is in minor.[15] The melodic line is comprised of repeated short motives, many small steps (usually seconds), a very simple rhythmic pattern of quarter - and eighth-notes, and a symmetrical up-and-down melodic contour, which reminds us of European liturgical pieces.

Example 1. "One Morning a Jew Went Out into the Street"

---

13 This song was printed in Yiddish, with the musical score, in the underground journal *Dror* in the summer of 1940. Its title was "Folk tune of 1940" – "Hashir shel 1940."
14 A. Rubin, *Songs of the Ghettos - Shirim Min Hagetaot* (Tel Aviv, 1988), 7.
15 E. Horowitz, *In Distress – Min Hamezar* (Tel Aviv, 1987), 12.

As in Warsaw, the songs of the Lodz ghetto are indicative of the atmosphere that prevailed there. Lodz was known for its textile industry, where the large halls of the factories and workshops enabled the spreading of new songs, which became popular instantaneously. Artists were encouraged by the head of the ghetto, Haim Rumkovsky, who also established a musical theater. In that theater, music played a very important role. In Rumkovsky's view, music and theater were important means of demonstrating that "things are under control." For this reason, most Lodz ghetto songs derive from excerpts of stage plays performed under Rumkovsky's supervision. But, despite Rumkovsky's own attempts to exercise a degree of censorship, a number of banned songs, those that reflect upon the horror and impossible conditions of the ghetto, were learned by workers and spread throughout the ghetto. One such song, which became widely popular, was "Mach tsu di Eygelekh" – "Close Your Eyes," in Yiddish, by I. Spigel and D. Beigelman[16] (Example 2).

Mach tsu di eygelekh,	Close your little eyes,
Ot kumen feygelekh	Soon little birds will fly
Un krayzn do arum	In circles everywhere,
Tsukopns fun dayn vig;	Around your cradle.
Dos pekl in der hant,	Your bundle in your hand,
Dos hoyz in ash un brand	Your house in ash and sand,
Mir lozn zikh, mayn kind,	We leave you, my child
Zukhn glik…	In search for luck…
Men hot undz naket-bloyz	Stripped naked
Faryogt fun undzer hoyz,	We were thrown from our home
In fintsternish	In the dark of night,
Getribn undz in feld;	Driven out into the open field,
Un shturem, hogl, vint	The wind and hail and storm
Bagleyt undz, mayn kind	Accompanied us, my child
Bagleyt inem opgrint	Accompanied us into
Fun der velt.	The depths of the earth.

---

16 Spigel wrote the poem, in Yiddish, as a lullaby for his departed five-years-old daughter Hava'le, who had been a beloved child in the ghetto. See G. Flam, *Singing for survival* (Urbana and Chicago, 1992), 146–49; A. Vinkovetzky and others, *Anthology of Yiddish Folksongs*, vol. IV (Jerusalem, 1987), 147-48. Musical transcription in E. Horowitz, *In Distress – Min Hamezar* (Tel Aviv, 1987), 50.

Example 2. "Close Your Eyes"

This song, like most Holocaust songs, is syllabic and is characterized by small intervals, simple melodic motives with a repeated rhythmic pattern, a slow tempo, and short phrases.

The music of the Krakow ghetto likewise reflects the social and spiritual identity of its inhabitants. Krakow, known as the historical and cultural center of Poland, was "preserved" by the Germans. They did not brutally destroy it, and many among the city's Jews were deluded in thinking that recent horrors would not return. This attitude is reflected in the ghetto's songs, many of which are optimistic, happy, and full of hope. Even in those songs where the text is sad, final lines are full of hope and the melody is cheerful. The songs are typically fast and in duple meter, which provides for an energetic impression. Rhythmic values are short, there are much syncopations, and melodic lines are built of skips of thirds, fifths and sixths. Two examples will illustrate this musical style, which represents the musical identity of the Krakow ghetto.[17]

The first is "Minutn fun Bitokhn" – "Moments of Confidence"[18] (Example 3), a song that describes humiliations, fights despair, and boosts the morale of ghetto inhabitants by comparing the enemy to Hamman. It expresses contempt toward oppressors, and it mocks the face of the enemy. The music is inspired by the spirit of Hassidic melodies:

Yidn. Zol zany freylekh,	Jews rejoice,
Shoyn nit lang ikh hof,	The day is not far off,
S'ekt bald di milkhome,	The war is drawing to a close
S'kumt bald zeyer sof!	The enemy's end is nigh!
Freylekh, nor nit zorgn	Be gay, do not grieve

---

17 Both songs were composed by M. Gebirtig. For more details see M. Lemm, Mordechaj Gebirtig Jiddische Lieder (Germany, 1994)
18 Transcribed in Horowitz, *"In Distress" – "Min Hamezar" (Tel Aviv,*1987), 14.

Un nit arumgeyn trib –   and be not melancholy
Hot geduld, bitokhn   Have patience and faith
Un nemt on altz far lib...   Accept all with fortitude...[19]

Example 3. "Moments of Confidence"

The second song, by M. Gebirtig, "S'iz Gut" – "It's good," was probably the last song written in the Krakow ghetto before its total liquidation. It is full of biting sarcasm:

S'iz gut, s'iz gut, s'iz gut,   It's good, it's good, it's good!
Di yidelekh shrayen s'iz gut.   The Jews shout: It's good!
Der soyne, dr vilder,   The wild enemy
Geyt groyzam un shnel   Goes horribly and fast,
Un vi nor er kumt, vert   And wherever he comes,
Funlebn a tel...   Life becomes death . . .
S'ken beser nisht zany...   It couldn't be better . . .[20]

The song is in major mode, which is quite unusual in this repertoire, and it contains short textual and musical phrases, each of which in a range of a fourth. This gives the impression of a joyous melodic line. The song's meter, three eights per measure, creates short spaces between the downbeats, and reinforces the overall impression of joy and courage (Example 4).

---

19 A. Vinkovetzky and others, *Anthology of Yiddish Folksongs*, vol. IV (Jerusalem, 1987), 157-59.
20 S. Kalisch, *Yes, We Sang!* (New York, 1985), 19; S. Leichter, *Anthology of Yiddush Folksongs*, vol. V (Jerusalem, 2000), 284-87. Musical transcription in E. Horowitz, *In Distress – Min Hamezar* (Tel Aviv, 1987), 16.

Example 4. "It's Good!"

The musical style of ghetto songs from the Soviet Union reflects not only the life of individual Soviet ghettos but also the mood of Jewish partisans. In the ghettos of Vilnius, Kovno, Shavly, and Kiev, we find two musical "faces" or repertoires. One consists of music that describes daily life in the ghetto. Its stylistic language is similar to that found in Polish ghettos, with one exception: Many songs are based upon Soviet popular melodies. The second repertoire is that of the partisans. Jewish Partisans were particularly widespread in the forests of Eastern Europe. They fought bravely, usually in mixed partisan units, maintaining a remarkable sense of Jewish identity. This was characterized by the use of the Yiddish language in military communications, in poetry, and in music. Some composers and poets managed to escape from the ghettos and join up with partisan bands fighting behind the Nazi line. Thus, cultural activities continued and music became part of the resistance movement, but its identity changed completely. Jewish partisan songs expressed homesickness, concern for family members still living in the ghetto, grief, desire for revenge, descriptions of militant resistance, and praise of the partisans' brave activities, but such music was no longer based upon traditional Jewish tunes. Instead, Soviet and Ukrainian melodies take over, stressing the march-like style. Most of these songs are short and include series of dotted rhythms in unison or seconds, with syncopations and large melodic leaps in between. The song "Shtey oyf tsum Kamf" – "Get Up and Fight," written by L. Svirsky, based on a Soviet folk tune (Example 5) is an example of such songs.

Shtey oyf dokh tsum kamf, du yidish folk,	Jewish people, rise up and fight!
Genug unterdrikt shoyn gevezn;	Too long have we been oppressed;
Mir zaynen keyn knekht, mir fodern rekht,	We won't be slaves, our rights we will claim,
Mir veln es keynmol nit fergesn...	And we will never, never forget...[21]

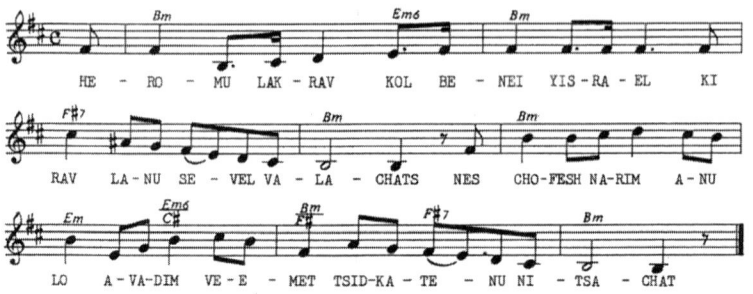

Example 5. "Get Up and Fight"

Another example is the song "Far wos" – "Why"[22] by L. Opeskin,[23] which is based on a Soviet tune by V. Byeli (Example 6).

Far vos iz der himl geven nekhtn loyter	Why was the sky yesterday so bright
Fun freyd hot geshaynt yede gas?	With happiness were the streets shining
Far vos iz di zun aza likhtike, royte,	Why is the sun so clear and red
Farkhmuret haynt, beyz un in kas?[24]	But today so cloudy and angry?

Example 6. "Why?"

---

21 The text quoted here is taken from the notes of the CD *Rise Up and Fight* (United States Holocaust Memorial Museum), 24-25. Transcription in E. Horowitz, *In Distress – Min Hamezar* (Tel Aviv, 1987), 94.

22 Transcription in E. Horowitz, *In Distress – Min Hamezar* (Tel Aviv, 1987), 20.

23 L. Opeskin was a partisan from the Vilnius ghetto. He died in battle in July 1944.

24 M. Gotlieb and Ch. Mlatek, 25 Ghetto songs – 25 Ghetto lieder (New York, 1968), 28-9.

The Jews of The Saloniki, in Greece, were forced into the ghetto in July 1942. The community was liquidated in August 1943. We have very little information about their musical activities. But survivors recall the performance of old liturgical and para-liturgical pieces, as well as popular songs in Hebrew and Ladino, of which they changed the texts from time to time to reflect contemporary events. This music was also performed by partisans who joined the Greek units, who also "adopted" songs of their partners, the Greek partisans, in Greek.[25]

– – –

The final stage of the war was marked by the deportation of Jews to concentration and extermination camps. Many songs of the ghettos disappeared with their liquidation, but those that survived were part of the "luggage" that Jewish prisoners took with them on their way to forced labor and death camps. Here it seems, that musical repertoires reflect, once again, Jewish identity through the prism of the present situation. At this stage, we can identify two sorts of music:

1. "Forced" music, performed according to the orders of the Nazis, for the purpose of deceit. Such music was sung and played to accompany prisoners while marching to work and returning to the camp, at executions, at ceremonial public punishments, and as aural "camouflage" at the entrances of extermination chambers. This music, mainly western art music, was broadcast at full volume through sound systems in order to drown out the infernal noises. Jewish musicians participated in all of these missions, as well as on concerts and parties of the Nazi commanders. The testimonies of survivors of the Auschwitz orchestras testify to this kind of music-making, which was based on non-Jewish material.[26] The only chance to perform Jewish traditional music was when the Jews of Greece were forced to sing in Ladino or in Greek. On such occasions they chose old traditional folk tunes and changed the original texts into curses for the enemy and expressions of longing for their homeland, The Saloniki. For these musicians, music was life saving, and performing as soloists or as members of the orchestra was liter-

---

[25] Oral testimonies of The Saloniki survivors inform us that the Partisan Greek song "The White Castle," which commemorates the brave activities of Jewish Partisan units, was sung also while preparing the revolt in Birkenau (to be discussed below).
[26] For descriptions of the life of the musicians in Auschwitz, see F. Fenelon, *Playing for Time* (New York, 1977); G. Knapp, *Das Frauenorchester in Auschwitz* (Hamburg, 1996); R. Newman and K. Kirtley, *Alma Rose – Vienna to Auschwitz* (Oregon, 2000); G. Greif, *We Wept Without Tears – Bachinu Beli Dmaoth* (Jerusalem, 1990); H. Rafael, *The Song of Haim – Shirat Haim* (Tel Aviv, 1997); and E. Barzilai, *The Destruction of Greek Jewry – Churban Jahaduth Javan* (Tel Aviv, 1998).

ally an act of survival, since it enabled them to be granted life by their captors for a few more days or months.

2. Music that was performed among the Jewish prisoners and reflects the Jewish spirit. Such music was performed secretly, far from the Nazi commanders, and included mainly old songs in addition to few newly composed ones.

An important component of this latter category is the collection of old Jewish songs, which were "transported" from the ghettos. This repertoire included excerpts from the Jewish liturgy as well as sacred tunes and songs that were popular in Jewish communities before the war. The texts of these songs were in Hebrew, Yiddish, or Ladino and the singing was typically responsorial, so that everybody could participate. The prisoners insisted on singing them as in as authentic a manner as possible, just as they remembered singing them at home, because these songs constituted, for them, a substitute for holy rituals and spiritual exaltations. Prayer books were not available to anyone, so singing itself became a declaration of Jewish identity. In testimonies collected from diaries and memory books of the period, we find many descriptions of such spiritual exclamation, in many cases carried out under mortal risk.

New, easily absorbed melodies were set also to liturgical and para-liturgical texts, thus enriching the traditional repertoire. An example from this corpus of songs is the poem "Ya Ribbon Alam" (Master of the Universe). The melody was composed by Arie Ben Erez Abrahamson in France's St. Cyprien concentration camp in 1940.[27] The text is taken from a popular ancient poem in Aramaic, frequently used during Sabbath meals.[28] This song was, once again, an overwhelming declaration of the religious spirit, which nothing could ever vanquish or destroy.

The new songs composed in labor and extermination camps were often sung while working, walking, and gathering. The language of these songs was typically Polish, Greek, Hungarian, or German, perhaps as a goodwill gesture to their gentile co-inhabitants. The musical pattern of such songs has no overly Jewish elements, and is also very simple. The songs are short, melodic lines include no more than three or four motives, and rhythmic patterns are simple and obsessively repeated. An example of such a "working" song is "The Chanting Horses,"[29] based on a Polish folk tune, and originally sung in Polish (Example 7).

---

27 Arie Ben Erez Abrahamson composed the melody on the first Sabbath eve of his captivity and sang it at the reunion with his family after his escape from the camp to Marseilles.
28 By the sixteenth-century poet Israel Najara; the line "May He free us from the jaws of the lion" had special meaning for the prisoner, and inspired a heroic melody. Abrahamson dedicated the song to his father.
29 Transcribed in M. Hoch, *Kolot Mitoch Hachoshech - Voices from the Dark* (Jerusalem, 2002), 136-37.

Wiesz ty co koniku, wiesz ty co?	Do you know what, my horse?
Ciagnij woz i nie pytaj gdzie i co!	Carry on the coach and do not ask where and why!
Czy ci dobrze , czy ci zle,	If you feel good or bad,
To usmiechaj zawsze sie!	Always smile to the world!
Smiech to zdrowie,	Smiling is health
Zapamietaj sobie to!	Remember it always!

Example 7. "The Chanting Horses"

Another example is "Shoin Genug" – "Enough is Enough,"[30] composed by I. Grodzanovsky after a Polish tune while she was paving a road in the Kromnnau camp (Example 8).

Yedn Fri, Yedn Fri	Every day, every day
Klapt dejn fus	Knocks you feet
yedn Tog ofn hartn brik	On the hard stones
Un di fis, deine fis	And your feet, yes youe feet
Fun dem gang ofn brik	Walking heavily on the stones
shoin geworn mjid	Are already worn out
Wu di gist zich nor a ker	If you turn here and there
Un di gist zich nor a drei	Or you move back and forth
Umetum alle tirn	All the doors and gates
Geshlossn nor far zei	Are closed in front of you
Shoin genug, shoin genug	Enough is enough is enough
Klapt dejn fus yedn Tog ofn hartn brik	Knocks your feet every day on the hard stones.

---

30 Text and transcription in E. Horowitz, *Min Hamezar - In Distress* (Tel Aviv, 1987), 32.

Example 8. Grodzanovsky, "Enough is Enough"

At gathering-times, while resting from the inhuman labor, Jewish prisoners composed songs such as the song of the Greek Jews, composed by D. Haim's "Siete dias encerrados" – "Locked inside for a week,"[31] which was written in ladino, in the Buna camp in 1944 (Example 9).

Siete dias encerrados	Locked inside for a week
En vagones de behemas	In a crowded cattle car
Una vez a los tres dias	They let us out to breathe air
Mos quitaban a airear…	Once in three days…
Padre, madre, hermanos y hermanicas	Brother, sister father and mother
Saliendo todos rejagis	Leave the heavens to clatter
A el Patron del mondu	From the Master please request
Que envie salud a mi	That He will send me health
Que me quite de estos	From the valley of death
Para vos echar kadis.	He'll take me to you to say Kaddish.

---

31 I. Kerem, "The Music of the Greek Jews in the Holocaust," in *Proceedings of the First International Conference on Jewish Music*, ed. S. Stanton (London, 1994), 46. Text and transcription in S. Weich-Shahak, *Ein boan siman* (Haifa, 2006), 137.

Example 9. "Siete dias encorreados" – "Locked for Seven Days"

Another such song is "Sweet Saloniki,"[32] composed by Y. Levi in Auschwitz in 1943 (Example 10).

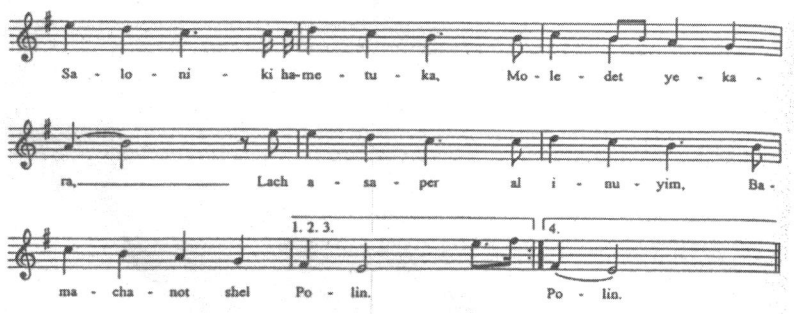

Example 10. Levi, "Sweet Saloniki"

Both of these songs feature very simple descending scale-like melodic patterns, with many repetitions and simple rhythmic values.

We should not conclude without noting that music also played an important role in the *Zonderkomando* revolt in Birkenau, Auschwitz, in October 1944. The women who supplied ammunition-powder for the revolt came as near as possible to the crematoriums where the *Zonderkommando* worked. They sang popular songs in Ladino (which the Germans did not understand), but the texts of their songs were altered to inform the prisoners about the materials that they had stolen, to be used in order to explode the crematoriums as part of the planned revolt. Indeed, music played a very important part in advancing the revolt, although it does not have any meaning in terms of projecting the Jewish identity.[33] Such music, though composed by Jewish prisoners principally for the benefit of

---

32 Transcribed in Hoch, *Kolot Mitoch Hachoshech - Voices from the Dark* (Jerusalem, 2002), 223. The only available printed text and recording are in Hebrew.
33 There are no recordings of this kind of music, but the facts mentioned here appear in the testimonies of the survivors.

their comrades, does not exhibit any salient marks of Jewish identity. It seems to me that at this point of oppression, when the Jewish essence had been so brutally humiliated, there was no need to manifest the Jewish spirit in newly composed songs. Jewish identity had been preserved in old songs that enabled Jewish prisoners to give voice to their faith and hopes for victory of the eternal Jewish spirit. It was enough, I believe to embody the physical destruction that surrounded the Jewish people in new, "non-Jewish" songs.

Jewish music during the holocaust has undergone a process of constant changes, carrying the musical traditional elements on one hand, while adopting foreign musical and textual components on the other hand. The rich repertoire, including traditional music, folk music and western art music, serves as a document of the period, and has a unique value. It is the expression of the victory of the Jewish spirit, embodied in composing, performing and preserving, in spite of the efforts of the enemy to destroy this Jewish identity.

Baltic Musics

Kevin C. Karnes

WHERE SPACE BECOMES TIME
Music, Landscape, and Memory in the Latvian Rock Opera Lāčplēsis

"It's not water that flows in the Daugava—it's time." Hearing these words, sung by a choir backed up by two of the country's leading rock bands, 180,000 Latvians began their journey through the rock opera *Lāčplēsis* in the summer and fall of 1988. That experience constituted a virtual rite of passage for those coming of age during the time of *glasnost'* and *perestroyka*. "Every Latvian considered it his duty to go see it," a pair of Latvian journalists recently recalled.[1] As foretold in the opera's opening line, the text and music of *Lāčplēsis* collapse space and time, extending the listener's experience of the here and now to imaginative places at once geographically, temporally, and mythologically distant. Like the Daugava River itself, the listener's mind is drawn from the Baltic Sea through the heart of Riga, and across the Latvian countryside into Russian (then Soviet Russian) spaces beyond. Listening to *Lāčplēsis*, we survey imaginatively the host of refashionings of the opera's epic story that have appeared since that story's first publication in 1888. And, immersing ourselves in words and music, we revisit the substance of the Bear Slayer ("Lāča-plēsis") epic itself, which has been a cornerstone of Latvian heritage and imagined cultural community for well over a century, and perhaps many more. In the opening chorus of what the opera's composer called, in a sketch for the work, its "time song" (*laika dziesma*), the words of the librettist, poet Māra Zālīte, continue:

I wish to thank Zigmars Liepiņš for his permission to publish excerpts from the score of *Lāčplēsis* in this essay. The piano-vocal score was originally published in two volumes, as *Dziesmas un rokopera "Lāčplēsis"* (Riga, n.d.), and is presently available online at http://www.zigmarsliepins.lv/ (accessed 15 May 2009). A recording of the complete opera is available as a free .mp3 download from the same site. I also wish to express my gratitude to Yayoi Uno Everett for her invaluable comments on an earlier version of this essay.

1 Džeina Tamuļeviča and Uldis Rudaks, "Rokopera Lāčplēsis atgriežas divdesmit gadu pēc pirmizrādes," *Diena* (22 June 2008): 10. I take the figure for total attendance at the opera's forty-three staged performances from Guntis Šmidchens, "National Heroic Narratives in the Baltics as a Source for Nonviolent Political Action," *Slavic Review* 66, no. 3 (2007): 484-508 (at p. 499).

Tas nav ūdens, kas Daugavā plūst.	It's not water that flows in the Daugava.
Tas ir Laiks.	It's Time.
Tā nav asins, kas dzīslās tev tek.	It's not blood that flows in your veins.
Tas ir Laiks.	It's Time.
Tas nav vilnis, kas apskalo mūs.	That's not a wave washing against us.
Tas ir Laiks.	It's Time.
Tas nav atvars, kas gredzenu griež.	That's not a whirlpool twisting in a circle.
Tas ir Laiks.	It's Time.[2]

To these lines, the music of Zigmars Liepiņš, singer and keyboardist with the rock band Opus, is performed by SATB chorus, drums, keyboard, and electric bass and guitars (Example 1).

Example 1. *Lāčplēsis*: opening chorus ("time song")

As Philip Bohlman has observed in one of a series of essays that has partly inspired my present exploration of landscape and memory in *Lāčplēsis*, music has an uncanny ability, even an inevitable proclivity, to "perform a place into being."[3] The performance of music and the act of listening to music—and

---

[2] Māra Zālīte, *Lāčplēsis*, in *Dzeja – Lāčplēsis* (Riga, n.d.), 152. The published title of this number is "Tas ir Laiks," or "It's Time." Liepiņš's compositional sketch for the score, cited here, is preserved in the Rakstniecības, Teātra un Mūzikas Vēstures Muzējs (Riga), inv. no. 619146, topogr. apzīm. Z. Liep. R1/3.

[3] Philip V. Bohlman, "The Remembrance of Things Past: Music, Race, and the End of History in Modern Europe," in *Music and the Racial Imagination*, ed. Ronald Radano and Philip V. Bohlman (Chicago and London, 2000), 644-76 (cited at p. 649). See also Bohlman, "Landscape—Region—Nation—Reich: German Folk Song in the Nexus of National Identity," in *Music and German National Identity*, ed. Celia Applegate and Pamela Potter

especially those musics, typically popular musics, that we carry around with us in our minds—has a power "to stem the ineluctable pull of forgetting."[4] It brings us back, when performed, heard, or conjured, to spaces once inhabited, collapsing the here and the now with the elsewhere and the once, and even with times and places only imagined. "The memory created by music may only evoke a sense of place," Bohlman writes, "a nostalgia about a place that can no longer be recovered. [But] the sites of memory nonetheless empower music to connect individual experiences to place. If indeed that place is not immediately retrievable, the memory that the musical monument represents is insistently a reminder that the possibility for such retrieval is not entirely lost."[5] Writing last summer in commemoration of the twentieth anniversary of the rock opera's debut, the journalists Džeina Tamuļevič and Uldis Rudaks recalled that this sort of active, creative remembering was an inherent part of the *Lāčplēsis* experience for Latvian youths of their generation. To assure that the imaginative experience of the opera would not be lost after its final chorus faded away, "we all picked up, like a relic, a tangible memento in the form of three vinyl discs."[6]

But as Bohlman also notes, memory is selective, and an act of forgetting, deliberate or otherwise, inevitably accompanies the act of remembering. It is within the dynamic interplay of remembering and forgetting, comprising a kind of messy dialectic, that our identities—historical, cultural, and personal—are continuously shaped and reshaped. "Music," Bohlman writes, "functions powerfully to facilitate both remembering and forgetting, but it is precisely that contradiction that makes it so suggestive as a means of interpellating the European racial imagination"[7]—or, I would argue, the European *historical* imagination. Or, in the present case, the *Latvian* historical imagination.

What I want to explore in the present essay is the interplay of space and time, landscape and memory, in the rock opera *Lāčplēsis*, and in particular the ways in which these various sorts of imaginative interplay have shaped and reshaped Latvian historical consciousness from the nineteenth century through the present day. We have, of course, long appreciated the fact that our tellings of our histories condition our experience of the present moment. More recently, we have also begun to acknowledge that the ways in which we describe the spaces we inhabit are not simply reflective of who were are or what we aspire to be (as

---

(Chicago and London, 2002), 105-27; and Bohlman, "The Final Borderpost," *Journal of Musicology* 14, no. 4 (1996): 427-52.
4 Bohlman, "The Remembrance of Things Past," 665. The link between popular music, memory, and what might best be described as aural or imaginative reliving are eloquently described in Simon Frith, *Performing Rites: On the Value of Popular Music* (Cambridge, MA, and London, 1996), 6-8.
5 Bohlman, "The Remembrance of Things Past," 664.
6 Tamuļeviča and Rudaks, "Rokopera Lāčplēsis," 10.
7 Bohlman, "The Remembrance of Things Past," 646.

maps of empire make plain), but that they are also *causal*. Those descriptions, like the historical narratives we construct, become in our minds imaginative forces that shape our identities in turn.[8] As water collapses into time and envelops the self in the opening chorus of *Lāčplēsis*, so too, I will argue, do the shaping forces of historical narrative and descriptions of place converge in numerous ways and moments in the opera, conditioning the listener's experience of the present moment, wherever and whenever that might be.

The Promise of Eternal Return

There is a more concrete theory behind what I propose with respect to *Lāčplēsis*, as my essay's title suggests. "Where Space Becomes Time": This refers, of course, to Wagner's *Parsifal*, and specifically to the "Transformation Music" (*Verwandlungsmusik*) that precedes the inexplicable morphing of Parsifal's surroundings from forest to Amfortas's castle, and that simultaneously marks the beginning of Parsifal's personal transformation from "pure fool" (*der reine Tor*) to savior of his people. "Time becomes space here," counsels Gurnemanz, Parsifal's guide, just as the here and the now begin to fade. In terms of plot, the parallels between *Parsifal* and *Lāčplēsis* are readily apparent, even after a cursory look at the latter. For Lāčplēsis the Bear Slayer also begins his journey as an innocent "little child" (*mazs bērniņš*), who ventures into a world filled with traps and trials, and who is ultimately transformed through his own epiphany into his people's savior.[9] Wagner completed *Parsifal* in 1882. The poet Andrejs Pumpurs, author of the original Lāčplēsis epic, published the latter in 1888.[10] Though separated geographically, their worlds were both places where time, memory, and the identities they engender were hotly contested across broad swaths of society. And the works of both artists confront some fundamentally similar positions on these issues.

From the 1820s through the turn of the twentieth century, the leading voice in German-speaking European discussions of time and history (and Latvia was still, intellectually, very much a part of German-speaking Europe) was Hegel's.

---

8 On this issue, see Jeremy Black, *Maps and History: Constructing Images of the Past* (New Haven and London, 1997), 83; and, more generally, Simon Schama, *Landscape and Memory* (New York, 1996).

9 Moreover, Lāčplēsis's transformation, like a mirror-image of Parsifal's, is concluded, rather than initiated, in a magical space: the castle of the mythical figure of Staburadze, located at the bottom of the Daugava River.

10 Andrejs Pumpurs, *Laçplésis, Latvju tautas varonis. Tautas epus. Pec tautas teikām sacerejis Pumpurs* (Riga, 1888). In the present essay, all citations from Pumpurs's epic will be taken from the critical edition by Jāzeps Rudzītis: Pumpurs, *Lāčplēsis. Latvju tautas varonis. Tautas epos*, ed. Jāzeps Rudzītis (Riga, 1988). For an English translation, see Pumpurs, *Bearslayer: The Latvian Legend*, ed. Arthur Cropley, Ausma Cimdiņa, and Kaspars Kļaviņš, trans. Arthur Cropley (Riga, 2007).

Though his philosophy of history is most commonly associated today with the notion of *Zeitgeist*, Hegel also drew a sharp distinction between two varieties of temporal experience. The passing of time in the natural world, as Hegel saw it, was essentially cyclical, characterized by sunrise and sunset, the changing of the seasons, and recurring cycles of birth and death in the animal and vegetable kingdoms. "The changes that take place in nature," Hegel wrote, "however infinitely manifold they may be, exhibit only a perpetually self-repeating cycle."[11] In contrast, spirit or *Geist*, the animating force in human action, thought, and civilization, manifests time as a linear, directed process. Human beings and societies, Hegel argued, experience non-repeating temporal development. Thus, in his view, they experience *history*.[12] As the British philosopher R.G. Collingwood nicely summarized Hegel's position, "there is no history except the history of human life."[13]

In Wagner's world, a deeply pessimistic variant of the Hegelian dichotomy between the temporalities of man and nature flourished, as formulated by the composer's philosophical idol, Arthur Schopenhauer. Schopenhauer, who despised Hegel and his work, turned the latter's privileging of human history over natural time upon its head, and drew a stark contrast between the phenomenon of perpetual rebirth in the natural world and what he identified as the inevitable corollary of Hegel's theory of linear human history. The processes of nature, Schopenhauer observed, recur again and again, eternally. Man, however, lives a unidirectional life that has a definite end point: death. "The earth rolls on from day into night," Schopenhauer wrote. "The individual dies; but the sun itself burns without intermission, an eternal noon."[14] This fact, for Schopenhauer, was just one of many indicators of what he called, speaking of human beings, the *vanity of life*. "This vanity," he wrote, "finds its expression in the whole form of existence; in the infinite nature of time and space as opposed to the finite nature of the individual in both . . . a man all of a sudden exists after countless thousands of years of non-existence and, after a short time, must again pass into a non-existence just as long."[15] And thus, given the inevitable sufferings that plague the brief life of every individual, Schopenhauer concluded, with respect to a man's life, that "it would be better not to have it."[16] Wagner took the Schopen-

---

11 Georg Wilhelm Friedrich Hegel, *Philosophy of History*, trans. J. Sibree (New York, 1902), 104. On *Zeitgeist* in Hegel's philosophy of history, see Terry Pinkard, *German Philosophy, 1760-1860: The Legacy of Idealism* (Cambridge, 2002), 296-300; and Leonard Krieger, *Time's Reasons: Philosophies of History Old and New* (Chicago and London, 1989), 53-62.
12 Hegel, *Philosophy of History*, 105-134.
13 R.G. Collingwood, *The Idea of History* (Oxford, 1946), 115.
14 Arthur Schopenhauer, *The World as Will and Representation*, trans. E.F.J. Payne (New York, 1958), 1:281.
15 Schopenhauer, *Parerga and Paralipomena*, trans. E.F.J. Payne (Oxford, 1974), 2:283.
16 Schopenhauer, *The World as Will and Representation*, 2:575.

hauerian view of existence with utmost conviction. One thinks, for instance, of the character of Kundry in *Parsifal*. Cursed with immortality after mocking Christ, she longs for death as release from the sufferings of everlasting life. Or of the *Flying Dutchman*, conceived before Wagner had ever even heard of Schopenhauer's work: Endlessly the Dutchman plies the turbulent oceans, seeking rest in death.

To make our way back to Pumpurs and *Lāčplēsis*, we must consider one more late-nineteenth-century thinker, whose work posed a remarkable answer to this Wagnerian-Schopenhauerian pessimism. In the study I cited at the outset of this essay, Philip Bohlman characterizes the inevitable disjuncture between imagined landscapes and attainable realities as symptomatic of what he calls "The Myth of Eternal Return."[17] As I will suggest below, the mythology of return has long been essential in shaping Latvian notions of cultural identity. But we should note that "eternal return" is also a specific theory of history, powerfully adumbrated by Friedrich Nietzsche and of profound importance to understanding the European historical consciousness of Pumpurs's time. Significantly, eternal return was, to Nietzsche's mind, not a myth at all, but reality and a promise. It was, as the philosopher wrote, was "highest formula of affirmation that is at all attainable" in a post-Schopenhauerian world.[18] That theory is a centerpiece of Nietzsche's *Thus Spoke Zarathustra*, where it first appears in the form of a parable.

Imagine a gateway, Nietzsche's Zarathustra urges, representing the present moment—a narrow gateway that straddles a road running to infinity behind us and to infinity ahead of us as well. "Must not whatever *can* walk have walked on this lane before?" Nietzsche asks, given the finite nature of matter and energy and the infinite nature of time. "Must not whatever *can* happen have happened, have been done, have passed by before?"[19] Zarathustra's musings prompt bewilderment in his audience. But later, he is understood perfectly well, though not by people—*by animals*. "O Zarathustra," Nietzsche's barnyard animals say to him consolingly,

> to those who think as we do, all things themselves are dancing: they come and offer their hands and laugh and flee—and come back. Everything goes, every-

---

17 Bohlman, "The Remembrance of Things Past," 667-69.
18 Friedrich Nietzsche, *Ecce Homo*, trans. Walter Kaufmann, in *On the Genealogy of Morals and Ecce Homo*, ed. Walter Kaufmann, trans. Walter Kaufmann and R.J. Hollingdale (New York, 1989), 295. For general considerations of Nietzsche's theory eternal recurrence, to which my discussion below is indebted, see Lawrence J. Hatab, "Shocking Time: Reading Eternal Recurrence Literally," in *Nietzsche on Time and History*, ed. Manuel Dries (Berlin and New York, 2008), 149-62; and Robert Gooding-Williams, *Zarathustra's Dionysian Modernism* (Stanford, CA, 2001).
19 Nietzsche, *Thus Spoke Zarathustra*, in *The Portable Nietzsche*, ed. and trans. Walter Kaufmann (New York, 1968), 270 (emphasis in original).

thing comes back; eternally rolls the wheel of being. Everything dies, everything blossoms again; eternally runs the year of being. Everything breaks, everything is joined anew; eternally the same house of being is built. Everything parts, every-thing greets every other thing again; eternally the ring of being remains faithful to itself. In every Now, being begins; round every Here rolls the sphere There. The center is everywhere. Bent is the path of eternity.[20]

As space and time begin to merge in the final lines of the animals' gloss, they pause to state Zarathustra's case for eternal return more clearly than the prophet himself can:

> Behold, we know what you teach: that all things recur eternally, and we ourselves too; and that we have already existed an eternal number of times, and all things with us. . . . the knot of causes in which I am entangled recurs and will create me again. I myself belong to the causes of the eternal recurrence. I come again, with this sun, with this earth, with this eagle, with this serpent—not to a new life or a better life or a similar life: I come back eternally to this same, selfsame life.[21]

In Nietzsche's *Zarathustra*, we find release from Schopenhauerian pessimism in deconstruction of Schopenhauer's terms. Man and nature are not mutually exclusive, but man *is* nature, and nature is man. The animals speak of the unity of all existence—*das All*—and the eternal rebirth of everything. And life and death are not distinct and opposed but two sides of the same coin; or, as Nietzsche observed, they are like the two glass vessels of an hourglass that is forever being turned over.[22]

In the final decades of the nineteenth century and the early years of the twentieth, aspects of Nietzsche's theory of eternal return literally pervaded German intellectual culture. One thinks, for instance, of Gustav Mahler's *Kindertotenlieder* (1901-04), with a text by Friedrich Rückert. The first song of that cycle begins by meditating on the Schopenhauerian dichotomy between eternal nature and mortal man: "Now the sun will rise again just as brightly, as if no misfortune"—the death of the child—"had happened in the night." Yet it concludes with the promise of salvation, attained through identification with the natural world and its eternally recurring processes. ("A little lamp has gone out in my dwelling; hail to the joyous light of the world!")[23] Or, one might think of the playwright and philosopher Maurice Maeterlinck, whose works were sensa-

---

20 Ibid., 329-30.
21 Ibid., 332-33 (emphasis in original).
22 Ibid., 332. On Nietzsche's work as deconstructing "the history of metaphysics" (though not considering Schopenhauer specifically), see Christopher Norris, *Deconstruction: Theory and Practice*, 3rd ed. (London and New York, 2002), 55-72 (cited at p. 72).
23 "Nun will die Sonn' so hell aufgehn, / Als sei kein Unglück die Nacht geschehn. . . . Ein Lämplein verlosch in meinem Zelt, / Heil sei dem Freudenlicht der Welt!"

tionally popular throughout German-speaking Europe around 1900.[24] Central to Maeterlinck's mature thought were the Nietzschean convictions that man and nature are identical in essence, and that the spirit of all living things persists eternally, participating the cycle of perpetual rebirth. "The genius of the Earth," Maeterlinck wrote, "which is probably that of the universe, acts, in the vital struggle, exactly as man would act."[25] And, recasting Nietzsche's parable of the arch and the infinite road, "the hands of our ancestors are clasped by the hands of our sons yet unborn. . . . Thus are we led by past and future."[26] And, transforming Nietzsche's sermon of the barnyard animals into a meditation on the lives of bees: "Your aim is clear to us, clearer far than our own; you desire to live, as long as the world itself, in those that come after."[27] As I will argue, this unabashedly affirmative, eternally recurring vision of history, nature, and one's place within them pervades the worlds both inhabited by and inscribed within the Lāčplēsis epic, and it receives perhaps its most powerful statement in the *Lāčplēsis* rock opera of 1988. For as the librettist Zālīte writes of the waters of the Daugava in the opera's opening chorus, "That's not a whirlpool twisting in a circle. It's time."

From 2008 to 1888

I saw *Lāčplēsis* performed in Riga in July 2008, at one of the city's major stadiums, in a show commemorating the twentieth anniversary of the opera's premiere. On that occasion, links between the present and the recent past were manifest everywhere one looked. When I told a friend, who writes for a leading Latvian music magazine, that I was going to see the show, she replied incredulously, "You are?" After which she told me that her parents had taken her to see the opera back in 1988, because "that's what people did in those days." In a similar way, that stadium in Riga in July 2008 was packed with thirty-somethings bringing their own children to the show, thus passing on the gesture described by my friend to a generation that had never known the Soviet experience to which the opera's creators had responded in their work. In this way, the performance of the opera connected three generations and two distinct ages in Latvian cultural history. I witnessed there the forging of a new link in the

---

24 See Stefan Gross, ed., *Maurice Maeterlinck und die deutschsprachige Literatur. Eine Documentation* (Mindelheim, 1985). On Maeterlinck's influence in Vienna particularly, see Paul Gorceix, *Maurice Maeterlinck. Le Symbolisme de la différence* (Mont-de-Marsan, 1997), 207-229.
25 Maurice Maeterlinck, *News of Spring and Other Nature Studies*, trans. Teixeira De Mattos (New York, 1913), 103.
26 Maeterlinck, *The Treasure of the Humble*, trans. Alfred Sutro (New York, 1898), 143.
27 Maeterlinck, *The Life of the Bee*, trans. Alfred Sutro (New York, 1905), 177-78.

Maeterlinckian chain being, in which "the hands of our ancestors are clasped by the hands of our sons yet unborn."

To hear *Lāčplēsis* performed in 2008 was indeed to be brought back to an earlier time. For when the chorus pronounced its opening words, "It's not water that flows in the Daugava—it's time," I was reminded that the Daugava was, in 1988, much more than just a river. Over the handful of years immediately preceding the latter date, the Daugava had become emblematic of the Latvian citizenry's nascent yet increasingly frequent and steadily growing protests against Soviet rule. In the process, the river had come to represent a great deal of Latvian history, culture, and identity. This was, indeed, the political context in which the libretto's invocations of the Daugava were penned, and also the context in which the opera's first listeners pondered its imagery.

With the advent of *glasnost'* in the Baltic states in the middle 1980s, the first round of large-scale protests in the recent history of Soviet Latvia were sparked by an environmental movement, whose spiritual leaders were a journalist and a computer programmer. In October 1986, the latter pair wrote, in the combined journal of the Unions of Soviet Latvian Artists, Writers, and Composers, an essay denouncing the government's planned construction of a hydroelectric dam on the Daugava River near the town of Pļaviņas. Their efforts soon combined with those of the republic's Environmental Protection Club (Vides aizsardzības klubs, or VAK) and, in that guise, embraced a host of preservationist causes, from protests against air and water pollution and the planned construction of the Riga metro to lobbying for the restoration of churches and other historic buildings.[28] The poster reprinted as Figure 1, distributed in 1987 and with a caption that reads "don't pollute the water!" (*nepiesārņojiet ūdeni!*), is exemplary of creative responses to and products of this movement.

The subtext that united the disparate activities of the VAK and its associated groups was the conviction that Latvia's environment, whether urban or rural, was itself an aspect and manifestation of its heritage. And, therefore, to protect that heritage, whether manmade or natural, was to preserve and to nurture awareness and respect for the republic's indigenous culture and its mostly non-Soviet history. "The first VAK members," write the Latvian historians Artis Pabriks and Aldis Purs, "considered society and people as a part of nature. . . . Consequently, oppressed Latvian culture came under the imagined protection of the Latvian Environment Protection Club."[29]

---

28 On these events and movements, see Artis Pabriks and Aldis Purs, *Latvia: The Challenges of Change* (London and New York, 2002), 51-53; Anatol Lieven, *The Baltic Revolution: Estonia, Latvia, Lithuania and the Path to Independence*, 2nd ed. (New Haven and London, 1994), 219-21; and Romuald Misiunas and Rein Taagepera, *The Baltic States: Years of Dependence, 1940-1990*, rev. ed. (Berkeley and Los Angeles, 1993), 304-305.

29 Pabriks and Purs, *Latvia*, 51-52.

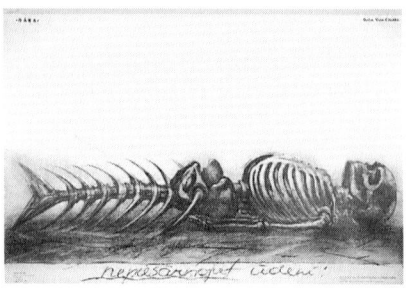

Figure 1. "don't pollute the water!" (poster, 1987)

Within this movement, the Daugava was cherished as emblematic of all that Latvia could be and had been. For its participants and many of their numberless sympathizers, the river was, as Simon Schama writes of his native Thames, "a line of time as well as space."[30] By invoking, at the very beginning of *Lāčplēsis*, an image of the Daugava as a living embodiment of the course of history itself, the librettist Zālīte offered a powerful commentary on this environmental discourse—and, by extension, on the contemporary Latvian political environment as well.

And, just as the memory of the environmentalist movement of the 1980s was brought to my mind by the opening chorus of *Lāčplēsis*, so too did that opera's reflections on the timelessness and sacred nature of the Daugava recall, for listeners in 1988, memories of a still-earlier period in Latvia's history. That earlier period, of the Latvian "National Awakening" (*tautas atmoda*), was the one inhabited by the poet and author of the original Lāčplēsis epic, Andrejs Pumpurs (1841-1902). We know that many such listeners recalled that earlier period because the literary critic Jānis Kalniņš reminded them of it, in an essay published that summer:

> These days, when the protection of the Daugava and the preservation of its splendor occupy such vital and important places in the life of our republic, it is perhaps worthwhile to remind ourselves that, to a significant extent, it was none other than Andrejs Pumpurs and [the nineteenth-century Latvian poet] Auseklis who created our image of the Daugava, whereby the Daugava is associated with the Latvian nation, its longings for freedom, and its ethical singularity.[31]

To hear the opera *Lāčplēsis* performed in 1988 was, for many, to be confronted with memories of an earlier century, when the air was filled with what

---

30 Schama, *Landscape and Memory*, 5.
31 Jānis Kalniņš, "'Lāčplēsis' sava laika kultūrvēsturiskajā situācijā," *Karogs* (September 1988): 13.

Latvian historians call "Latvian Romanticism"—a mode of perception and creative activity in which "nature and god were regarded as identical notions."[32] It was, significantly, within this Latvian Romantic culture that notions of Latvian national heritage and identity were first cultivated and publicly debated. In that discussion, as recorded in the writings of its original participants, the industrializing modernity of the late nineteenth century often merges with an imagined, distant past, with the pastoral Latvian landscape, and the Daugava River in particular, providing the link between myth and reality, and between the Latvian people's forgotten histories and their longed-for future. "Latvians, where have you hidden your folksongs," asked Jēkabs Zvaigznīte, a full-blown Romantic, in an essay of 1860. "Turaida's hills, have you no echoes recalling the events of the old days? Daugava, Gauja, Venta"—three great rivers in what was then Latvian-speaking Baltic Russia—"do you not carry out to sea, upon your famous waves, the stories of our grandfathers' famous deeds?"[33] And Pumpurs too, in the foreword to his Lāčplēsis epic of 1888, hinted at the places in which he had found the timeless materials that provided the basis for his work. In doing so, he forged a link between the modernity of his poetic creation and the mythological past, and, in turn, he dissolved that past into the landscape of the Latvian present.

> Around the banks of the Daugava one hears tales told and songs sung about gods and [the thunder-god] Pērkons, about the sons of gods and the daughters of the Sun, about sturdy sons of the folk and daughters of the folk, about fate and about struggles full of heroic deeds. These tales and songs take us back into the distant past, and to myths of nature and gods.[34]

In what some regard as the perplexing finale of his Lāčplēsis epic, Pumpurs's Bear Slayer, having been transformed into his people's savior, dies, falling with his nemesis, the Black Knight, into the waters of the Daugava.[35] But

---

32 Biruta Gudriķe, "Nacionālās atmodas laika literatūra. 19. gs. 50. gadu vidus-19. gs. 80. gadi," in *Latviešu literatūras vēsture*, vol. 1, *No rakstītā vārda sākumiem līdz 1918. gadam*, ed. Viktors Hausmanis *et al* (Riga, 1998), 170.
33 Jēkabs Zvaigznīte, "Par Latviešu tautas dziesmām," *Sēta, daba, pasaule* 3 (1860): 11-12. For more on Latvian cultural activism during this period, see Kevin C. Karnes, "A Garland of Songs for a Nation of Singers: An Episode in the History of Russia, the Herderian Tradition and the Rise of Baltic Nationalism," *Journal of the Royal Musical Association* 130, no. 2 (2005): 197-235; Latvian trans. in *Mūzikas akadēmijas raksti* 3 (2007): 7-31.
34 Pumpurs, *Lāčplēsis*, 141-42.
35 The meanings of this ending have recently been debated in the *Journal of Folklore Research*. See Sergei Kruks, "The Latvian Epic *Lāčplēsis*: *Passe-partout* Ideology, Traumatic Imagination of Community," *Journal of Folklore Research* 41, no. 1 (2004): 1-32; and Guntis Šmidchens, "Notes on the Latvian National Hero, Lāčplēsis," *Journal of Folklore Research* 43, no. 3 (2006): 271-80.

the final lines of Pumpurs's poem suggest that here too, as in the natural world surrounding the river itself, time is cyclical, and that Lāčplēsis will someday return:

Laik' no laika laivinieki, Braukdami pa Daugavu, Pusnaktī redz divus vīrus Stāvā krastā cīkstoties.	Every now and then, boatmen, traveling down the Daugava, see two men in the middle of the night, fighting on the bank.
[...]	
Tas ir Lāčplēs's, kas te cīkstas Vēl ar svešo naidnieku.	That's Lāčplēsis, still fighting there with the foreign enemy.
[...]	
Un ar reizi nāks tas brīdis, Kad viņš savu naidnieku, Vienu pašu lejā grūdis, Noslīcinās atvarā, – Tad zels tautai jauni laiki, Tad būs viņa svabada!	And one day, a time will come when he will strike down his enemy, who will drown in the whirlpool. Then a new age will flourish for the people; then, he will be free![36]

Though drowned in the Daugava, Lāčplēsis, in Pumpurs's epic, suffered no Schopenahuerian end; his death was not followed by an eternity of absence, but by the promise of return. He will, Pumpurs assures us, reawaken someday to fight again for the Latvian people and their dreams of freedom.

As we will see, the figure of Lāčplēsis has indeed returned, over and over again. For the story of the epic since its first publication in 1888 has been one of perpetual rounds of forgetting and remembering, in which the legend of the Bear Slayer has repeatedly gone dormant, only to re-emerge and to be re-imagined at pivotal moments in Latvia's history. As much as any recitation of political or social transformations, these artistic re-imaginings document a century of Latvian efforts to define and comprehend their places in a constantly shifting world. Having traversed a path backwards, in the present essay, from 2008 to 1888, I would like now to reverse our course, and to journey from there back to the present, pausing at those moments of the epic's re-emergence, which we might call "Lāčplēsis Years." Over the course of reviewing the ensuing twelve decades of collective forgetting and remembering, we experience what the poet Zālīte describes as the whirlpool of Latvian cultural history. We encounter successive incarnations of Pumpurs's Bear Slayer, always made modern, yet always reminding us, at the same time, of the living presence of the past, and of the

---

36 Pumpurs, *Lāčplēsis*, 260. For an English translation different from my own, see Pumpurs, *Bearslayer*, 286-87.

power of that past and our tellings of it to shape our understandings of wherever we are in the moment.

Lāčplēsis Years

If we dwell for just a moment longer in the world of Pumpurs himself, we find that the origins of his epic are more fraught than they first appear. For although Pumpurs's *Lāčplēsis* has been celebrated as "the pinnacle, the quintessence of [Latvian] national Romanticism," the age in which it was created was no longer a Latvian-Romantic one.[37] Its publication responded, at least in part, to a challenge that had been voiced by skeptical members of the Baltic German community for decades before Pumpurs picked up his pen. As the Baltic German historian Karl Ulmann argued in Baltic Russia's leading literary journal in 1877, the Latvian people did not constitute a legitimate cultural nation, precisely because they lacked a heroic epic comparable to the *Odyssey* or the *Nibelungenlied*. "Why does it not have one?" Ulmann asked his readers about the Latvian *Volk*. "Simply because it has, as yet, no history worth singing or telling, because its life is merely lived with nature, and is not a life in any way comparable to the lives experienced by other *Völker*."[38] Ulmann's position is Hegelian, of course, and its implications for a people still coping with the effects of centuries of serfdom were surely hard to miss. To the mind of a Hegelian, as Collingwood summarized, only human beings have histories. Those who do not possess histories of their own are simply not—or not fully—human.

And so, Pumpurs wrote his Latvian epic, and published it in 1888.[39] But by that time, as I just mentioned, Latvian Romanticism was essentially over as a literary movement and a cultural force. That same year, the writer Jēkabs Lautenbahs delivered a lecture to the Riga Latvian Association on "scientific" methods for the collection and analysis of folklore—methods well known to scholars in Germany, Russia, and the Baltic as well, but of which Pumpurs himself seemed hardly to have been aware.[40] Picking up on this same theme in a

---

37 Kalniņš, "'Lāčplēsis' sava laika kultūrvēsturiskajā situācijā," 10.
38 Karl Ulmann, "Volkslied und Volkscharakter," *Baltische Monatsschrift* 25 (1877): 713. Without mentioning Ulmann, Pumpurs acknowledged the prevalence of such views in the preface to his epic; see Pumpurs, *Lāčplēsis*, 141. On prevailing Baltic German understandings of Latvian culture and identity during this period, see Anders Henriksson, *The Tsar's Loyal Germans: The Riga German Community, Social Change, and the Nationality Question, 1855-1905* (New York, 1983), esp. pp. 9-26.
39 The most detailed history and analysis of Pumpurs's work and creative process published to date is Jāzeps Rudzītis, "A. Pumpura eposs 'Lāčplēsis,'" in Pumpurs, *Lāčplēsis*, 7-137. A concise summary in English is provided in Šmidchens, "National Heroic Narratives," 496-97.
40 "Ievedums Latviešu mitoloģijā jeb Latviešu ticībā, no lektora J. Lautenbaha," *Rigas Latviešu Biedrības Zinību Komisijas rakstu krājums* 4 (1888): 33-44.

review of *Lāčplēsis* itself, an anonymous critic for the literary journal *Austrums* charged that Pumpurs's fantastical transformations of his folklore sources rendered his work preposterous as a folk epic or a storehouse of cultural memory. "An artistic poet creates artistic poems," not expressions of collective imagination. Thus, *Lāčplēsis* is a personal statement; "it is not and cannot ever become a national epic."[41] In 1902, a more sympathetic Latvian critic tried to elucidate Pumpurs's work to his readers by introducing them to the concept of Latvan Romanticism itself, "since," he noted, "that movement . . . has become, for children of our time, foreign and incomprehensible."[42] At the time *Lāčplēsis* appeared in print, the self-image of the Latvian intellectual main stream was modernizing and international, with little use for the Romantic imaginings that Pumpurs's work enshrined.

Shortly, however, Latvian society would be swept by new form of Romantic imagining, which likewise had roots in Hegel: the Socialism of Marx and Engels. And in 1905, with the first Russian Revolution, we arrive at what we might call the second Lāčplēsis Year, if we count the first at 1888. That year, the poet, essayist, and Socialist activist Jānis Rainis completed his first play, *Uguns un nakts* (Fire and Night).[43] There, Rainis recast Pumpurs's Lāčplēsis epic as a deeply psychological drama, imbued with the political idealism of the age. In his play, Lāčplēsis calls upon the Latvian people to throw off the yoke of their oppressors, foreign and domestic, social and political. As he does so, the Bear Slayer transforms himself into a model of avowedly non-violent political idealism.[44] And as in Pumpurs's epic poem, so does Rainis promise the return of the hero at the end of his play. After Lāčplēsis tumbles into the Daugava, his companion and helper Spīdola has the final word, brimming with revolutionary optimism: "The fight is not over and will not end. Spīdola is coming, Lāčplēsis, to your aid!"[45]

The Bear Slayer's re-emergence in the third Lāčplēsis Year, 1919, grew upon the foundations of the second. For it was then that the composer Jānis Mediņš cast Rainis's play, nearly verbatim, as an opera of Wagnerian proportions, spanning two full nights in performance. Mediņš's opera, also called *Uguns un nakts*, was completed in November 1919, coinciding, perhaps exactly,

---

41 "T," "Lāčplēsis, Latvju tautas varonis," *Austrums* 4 (1888): 1275.
42 Andrievs Niedre, "A. Pumpura 'Lāčplēsis' kā romantisma piemērs," *Peterburgas avīžu literāriskais pielikums* (3 July 1902): 419.
43 Jānis Rainis, *Uguns un nakts. Sena dziesma – jaunās skaņās*, in *Jānis Rainis: Kopoti raksti 30 sējumos* (Riga, 1980), 9:165-314. An English translation, by Alfreds Straumanis, is given in Straumanis, ed., *Fire and Night: Five Baltic Plays* (Prospect Heights, IL, 1986), 1-89.
44 On the crucial trope of non-violence in Rainis's play, see Šmidchens, "National Heroic Narratives," 497-99; and Šmidchens, "Notes on the Latvian National Hero, Lāčplēsis."
45 Rainis, *Uguns un nakts*, 314. For an alternate English translation, see Straumanis, *Fire and Night*, 89.

with the one-year anniversary of the founding of the independent Republic of Latvia on 18 November 1918.[46] The monumental length of Mediņš's opera, however, is not its only Wagnerian trait, for its harmonic language also harkens back to that of Wagner's early operas (Example 2).

Example 2. Jānis Mediņš, *Uguns un nakts*: Prologue (Riga, n.d.)

One cannot help, when pondering Mediņš's work, but to feel that both its scale and its musical language testify to the ambitions of the newly founded Latvian political nation.[47]

The fourth Lāčplēsis Year was one that conjures very different memories for most Latvians today: 1943. And the artwork that marked that Lāčplēsis Year was unconcerned with the sorts of epic quests and psychological transformations given mythological treatment by Pumpurs and Rainis. Instead, the Bear Slayer was, in this latest guise, a symbol of overtly nationalistic, militaristic strength of a type widely cultivated by military propandists on all sides of the Second World War. After Soviet forces had occupied Latvia and terrorized much of its citizenry in 1940-41, they were driven out by the German army, which inflicted innumerable terrors of its own. Writing in 1943 from Moscow, where, as a Soviet sympathizer, he had fled Hitler's advancing forces, the poet Jānis Sudrabkalns published his own *Lāčplēsis* in the Soviet émigré press.

---

46 I take the date of completion of Mediņš's opera from a photocopy of the manuscript piano-vocal score preserved in the Music Section (Mūzikas nodaļa) of the Latvian National Library in Riga (Latvijas nacionālā bibliotēka), cat. N91-3/513-514, p. 468. Mediņš gives simply November 1919, without specifying a day.
47 Indeed, reviews of the 1921 premiere of the opera frequently called attention to its aural traces of Wagner. See Baiba Jaunslaviete, "Latviešu mūzika cittautu kritiķu skatījumā. Izlase. I. sējums 1873-1926," *Mūzikas akadēmijas raksti* 1 (2004): 106-111.

Sudrabkalns's poem begins by invoking the specter of life under German rule, which had already been a prominent theme in Pumpurs:

Brīva bij Latvijas tauta,	Free were the Latvian people,
to vāciešu vara iekala važās,	whom German powers put in chains.
Brīva tā atkal reiz kļūs,	Free they will become once again,
vāciešu vara kad grūs.	when German power collapses.[48]

In the ongoing war against German aggression in Latvia and elsewhere in Eastern Europe, Sudrabkalns allied the Bear Slayer's mythic resolve with that of the Soviet Army, hailing the foreseen reconquest of Latvian territory as the fulfilment of Lāčplēsis's promised return:

Lāčplēsis latviešus sauc:	Lāčplēsis calls to the Latvians:
"Likteņa stunda ir klāt!"	"The hour of destiny is upon us!"
Padomju piecstaru zvaigne	The five-pointed Soviet star
varonim vairogā staro,	shines upon the hero;
Latvijas saule tur aust,	Latvia's sun is rising,
mūžīgas brīvības rīts.	the dawn of everlasting freedom.[49]

The return of the Soviets did come, of course, and with it the Stalinization of Latvian society at the end of the World War II. For the next four decades, there were no more Lāčplēsis Years. A deluxe edition of Pumpurs's epic was issued in 1947, with beautifully painted illustrations and illuminations and a preface by Andrejs Upīts, chair of the Union of Soviet Latvian Writers, to commemorate the Red Army victory that supposedly had, as Sudrabkalns's poem anticipated, brought freedom from oppression to the Latvian people.[50] A decade later, the beginnings of the Khrushchev "Thaw" in the republic were accompanied by renewed interest in the music of Jānis Mediņš, who had fled the return of Soviet forces to begin a new life in Sweden.[51] And, in 1966, Mediņš's *Uguns un nakts* was staged, for the first time since 1921, by the Latvian Opera.[52] All of these events were retrospective, however, republishing and restaging variants of the Lāčplēsis epic that had been created in earlier times. The creative refashioning, the re-imagining, the cyclical renewal of the Lāčplēsis epic that had characterized the first half-century of its existence lay dormant throughout most

---

48 Jānis Sudrabkalns, "Lāčplēsis," *Karogs* 3 (1943): 11.
49 Ibid., 12.
50 Pumpurs, *Lāčplēsis. Latvju tautas varonis* (Riga, 1947).
51 See Jēkabs Vītoliņš, "Jāņa Mediņa jaunākos skaņdarbus klausoties," *Māksla* (January 1959): 26-28.
52 See Vītoliņš, "'Uguns un Nakts' tēli uz operas skatuves," *Māksla* (April 1966): 29-32; and Ligita Viduleja, "Par Raiņa 'Uguns un nakts' muzikālo traktējumu," *Karogs* (January 1967): 161-62.

of its second. Māra Zālīte, author of the rock opera libretto, lamented this situation in 1988:

> If traditional symbols are not developed and interpreted over and over again, they devolve into stereotypes. It is surprising and sad that we have neither ballets rooted in the [Lāčplēsis] epic nor different versions of the epic performed in theaters, nor a serialized movie or even an animated film for children. We have not made use of the potentialities of the epic or taken up the challenge posed by Pumpurs and his work, and its marvelous, creative provocations. . . . Although the epic is taught in schools and Lāčplēsis's name is foreign to no one (but what of his constantly evolving essence?), the epic has assumed a passive role in the living process that is our culture.[53]

Eventually, another Lāčplēsis Year did arrive—or, more precisely, a Lāčplēsis *season*. Made possible by the advent of *glasnost'* and *peretroyka* and culminating with republic-wide celebrations of the epic's centennial, the second half of the 1980s was marked by a full-blown flowering of Lāčplēsis revivals and re-imaginings, of new rememberings and attendant forgettings. The season was begun in September 1987, when, for only the second time since the 1920s, Mediņš's *Uguns un nakts* was staged by the Latvian Opera. In the program book for the performance, we find a half-page photograph of the elderly Mediņš, then residing in Swedish exile, visiting the former home of the most famous Latvian émigré composer of all, Jāzeps Vītols (1863-1948), during a visit to Latvia in 1966.[54] In this image, a contemporary embodiment of Latvia's non-Soviet culture is shown paying homage to a non-Soviet icon of Latvian history, and the performance of Mediņš's long-silenced opera becomes a tribute to a vision of Latvian culture in which all that is great and pure in the republic's history is untouched by the Soviet experience. The following year, Latvia's principal academic publishing house, Zinātne, issued a new critical edition of Pumpurs's epic, the release of which was timed for 30 June 1988—exactly 100 years, to the day, after Pumpurs's work first appeared in print.[55] In that volume, the literary historian Jāzeps Rudzītis provided over 200 pages of historical background, textual analysis, and critical commentary, in which he took pains to demonstrate

---

53 Zālīte, "Taka mūžamežā," in *Dzeja – Lāčplēsis*, 143-44. This essay was originally published in the program book distributed at performances of the rock opera in 1988, a copy of which is preserved in the Rakstniecības, Teātra un Mūzikas Vēstures Muzējs (Riga), inv. no. 378658, topogr. apzīm. M. Zāl. 11/1.

54 A copy of the program book is preserved in the Rakstniecības, Teātra un Mūzikas Vēstures Muzējs (Riga), inv. no. 433938, topogr. apzīm. OBT 11/16. On Soviet-era views of Vītols's emigration, see Karnes, "Soviet Musicology and the 'Nationalities Question': The Case of Latvia," *Journal of Baltic Studies* 39, no. 3 (2008): 283-305.

55 On the timing and idea behind this publication, see I. Riekstiņš, "'Lāčplēsis' – jaunā zinātniskā izdevumā," *Literatūra un māksla* (8 July 1988): 3.

the folk-cultural authenticity of Pumpurs's sources and poem.[56] Unquestionably valuable as a work of literary criticism, Rudzītis's volume is, like the program for the performance of Mediņš's opera, also an excercise in disciplined forgetting, cleansing the epic of the undesirable meanings it had accrued in such works as Sudrabkalns's *Lāčplēsis* poem and the 1947 edition of Pumpurs's epic published to commemorate Stalin's wartime successes.

A more overtly mythologizing tone was struck in other commemorative events. In June 1988, a Lāčplēsis festival was held in the town of Burtnieki, complete with costumed reenactments of episodes from the Bear Slayer's epic journeys.[57] And the following month, the Lāčplēsis centennial was feted at the folklore festival Baltica '88. In an essay published in the festival's daily newsletter, a historian of literature explained that *Lāčplēsis* was "received as a brilliant expression of national romanticism by the democratic sector of Latvian society" of Pumpurs's time—thus forgetting not only the fraught contemporary reception of the epic but also the fact not even the most liberal segments of Latvian society had lobbied for anything resembling democracy in nineteenth-century Imperial Russia.[58]

At the Burtnieki Lāčplēsis festival, an unstaged premiere of the rock opera based on the epic was given to an overflow crowd. And on 23 August, precisely forty-nine years after the signing of the Nazi-Soviet non-aggression treaty that assured Latvia's absorption into the USSR, the first performance of *Lāčplēsis* was staged in a Riga arena.[59] With this, the creative rebirth of the Bear-Slayer epic, after half a century of slumber, had occurred yet again. In the whirlpool of events that had engulfed Latvian society in the age of Gorbachev's reforms, the cyclic renewal of historical experience was felt with Nietzschean power.

---

56 Pumpurs, *Lāčplēsis*, ed. Rudzītis, 7-137 and 267-338.
57 See Anita Jansone-Zirnīte, *Laikam klāt laiks* (Riga, 2008). Photos of these reenactments are given on pp. 42-51.
58 Ojārs Zanders, "Lāčplēsis (Bearslayer) and Other Centenarians," *Baltica '88*, no. 1 (10 July 1988): 7 (published in English).
59 The significance of the correspondence of these dates is explored in Andra Rutkēviča, "Nācijas modināšana. Rokoperas 'Lāčplēsis' iestudējums, tā attiecības ar sociālpolitiskajiem notikumiem valstī," *Platforma* 2 (2004): 195-202. On the Burtnieki performance, see Jansone-Zirnīte, *Laikam klāt laiks*, 94-131. From the perspective of genre, *Lāčplēsis* was, of course, only the latest of many rock operas staged and composed in the USSR since Andrew Lloyd Webber's *Jesus Christ Superstar* had its Vilnius premiere in 1973. On the phenomenon of the Soviet rock opera generally, see Peter J. Schmelz, "'Crucified on the Cross of Mass Culture': Late Soviet Genre Politics in Alexander Zhurbin's Rock Opera *Orpheus and Eurydice*," *Journal of Musicological Research* 28, no. 1 (2009): 61-87. Zigmars Liepiņš, the composer of *Lāčplēsis*, wrote on the place of his own work within this broader context an essay entitled "Kas ir rokopera?" (What is a rock opera?), published in the program book distributed at the opera's 1988 premiere. A copy of this program book is preserved in the Rakstniecības, Teātra un Mūzikas Vēstures Muzējs (Riga), inv. no. 378658, topogr. apzīm. M. Zāl. I1/1.

Bear Slayer's Return (Again)

Along the lines of other commemorations and re-imaginings of the epic that occurred in the Lāčplēsis season of 1987-88, the rock opera by Māra Zālīte and Zigmars Liepiņš refashioned the story told in Pumpurs's poem so as to engage, to the extent that was politically feasible, the snowballing anti-Soviet sentiment within Latvian society of the period. They too suggest, through the medium of their work, that the republic's Soviet experience was a foreign imposition, an anomaly and a crime in Latvian cultural history—despite the fact that it was implemented, in large part, by Latvians like Sudrabkalns and Upīts.[60] In the rock opera, as in Pumpurs's, poem, the mythic leader of the Latvians' enemies is named Dīterihs—Latvianized *Dietrich*. But in the opera, those enemies are no longer identified as Germans, as they had been by Pumpurs. Instead, the invaders of the Latvian lands are simply "foreigners" (*svešnieki*), with Dīterihs no longer a Lutheran evangelist but simply the "foreigners' leader" (*svešnieku vadonis*). And, in the opera's staged performances of 1988, those foreigners were clothed in red. Likewise, the character of Kangars, who begins the opera as Lāčplēsis's trusted friend, wears white in the opera's first act. But as he is turned, through his own thirst for power, into Lāčplēsis's betrayer in the second, his visual appearance changes as well, and he too dons a red uniform.[61]

What I want to explore in the remainder of this essay, however, is the way in which processes of mythic and historical renewal are manifested not only in the *fact* of the rock opera's appearance in 1988, but also *within* the work itself. In other words, the story of the Bear Slayer is re-imagined over the course of the opera's unfolding. The process of historical re-imagining is thus inscribed within a product of that very process. It is this aspect of the work, I would argue, that has made the opera such a powerful and enduring stimulus for re-imagining Latvian historical and cultural identity in the late- and post-Soviet eras.

In a literal way, *Lāčplēsis* is a cyclic construction, its two acts framed by a complex of musical numbers that both open and close the work (see Table 1). The numbers that comprise these musical bookends are arranged so that each of these framing complexes unfolds as an approximate mirror image of the other. Act 1 opens with the sequence *Prologue–Chorus/Narration–Lāčplēsis Solo*, while Act 2 closes with *Lāčplēsis Solo–Chorus/Narration–Epilogue*.

---

[60] For a thoughtful and sensitive consideration of this distinct variety of late- and post-Soviet forgetting in a Latvian context, see Irēne Šneidere, "Padomju okupācijas režīms Latvijā: pētniecības virzieni un problēmas," in *Padomju okupācijas režīms Baltijā 1944.-1959. gadā: politika un tās sekas* (Latvijas vēsturnieku komisijas raksti 9) (Riga, 2003), 25-34.

[61] See the original cast video recording, *Rokopera Lāčplēsis*, Radio SWH Productions, RSWH 058 (1988).

Act 1

Prologue: "The sun was weeping bitterly" (*Gauži raud saulīte*), A minor

1a. Chorus: "It's Time" (*Tas ir Laiks*), A minor

1b. Narrator's opening words

2. Lāčplēsis's theme song, "I hear" (*Es dzirdu*), D minor

3. Lielvārdis: "Little child at the crossroads" (*Krustcelēs mazs bērniņš*), D minor

[...]

Act 2

[...]

29. Lāčplēsis: "What are you?" (*Kas tu esi?*) → "Little child at the crossroads," A minor

30a. Chorus: "It's Time," A minor

30b. Narrator's closing words

Epilogue: "The sun was weeping bitterly," A minor

Table 1. Cyclic construction in *Lāčplēsis*

Within this overarching framework, the prologue and the epilogue lend an aspect of literal cyclicity to the whole, since they consist of identical musical settings of a single text:

Gauži raud saulīte	The sun was weeping bitterly
ābeļu dārzā.	in the apple garden.
Ābelei nokrita	From the apple tree,
zeltābolītis.	a golden apple had fallen.
Neraudi, saulīte,	Don't cry, sun,
Dievs dara citu.	God will make another—

No vara, no zelta,
no sudrabiņa.

Of copper, of gold,
of silver.[62]

The music that sets these verses, scored for a single, nameless voice and sparsely accompanied by keyboard, begins as in Example 3:

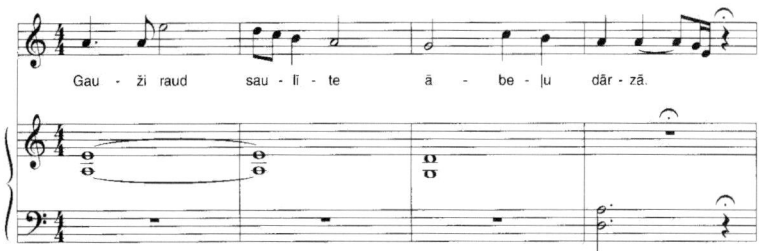

Example 3. Prologue and Epilogue: "The sun was weeping bitterly"

The text, of course, speaks directly of the phenomenon of perpetual renewal in the natural world. But it also invokes images of renewal of a different kind. For while Liepiņš's musical setting is original, Zālīte's poetic text is borrowed from a Latvian folksong. Admittedly, it is a folksong of obscure origin and provenance, but it was a folksong canonized in performances and recordings by the folk-music ensemble Skandinieki, an outfit that was one of the leading forces in the Latvian folk-music revival of the middle and late 1980s, a movement closely associated with the activities of the Latvian independence movement.[63]

---

62 Zālīte, *Lāčplēsis*, 152, 189.

63 The song is not included in Krišjānis Barons's *Latvju dainas* (1894-1915), the largest corpus of Latvian folk song texts; see the online catalog of Barons's collection, maintained by the Archives of Latvian Folklore (Latvijas folkloras krātuve), http://www.dainuskapis.lv (accessed 17 May 2009). Skandinieki's recording of *Gauži raud saulīte* can be heard online at http://www.upe.lv/mp3/ltmk/gauzi.mp3 (accessed 17 May 2009). On Skandinieki and the Latvian folklore revival movement of the middle and late 1980s, see Martin Boiko, "Volksmusikbewegung im Baltikum in den 70er und 80er Jahren – Kontexte, Werte, Konflikte," in *Verfemte Musik. Komponisten in den Diktaturen unseres Jahrhunderts*, 2nd ed., ed. Joachim Braun, Heidi Tamar Hoffman, and Vladimír Karbusický (Frankfurt am Main, 1997), 349-57; and Šmidchens, "A Baltic Music: The Folklore Movement in Lithuania, Latvia, and Estonia, 1968-1991," (Ph.D. diss., Indiana University, 1996), esp. pp. 178-81 and 218-23. To those familiar with the epic's history, yet another memory is conjured by the words of the prologue, for mythical golden apples also figure prominently in the fourth act of Rainis's *Uguns un nakts*. There, they are associated with the transformation of the character of Spīdola from Lāčplēsis's enemy to his most valued helper, and also with Lāčplēsis's crucial decision to spare the life of his onetime betrayer. See Rainis, *Uguns un nakts*, 257-60; trans. in Straumanis, *Fire and Night*, 56-58.

The choral "time song," which begins with the line "It's not water that flows in the Daugava—it's time," is likewise repeated literally at the beginning and the end of the opera (numbers 1a and 30a in Table 1; the music is given in Example 1). And the Narrator (*Teicējs*), who speaks over the second half of the "time song" both times it is performed (1b and 30b in Table 1), plays another historically grounding role. For the Narrator's words, at the beginning of Act 1, are taken directly from the opening lines of the second canto of Pumpurs's Lāčplēsis poem, in which the Bear Slayer makes his first appearance (the epic's first canto is cosmogonic):

Sensenos laikos, Baltijas zemē,	In ancient times in the Baltic land,
Kur teka Daugava līčotiem krastiem,	where the Daugava flowed along its twisting banks,
Kur miežu līdumi liesmoti dega,	where barley fields burned brilliantly,
Dzīvoja laimīga latviešu tauta.	there dwelled the joyful Latvian people.[64]

And at the end of Act 2, the Narrator recites exactly those words that conclude Pumpurs's epic, which were cited earlier in this essay, and which promised the Bear Slayer's eventual return, despite his apparent defeat. ("Every now and then, boatmen traveling down the Daugava see two men in the middle of the night, fighting on the bank.")[65] Thus, through the role of the Narrator, Zālīte literally inscribes the voice of Pumpers within the libretto of the opera. And one might say that she accomplishes the inverse as well: In using the poetic frame of Pumpurs's epic as the frame for her libretto, she inscribes the body of her own Lāčplēsis epic within the body of Pumpurs's.[66]

While both of the framing devices considered thus far invoke memories of earlier fashionings of the Lāčplēsis epic and ground the work in the mythological past conjured by Pumpurs a century earlier, both are, nonetheless, essentially static devices. In both cases, something recalled at the beginning of the opera's first act is recalled again at its end. Both of these references reflect upon history as it exists outside of the rock opera itself; they do not evolve in any essential way over the opera's course. Within this static frame, however, dynamic forces are also at play, forces that mimic through musical means the processes of perpetual re-imagining and renewal that the creation of the opera

---

64 Zālīte, *Lāčplēsis*, 153; Pumpurs, *Lāčplēsis*, 153. For an alternate translation, see Pumpurs, *Bearslayer*, 39.
65 Zālīte, *Lāčplēsis*, 189; Pumpurs, *Lāčplēsis*, 260.
66 Moreover, the librettist's act of inscribing the voice of Pumpurs within her telling of the Lāčplēsis epic constitutes, in itself, the renewal of yet another tradition. In a similar literary move, Rainis invoked the figure of Pumpurs by name in *Uguns un nakts*, and Jānis Sudrabkalns invoked both Pumpurs and Rainis in his Lāčplēsis poem of 1943. See Rainis, *Uguns un nakts*, 277; trans. in Straumanis, *Fire and Night*, 69; and Sudrabkalns, "Lāčplēsis," 11.

itself represents. This dynamic process is realized in the remaining numbers listed in Table 1: in Act 1, Lāčplēsis's theme song, "I hear" (*Es dzirdu*), followed by the elder Lielvārdis's summoning of the young Bear Slayer to his destiny ("Little child at the crossroads": *Krustcelēs mazs bērniņš*); and, at the end of Act 2, the Bear Slayer's recollection of Lielvārdis's song, "Little child at the crossroads," from the beginning of the first act.

Lāčplēsis's signature number, "I hear," in D minor and scored for assertive, distorted electric guitars, opens as shown in Example 4. In this number, we come to identify the Bear Slayer's strength with his mythical bears' ears, which symbolize his ability to "hear" the longings of the Latvian people.

Example 4.   Lāčplēsis, "I hear" (beginning of Act 1)

This number, essentially functioning as Lāčplēsis's introduction aria, is followed by a song sung by Lielvārdis the father-figure, who counsels the "little child" in his care that the wheels of time and destiny have more in store for the young Bear Slayer than he is yet aware:

Krustcelēs mazs bērniņš rotaļājas.	Little child, playing at the crossroads,
Zem ratu riteņiem, zem pakaviem,	under the wagons' wheels, under the horses'
Zem dzelžu pēdām.	iron-shod hooves.
Mazs bērniņš krustcelēs.	Little child at the crossroads,
Kā laiks tam smiltis	sand runs between your fingers
Tek caur pirkstiem.	like time.

Tā mūsu dzīvība. Such is our life.
Tā mūsu brīvība. Such is our freedom.[67]

The music Lielvārdis sings, in Lāčplēsis's key of D minor, is shown in Example 5.

Example 5. Lielvārdis: "Little child at the crossroads" (beginning of Act 1)

The context in which these numbers return in the finale of Act 2 is crucial, for immediately after Lāčplēsis signals, by singing once again his powerful theme song "I hear," his acceptance of the hero's role for which he is destined, he is drawn into fateful combat with his mythic arch-enemy, the Black Knight. As in the tellings of the Lāčplēsis story by both Pumpurs and Rainis, in the rock opera too the hero is caught off-guard by the strength of his opponent; thus the bewildered number "What are you?" (*Kas tu esi?*), the first half of number 29 in Table 1 above. And it is halfway through that number, when the dire reality of Lāčplēsis's personal situation becomes apparent to him, that the creative re-imagining of the Bear Slayer's history takes place within the musical substance of the opera itself. Just before the wounded hero is overcome completely by his adversary, he recalls Lielvārdis's Act 1 song, in what might be taken, at first, as a moment of halucinatory escape (Example 6).

---

67 Zālīte, *Lāčplēsis*, 153.

Example 6.   Lāčplēsis: "Little child at the crossroads" (end of Act 2)

The real significance of Lāčplēsis's singing, however, is first suggested by his tonality. For he sings no longer in the key of D minor, the key of his signature "I hear," which had been closely associated with his character since the beginning of the opera. Instead, Lāčplēsis echoes Lielvārdis's summons in the tonality of the chorus, A minor. (I have given the keys of all of these numbers in Table 1 above.) As this shift suggests, we hear, at this moment, the hero on the cusp of death, handing off his heroic mission to the crowd, the *turba*, his audience. As Lielvārdis had earlier directed these words to Lāčplēsis by singing them in Lāčplēsis's key, so Lāčplēsis now directs them to the numberless crowd of the chorus by singing it to them in theirs. And this redirection, at first signalled only by way of tonality, is soon made concrete by a subtle shift in the grammar of Lāčplēsis's appeals. After singing, in the key of A minor, the complete chorus of Lielvārdis's Act 1 summons, Lāčplēsis continues with words of his own, appealing, to whoever might be listening, to call upon him, and to keep calling:

Sauc mani skaļāk, bērniņ, sauc!	Call my name more loudly, little child, call my name!
Es dzirdu vēl!	I still hear!
Man vēl ir valoda un vārds!	I still have language, and a name!
Sauc mani, bērniņ!	Call my name, little child!
Sauciet mani skaļāk!	Call my name more loudly![68]

It is in Lāčplēsis's final two lines that the linguistic shift occurs. The imperative form *sauc*, from *saukt*, to call or name, is singular and familiar; it is the form of the verb that one would use to address a "little child," as Lielvārdis calls the young Bear Slayer at the beginning of Act 1. *Sauciet*, in contrast, is formal or plural. It is the form one would use to address the chorus, the audience *en masse*, or whoever might happen to be listening. And immediately after Lāčplēsis makes this appeal, the chorus indicates that they do hear the hero's appeal, and that they will indeed take up his charge. For they answer the Bear

---

68 Ibid., 188.

Slayer in the vocative case, thus directing their impassioned response unambiguously to the hero: "Lāčplēsi! Lāčplēsi!"[69] (Example 7).

Example 7. Lāčplēsis: "Call my name more loudly!" Chorus: "Lāčplēsis!" (end of Act 2)

At the end of the opera, the fallen Bear Slayer does something more than promise his eventual return. He charges anyone and everyone who hears his singing to call upon him with his or her own voice. In doing so, he challenges us, his listeners, to *remember*—to remember who he is and what he has been, for Pumpurs and Rainis, for Mediņš and Sudrabkalns, for ourselves and for a century of Latvians who have been touched, in whatever ways, by those artists' works. For Lāčplēsis, as Liepiņš and Zālīte make clear in their work, is more than a character in an epic tale. Lāčplēsis is an idea, he is memory itself, as forgettable and indelible and selective and persistent and apt to shape our present experiences as any memory can be. The story of Lāčplēsis is a story of Latvia, its inhabitants, and the Latvian people, not because of the deeds it recounts but because all of us who hear it, sing it, and read it also carry it within

---

69 Ibid.

ourselves, in countless variants, each essential and incomplete. "He never was," the librettist Zālīte wrote of the mythical Bear Slayer. "But he always is."[70] And, one might add, although he exists in no single place, Lāčplēsis resides everywhere—or, at least, wherever his readers and listeners might be.

2008 (Again)

As Philip Bohlman writes in the essay I have quoted throughout the foregoing discussion, "As a performative medium, music fills and then empties a temporal moment; depending on what experience that performativity evokes, music may give very different meanings to history itself."[71] As I have tried to show over the course of this essay, this is certainly the case with the rock opera *Lāčplēsis*. But in closing, we should take note of the fact that the histories invoked by the creators of the opera, like all of those works marking what I have called Latvia's "Lāčplēsis Years," were predominantly histories of oppression. For Pumpurs, the Bear Slayer's arch-villian, the Black Knight, was Teutonic, and clearly associated with the landed Baltic German nobility that ruled the Latvian lands until the Revolution of 1917. For Sudrabkalns, the Knight was a Hiterlite, a National-Socialist. For Liepiņš and Zālīte, the enemy was Soviet, whether Latvian or Russian. Today, however, Latvia is once again an independent republic, oppressed by neither foreign rule nor the executors of totalitarian ideology. If Lāčplēsis is still challenging us to call upon his name and memory, as he did once again in performances of the work given in the summer of 2008, then who or what, exactly, is he challenging us to resist? What lessons is he asking us to draw from history in the present context?

In February 2008, Anita Jansone-Zirnīte, documentarian of the Burnieki Lāčplēsis festival of twenty years earlier, posed these questions to Zālīte. "The Dark Knight," the librettist responded, "is an ingenius symbol. . . . The symbol's genius is hidden in plain sight. It can be interpreted in any way, as appropriate to any time. What sorts of dangers are threatening, what is today's evil, what is the Dark Knight in the present moment? Every age must define these things anew." And just what, Jansone-Zirnīte pressed, do *you* regard as the meaning of the Black Knight in the year 2008? To this, Zālīte replied:

> It's been a long time since I was young enough to think that everything dark, everything evil resides only outside of ourselves. Indeed, such things reside within each and every one of us. We portray these things in symbolic guises only to separate them from ourselves, to distill them down to their essence. One might think of today's Dark Knight as a kind of dark substance that we breathe in, drink, inhale. The level of this "Dark Knight" substance in society

---

70 Zālīte, "Taka mužamežā," 142.
71 Bohlman, "The Remembrance of Things Past," 646.

is like the level of sugar in the blood. And its level in our society's blood is elevated. It is comfortable and dangerous to locate evil only outside of ourselves. Darkness is in our tissues, and we must be ever-vigilant in our efforts to cleanse ourselves ethically.[72]

And so the present danger, as Zālīte sees it, is moral and psychological, a danger lurking within ourselves. And perhaps it has always been that way. As the tenor Jānis Sproģis, singing the role of Lielvārdis, put it in an interview last summer, "although twenty years have passed, the battle between the Dark Knight and the Light has not ended; it has merely assumed a new form."[73] The whirlpool of history, Lāčplēsis reminds us, has not ceased its spinning. Just as surely as there will always be darkness, there is always the chance for light. It just might be that the cycle of mythic, historical return is, after all, eternal.

---

72 Jansone-Zirnīte, *Laikam klāt laiks*, 97.
73 Tamuļeviča and Rudaks, "Rokopera Lāčplēsis," 10.

Mikus Čeže

LATVIJAS NACIONĀLĀ OPERA UND IHRE GEBURTSDEUTUNGEN
Das Problem von Deplazierten Jubiläen

Seit der Gründung des lettischen Opertheaters wurde jedes Jahrzehnt seines Bestehens mit monumentalen Festakten gefeiert. Nur die Meinungen, wann eigentlich diese Festlichkeiten zu veranstalten wären, sind immer gespalten gewesen. Im Programmheft für das zehnjährige Jubiläum der *Latvijas Nacionālā opera*[1] 1929, ist folgendes zu lesen:

> Erst als der lettische Staat gegründet wurde, brachten Professor Jāzeps Vītols und Andrejs Frīdenbergs, die im Herbst 1918 in Russland und in Lettland zerstreuten Sänger zusammen und eröffneten im heutigen Nationaltheater die "Latvju opera"[2]. ... Als Riga von Kommunisten erobert wurde, hat die Oper ihre Tätigkeit unter Leitung von Teodors Reiters wiederaufgenommen. ... im August hat das Bildungsministerium beschlossen, die "Nacionālā opera" als eine staatliche Institution zu organisieren. Alle Vorbereitungen und die Bildung eines Repertoires brauchten viel Zeit, und so wurde die breite Öffentlichkeit erst am 2. Dezember 1919 Augenzeugin der Tatsache, dass die "Nacionālā opera" entstanden ist. An jenem Abend fand die erste Aufführung des jungen Opernhauses statt mit dem "Tannhäuser" von Wagner.[3]

---

1 *Latvijas Nacionālā opera* = Lettische Nationaloper. Die Eröffnung mit diesem Namen erfolgte am 27. November 1918 mit einem Symphoniekonzert und am 2. Dezember mit *Tannhäuser* von Richard Wagner (alle lettisch-deutsche Übersetzungen sind vom Author).
2 *Latvju opera* = Lettische Oper. Die Eröffnung mit diesem Namen erfolgte zweimal: am 15. September 1918 mit einem Symphoniekonzert und am 15. Oktober mit der lettischen Premiere des "Fliegenden Holländers" von Richard Wagner. Hier soll bemerkt werden, dass in der damaligen lettischen Presse die Bezeichnung der Truppe *Latvju Opera* 1918 sehr oft mit der Bezeichnung *Latviešu opera* verwechselt wurde, obwohl das institutionell gesehen ein Fehler ist. *Latviešu opera* stand zwischen Ende Dezember 1912 bis Juli 1915, dann von Januar bis März 1918 unter der musikalischen Leitung von Pāvuls Jurjāns. *Latvju opera* bezieht sich auf den Zeitraum zwischen September 1918 bis Februar 1919, dann von Mai bis August 1919; es war eine Truppe, die unter der musikalischen Leitung von Teodors Reiters gewirkt hat. *Latviešu opera* und *Latvju opera* kann man nur als *Lettische Oper* übersetzen. Die Form *latvju* klingt nur ein wenig altertümlicher als *lat-viešu*, sprachlich bedeutet sie aber dasselbe. Der Unterschied zwischen *latviešu* und *latvju* ähnelt dem Unterschied zwischen *deutsch* und *teutsch*.
3 *Nacionālās operas darbības desmit gadi* [Zehn Jahre der Tätigkeit der Nationalen Oper], (Riga, 1929), S. 3.

In einem Text, der 1932 von Kārlis Dziļleja geschrieben wurde, kann man eine vermeintlich ehrliche Antwort lesen, warum dieser "Tannhäuser" in der lettischen Übersetzung so spät, also nur am Ende des Jahres 1919, sein Publikum erreichen konnte: *In der Sowjetischen Zeit . . . organisiert sich auch die Oper. Die Premiere von "Tannhäuser" ist für den 22. Mai geplant, aber an jenem Tag wird Riga von Landeswehrtruppen unter Andrievs Niedra eingenom-men, und die Oper öffnet ihre Türe nicht.*[4] Diese Information aus der Zwischenkriegszeit der bürgerlichen (Ersten) Republik Lettland wäre auch heute akzeptabel, wenn da einige Details nicht stören würden.

Derselbe lettische "Tannhäuser" – in denselben Räumlichkeiten des ehemaligen deutschen Rigaer Stadttheaters, mit demselben Chor und Orchester unter Leitung von Teodors Reiters, im Bühnenbild von Jānis Kuga – hatte die Premiere schon in der *Padomju Latvijas opera*[5] am 10. Mai 1919 erlebt. Alle Interessenten hatten sogar die Möglichkeit, durch das Rigaer Komitee der Kommunistischen Partei kostenlose Einladungen für eine Vorlesung über Richard Wagner erhalten. Kārlis Fiņķis, ein Arbeiter aus der Gasfabrik in Riga saß dabei. Seine Reaktion in der wichtigsten kommunistischen Zeitung Lettlands *Cīņa* war mehr als zurückhaltend:

> Das ganze Leben habe ich gearbeitet, geschmiedet, gesägt und gefeilt – ich kenne mich mit meiner Arbeit aus, weil ich das Schmieden und Feilen gelernt habe. . . . Am Sonntag, den 4. Mai, wurde eine Vorlesung über den großen Musikschmied Richard Wagner und seinen "Tannhäuser" veranstaltet. Ich weiss nicht, ob der Lektor den Wagner nicht verstanden hat, oder ich den Lektoren nicht, aber – so klug wie ich kam, so dumm sollte ich nach dem Vortrag weggehen. . . . Ich habe auch früher Vorlesungen über Musik besucht, und obwohl ich wenig davon verstehe, aber etwas verstehe ich doch. Verzeihung, aber diesmal habe ich nichts verstanden.[6]

Nicht nur jene Einladungen für die Vorlesung, sondern auch Eintrittskarten für die Premiere wurden unter den Arbeitern Rigas kostenlos ausgeteilt: damit sollte demonstriert werden, dass in der neuen sowjetischen Ordnung die Kunst dem Volke gehört. Wenn man das mit dem gutbürgerlichen deutschen und lettischen Publikum vergleicht, das den Saal des Rigaer deutschen Stadttheaters bis zum Ersten Weltkrieg besuchte, ist die Zusammensetzung des Publikums im ersten lettischen "Tannhäuser" in der Premiere am 10. Mai ziemlich merkwürdig gewesen: *Ungeachtet aller Anweisungen sind in der Premiere von "Tannhäuser" viele Frauen mit Schoßkindern gekommen, die einen solchen Lärm machten, dass das Orchester in der Mitte der Ouvertüre zu spielen*

---

4 Kārlis Dziļleja, *Rīga – teātru pilsēta* [Riga – Stadt der Theater], in: *Rīga kā Latvijas galvaspilsēta* [Riga als die Hauptstadt Lettlands], Riga 1932, S. 711.
5 *Padomju Latvijas Opera = Oper von Sowjet Lettland.*
6 *Cīņa*, 14. Mai 1919.

aufhörte und die ganze künstlerische Atmosphäre der Aufführung ruiniert wurde.[7] Es gibt in der Presse keine Angaben, ob die Stimmung eines Kindergartens sich auch im "Tannhäuser" der bürgerlichen Republik Lettland am 2. Dezember 1919 ausgebreitet hätte. Aber, wie es auch gewesen wäre, die soziale Zusammensetzung und der Bildungsstand des Publikums entscheidet nicht die Frage, wann ein Opernhaus gegründet worden ist.

Die Geburt einer Theaterinstitution basiert auf der Annahme, dass für unsere Aufmerksamkeit etwas Neues, nie Dagewesenes im Bühnenlicht steht; eine neu zusammengestellte Truppe bietet für die Öffentlichkeit ihre erste Inszenierung, es kommen dann später weitere Inszenierungen, die für eine Kontinuität der Institution sorgen. In der Entstehungsgeschichte der *Latvijas Nacionālā opera* kann der erwähnte "Tannhäuser" keine Rolle eines Erstgeborenen spielen, da am 2. Dezember 1919 diese Inszenierung schon das fünfte Mal gezeigt wurde: seit dem 10. Mai gab es in der *Padomju Latvijas Opera* drei Vorstellungen, die vierte fand am 7. Juni statt, nach dem Sturz der Sowjetmacht in Lettland am 22. Mai, als die Truppe wieder seine vorsowjetische Bezeichnung *Latvju opera* zurücknahm.

Am Ende des Jahres 1919 war die lettische Operninstitution keine schaumgeborene Jungfrau. Die *Latvijas Nacionālā Opera* als Truppe war schon wie eine Dame mit sieben Kindern aus zwei vorigen politischen Ehen: wenn man mit Aufmerksamkeit das erste Jahr der *Latvijas Nacionālā Opera* betrachtet, kann man konstatieren, dass in der sogannannten ersten Spielzeit 1919/1920 nur zwei Werke (*Carmen* von Georges Bizet und *Baņuta* von Alfrēds Kalniņš) echte inszenierungen für diese lettische Truppe bedeuteten. Alle anderen sieben sind aus der vorigen (im Bruckner'schen Sinne kann man sogar sagen, aus der Nullten) Spielzeit genommen.

Falls wir den 2. Dezember 1919 zum Geburtsdatum der *Latvijas Nacionālā Opera* erklären möchten, bedeutet das – da sich die neue *Tannhäuser*-Inszenierung ja als Produkt aus den fünf Sowjet-Monaten entpuppte - nur eine Ehrung der neuverliehenen Bezeichnung *Latvijas Nacionālā Opera*. Hier darf nicht unerwähnt bleiben, dass die wichtigste lettische Operninstitution mehr als die Hälfte ihres 90-jährigen Bestehens unter verschiedenen offiziellen Namen bestand. Einige von ihnen waren kurz und elegant wie *Rīgas Opera* in den Spielzeiten 1941/42 bis 1943/44.[8] Andere wiederum klingen erschreckend unbeholfen. Zum Beispiel war die offizielle Benennung dieses Theaters von 1956 bis 1989 *Latvijas PSR Valsts ar Darba Sarkanā Karoga ordeni Apbalvotais Akadēmiskais operas un baleta teātris*.[9] Aber auch in jenen Jahren, die in die

---

7 *Cīņa*, 13. Mai 1919.
8 Deutsche Parallelbenennung der *Rīgas opera* = Rigaer Opernhaus.
9 Latvijas PSR Valsts ar Darba Sarkanā Karoga ordeni Apbalvotais Akadēmiskais operas un baleta teātris [Akademisches mit dem Arbeitsbanner der Roten Flagge ausgezeichnetes Staatstheater für Oper und Ballett der Lettischen SSR].

Geschichte der *Lettischen Nationaloper* unbestreitbar hineingehören, sind herausragende Persönlichkeiten unter Solisten und Dirigenten zu finden. Beim öfteren Wechsel von Mächten und Hausbenennungen ist die Haupt-funktion dieses Theaters unverändert geblieben. Die notwendige Kontinuität wurde durch dieselbe lettische Opern-und Balletttruppe mit ihrem Stil und goldenem Repertoire gesichert.

Nach dem zweiten Weltkrieg, als sich Lettland bereits zum dritten Mal unter sowjetischen Herrschaft befand, wurde das Geburtsdatum des lettischen Opernthesters auf den 23. Januar 1919 festgelegt, d. h., in Monaten der ersten Sowjetrepublik Lettland. Mit folgender Begründung: es ist der Tag, an dem die Letten zum ersten Mal im ehemaligen 1. (deutschen) Rigaer Stadttheater, im Hause der heutigen *Latvijas Nacionālā Opera*, den "Fliegenden Holländer" Richard Wagners auf lettisch gespielt haben. Hier hat man aber mit einem ähnlichen Problem wie im Falle des "Tannhäusers" zu tun. Denn am 23. Januar 1919 wurde eine Inszenierung gezeigt, die mit denselben Solisten, mit demselben Dirigenten, Regisseur, Szenograph, Chor und Orchester ihre Premiere im ehemaligen 2. (russischen) Rigaer Stadttheater am 15. Oktober 1918 erlebt hatte.

Latvju opera (1) → *Padomju Latvijas opera*

> Die lettische Oper, der ein paar symphonische und Kammer-Musik-Konzerte vorangegangen waren, eröffnete unter Professor I. Wihtols Direktion ihre Saison am 15. Oktober mit einer Aufführung von Richard Wagners "Fliegender Holländer," die zugleich die Uraufführung des Werkes in lettisch-er Sprache war. . . . Neben der Darstellung erfüllte sowohl die dekorative In-szenierung, wie auch das Orchester unter der Leitung des Kapellmeisters Theodor Reiter derart alle Forderungen, dass ein starker Besuch nicht nur von Letten, sondern auch von Hebräern und sogar von Deutschen zu verzeichnen war.[10]

> Aber mit voller Anerkennung darf es ausgesprochen werden, daß die schwierige Aufgabe nach musikalischer Richtung hin von seiten der Beteiligten mit sichtlicher Hingebung und Arbeitsfreudigkeit gelöst worden ist. . . . Die Regie muß noch mehr darauf bedacht sein, die szenischen Vorgänge aus

---

10 "-atis," *Die jüngste Entwicklung der lettischen Schaubühne*, in: *Baltische Blätter für Theater und Kunst* II, S. 64. Man kann sicher sein, dass sich hinter *"atis"* der lettische Schauspieler und Theaterkritiker Ernests Kārkliņš verbirgt, der unter dem Pseudonym Zeltmatis gewirkt hat. Den Anlass dazu gibt ein Brief an Wolfgang Hoffmann-Harnisch, der als letzter Dramaturg des 1. Rigaer Stadttheaters tätig war. Der Engagementvertrag mit Hoffmann-Harnisch wurde vom deutschen Theater-Direktor Stanislaus Fuchs am 8. April 1918 unterzeichnet (aufbewahrt in der Theatersammlung der Universität Köln unter Signatur Au 4431, Inv. Nr. 34193434 in Porz-Wahn). Hoffmann-Harnisch war gleichzeitig auch der Herausgeber von *Baltischen Blätter für Theater und Kunst*. Der handschriftliche Brief von Zeltmatis ist ebenfalls in Porz-Wahn unter Signatur Au 9674 auffindbar, spricht gerade von einer kürzlich verfassten Übersicht.

dem Geist des Dramas heraus zu schaffen, so manches Mißverständnis könnte leicht beseitigt werden, wenn in der Gebärdensprache des Einzelnen und in den Gruppenbewegungen das "Opernhafte" nicht zu stark in den Vordergrund gerückt würde.[11]

Am 19. November 1918 spielte man diesen "Fliegenden Holländer" in Dekorationen des vorigen Abends: am 18. November wurde auf der Bühne des ehemaligen 2. Rigaer Stadttheaters die bürgerliche Republik Lettland proklamiert. Die Presse berichtet, dass der lettische Opernchor und Publikum vor der Ouvertüre dreimal *Dievs, svētī Latviju* (Gott, segne Lettland)[12] von Baumaņu Kārlis gesungen haben. Paradoxerweise – ohne die Bühne zu wechseln – wurde diese lettische Inszenierung des "Fliegenden Holländers" auch am 5. Januar 1919 in demselben Hause des 2. Stadttheaters gespielt. Die einzige Änderung war das Stück vor der Ouvertüre: da schon drei Tage die Erste Sowjetrepublik Lettland *de facto* existierte, noch aber keine eigene lettisch-sowjetische Hymne komponiert worden war, erklang diesmal vor Richard Wagners Oper die *Marseillaise*. Man kann sehen, dass das Publikum wie auch die lettische Operninstitution sehr flexibel war, wenn es ums Überleben ging.

Vom 5. bis zum 21. Januar konnten die Besucher der *Latvju opera* im 2. Stadttheater Werke von Wagner, Gounod, Čaikovskij und Verdi sehen. Am 23. Januar 1919 ging die lettische Truppe mit dem Segen des sowjetischen Bildungskommissariats[13] in das ehemalige 1. Rigaer Stadttheater. Für die Vergangenheit und für die Gegenwart der *Latvijas Nacionālā opera* ist dieses Gebäude aus dem Jahre 1863 sehr bedeutend, es ist für Letten inzwischen zum Inbegriff der Nationaloper geworden. Aber wenn man diese Frage emotionslos angeht, darf man nicht vergessen, dass die *Latvijas Nacionālā opera* etwas mehr bedeutet und darstellt, als nur ein schönes Haus mit Säulen. Die Kontinuität der Geschichte der Nationaloper ging im Zeitraum 1990 bis 1995 nicht verloren, als wegen der kapitalen Rekonstruktion die *Latvijas Nacionālā Opera* in anderen Räumlichkeiten gespielt hat. Die bestimmte Haussubstanz ist für Identität einer Institution wichtig, aber ist letztendlich nicht ausschlaggebend.

Man kann feststellen, dass sich am 23. Januar 1919 für die *Latvju Opera* einiges änderte: aus dem Theater mit einem kleinen Orchestergraben zog die Truppe in ein Theater mit einem größeren Graben. Das heisst allerdings nicht, dass gerade durch Häuserwechsel im Moment des Umzuges ein neues lettisches Opernhaus als Institution geboren wurde! Viel wichtiger sind die Metamorpho-

---

11 Carl Waack, *Lettische Oper*, in: *Rigasche Zeitung*, 16. Oktober 1918.
12 Damals hatte *Dievs, svētī Latviju* allerdings noch keinen offiziellen Status als Nationalhymne: eine Erklärung zur Hymne der Republik Lettland erfolgte nur am 4. Juni 1920 (publiziert in der Zeitschrift *Valdības Vēstnesis*, 7. Juni 1920).
13 Alles spielte sich sehr rasch ab, da beim Bildungskommissar von Sowjetlettland auch der an diesen Räumlichkeiten interessierte Operdirigent Teodors Reiters als Leiter der Musikabteilung arbeitete.

sen, die im Februar 1919 stattfanden, als die zuvor auf kooperativen Grundlagen privat betriebene *Latvju Opera* mit dem Dekret der *pro-russisch* orientierten Sowjetregierung Lettlands unter Pēteris Stučka verstaatlicht wurde.[14] Umbenannt in *Padomju Latvijas opera* hat die Truppe ihre alten Inszenierungen gezeigt und an neuen gearbeitet. Das deutsche 1. Rigaer Stadttheater, das seine letzte Aufführung noch am 31. Dezember 1918 zeigte, versteckte seine Notenbibliothek: diese Sammlung wurde erst bei der grossen Rekonstruktion des Theaters in 1990-er Jahren entdeckt.[15] Die Arbeitsbedingungen waren im Ganzen keineswegs ideal, da am 2. Januar, in Kämpfen der kommunistischen Machtübernahme, Teile des hinteren Bühnenbereichs des Theaters ausgebrannt waren. Die Schuld für diesen Brand wurde ohne genauere Beweisführung den wegrückenden deutschen Truppen gegeben. Ansis Gulbis (1873-1936), der den Posten des Generaldirektors der *Latvijas Nacionālā opera* im Zeitraum vom 26. März 1926 bis zum 1. Juni 1927 eingenommen hat, schrieb 1923 seinen Roman *Fantasti* (*Die Fantasten*), in dem folgende Episode zu finden ist:

> Das Erste Stadttheater, die Festung der deutschen Kultur, brannte . . . "Angezündet! Die haben selber ihr Theater angezündet!," sprachen die Beobachtenden. – "Die deutschen Soldaten?" – "Wer sonst, wenn nicht deutsche Soldaten! Sie haben ein neues Leuwen gebraucht." – "Die haben ein altes Spric-wort: Falls nicht mein, dann auch nicht dein! Das liegt in ihrem Charakter. Deshalb haben sie das Theater im Brand gesteckt."[16]

Für Menschen mit Kriegserfahrung waren diese Brandfolgen wahrscheinlich ziemlich unangenehme, aber unbedeutende Kleinigkeiten:

> Vom Brand ist die Bühne nicht betroffen, nur scheint es, dass die ausgebrannte Wand kalte Nordwinde frei walten läßt, die manchmal den Vorhang schütteln und auf das Publikum kühle Lüfte wehen. Den Zuschauern macht das nichts aus – aber was werden die Sänger dazu sagen? Im Saal ist ein Brandgeruch zu merken. Sonst aber ist alles in Ordnung.[17]

Latvju Opera (2) → *Latvijas Nacionālā Opera*

Nach dem Fall der sowjetischen Regierung unter Pēteris Stučka am 22. Mai 1919, als die *pro-deutsche* Regierung Lettlands unter Andrievs Niedra die Stadt

---

14 Die staatliche Übernahme der *Latvju opera* erfolgte Anfang Februar 1919. Information über diese Übernahme wurde publiziert am 8. Februar 1919 in *Cīņa*, auf den Programmzetteln und in der Presse kommt diese neue Bezeichnung erst seit dem 15. Februar vor.
15 Mikus Čeže, *Die Geschichte der Sammlungsbestände des Rigaer Stadttheaters*, in: Erik Fischer (Hrsg.), *Musik-Sammlungen – Speicher interkultureller Prozesse* (Stuttgart, 2007), Teilband A, S. 182-94.
16 Ansis Gulbis, *Kopoti raksti*, Riga 1938, Band 3, S. 355.
17 "Oktāvs," *Latvju Opera,* in: *Uz priekšu*, 30. Januar 1919.

Riga einnahm, kehrte die *Padomju Latvijas opera* zur Benennung *Latvju opera* zurück. Damit die eingenommenen Positionen nicht verloren gehen würden, hat die Operntruppe auch im Juni und Juli aufgetreten. In einigen Fragen half das aber nicht, da das Haus des ehemaligen deutschen Stadttheaters den Letten wieder aus den Händen glitt. Aus der Sicht des vorsowjetischen Rechtes lag das deutsche Rigaer Stadttheater unter Verwaltung der großen Gilde, die hauptsächlich aus reichen deutschen Kaufleuten bestand und allergisch gegen Auftrittsbemühungen der lettischen Operntruppe auf der deutschen Bühne reagierte. Der sichernde Status einer Staatsoper war zusammen mit dem Statusgeber, also mit der Sowjetrepublik Lettland, verschwunden und die erste Sowjetlettand blieb mit allen ihren staatlichen Gründungen nur als die ideologysche Matrix für zwei weitere sowjetische Episoden in der Geschichte Lettlands bestehen.

Am 8. Juli 1919 wurde die unter Andrievs Niedra geleitete *pro-deutsche* Regierung Lettlands von der *pro-lettischen* Regierung unter Dr. Kārlis Ulmanis verbannt. Im Chaos vieler Ereignisse, ohne Haus und ohne Geldgeber, wurde die Operntruppe zur 1. Kurländischen Division zukommandiert. Das wurde als ein Mittel gegen möglichen Verfall der *Latvju Opera* organisiert. Die Zukunftaussichten waren unklar. Die große Gilde, die jahrzehntelang zusammen mit der Stadt Riga die Verwaltung des Rigaer Stadttheaters geleistet hat, bestand verständlicherweise darauf, dass die alten (seit 1887 mehrmals verlängerten) Kontrakte auch in neuen historischen Begebenheiten ihre Gültigkeit nicht verloren haben. Das unerwartete Bündnis der lettischen Operntruppe mit der lettischen 1. Division ließ die alten Kontrakte brüchig erscheinen. Am 16. August schrieb die Kulturabteilung der Stadtverwaltung an die große Gilde:

> In der Annahme, dass die deutsche Einwohnerschaft in Riga kleiner geworden ist, wäre die Benutzung des Stadttheaters für diese Einwohner schwieriger geworden, d. h., es ist der Wunsch entstanden, dieses Theater den lettischen Einwohner zu geben. Nämlich, es ist die Intention, den Letten so ein großes Haus, wie das Haus des 1. Rigaer Stadttheaters eben ist, zu geben. Wir bitten Sie, schriftlich zu erklären, unter welchen Bedingungen die große Gilde bereit wäre, auf den bestehenden Vertrag mit der Stadt zu verzichten.[18]

Es begann ein unfruchtbarer Briefwechsel, aber schon an demselben Tag wurde in der Stadtverwaltung bekannt, das die 1. Kurländische Division die Häuser der beiden Stadttheater zugunsten der lettischen Aufführungen und Konzerte enteignet hat.

Die deutschbaltische Reaktion war verständlicherweise reserviert. Die deutschen Kritiker in Riga der Zwischenkriegszeit würdigten oft die hohen künstlerischen Leistungen der Lettischen Nationaloper. Aber es sind auch einige

---

18 Kārlis Dziļleja, *Rīga–teātru pilsēta*, in: *Rīga kā Latvijas galvaspilsēta*, Riga, 1932), S. 707.

Texte zu finden, wo eine ganz klare Postition zu damaligen Ereignissen gezogen wird:

> . . . .schon 1919 mußten die Deutschen feststellen, daß deutsches Eigentum plötz-lich lettisches Gemeingut war. . . . So kann hier der Verlust einiger Bauten verzeichnet werden, der durch übelste Machenschaften entstanden ist . . . . Die deutsche Oper stellt heute die lettische Staatsoper dar. . . . Durch diese Verän-derungen sind dem Deutschtum schwerste wirtschaftliche und kulturelle Schäden zugefügt worden; fortan zeigten Letten den in Riga weilenden Aus-ländern die deutschen Bauten und Denkmäler als die Ergebnisse ihrer Kultur.[19]

Am 23. September 1919 waren letztendlich von Ministerpräsidenten Dr. Kārlis Ulmanis und Bildungsminister Dr. Kārlis Kasparsons die historischen *Noteikumi par Nacionālo Operu* unterschrieben.[20] Die Operntruppe hatte wieder das gesetzlich garantierte Haus und eine staatliche Finanzierung, die für eine Fortsetzung der regen Tätigkeit willkommen war. Es wurde aber ziemlich bald bei einigen schon am Anfang zitierten Geschichtsschreibern der Zwischen-kriegsperiode beschlossen, dass aus patriotischen Gründen diese Fortsetzung besser zu einem Neuanfang zu deklarieren wäre. So geschah das, obgleich Ver-zeichnisse der Mitglieder dieser Truppe und die Inszenierungen in beiden Spiel-zeiten 1918/19 und 1919/20 eine unverkennbare Einheit bilden: *Latvju Opera = Padomju Latvijas Opera = Latvijas Nacionālā Opera*. Die Statusfrage einer Staatsoper (obgleich bei zwei verschiedenen Staatssystemen) läßt die historische Gleichung noch kürzer erscheinen: *Padomju Latvijas Opera = Latvijas Na-cionālā Opera*.

Das zehnte Jubiläumsjahr der *Latvijas Nacionālā Opera* in der Republik Lettland wurde nur mit einem festlichen Programmheft bedacht. Im Theater waren 1929 keine Feierlichkeiten im großen Stil möglich, da die schwierigste Weltwirschaftskrise des 20. Jahrhunderts im vollen Gange war.

Das zwanzigste Jubiläumsjahr der Nationaloper wurde am 2. Dezember 1939 mit einer festlichen Aufführung zelebriert: diemal war es aber kein "Tann-häuser" Richard Wagners (wie am 2. Dezember 1919). Um die Pros-perierung der lettischen Nationalkultur zu zeigen, wurde *Baņuta* von Alfrēds Kalniņš ges-pielt.

Das dreißigste Jubiläum des lettischen Opernthesters im Jahre 1949 bietet prognosierbare Variationen über die Geschichte des Hauses. Der Poet Fricis Rokpelnis, ein strebsamer Karrieremacher im stalinistischen Sowjetlettand, schrieb im Rückblick über das Jahr 1919: *Für die Oper wurde das beste Rigaer*

---

19 Hans-Bernhard Peege, *Lettische Angriffe auf die kulturelle Herrschaftsstellung der Deutschen in Lettland*, Dissertation an der Ernst-Moritz-Arndt-Universität, 1938, S. 46.
20 Diese "Noteikumi par Nacionālo Operu" (Regelungen über die Nationaloper) sind in der Zeitschrift *Valdības vēstnesis* am 30. September 1919 publiziert.

Theater gegeben, in dem jahrzehntelang das deutsche Theater hauste, volksfeindliche Ideen der Herrscherklasse brütend. Die neue Kunststätte heißt jetzt offiziell "Padomju Latvijas Opera," und von diesen Tagen beginnen wir mit der Zeitrechnung des Staatstheaters für Oper und Ballett.[21] Er schreibt also über Januar 1919. Merkwürdigerweise wurden aber alle Jubiläen dieses Operntheaters zwischen 1949 bis 1999 in der zweiten Hälfte des Aprils mit Festkonzerten gefeiert. Nirgendwo in der Literatur habe ich Hinweise darauf gefunden, warum diese Jubiläumskonzerte gerade im Geburtsmonat Lenins stattfanden. Aus der geschichtlichen Perspektive ist der Monat April für beide ersten Spielzeiten der *Latvijas Nacionālā Opera* eigentlich ganz farblos. Es ist eigenartig, dass in der stalinistischen Zeit gewählter Monat für die Feierlichkeiten der lettischen Operninstitution so langlebig sein konnte. Die Unterschiede sind nur in verschiedenen Referenzen und Vektoren des kollektiven Gedächtnis spürbar. Von 1949 bis 1979 wurde im April gefeiert, mit dem vermeintlich richtigen Hinweis auf den 23. Januar 1919. Im Jahre 1999, wurde auch im April gefeiert, aber jetzt schon mit dem vermeintlich korrekten Hinweis auf den 2. Dezember 1919.

Das Jahr 1989 fällt besonders auf, weil das Theater sein Jubiläum damals sogar zweimal arangiert hat. Am 22. Januar wurde die 70-Jahre-Feier des *Latvijas PSR Valsts ar Darba Sarkanā Karoga ordeni Apbalvotais Akadēmiskais operas un baleta teātris* mit einem Festkonzert ausgezeichnet. Drei Monate später, am 24. April, wurde die 70-Jahrfeier der *Latvijas Nacionālā Opera* mit einem Jubiläumsabend begangen. Schon zwei Jahre vor dem definitiven Zusammenbruch des Sowjet-Lettlands wurde also noch im Rahmen des bestehenden Sowjet-Lettlands für die Bezeichnung des Opernhauses die historische Variante aus der bürgerlichen Republik Lettland genommen, es wurde damit unverkennbar ein Vorzeichen der Wende gesetzt.

Das lettische Opernhaus hat sich unter verschiedenen Mächten entwickelt, aber alle haben auch etwas Gemeinsames gehabt, nämlich die Vorstellung, dass man eine Institution nur umbenennen soll, um denken zu können, dass dabei etwas ganz Neues entstanden ist. Solche Einstellung und Vorgehensweise gibt für Ideologen aller Färbungen freie Hand. Zu jeder Zeit hat die jeweils herrschende Macht versucht, die ersehnte Gründung einer repräsentativen kulturellen Institution sich zuzuschreiben.

Am 3. September 1917 wurde Riga von der Armee des kaiserlichen Deutschlands eingenommen, am 6. September kam Wilhelm II höchstpersönlich, um seinen späten Triumph zu genießen. In der deutsch-besetzten Stadt kam im August 1918 aus Petrograd ein Zug mit *Latvju Opera* an, mit jener Truppe, die in einem Jahr zur *Latvijas Nacionālā Opera* wurde. Wie schon oben beschrieben, gab am 15. Oktober 1918 die Oper unter Leitung von Jāzeps Vītols

---

21 Fricis Rokpelnis, *Trīsdesmit darba gadi* [Dreissig Jahre der Tätigkeit], in: *Latvijas PSR Valsts Operas un baleta teātra 30 gadi*, Riga, 1949, S. 11-12.

und Teodors Reiters ihre Gründungsaufführung, den "Fliegenden Holländer." Dieser 15. Oktober 1918 war aber weder für die Republik Lettland, noch für das Sowjet-Lettland von großem Interesse. Keiner wollte den deutschen Hauptmann Paul Hopf, der als Kriegsverwalter der Stadt Riga agierte, in Erinnerung behalten: er war es, der der lettischen Operntruppe Erlaubnis gab, im ehemaligen russischen 2. Rigaer Stadt-Theater ihre Tätigkeit aufzunehmen.[22] Das wilhelminische Deutschland, das an die künftige Jubiläumsfeierlichkeiten am 15. Oktober in späteren Jahren vielleicht interessiert gewesen wäre, hat schon im November 1918 sein Ende erlebt.

Das 90-jährige Jubiläum der *Latvijas Nacionālā opera* wurde nicht für den 15. Oktober 2008 oder für den 23. Januar 2009, sondern – nach den traditionellen Geschichtskoordinaten der ersten Republik Lettland – für Dezember 2009 eingeplant. Das Beispiel der *Latvijas Nacionālā opera* zeigt deutlich, dass ein Operntheater in dieser Region nur scheinbar seine Jubiläen aus der puren Eigeninitiative feiert. In Wirklichkeit ist es in den vergangenen 90 Jahren bis heute immer die bestehende Machtordnung gewesen, die sich durch die Oper feiern läßt.

Anhang

Zwei Abbildungen – *Lyra mit dem Stern* (1863 bis 1991 und seit 2000) und *Lyra ohne Stern* (1991 bis 2000) – zeigen deutlich, dass nicht nur Jubiläen einer Operninstitution in Abhängigkeit von ideologischen Stand-punkten verschoben werden können. Selbst kleine architektonische Elemente wurden der jeweiligen politischen Situation angepasst.

Bei der Rekonstruktion der Lettischen Nationaloper von 1991 bis 1995 wollte man sich von sowjetischen Machtsymbolen trennen. Der sechszackige Stern auf dem Kopf der allegorischen Figur des jungen Genius, das mit seiner Theaterkunst (Maske in der Hand) die wilden Instinkte (Figur des Panthers) zähmt, schien unpolitisch – und wurde deshalb beibehalten. Der fünfzackige Stern, der die auf dem Dach positionierte Lyra krönte, wurde aber entfernt, weil man glaubte, dass dieses ungeliebte Symbol erst 1945 angebracht worden sei und die von Komödie und Tragödie eingerahmte Lyra gleichsam "besetzt" habe.

---

22 Näheres darüber im Bericht über die künftige Spielzeit des Lettischen Theaters: *Latviešu teātra nākošā sezona*, in: *Rīgas Latviešu avīze*, 30./17. August 1918

Abb. 1   Die Leier mit dem fünfzackingen Stern aus dem Czarnikow-Album (1863) bis etwa 1900

Besonders stark ist diese Assoziation durch ein vom staatlichen Komponistenverband Lettlands initiiertes und 1980 von Arvīds Darkevics herausgegebenes Album geworden. Unter dem in drei Sprachen angegebenen Titel *Mūzikas dzīve Padomju Latvijā / Muzikal'naya zhizn' v Sovetskoy Latvii / Music Life in Soviet Latvia* ist die Lyra des lettischen Opernhauses unverkennbar abgebildet. Die dreifache Wiederholung *Padomju / Sovetskoy / Soviet* im Zusammenspiel mit dem fünfzackigen Stern schafft ein in ideologischer Hinsicht durchdachtes Gesamtbild:

Abb. 2   "Titelblatt des Albums herausgegeben vom Lettischen Komponistenverband (1980)"

Joachim Braun, der in einer bedeutenden analytischen Studie die ideologischen und politischen Hintergründe des sowjetlettischen Musiklebens aufgespürt hat, deutete das für die baltische Musik in den sechziger und siebziger Jahren des 20. Jahrhunderts typische Interesse an lateinisch-italienischen Werktiteln folgendermaßen: *Es symbolisiert hiermit eine Distanzierung von russischer Dominanz und eine Solidarisierung mit dem Westen.*[23] Diese Feststellung wäre auch auf das vom Dach entfernte plastische Element zutreffend. Hier hat man einfach mit anderen Mitteln versucht, sich von russischer Dominanz und der sowjetischen Vergangenheit Lettlands zu distanzieren.

1998 wurde in der Akademischen Bibliothek Lettlands ein Album aus der *Kunst-Stein-Gießerei und Zinkguss-Anstalt von Czarnikow* entdeckt. Alle Skulpturen und dekorativen Elemente, die von Moritz Czarnikov aus Berlin für die Rigaer Theaterfassade zugeliefert wurden, sind dort abgebildet.[24] Die Aufnahmen zeigen unmissverständlich, dass der fünfzackige Stern schon seit Eröffnung des Rigaer Stadttheaters 1863 da war:

Abb. 3   Figur der Lyra ohne füfzackigen Stern (1991-2000)

Aus diesem Grund wurde er im Jahre 2000 ganz still auf die Lyra zurückgestellt. Jene Photos mit der "ent-stemrnten" Lyra aus den Jahren 1990-1995, bleiben, ungeachtet dieses Triumphes der historischen Wahrheit, in der lettischen Theatergeschichte als kurze Episode einer post-sowjetischen Hermeneutik in Riga zu betrachen.

---

23 Joachim Braun, *Zur Hermeneutik der sowjetisch-baltischen Musik. Ein Versuch der Deutung von Sinn und Stil*, in: Joachim Braun, *Schriften. Musik in Lettland*, Hrsg. M. Boiko (Riga, 2002), S. 211.
24 Der allgemeine Firmenkatalog *Modell-Ansichten sowie Preis-Angaben der Kunst-Stein-Giesserei und Zinkguss-Anstalt von Czarnikow in Berlin* wurde dann im Jahre 1865 in Berlin herausgegeben.

Dagmāra Beitnere

MUSICOLOGY AND POWER IN THE DISCOURSE OF SOVIET LATVIAN HISTORY AND MEMORY

Music has a power of its own, and to study the musicologist's relationship with power is an attempt to explain this phenomenon from the point of view of an individual's life. In examining social and cultural relations from a sociological perspective, we may say that power is present in any relationship. And the sociology of music is raises questions about the ways in which power influences the art form's elites—composers and musicologists, both interpreters of the musical "universe." During the Soviet era, composers and musicologists were involved not only with the operations of the Conservatory of Music (now the Jāzeps Vītols Latvian Academy of Music) and the Composers' Union, but also with the planning of song and dance festivals and the writing of reviews for publication in the popular press. For many, creative work was closely associated with research, which accounts for the musicologist's high status in the Latvian intellectual elite, and also for the fact that their lives and professional work took place within diverse and overlapping socio-political orders. The goal of this paper is to identify those attitudes about musicology and its attendant relationships of power that prevailed during the various periods of Soviet rule, and to pinpoint those attitudes from those periods that survive in the intellectual elite of Latvia today, specifically among composers and musicologists. I am interested especially in the ways in which members of the present elite view Latvia's socialist past, and their own role in the relationship between Latvian musical culture and Soviet power.

In recent years, interest has grown in attempts to understand the influence of historical events in a person's everyday life, his or her world view, his or her relationship with diverse structures of power, and those broader cultural resources that help to form harmonized relationships with one's environment, whether visible or otherwise. For some time now, researchers in Western Europe and North America have been studied the experience of the Soviet era in the so-called post-Soviet space. In the past twenty years, a critical discourse about the republic's Soviet experience has also been evident in Latvian society. The time seems ripe for analysis of this topic that does not place itself in opposition to past events, but rather attempts to understand what is was like to live and work under the conditions of the Soviet regime. How did people maintain a relationship with official Soviet ideology in their personal and professional lives? What experiences justified apparent cooperation with the regime? And, how did musicologists acquire or fail to acquire the essential skill of so-called "double-speak"? Prior research has shown that, in addition to collaborators, there were many people whom the Soviet system genuinely influenced and subjugated. But there were also people who were able to use the regime's inability to fully control everything and everybody in order to advance their own and others' creativity, both scholarly and musical.

Methodology

This study relies upon life stories. In recording and interpreting these stories, I make use of Niklas Luhmann's theory of auto-referential systems, which describes society as a system in which participants are self-observing; through self-observation, participants create a profile of themselves, which, over a period of time, eventually become self-referential. Such profiles constitute identities confirmed by actions, which in turn figure in a process of *autopoeisis* or self-creation.[1] My concern is with the way in which participants in a society see and understand themselves, and they ways in which those understandings give rise over time to action. In his work *Art as a Social System*, Luhmann argues that artistic communication provides structures of connectivity between individual consciousness and society.[2] His approach endows artistic communication with great significance within society as a system. It is a means of forming invisible connections, and therefore also of preserving values.

The interviews of which I make use in this essay are analyzed by way of an approach that is founded upon theories of narrativity, as they relate to the self. My research materials consist, for the most part, of interviews with composers and musicologists. These interviews constitute fragments of individual life stories, and, as such, they comprise an original discourse in which are reflected personal experiences and understandings of both the self and society. In all life stories, memory and narrative (the manner of telling; what is remembered or kept to oneself) play important roles. The use of life stories to reconstruct events is therefore limited, since every life story is, fundamentally, an interpretation of the self, a infusion of the self with meaning, which creates new relationships between past and present, and which is the product of a specific culture.[3] If this idea is applied to a larger social group and one considers the life stories of a group of contemporaries, then we may come to recognize that a common set of themes dominates the life stories and self-understandings of the members of that group, whether large or small. In this way, we can recognize groups of life sto-

---

This essay has been translated from the Latvian by Amanda Māra Jātniece, Aviva Braun, and Anita Liepiņa.

1 See Niklas Luhmann, *Social Systems* (Stanford, CA, 1999).
2 Luhmann, *Art as a Social System* (Stanford, CA, 2000), 52.
3 See Mark Freeman, *Rewriting the Self* (London, 1993), 28-29.

ries as narratives belonging to a particular social time and place. In the present study, those times and places correspond to the four periods of Soviet rule in Latvia, which I will label according to the name of the General Secretary of the Communist Party of the Soviet Union who ruled at those particular times (Stalin, Khrushchev, Brezhnev, Gorbachev).

Societies often regard the stories of one or another generation, whose members are united through historical events and experiences, as paradigmatic for that generation's—and even a whole culture's—system of values, norms, and symbols. In this respect, one can say that the present paper attempts to uncover a kind of social or collective memory, which itself assumes an important position in the construction of a society's history.[4] Individuals' memories of historical events differ because memory often tunes out and excludes those events or attitudes that seem unpleasant or traumatic to the narrator. The use of life stories in historical research is therefore inherently subjective. Moreover, people tend to view their lives and personal histories differently at different periods in their lives.

The study of life stories emphasizes individuals' relationships with the past, the ways in which they understand and interpret the events of their pasts in the mind of the present, and their evaluations of themselves and their actions. Examined collectively, life stories are like unwritten histories experienced by a community, with each individual's experience forming one of the stories that together constitute some collective experience. In the present study, I located subjects to share their life stories with me according to the so-called "snowball method": Each interviewee suggested other musicians or musicologists whom they felt I ought to contact. Thus, a small group of respondents was formed. In addition, some respondents were selected in order to gain further context.

In researching the experiences of the Soviet era, it is important to remember the words of the philosopher Isaiah Berlin, who notes that the researcher must be aware that we are studying people who have lived and worked in dangerous situations.[5] In this case, Berlin's cautionary statement holds true for those who lived and worked in not only under Stalin but also in Latvia's Khrushchev, Brezhnev, and Gorbachev periods.

In the view of the media scholar Sergei Kruks, an unsystematic approach has thus far dominated research on the cultural history of Latvia's Soviet era. The most common approach taken by post-Soviet scholars has been to interpret the political environment in terms of struggle between a despotic power and a lone, brilliant artist, whose works are regarded as dangerous to the regime. Influenced by the Romantic intellectual tradition, this approach regards culture as fundamentally separate from society, and assigns a greater significance to cul-

---

4 See Peter Burke, "History as Social Memory," in *Memory: History, Culture and the Mind*, ed. Thomas Butler (Oxford, 1989); cited from the Latvian translation: "Vēsture kā sociāla atmiņa," in *Atmiņa un vēsture* (Riga, 1998), 31.
5 Steven Lukes, interview with Isaiah Berlin; Latvian trans. in *Diena* (25 September 1998).

ture than to society in people's lives.[6] Following Kruks's lead, I would argue that a new outlook on the processes of cultural politics may be obtained by bringing an analysis of sociological factors into our scholarship. These sociological factors include such things as the goals of consumers of art, the dominant discourses of aesthetics, the utilitarian tasks of the arts in communication, the economic interests of artists, and the tactical uses of artistic issues in political struggles.

The Totalitarian System and the Creative Spirit

To date, several researchers have produced important studies that have sought to open doors for the sociological study of Latvian musical culture. One in particular must be mentioned: Joachim Braun's 1982 article "Zur Hermeneutik der Sowjetischen-Baltischen Musik. Ein Versuch der Deutung von Sinn und Still."[7] Braun's article was the first to examine musical life in the Baltic States under Soviet rule from a perspective that transcended the "blindness of the system." As Luhmann argues, society as a system is not able to observe or produce self-characterizations of itself because it is impaired by the "blindness of the system"; in other words, society is not able to transcend its own ideological assumptions, as it would have to do if it were to to understand itself.

Braun himself belonged to the Latvian musical community until his emigration to Israel in 1972. Once he left the Soviet system, he had the opportunity to provide those remaining in Latvia with a theoretically grounded understanding of Baltic musical languages and about the semantically loaded musical codes that the Baltic creative intelligentsia had developed. In retrospect, we can appreciate that the creative elite in all three Baltic States both cooperated with the regime and at the same time made use of latent or indirect modes of resistance to Soviet totalitarian ideology. All branches of art are important in understanding a society's communications about itself, because new self-images and self-understandings are constantly created and existing ones renewed, providing society with opportunities to reflect upon and understand itself, and to coordinate auto-referential systems. As an art form, music has a high degree of abstraction, which allows it to speak indirectly about values that were invisibly maintained in all three Baltic States during the period of Soviet rule. Braun's study sheds light on precisely such a situation.

It is important to note, however, that official attitudes toward the creative professions were not constant during all periods of Soviet rule. But during each period, freedom of expression was allowed up to a certain point, as was a certain ig-

---

6 Sergejs Kruks, *"Par mūziku skaistu un melodisku." Padomju kultras politika, 1932-1964* (Riga, 2008), 16.
7 Joachim Braun, "Zur Hermeneutik der sowjetisch-baltischen Musik: Ein Versuch der Deutung von Sinn und Stil," *Zeitschrift für Ostforschung* 1 (1982): 76-93; repr. in Braun, *Studies: Music in Latvia* (Riga, 2002), 204-224.

norance of the terms of Soviet ideology. In one's professional work, one generally assumed the attitude expressed in the Gospel of Matthew: "Give to Caesar what is Caesar's, and to God what is God's" (Matth. 22:21). Many creative professionals felt some degree of ambivalence, because the Soviet era made a lasting impression on the cultural environment during every decade of its existence in Latvia.

The Soviet Era

In Latvia, the Soviet era can be divided into four periods: the Stalin era, beginning with Latvia's annexation in 1940 and ending in 1953; the Khrushchev era, from 1953 to 1964; the Brezhnev era, from 1964 to 1982; and the Gorbachev era of *perestroyka*, from 1985 to 1991. Each of these periods was marked by specific ideological systems and political and social processes, and each differs from the others with respect to prevailing attitudes towards music. As Kruks observes,

> Cultural policy lacked consistency, having been left without definite guidelines. Practically speaking, it was not possible to incorporate art into the Procrustean bed of Socialist Realism, since the resolutions of the Party gave contradictory orders. . . . Documents from the archives of the Ministry of Culture, the Central Committee of the Communist Party, and the creative unions attest to the fact that cultural life—to say nothing of aesthetics—was also dictated by political and tactical factors: the actions and counter-actions of various interests, the vacillations of the Party apparatus, the sacrifices of artists, or the denunciations of colleagues.[8]

In analyzing Soviet-era cultural policy, I believe that the researcher must be aware of the difficult conditions under which intellectuals lived and worked. Not only did various human passions influence the work of the creative unions and those artists involved with them (often as simple as who likes or dislikes whom, and so forth), but we must also be aware that the denunciations, arrests, and deportations that were implemented during the Stalin period irreversibly changed people's lives and influenced (even branded, put a stamp on) their creative work. When the Soviet army entered Latvia in 1944, it brought with it a culture of distrust, suspicion, persecution, and something that had not been known in the republic before that time: the "cult of showing one's love towards the great leader," a love that had to be demonstrated in one's artwork.

In his recent book *Stalin i pisateli* (Stalin and writers), the Russian literary scholar Benedikt Sarnov brings a hermeneutic approach to bear upon the relationship between twentieth-century Russian poets and the Soviet regime, and in particular Josef Stalin. Sarnov argues that intellectuals of the Stalin period allowed themselves little doubt the regime and "branded" the dogma of consensus onto their minds, allowing self-hypnosis to grind their souls up in the name of

---

8   Kruks, *Par mūziku skaistu un melodisku*, 15.

the unified standard of "the great principle."⁹ In whose name did they undertake this blood-chilling transformation? What gave Stalin the ability to acquire a monopoly of power over the spiritual life of each individual? Sarnov's answer: The poets' enchantment with Stalin's power, or the "hypnosis of power" that constitutes a continuation of the Russian tradition of believing in an all-powerful ruler, the tsar. Poets surrendered to Stalin's power, even if it brought death. By using the old tactic of "punish a couple of witches in order to intimidate the rest of the heretics," Stalin's regime created an atmosphere of fear and distrust, and of the complete deferral of creative intellectuals to the desires of political regime.

This relationship of creative intellectuals to Soviet rule was brought to Latvia after its annexation and incorporation into the Soviet Union. The deportations of 1941 and 1949 were used to intimidate the population, and those deportations were supplemented by repressions against Latvian intellectuals and direct and indirect incitement, all of which changed the creative atmosphere in the occupied territory.

The Stalin Era: Fear and Distrust

With Soviet annexation, Latvia—indeed, all three of the Baltic States—had not only lost its independence and been subjugated to a foreign rule; its entire intellectual life and value system had been changed. The model of the Soviet Russian creative unions was mechanically replicated in the Baltic States, bringing with it the terrifying feeling of dependence and danger. When reconstructing the events of those days and quoting the works of musicologists, researchers are not always able (due to the academic goals of their work) to take account of an individual's writer's personal situation after the events of 14 June 1941, when a foreign power and its army entered Latvia territory and implemented mass deportations. Stories of the arrest, torture, and deportation of tens of thousands of peaceful citizens to Siberia remain an unforgettable emotional experience to this day. The influence of these events—the fear and the distrust—remained with the older generations of Latvian intellectuals until the restoration of the republic's independence in 1991.

The fear experienced by artists themselves, and their loved ones' stories of fear and betrayal, entered either directly or indirectly into the present study by way of life stories. Ludvigs Kārkliņš, One of Latvia's leading music theorists and a former vice-chancellor of research at the Latvian Academy of Music (then the Latvian National Conservatory), responded tentatively to my call for interviews for this study.¹⁰ At first he agreed to an interview, but then canceled three

---

9 Benedikt Sarnov, *Stalin i pisateli* (Moscow, 2008), 427-433.
10 Ludvigs Kārkliņš (b.1928) studied composition theory at the Jāzeps Mediņš Music School from 1947 to 1951. He was not accepted into the Latvian Conservatory. Instead, he entered and graduated from the Russian Music Academy in 1982 (Dr. art.) with a concentration in musicology. He earned a Dr. habil art. in 1992, and served as vice-chancellor for

days later and sent instead a manuscript entitled "A Life Story Characteristic of the Latvian Nation" (*Latviešu tautai raksturīgs dzīvesstāsts*), a literary autobiography about his parents and a synopsis of the life stories of his brother and himself, including memories of the composer Jānis Līcītis, who was repressed in 1950. Research in clinical psychology shows that traumatic experiences in the past can lead to amnesia, or to a dissociative protective reaction. If an experience is particularly traumatic, it can cause various psychological reactions, such as the splitting of memories.[11] The traumatic event in effect prohibits a memory from returning to the subject, thus protecting the person from reliving it. The culture of memory is a complicated witness to social life, and this is particularly true in the case of an unfairly repressed person's relationship to what he or she experienced when deported and forced to live in exile. Therefore, the text that Professor Kārkliņš sent me speaks for him.

Kārkliņš's parents were deported on 25 March 1949. In his manuscript autobiography, he asks: "And what was it all for? For their hard work from morning until late at night, year in and year out, to raise their children, for their education . . . Fate is often unfair, too." Kārkliņš himself was denied the opportunity to study at the Latvian Conservatory for the same reason that his parents had been deported: because they were considered enemies of the Soviet regime.

> For several years after graduating from the Jāzeps Mediņš Music School in Riga, I knocked in vain at the door of the J. Vītols Latvian National Conservatory, even though I had the best grades on the entrance exams. When I asked Party secretary V. Kaupužs why I had not been admitted, he answered cynically, "We had not become sufficiently acquainted with your biography before the exams . . ."

Representatives of the Soviet regime were careful to allow only those people who were loyal to the Communist Party to participate in public life. Loyalty was proven not just by "correct" biographies; the system also demanded and expected specific "levies."

Arrests Accompanied by Music

Did composers in Latvia experience the sort of brutal indoctrination into the Soviet system that Sarnov describes in his study of Russian poets during the years of Stalinist terror? Sergei Kruks's recent study of the influence of Soviet ideology on musical life from 1932 to 1964 shows that Party functionaries meddled

---

research and creative work at the Jāzeps Vītols Latvian Academy of Music from 1990 to 1994.
11 See Colin A. Ross, "History, Phenomenology, and Epidemiology of Dissociation, in *Handbook of Dissociation: Theoretical, Empirical and Clinical Perspectives*, ed. Larry K. Michelson and William J. Ray (New York, 1996), 3-23.

profoundly in the creative work of composers as well.[12] Kruks's research reveals that local schemes and mutual spats and quarrels, sometimes on the level of simple personality differences, became the norm in the activities of Latvia's creative unions. But isn't this an oversimplification, putting the insignificance of individual people's personal lives before the will of the Stalinist Soviet regime? How can we understand the events of that time and the writings of musicologists working under the pressure from the regime? Have we adequately analyzed the situation faced by Latvian intellectuals and members of the creative professions?

The experience of the first generation of Latvian intellectuals was unique, since its members had been educated in the universities of tsarist Russia and had occupied high positions in various Latvian offices before the republic's annexation to the USSR. For these reasons, the shock was acutely felt when Soviet authorities began violently introducing its ideology, which had to be obeyed without protest. Part of the Latvian intellectual community re-orientated itself fairly quickly to the new ideological conditions, adopting both visible (collaborationist) and encoded ("double-speak") codes of communication between themselves and society. Of course, there were also left-leaning intellectuals who actively cooperated with and enabled Soviet authority. The Soviet regime did not absolve a single review or musicological study that had been written during the war years. It made clear that no one's prior experiences and achievements were of worth, and it constantly demanded statements of loyalty in the form of creative work.

When reconstructing events in Latvia after the Second World War, Western researchers often analyze texts as their principal historical sources. Here we must mention Kevin Karnes's detailed article "Soviet Musicology and the 'Nationalities Question': the Case of Latvia."[13] Karnes article places much importance on so-called *zhdanovshchina*; in other words, it analyzes the totalitarian tactics of intimidation, threats, and the cultivation of terror that influenced the work of all creative unions in the former Soviet Union. The creative unions of all the occupied republics were compelled to serve Soviet ideology and to participate in its main task—namely, the education of the populace in the spirit of Marxism-Leninism-Stalinism. Karnes's article also introduces the reader to the achievements of those musicologists who sought to "guard" the timeless values of Latvian music during the Soviet period, thereby preserving cultural continuity (he examines, for example, the legality of Jāzeps Vītols's musical heritage within the Soviet system).

In Latvia, the *zhdanovshchina* was not only a theoretical attack. Musicologists were actually arrested and tried for "bourgeois nationalism," intimidated, and deported. Some escaped by fleeing into exile. Arrests "accompanied by music" began. For example, through life stories we learn about the fate of the pian-

---

12 Kruks, *Par mūziku sakistu un melodisku.*
13 Kevin C. Karnes, "Soviet Musicology and the 'Nationalities Question': The Case of Latvia," *Journal of Baltic Studies* 39, no. 3 (2008): 283-305.

ist Jāzeps Lindbergs, who was allowed to play his graduation concert at the Conservatory, but who was immediately escorted out of the hall and arrested by KGB. Likewise, young pianist Regīna Pumpure had been accepted into the Paris Conservatoire in the autumn of 1941, but was deported to Siberia on 14 June of that year. She recalls this experience: "They told me to take lots of warm clothing along. I took a bed sheet and put all of my most important musical scores and books in it. Then I went to the piano, opened it, and told everyone, 'Sit down.' I played Lūcija Garūta's *Meditācijas*, closed the piano, and said, 'Now we can go.'"

In his study of the cultural situation in the Soviet Union in the 1930s, Sarnov argues that the totalitarian system destroyed all disobedient and non-compliant intellectuals not only physically but also intellectually—by destroying their work and relegating it to oblivion.[14] The musicologist Oļģerts Grāvītis recounts many examples of composers being silenced and their work being banned. "As soon as one is barred from the Composers' Union, one's music is no longer played on the radio or in concerts. For example, Oskars Stroks was banned from the Composers' Union in 1952, and he was rehabilitated only a couple of years ago."[15]

Those Arrested and Deported

According to the private records of professor Oļģerts Grāvītis, between 1941 and 1950 more than fifty individuals from the community of Latvian composers, musicologists, and performers were arrested, interrogated and convicted.[16] It is impossible to describe, within the scope of this article, the absurdity of the incriminating accusations. Among musicologists and composers, the best known and most frequently mentioned cases (on account of the detailed records of their arrests and persecutions) are those of Jēkabs Graubiņš (1886-1961) and Jānis Līcītis (1913-78). Both of their cases suggest that the persecution of musical in-

---

14 Sarnov, *Stalin i pisateli*.
15 The Soviet system of punishment included having bans placed on the performance of one's music, having references to one's name banned or removed from encyclopedias and scholarly publications, and being barred from the Composers' Union. Among the Union's once-barred and now rehabilitated members are Oskars Stroks, Jēkabs Graudiņš, Joachim Braun, and Lolita Vambute.
16 Grāvītis's records mention fifty-seven musicians, musicologists, performers, and composers who were persecuted, deported, tortured, or killed under the Bolshevik and Nazi regimes. Under the Soviets, many were marginalized and not allowed to continue working. Those killed by the Soviets include J. Vītiņš (1897-1941), E. Samts (1909-41), and O. Kreišmanis (1909-48; shot in Moscow). Those shot by the Nazis in Rumbula include A. Mecs (1888-1941) and S. Rašins (1920-41). The following died in Siberia: N. Vidulejs (1890-1949), A. Sīlis (1904-43), J. Muške (1893-1943), K. Līdaks (b.1893; died at an unknown time in the 1940s), E. Kalniņš (1893-1948), A. Feils (1902-1942), A. Frīdenbergs (1875-1941), and A. Auziņš (1899-1941).

tellectuals was inspired by the 1948 discussion and decree by the Central Committee of the Communist Party regarding the opera *The Great Friendship* by Vano Muradeli. This decree was a signal for local authorities to begin a campaign against formalism in all of the USSR. This provided an opportunity for Latvian culture inspectors to cull and punish the politically disloyal and to intimidate all others.

The arrest of the pianist and Conservatory student Jāzeps Lindbergs (1922-94) is only one example of this method of intimidation. Only in 1990 did Lindbergs dare to disclose that the KGB *troika*'s accusation against him: his refusal to speak Russian. For this, he received a sentence of five years in prison. The arrests in Latvia in 1950 were connected to the arrival from Leningrad of Vladimir Muzalevskiy (pseudonym for Bunimovich). In a conversation with Grāvītis, Lindbergs affirmed that, in addition to the denunciation of him by Muzalevskiy, he also saw two other denunciations in the Cheka (State Security Committee) files: he saw two other denunciations, one by a member of the Conservatory staff, and another by a student.

In my interviews with composers and musicologists, nobody was willing to name Latvian informers, because that would mean diminishing the prestige of a number of staff members working at the Conservatory during those years, who have since gained a place in Latvian music history. This is a sensitive issue in the Latvian political discourse, because, since regaining independence, the Cheka archives have never been opened, and thus there has been no reconciliation with this aspect of Latvia's past. The files have been kept closed in order to avoid confrontations among members of the community and suffering for children and family members of informers and victims alike. Latvian history in the twentieth century is, certainly, not clear cut, black and white. There are many shades and nuances. The present financial, economic, and political crisis in Latvia has raised anew timeless moral questions: Mistakes must be recognized. Should the names of people who knowingly denounced others during the Soviet period therefore be made public? As Rūta Līcīte, daughter of Jānis Līcītis, told me in her interview, her father first spoke of his arrest and time in Siberia only in 1973. He begged his daughter not to speak of it to anyone. Just as Lindbergs kept silent after his return from Siberia, so did Jēkabs Graubiņš and Jānis Līcītis. Upon their release from prison, they were made to sign a pledge not to reveal anything of their experience: "not a word or you will return here."

How to Write "Correctly"

The patriarch of Latvian musicologists, Oļģerts Grāvītis, began his interview by recounting the beginnings of his studies in 1947. His account includes the story of the musicologist Jēkabs Vītoliņš, mentioned in the article by Karnes:

I remember hearing Jēkabs Vītoliņš speak on the radio when I was a boy. He was introducing concerts during the first period of Latvia's independence. At the Conservatory I found myself in his class. He was a very intelligent, shrewd individual, with a refined taste in clothes, who told us about concerts he had heard in Paris and Vienna. He was interested in the music of W.A. Mozart, L. van Beethoven, and R. Wagner. The professor encouraged me to write the thesis for my diploma on Andrejs Jurjāns.

That is when the future professor Grāvītis received his first instructions on how a student in Soviet times had to write. "At the beginning and at the end there must be quotations from Lenin and Stalin. Professor Jēkabs Vītoliņš taught that it was proper form and I taught that to my students up to 1990." Can we question today why such a brilliant intellectual as Vītoliņš opted for this way of collaborating with the Soviet authorities? He had witnessed personally the deportations of 1941 and 1949, the arrests of countless colleagues at the Conservatory, as well as the double standard adopted by Soviet authorities with respect to history. He probably assessed the situation as an individual concerned with his long-term future. Grāvītis provides an example of the false double standards of Soviet ideologues. In 1941 the Untion of Soviet Latvian Composers founded on the model of similar unions throughout the USSR. By order of the Supreme Soviet, Jāzeps Vītols was appointed president. After the Soviet army returned to Latvia in 1944, the Composers' Union was renewed, but this action was called its "founding," thereby completely ignoring the fact that this same Union had been founded in 1941. The reason was that its former president, Vītols, had gone into exile, a sin that Soviet authorities could not forgive. Thus began a series of textual manipulations by musicologists enployed to rehabilitate Jāzeps Vītols in the Soviet era. This process has been described in a study by Kevin Karnes.[17]

Inevitably, one set of lies and falsified histories necessitated another set of the same. Against a background of fear and violence emerges the realization that one must always wear a mask. Communications with Soviet authorities must be undertaken in this same way, according to a double standard, in order to assure the continuation and existence of Latvian musical culture. To date, one of the more extensive studies of the "re-education" of composers, music theorists, and musicologists under the Soviet system is Vizbulīte Bērziņa's *Daudz baltu dieniņu* (Many bright days), dedicated to the life story of musicologist Jēkabs Graubiņš.[18] Bērziņa's monograph reconstructs in detail the mood in the Latvian Composers' Union and the Latvian Conservatory immediately following World War II, as many Latvians returned from Russia. These former émigrés had experienced first-hand the years of Stalin's terror in the USSR. In addition, special "emissaries" of the "great brotherly nation" (Russia) arrived in order to establish a department of music history, and also to to teach by intimidation the ideology

---

17 Karnes, "Soviet Musicology and the 'Nationalities Question,' " 294-298.
18 Vizbulīte Bērziņa, *Daudz baltu dieniņu. Jēkaba Graubiņa dzīvesstāsts* (Riga, 2006).

of the new regime. Among other valuable materials, Bērziņa's study includes an account of the minutes taken during KGB interrogations and of the guidelines distributed at department meetings of the Conservatory, and it provides much food for thought about the conduct of some well known individuals in the musicological community.

The Khrushchev Era: Was There a "Thaw" in Latvia?

The Twentieth Congress of the Communist Party was important in Latvian history because it charted a new ideological course, characterized by condemnation of Stalin's dictatorship and the illusion of relaxed ideological control. The period nicknamed the "Khrushchev Thaw" was never quite experienced in Latvia, because as early as 1957, after the visit of the Secretary General of the Communist Party of the USSR, the mood changed abruptly. In Latvia, those in government had taken Khrushchev's changes seriously and had begun working to develop cadres who would support policies based on the interests of the republic. And so the dismissal of Eduards Berklāvs, General Secretary of the Latvian Communist Party, was a grave signal, an indicator that, for all the talk of a "Thaw" in Soviet society, nothing could change without the approval of "big brother." The newly installed Latvian Party Chairman, Arvīds Pelše, was a typical career Communist who diligently supervised cultural movements. He is remembered for his ban on the celebration of Latvia's traditional Midsummer's Night Festival (*Līgo svētki*). No written records of this prohibition have been found, however. It was characteristic of the Soviet regime to give such instructions by telephone or by insinuation, and they were often misunderstood.

Soviet authorities paid careful attention to the selection of cadres to undertake the indoctrination of others. Musicologists had an important role in this activity. Even if a student had arrived at the point where he had written his graduation thesis, he was not assured of a diploma without complications. In 1961, the thesis of the musicologist Arnolds Klotiņš, *The Original Works of Alfrēds Kalniņš*, was deemed ideologically harmful. "It was said that my work contained *narodnik* [nationalist] ideology." His thesis supervisor was Lūcija Garūta, a figure not trusted by Soviet authorities. Moreover, and Klotiņš's father was a Baptist minister.[19] Klotiņš himself was not to be trusted not only because of his family, however, but also because he knew foreign languages and was an independent thinker. He graduated from the Conservatory one year late, and only because of the intervention by the musicologist Nils Grīnfelds, a professor trusted by the Soviets. During the period of Soviet rule, there were very few graduates in mu-

---

19 The biography of the composer Pēteris Vasks presents a similar case. His father's profession as a minister prevented his admission to the Latvian Conservatory. Instead, Vasks entered and graduated from the Lithuanian Conservatory in Vilnius in 1970. Thereafter, he returned to Riga, where he was permitted to take conservatory classes in composition.

sicology from the Latvian Conservatory. It is understandable that events like this, involving one graduate student, affect all others studying, or thinking of studying, in the field. All were aware that the would be closely watching.

The Brezhnev Era and Soviet "Double-Speak"

Like elsewhere in the Union, the period of Leonid Brezhnev's rule in Latvia was characterized by stagnation, with certain routine "demonstrations of loyalty" to Soviet authority. Composers came to exploit this phenomenon liberally, but the work of musicologists remained closely supervised, and all published texts were censored. Academic staff kept an eye on one another within Conservatory department, and all were watched by Glavlit (the State Censor), heads of the Party's various cultural departments, and countless representatives of the KGB. In all, the number of one's supervisors was huge. There seemed to be unwritten rules as to what could and could not be written. Since texts were carefully scrutinized throughout the period, music, among the most abstract of all art forms, became endowed with a sort of double message of its own. Artists in many disciplines created artistic images to convey ideas that their own people recognized and could interpret. A kind of Aesopian language flourished during the Brezhnev era. It was, in effect, a game: Would the Soviet authorities recognize the hidden meaning in a new opus? Would it be possible to send the hidden meaning out to the people?

An excellent example of this Aesopian language is found in the music of Marģers Zariņš. Zariņš wrote many works that pleased the system, and he used them as cover for other works that have became classics during the Brezhnev years. Grāvītis recounts an anecdote about Zariņš whispering the following to young composers:

> "Is it so hard for you to compose something to take to the Ministry of Culture. You may have a score entitled Fall Evening. They reject it. Take it back the next day and call it November Evening. Now that's different! They buy this work and pay you good money for it." Marģers Zariņš himself secretly taught us this. Be smart! Does it hurt you to write a song?

Grāvītis remembers that composers were always short of money, but they also knew that the Ministry of Culture made funds available for buying works, and it was relatively easy to apply. "A case in point," he recalls, "was an oratorio entitled *Lenin's Mother*, with lyrics by Mirdza Ķempe. When a work was registered you could get a 25% advance payment immediately. Even if the work was not finished a year later, it was possible to substitute a few songs and the debt was cancelled." The ministry of Culture watched carefully to assure that titles of compositions conformed to the demands of the authorities. If they did not, then titles were simply "adjusted" in order to make the work conform to proper ideology.

Grāvītis remembers a commission given to composer Valters Kaminskis for a work intended for performance at a song festival, with lyrics by Ojārs Vācietis. The Ministry of Culture insisted on including the phrase "Soviet Latvia" in the text. Both the composer and the poet protested, opposing the bureaucrats at the Ministry. But in the end they lost, and the refrain "Soviet Latvia" was added to the cantata. Grāvītis also recalls the fact that, during the Soviet era, one could learn to write a review of a work without ever seeing or hearing it:

> I can write a review in the middle of the night about a symphony, without ever hearing it. It all depends what is required—a positive or a critical review, mentioning that it is too slow here and there, not enough colour, the form could be improved. In this way the musicologist Nils Grīnfelds had "heard" my opus *Lenin's Mother* and included the work in his book of reviews. The work had been registered and money had been paid, but it was never written. At the time I wrote about twenty-five songs for choir to replace it. Clearly, we are the corrupted people of that era.

Grāvītis tells of his first major foreign trip, to the United States in 1972, where he served as part of a delegation of figures working in cultural fields in Latvia. Their mission was to tell Latvians in exile about the cultural achievements of the Latvian SSR. The professor recalls:

> Upon his return Grāvītis must give an account of his trip at the plenum of the Conservatory. There are many questions . . . and for the first time in my life I felt like a "smart Antiņš." I had been able to save a few LP records (they confiscated everything in customs), including the recording of the cantata *Garā nakts* (The long night), with lyrics by Velta Toma. The music and subject were good—a long black night enveloped Latvia, the sun went down, the flag of the independent republic disappeared . . . but the time will come when we shall return home. I illustrated my lecture with music from the recording, saying, in the presence of the plenipotentiary of the Party, Partordze, that J. Kalniņš also writes songs dealing with politics, about free Latvia. For sixteen minutes I played the recording, and the audience heard the message . . . we shall soon return.

Grāvītis explained, in his lecture, that those in exile also wrote works of a political nature. Proceeding in this manner, he was allowed to repeat the lecture several times to different audiences. A code for communication has been established. Now, he realized, there was a way to speak about compositions written in exile, by composers otherwise unmentioned and largely forgotten in Soviet Latvia.

Grāvītis also remembers, however, that the situation changed after Jurģis Skulme, lecturer at the Academy of Art, was arrested and sent to Daugavpils for distributing literature forbidden by the Soviet authorities to his students:

> The scandal touched all institutions of higher education. Here at the Conservatory, some ladies arrived to assure great accountability, and they sealed J. Vītols bookcase [which contained the departed composer's personal library] and labelled it "SF" [*specfonds*, restricted collection]. Thereafter, a student had to get a special permit from the rector in order to see the sheet music contained in the bookcase.

As Kruks observes, since the Latvian Conservatory was intended to educate its students along Soviet lines, it bore an added responsibility vis-à-vis the authorities. Thus, its teaching materials were severely restricted. Generally speaking, the Composers' Union was more moderate in its evaluation of musical works and published scholarship.

In retrospect, the double standard of the Soviet era gave rise to a double standard in the minds of those individuals who participated and collaborated in the system. In me interview with the composer Imants Kalniņš about his own relationship with the Soviet authorities, he concluded that he had not experienced any special repression. With respect to collaborating with the regime, he mentioned one song he had written for choir, dedicated to Lenin's centenary. It was written, he explained, to earn money. He has no regrets, because one has to live under all regimes. Kalniņš pointed out that, historically, totalitarian regimes have seen great advances in music. "And the free market does not protect me, as an artist, from receiving orders from the subculture. Now it seems that august academic art has become an outcast. Over a long period of time, in the realm of culture, authoritarian regimes benefit society more than democracy does."

National in Form, Socialist in Content

During every decade of Soviet rule, the artistic unions related in varying ways to the Latvian Communist Party and the KGB. Pauls Dambis (secretary of the Composers' Union from 1968 to 1979, president from 1984 to 1989) remembers that a change in the political discourse was inevitably accompanied by a change in one's supervisors. By the end of 1970s, his supervisors had clearly become open, tolerant, and loyal to the concerns of artists:

> We had curators from the Central Committee who began supervising our work at the end of 1970s. They were very tolerant individuals. They were normal people, like A. Goris. He was very tolerant with musicians. I can't think of any occasion where a performance was forbidden or a program was concert changed. It was as if we were protected by a warm glove of tolerance. . . . On the other hand, local cadres were very active, those who wanted to gain recognition and advance their positions. It was more work dealing with them than with the curators, who were responsible to the Central Committee for ideology.

As he remembers it, Imants Kalniņš was accused of being ideological suspect by individuals at the local level, his colleagues. In response, he "hid" himself in the provincial city of Liepāja, which greatly helped him to advance his career.

Dambis remembers that one KGB operative tried to recruit him in 1983, but that he was advised by the curator of the Central Committee of the Latvian Communist Party, Dzidra Bokālova, not to become involved with the organization. This occurred in the midst of a period of transition. Brezhnev had died and there was great uncertainty in society. With the turnover of General Secretaries, the Composers' Union received numerous visits from KGB officials who asked many questions about members' trips abroad. Composers never received royalties directly when their works were performed abroad; in such cases, Moscow kept the royalties up until the time of the Soviet Union's collapse. Instead, composer received monies in a curious way: A small percentage of one's royalties were paid out in so-called *certificates.* This was a system that exploited composers, and disregarding an artist's rights to his or her own work. "Yet Soviet power lost," Dambis explains,

> because there was a fundamental mistake in Socialist Realism. [Official ideology] stated that Social Realism is a reflection of national identity, that Soviet art is socialist in substance and ethnic in form.[20] [With this definition as a guide,] it was difficult to find fault with any music. Then came the new folklore wave [of the mid-1980s], and there was absolutely nothing to complain about.

Today the Composers' Union is headed by Uģis Prauliņš. In his interview with me, he claimed that he never experienced any repressive action taken against him by Soviet authorities. The Lyrics for some of his songs sometimes created difficulties, concert programs were strictly regulated, and a performers were not permitted to improvise freely during concerts. Aso, the audience's taste had to be considered.

The "Last Chance," and an Attempt at a Conclusion

After the death of Brezhnev, several changes were made in the leadership of the Communist Party, which resulted in alternating periods of greater and lesser control. In retrospect, certain fundamental changes were already evident in 1985. Gorbachev was in power and *perestroyka* has begun. A musicologist of the younger generation, Daiga Mazvērsīte, recalls that as late as 1985 she was summoned before the Conservatory pro-rector, Dz. Kļaviņš. Supposedly, information had surfaced that Mazvērsīte admired the cultural achievements of Latvia's bourgeois period had denigrated those of Soviet Latvia. The pro-rectors

---

20 In contrast to Dambis's characterization of it, official Soviet ideology defined social realism as art that is socialist in content and national in form.

threatened to expell her from the institution, because musicologists must regarded as champions of Soviet ideology. Their charge was to educate the populace and serve as intermediaries between the people and the Party. Since music itself is semantically ambiguous, it was difficult to control it. Therefore, the proper education of young musicologists must be assured.

So much for the issue of freedom of thought and expression in the Soviet State. A crucial question remains, however, which Karnes raises in his latest article.[21] He quotes a statement made by the Latvian historian Irēne Šneidere concerning the problem of collaborationism, denunciations, and treachery, in Latvians themselves were involved. Indeed, the questions posed by these historians has not yet been confronted. The Cheka archives have not been opened, and thus nearly all information about KGB agents and informers remains hidden. This question has been raised countless times since Latvia regained its independence, usually before elections. However, decisions have always been postponed. As a result, coming to terms with our history has remained but a wish, since the prevailing view in Latvian society is that although the Soviets are gone, they left behind a kind of Stalinist "time bomb" in the form of the Cheka archives. Opening them, it is argued, will hurt innocent people, mainly surviving family members, because many of the guilty are already dead. The information gained in the present study, both direct and indirect, suggests that Soviet authorities compromised many people in an effort to divide groups of intellectuals and to cultivate an atmosphere of distrust among individuals.

Considering the situation in Latvia today, I would suggest that a brave and honest confrontation with our history would provide a new opportunity for society to understand itself, describe itself, and solidify a collective sense of identity. This in turn would encourage *autopoiesis*, fostering growth and development of the society as a whole.

Conclusion

The life histories considered in this article reveal that the four periods of Soviet rule in Latvia were characterized by different attitudes toward the creative unions. Stalin's era has left memories of violence, deportations, arrests, and persecutions of dissenters. Brutal re-education forced people to observe outward loyalty to the Soviet ideology. People's emotional experiences may be understood in terms of their instinct for survival. And there were frequent examples of altruism. One should remember the words of Isaiah Berlin: that in our day, living in relative safety, it is all too easy to judge.

The Khrushchev era has gone down in history as the period of "the Thaw," characterized by denounciation of the Stalin cult, which encouraged people to

---

21 Karnes, "Soviet Musicology and Contemporary Practice: A Latvian Icon Revisited," *Musikgeschichte in Mittel- und Osteuropa* 12 (2008): 14-25.

return to the patterns of normal life. However, the artistic values still had to accord with Party guidelines. In Latvia, the effects of the Thaw were negligible. After the national Communist Berklāvs was removed from office and exiled in 1957, his replacement, Pelše, began his rule of intrigue. Although there was no longer the threat of brutal deportations, Pelše nonetheless victimized the citizenry.

L. Brezhnev's rule was the longest and became known as the era of stagnation. Creative professions were able to use this time to communicate with members of the societ via a kind of Aesopian language. Composers wrote works that did not comply with Party directives, and Soviet authorities largely accepted that, for their authority no longer scared people. New means of repression were milder than they had been earlier.

With Gorbachev came with the era of *perestroyka*, and an attempt to humanize Soviet authority. However, the Soviet system did not survive this test. It collapsed by itself. For members of the Latvian creative intelligentsia, as they were called in Soviet times, how to deal with their recent Soviet past remains an open question.

Interviews cited in this essay (all in Riga):

Pauls Dambis, 5 December 2008; Oļģerts Grāvītis, 12 November 2008, 3 December 2008; 14 January 2009; Valda Kalniņa, 26 January 2009; Imants Kalniņš, 3 December 2008; Arnolds Klotiņš, 5 December 2008; Ruta Līcīte, 6 January 2009; Daiga Mazvērsīte, 8 January 2009; Uģis Prauliņš, 4 December 2008.

Manuscripts cited in this essay (all in private collection):

Ludvigs Kārkliņš, autobiography; Jānis Līcītis, reminiscences

Rūta Stanevičiūtė

ÉCRITURE FÉMININE?
On Some Intertextual Gestures in Works by Contemporary Lithuanian Women Composers

An investigation of changes that occurred in the Lithuanian musical scene by the turn of the twenty-first century reveals a true boom of creative activity among women composers. At the present time, women composers make up one-third of the Lithuanian Composers' Union, while the percentage of female students at the Lithuanian Academy of Music and Theatre exceeds fifty percent. Moreover, women composers hold half of the artistic director seats of contemporary music festivals. Indeed, the changes relating to the place of women composers in Lithuanian society have been both quantitative and qualitative. It should be noted that, in recent years, works by women have received major prizes at the annual Best Work of the Year Awards held by the Composers' Union, and they have also been received considerable recognition at the International Rostrum of Composers in Paris. In the words of Lithuanian musicologist Asta Pakarklytė,

> Today it would be hard to imagine Lithuania's most important and largest contemporary music festival, *Gaida*, without the names of Onutė Narbutaitė and Raminta Šerkšnytė, whose compositions have been included in the CD collections of the best Lithuanian works for several years in a row, and have been recognised several times as the best works at the Work of the Year Awards organised by the Lithuanian Composers' Union. Their names appear in Lithuanian music repertoires just as often as the names of male composers, and they are perhaps even more well known to the international music community. [Other] composers of the young generation walk similar paths, in both local and international musical arenas.[1]

We should not fail to mention that, prior to the 1970s, when Onutė Narbutaitė made her debut on the Lithuanian musical scene, Konstancija Brundzaitė (1942-71) was the only Lithuanian woman composer to have achieved broad recognition. Indeed, it was the 1970s that marked the turning point in the history of women composers in Lithuania. Since then, four or five women composers have become recognized in each decade. And presently, there are more than

---

[1] Asta Pakarklytė, "A Broken Glass—*cherchez la femme*. The Social Roles of Lithuanian Women Composers and Their Transformations," *World New Music Magazine* (18 October 2009), 90-91.

twenty women composers figuring prominently in the contemporary Lithuanian musical scene.

To be sure, a number of expectations, affected by the radical political and cultural changes experienced by Lithuanian society, have taken root in the Republic's contemporary-music environment in the years since regaining independence. These expectations have shaped hermeneutical approaches to understanding music in such a way that one is inclined to look for reflections of the changing social and cultural reality in the works of contemporary composers themselves. Such approaches have also determined the critical reception of music composed by women. However, the aesthetic and stylistic diversity of creations by women has hindered the identification of a common musical tendency in their works. And thus, their gender-defined, socio-cultural positions and their specific "feminine sensitivity" have been regarded as the foundation of their musical imagination, a kind of common denominator. Such quasi-feminist readings are common even in music criticism that has no relation to the feminist tradition. (In this context it should be noted that the feminist tradition is generally quite weak in Lithuania, and there are no manifestations of feminist musicology whatsoever.) I shall cite a few examples that typify this trend in Lithuanian music criticism:

> [Narbutaitė's music] radiates subtle lyricism and testifies to the extraordinary sensitivity of the composer, as well as to the discipline that directs the repetitive, permutational flow of her masterful sound constructions.[2]

> The metaphorical, poetically evocative, or philosophically perplexing titles of recent works by Loreta Narvilaitė impart a certain mysterious or ineffable aura to her music, thereby becoming a distinctive sign for this young Lithuanian composer.[3]

> Onutė Narbutaitė's music has a remarkable power of attraction. The composer seems to be fully transfused with imaginary sounds, which she then conveys to the audience. The power of her work depends upon the sincerity of experience.[4]

---

2 Danuta Mirka, "IV polsko-litewska sesja muzykologyczna," in *W kręgu muzyki litewskiej*, ed. Krzysztof Droba (Kraków, 1997), 223.
3 Eglė Gudžinskaitė, "Loreta Narvilaitė's Aural Metaphors," *Lithuanian Music Link* 7 (October 2003/March 2004) (online; available at http://www.mic.lt/en/classical/info/330) (accessed 13 May 2009).
4 Reinhard Schulz, review published in the *Süddeutsche Zeitung*; cited Linas Paulauskis, "Onutė Narbutaitė: The Power of the Sincerity of Experience," *Lithuanian Music Link*, 13 (October 2006/ March 2007) (online; available at http://www.mic.lt/en/info/117) (accessed 13 May 2009).

The composition [*Sense Six* (2004) by Raminta Šerkšnytė] touches all five physical senses in turn, and thereby reaches the transcendental sixth—the emotional climax of the work.[5]

For half an hour, the audience [listening to the oratorio *Songs of Sunset and Dawn* by Raminta Šerkšnytė] is invited to dive into a relaxing ritual of sound, to experience the pleasure of listening (rare enough in modern works), to forget mundane life, and to wander into spheres of exalted poetry and music.[6]

A blank sheet of paper that starts wrinkling when a few drops of water are sprinkled over its surface, a wrinkling that forms some kind of pattern or contour: this is the image that has been recently haunting the imagination of Justė Janulytė, whose music is propelled by the need to embody in sound her most utopian ideas, fantasies, and impressions. . . . In all of her distinctly intimate and introspective pieces, Janulytė carefully moulds the overall form, swarming with tiny, hardly perceptible musical events.[7] (Veronika Janatjeva)

Tastefully strung together out of a number of different styles and moods, [Diana Čemerytė's *Lamentation: A Sound-Rose in Memory of the Women of Ravensbrück*] is most hypnotic in the fragile moments bordering on silence. For this piece, the author chose the expression of a cold beauty, avoiding the straightforward reflection upon its atrocious subject.[8]

Raminta Šerkšnytė's *Mountains in the Mist*—an elevated, colourful and dramatically intense neo-romantic soundscape—displays her particular skill at orchestral writing. Ugnė Giedraitytė tends more toward chamber expression; her *Panneau* reveals her typical warm, serene moods and a certain "French" elegance. . . . Justė Janulytė's music . . . is described both as "monolithic" and "organic"; her *Aquarelle* is like a long and deep breath, a continuous dynamic wave. (Linas Paulauskis, liner notes to the CD *ZoomIn7*, a compilation of works by young Lithuanian women composers)[9]

---

5 Justė Janulytė, "Raminta Šerkšnytė's Stunt Flight from Norway to Argentina," *Lithuanian Music Link* 9 (October 2004/March 2005) (online; available at http://www.mic.lt/en/classical/info/287) (accessed 13 May 2009).

6 Paulauskis, "Raminta Šerkšnytė: Songs of Sunset and Dawn" *Lithuanian Music Link* 14 (April/September 2007) (online; available at http://www.mic.lt/en/classical/info/166) (accessed 13 May 2009).

7 Veronika Janatjeva, "Justė Janulytė: Water on Blank Paper," *Lithuanian Music Link* 11 (October 2005/March 2006) (online; available at http://www.mic.lt/en/classical/info/252) (accessed 13 May 2009).

8 Ramunė Kazlauskaitė, "Diana Čemerytė: Thirty Percent of Silence," *Lithuanian Music Link* 9 (October 2004/March 2005 (online; available at http://www.mic.lt/en/classical/info/294) (accessed 13 May 2009).

9 Paulauskis, "Generation of 21st Century: Young Lithuanian Composers," liner notes to CD *Zoom In 7: New Music from Lithuania* (Lithuanian Music Information and Publishing Centre LMIPCCD 054, 2008).

As one can see from these quotations, works by Lithuanian women composers are often characterised by identifying some particular imprint that the creator's personality has made upon them. Symptomatically, feminine creativity is associated with a specifically feminine sensitivity, as well as with such qualities as lyricism, subtlety, intimacy, empathy, elegance, refinement, elaboration, and so forth. Indeed, when a work does not match this established conception of feminine creativity, it is typically interpreted as symptomatic of the same in its declarative opposition to these very stereotypes.

Such quasi-feminist readings of works by Lithuanian women might be dismissed as superficial and based on cultural fiction. Nevertheless, as noted by musicologists coming from diverse theoretical backgrounds (such as Mieczysław Tomaszewski, Richard Taruskin, or Jean-Jacques Nattiez), even the most liberal interpretations of music are related to certain structural characteristics of musical compositions.[10] With this in mind, I shall investigate what lies behind the concept of specific feminine sensitivity supposedly serving as a foundation for musical imagination, in an attempt to find an answer to the question of whether works by Lithuanian women composers really do represent the "Other" in the contemporary Republic's musical life.

2.

When speaking of specific feminine sensitivity or mere femininity, it is worthwhile to look at the classical feminist definitions of the terms. Especially influential concepts, suitable for the analysis of female self-expression in art, were formulated in French feminist theory in the 1970s. In the work of Hélène Cixous, Monique Wittig, Luce Irigaray, and Julia Kristeva, femininity is defined through psychosexual difference from masculinity. The specificity of feminine consciousness and experience, the feminine "I," and the authenticity of her personality in the works these authors is related to the concept of "feminine writing" (*écriture féminine*). American feminist Elaine Showalter defines feminine writing as "the inscription of the feminine body and female difference in language and text."[11] Such feminine writing is identified with strategies "that defer and differ from male methods" and "emphasize the feelings and experiences of women." "On the one hand," as Cixous observes, "there is the masculine position of obedience with its concomitant fear and desire for control; on the other,

---

10 Cf. Mieczysław Tomaszewski, *Interpretacja integralna dzieła muzycznego* (Kraków, 2000); Richard Taruskin, *Text and Act: Essays on Music and Performance* (Oxford and New York, 1995); and Jean-Jacques Nattiez, *Music and Discourse: Toward a Semiology of Music* (Princeton, NJ, 1990).
11 Elaine Showalter, "Feminist Criticism in the Wilderness," in Elaine Showalter, ed., *The New Feminist Criticism: Essays on Women, Literature, and Theory* (London, 1986), 249.

there is the feminine position of risk, characterized by openness, generosity, and a refusing to destroy."[12] However, this distinction between the feminine and the masculine is not automatically attributed to correspondingly masculine and feminine creative works. Rather it represents an ideal model of gendered creativity.

The concepts of femininity and "feminine writing" developed in the works of these writers are problematic and have frequently been criticised by representatives of feminist theory as well as scholars from other fields. Nevertheless, I have drawn attention to the concept of feminine writing not because of its feminist context, but on account of the relationship between this concept and post-structural concepts of writing and text, since I find this reference to be significantly more productive when searching for representations of femininity within the artistic work. In its peculiar ways, feminist criticism develops the post-structuralist concepts of a polyphonic, heteroglossic text (Mikhail Bakhtin) and of polysemic texts, writing, and intertextuality (Roland Barthes), essentially defining feminine writing as "a writing of the other."[13] So-called feminine strategies turn this intertext into an instrument for listening closely to the Other. Paraphrasing Barthes, one might say that, in music, this way of creation produces writing-listening or text-listening.[14]

Such a position, whereby the creator acts as an attentive, open, and non-confronting reader/listener of cultural texts, is especially common among Lithuanian women composers of the present day. First of all, this position manifests itself through numerous cultural inspirations and connotations in their works. This is characteristic not only of those works that openly recompose the music of other composers (such as the series of works dedicated to classical composers by Onutė Narbutaitė), but also of those frequently appearing cases in which the composer uses well known, previously written compositions as a point of reference, while neither promoting nor disguising the original source of inspiration.

I would like to illustrate this latter statement by taking a look at some typical musical examples. As the "source of inspiration," I took two pieces by Bronius Kutavičius: the cantata *Two Birds in a Thick of the Woods* for soprano, oboe, piano and tape, set to a text by Rabindranath Tagore (1978); and *Three Sonnets by A. Mickiewicz* for soprano and strings (1992). I shall focus upon paraphrases of musical gestures evident in these works as exemplified in three compositions by two Lithuanian women of different generations: *Sonnet à l'amour* for tenor and guitar (1999), set to a text by Oscar Milosz, and *Pas de deux* for mezzo-soprano

---

12 Quoted after Susan Sellers, "Écriture féminine," in Cheris Kramarae and Dale Spender, eds., *Routledge International Encyclopedia of Women: Global Women's Issues and Knowledge* (New York and London, 2000), 469-70.
13 Ibid.
14 On Barthes's concept of writing-reading, see his *S/Z: En Essay*, trans. Richard Miller (New York, 1974).

and cello (2006), set to a text by Jacques Prévert, both by Onutė Narbutaitė (b.1956); and the cantata-oratorio *Songs of Sunset and Dawn* for soprano, mezzo-soprano, tenor, bass, choir, and symphony orchestra (2007), based on texts by Rabindranath Tagore, by Raminta Šerkšnytė (b.1975).

3.

The two works I have selected by Kutavičius, *Two Birds* and *Three Sonnets*, were composed at different times and for very different reasons, yet they feature similar themes and share aspects of structure. The thematic axis of both works is the loss of a love that represents meaning in life, a resultant longing that turns into desperation, and a final withdrawal and seclusion suggestive of existential loss. Although the cantata, *Two Birds*, narrates the encounter of two persons and the sonnets meditate on yearning for one's homeland, the musical settings suggest a searching for a deeper, transcendental essence hidden behind seemingly traditional instances of intimate lyricism. One should note that, in spite of composer's nationalist aspirations, which come to the fore in his famous series of so-called "pagan oratorios," Kutavičius's worldview was formed by the Christian tradition. It is within the context of this tradition that I will interpret several exemplary musical gestures found in these two works.

In cantata *Two Birds in a Thick of the Woods*, the drama reaches its climax in the third movement, a climax signalled by the very first lines of poetic text: "It was midday when you left." Using sparing means, the composer manages to reproduce both the grief of the lyric character and the seemingly contrasting background of reality. Midday represents the time when the abundance and plenitude of the natural world blossoms, when all gifts, both natural and supernatural, are displayed with especial clarity. Loss and rejection are even more clearly revealed against such a background. The composer conveys such images, suggested by the poetic text, by employing the iconic symbolism so characteristic of his music. The "exploding" radiance of the sun and the flourishing of nature are expressed through a minutely varying instrumental pedal, most often based on the interval of an open fifth, while the singer's grief and her sense of rejection are revealed through a repetitively expanding melodic line that is formed from two symbolic intervals—the fifth (emptiness) and the second (complaint)—ornamentally woven around the sustained pedal G. These techniques reveal the major contrast in the work, between the feeling of loss against the background of daily routine, the image of which is created through the imitation of an unsophisticated, nearly homely kind of music-making (Example 1).

Example 1. Bronius Kutavičius, Two Birds in a Thick of the Woods (1978), beginning of third movement

This linking of existential event, state of mind, and a specific time of day is common in Kutavičius's music. One might even regard it as a certain consistent element, a particular vocabulary of musical gestures that recur in a number of works by the composer. In this respect, his symbolism resembles the logic of the liturgical cycle of hour, when the time of day is linked to a particular religious event, as well as to the act of worship.

Let us now consider another example of Kutavičius's stylistic language, taken from the *Three Sonnets by A. Mickiewicz*: the first movement, entitled "The Akkerman Steppe." The poetic text depicts an evening landscape; all of nature becomes quiet, and the lyric character captures even the slightest sound heard in the twilight silence. The singer strains his ears in a desperate attempt to hear a voice from Lithuania. His longing turns to despair as "nobody calls. . ." In Kutavičius's works, the evening symbolism encountered in this song has a fairly stable circle of connotations. On the one hand, evening is the time when all daily events and works, as well one's present stage of life, are reviewed. On the other hand, evening represents a borderline of transition into another dimension, a time of night, which is also a time of repose and metaphysical encounters. Within such a context, the inability to hear the longed-for "voice" acquires a deeper or even supernatural dimension. This situation, an attempt to hear a voice of affirmation from "the beyond" is emblematic in Kutavičius's music, where it is invoked most often in the endings of works or in the codas of middle movements. In "The Akkerman Steppe," this act of listening (expectation) and the subsequent sense of despair (lack of fulfilment) are expressed the same way, by means of melodic dissolution and *Sprechgesang*. This is seen in the contour of the question, and in the repetition of just a single sound, imitating steps (Example 2).

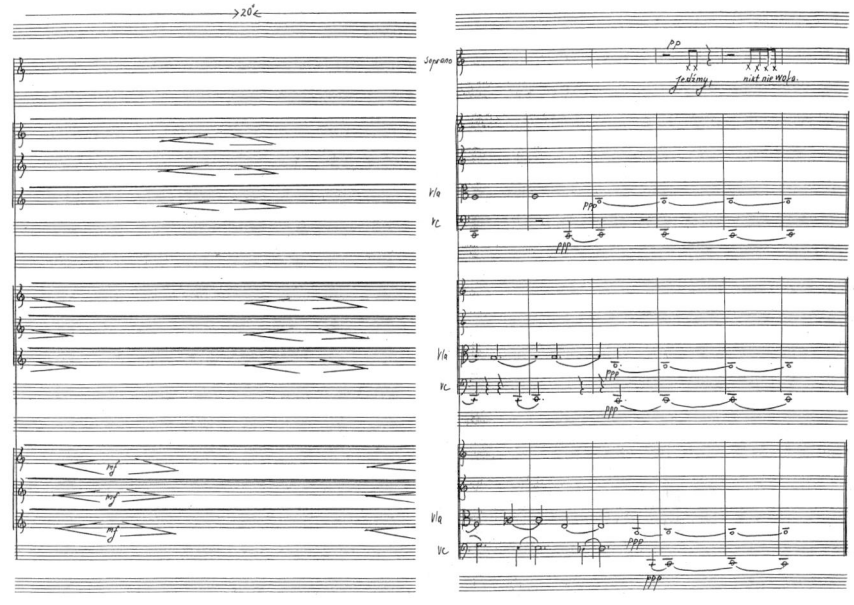

Example 2. Kutavičius, Three Sonnets by A. Mickiewicz (1992), first movement (fragments)

4.

Both *Pas de deux* and *Sonnet à l'amour* by Onutė Narbutaitė narrate stories of love, or, more precisely, of the impossibility and destructive power of love. This is revealed with especial clarity in *Pas de deux*, an original paraphrase of the "song without words." Most of the vocal part consists of vocalisations on the letters "a" and "m"—as "remainders," as it were, of the word *amour* (Example 3).

The vocalisation then unfolds from lamenting, stepwise intonations into lengthy, extended sighs, and bursts into full-blown melody on only three short occasions: twice in the vocalist's short "post scriptum," and once in the extended, summarizing cello monologue. At the end of the piece, following that monologue, we can identify a paraphrase of the scene enacted in Kutavičius's "The Akkerman Steppe"—the question ("Who is there?") followed by silence ("Nobody"), and the desperation born of unfulfilled expectations, symbolically expressed through repetition of a single note, this time imitating heartbeat (Example 4).

177

Example 3.   Onutė Narbutaitė, Pas de deux (2006), beginning

Example 4.   Narbutaitė, Pas de deux, excerpt

Narbutaitė has always admitted the influence of Kutavičius upon her music. However, such an obvious reconfiguration of a specific musical gesture borrowed from him is a fairly rare occurrence in her music. And undoubtedly, Narbutaitė is the most refined and subtle reader and reinterpreter of cultural texts by other Lithuanian artists. Such inspiration can even be seen as providing a principal source for her music, and her dialogue with tradition unfolds in her works in the variety of ways. Speaking of Kutavičius's influence, one may trace a number of "borrowed" intonations in Narbutaitė's compositions, musical gestures and other elements that have, in her works, become somehow naturalized. And in any case, it is much more common that the relationship between works by Narbutaitė those of her predecessors is barely tangible. We find such an instance in the relationship between her *Sonnet à l'amour* and those same, the above-mentioned works by Kutavičius. We can identify similar intonational cells, but the aesthetics and style of the works differ significantly. Nonetheless, Narbutaitė seems to "borrow" the imitation of homely music-making from her predecessor. Yet even here, she uses this similar intonation to create an entirely different atmosphere, one that invokes the music of the troubadours and thus creates a refined interpretation of perhaps that most complex of poetic genres, the sonnet (Example 5).

Example 5. Narbutaitė, *Sonnet à l'amour* (1999), third movement

5.

In this context, we might recall another piece by a Lithuanian composer based on texts by Oscar Milosz: *Le Silence*, written by Osvaldas Balakauskas in 1984. Later on, in 2002, the composer returned to Milosz's texts to compose the opera *La Lointaine*. These are emblematic compositions by Balakauskas, with respect to the influence of the French cultural tradition on his works. Nevertheless, it is obvious that, in selecting texts by this famous expatriate poet—who is so important for Lithuanian cultural self-consciousness—for her *Sonnet à l'amour*, Narbutaitė is in fact confronting Balakauskas's interpretations of Milosz's work. She rejects the instrumental treatment of voice that is so characteristic of Balakauskas's work, as well as the cultural connotations carried by both the poet and Balakauskas himself. Indeed, Narbutaitė reads Milosz's poetry and transforms it into mere sounds, thus treating it as a primary, sonic resource text. And in doing so, she effectively rejects more common, semantically loaded readings of it. Such a manner of "reading" cultural texts is characteristic of her work in general. The composer always strives to reveal what one or another text or image means to her personally.

That is why I have related the vocal compositions by Narbutaitė to the creative impulse of Kutavičius, since these two composers cross paths with respect to their exceptional representations of subjectivity in music, which, in turn, determine the functions of voice in their works. Within this context I would like to refer to Gary Tomlinson's book *Metaphysical Song* (1999), in which he profoundly outlines how, on the one hand, "voice locates subject in the world," and, on the other, how "this general function of envoicing subjectivity through singing" manifests itself.[15] Within the context of those musical works I have discussed above, Tomlinson's remark that "in the whole history of human society . . . voice opens to perception invisible realms" seems to be very important. This enables one to define "singing as a potent experience of a metaphysics as well as of a physics."[16]

With respect to the compositions in question, the experience of "a metaphysics through singing" might help to explain the shifting in expressions and representations of subjectivity that characterize their relation to Lithuanian musical culture as a whole. Both Kutavičius and Narbutaitė clearly confront the forms of vocality established in contemporary music, which represent the "non-identity of self" (Theodor W. Adorno).[17] The said instrumental use of the voice in Balakauskas's music might be one of the many vocal forms common in modern music, representing this type of subjectivity. Kutavičius and Narbutaitė both revert to tradition by relating metaphysical experiences with love poetry. However, the dramatic tensions of present-day culture are reflected in their use of new vocal forms and semantics.

Rejection: This state of mind, which is common to all four compositions considered above, is symptomatic in itself. Taking into account the fact that, in the Christian tradition, *love* is regarded as a fundamental attribute of God, it becomes clear just how differently Kutavičius and Narbutaitė express their longings for metaphysical closeness, and their despair that results from the subsequent lack of fulfilment of expectations. In Kutavičius's music, the state of rejection is expressed by way of the fragmented melody, while expectation is communicated by way of the metaphor of longing for the "voice from beyond." In Narbutaitė's works, rejection is expressed by the inability to sing, and divine closeness is associated with matters that cannot be represented in music. This is

---

15 Gary Tomlinson, *Metaphysical Song: An Essay on Opera* (Princeton, NJ, 1999), 6.
16 Ibid., 4.
17 Quoted after Tomlinson, *Metaphysical Song*, 129.

especially evident in *Pas de deux*, where *touch* or *feel* become attributes of closeness.

6.

Before finishing, let us briefly look at the score of the cantata-oratorio *Songs of Sunset and Dawn* by Raminta Šerkšnytė. First of all, it is worth noting that this representative of the youngest generation of Lithuanian composers studied composition with Balakauskas and later took master courses with a number of famous composers throughout the world. Despite these circumstances, it is perhaps most interesting to examine the ways in which the influence of Kutavičius, acknowledged by the composer herself, can be traced within her works, which embody an entirely different aesthetic and stylistic orientation.

The link to Kutavičius is, first of all, indicated by Šerkšnytė's choice of text. When Kutavičius selected texts by Tagore for his *Two Birds in a Thick of the Woods* in the 1970s, they had a certain cult status in Lithuania. They were new translations of foreign poetry, and they reflected the popularity of Eastern cultures and aesthetics at that time. Today, Tagore's poems and the cultural tendencies they represent seem to exist beyond the borders of Lithuanian culture itself. But a deliberately non-confrontational relationship to Lithuanian musical traditions and even to the cultural images fancied by her teachers is characteristic of Šerkšnytė in general. In this respect, she is quite different from many representatives of her generation. She avoids experimentation, feeling more at home with traditional scenes and academic contexts.

Šerkšnytė's *Songs of Sunset and Dawn* is related to Kutavičius's work not only by virtue of its poetic source, however, but also by its more general framework—the linkage of emotional states with the hours of the day. Just like Kutavičius, she employs a tripartite form, creating musical images of day/evening, night, and morning. As in some works by Narbutaitė, the influence of Kutavičius is evident. But the overall direction adopted by Šerkšnytė is entirely different from that chosen by Narbutaitė. While Narbutaitė's reinterpretations of predecessor might be referred to as a kind of "deep listening," Šerkšnytė walks an entirely opposite path, heading towards something that might be called "easy listening." Her impressive, quasi-programmatic compositions often remind one of a movie soundtrack. (I would not, however, make any distinction in value between their works.) To illustrate Šerkšnytė's different direction, we should consider more closely an example from her cantata-oratorio.

The third *Songs of Sunset and Dawn* is entitled "Morning. Eternal Morning." While the *actual* morning in this music is expressed through a kind of repetitive jubilation, with numerous iconic imitations of natural sounds characteristic of the works of Kutavičius and others, Šerkšnytė's musical image of *eternal* morning stands in sharp contrast to the character of the rest of the piece. Paradoxically, this latter music is based upon a musical gesture I discussed earlier—that is, the repetition of a single note with the use of *Sprechgesang*. Imitations of the "harmony of the spheres," briefly heard in the background, also prompt one to recall another musical gesture that is also frequently employed by Kutavičius in order to express the encounter with a kind of supernatural mystery (as at the end of his opera *The Bear*, for instance). And yet, in Šerkšnytė's music the use of this gesture assumes an entirely different meaning than in all of the above-mentioned works. "Eternal Morning" stands in such marked contrast to the surrounding music of both the movement itself and the multi-movement work as a whole that one comes to feel that this part of the experience represents something that the composer has not yet fully realized, and that, in order to represent it, she has had to rely upon this quasi-quotation, using images and sounds construed by others (Example 6).

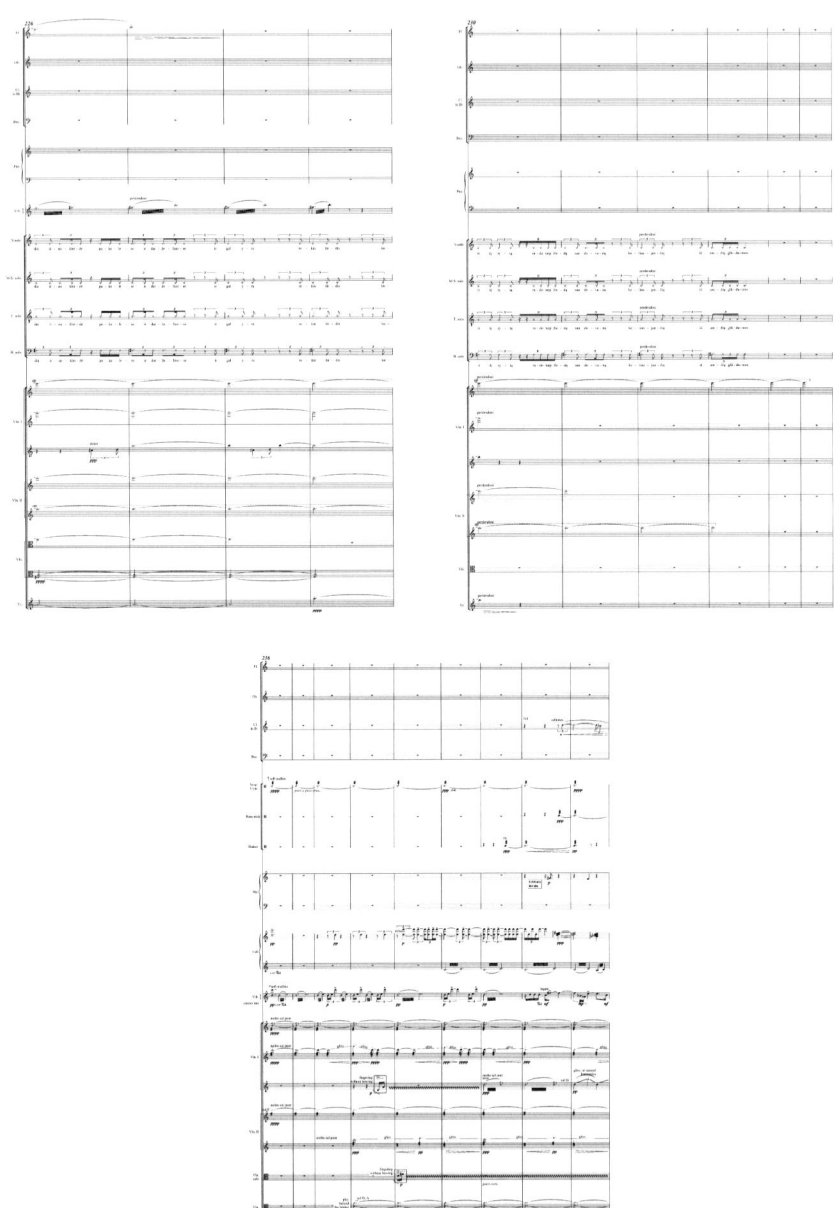

Example 6a. Raminta Šerkšnytė, *Songs of Sunset and Dawn* (2007), third movement: "Eternal Morning" (fragment)

7.

In this essay, I have presented several examples of musical reinterpretations in works by Lithuanian women composers in order to emphasise that "feminine writing" may be qualified not as a *confrontation* with the "Other," but, on the contrary, as an attentive or even deliberately non-confrontational *listening to* the "Other." Although the idea of such "feminine writing" extends well beyond those kinds of cases considered here, this notion seems, in the case of Lithuanian women composers especially helpful in our attempt to define certain tendencies. These tendencies, I would suggest, arise not on account of psychosexual feminine differences, but rather on account of socio-cultural circumstances. I would say that, first of all, they reflect the fact that women composers today represent the most active segment of Lithuania's culture-consumers, naturally deploying their deep knowledge of tradition for the purpose of individual artistic expression. Therefore, one should always be careful when analysing the manifestations of intertextuality in works written by women. To be sure, intertextual strategies do not always result in the creation of distinctly individual artists or works. Yet as the Russian cinema critic and culture theorist Almira Ousmanova observed when commenting on similar phenomena in women's cinematography, "theorists understand that to realise 're-vision,' to look at the past with clear and fresh eyes, and to see difference differently are especially important tasks of women's cinema."[18]

---

18 Almira Ousmanova, "Re-Making Love: Love and Sexual Difference in Soviet and Post-Soviet Cinema," in *Gender, Media, and Mass Culture* (Vilnius, 2005), 188 and 190.

Vizbulīte Bērziņa

"ON A ROAD TO HELL"
Jēkabs Graubiņš and the Soviet Regime

"Militarism overwhelmed pacifism. Brutal force suppressed human honor, human rights and human kindness... Broadcasting and sound-films overflowed with the screaming of Hitler, Musolini, and Stalin, screaming with hoarse or croaking voices... The world was on a road to hell!" This is how the Latvian historian Edgars Andersons described the situation in Europe at the end of the 1930s.[1] For Latvia, this "road" commenced on 5 October 1939, with the establishment of Soviet military bases, which had been forced upon Latvia as a result of the Molotov-Ribbentrop Pact, concluded between the Soviet Union and Nazi Germany. The final stretch of this road, which led to the destruction of the Republic, was cloaked in a heavy cult of personality. "The people's leader, with his clever mind and vast experience, will know how to defend the Latvian nation from external menace, as well as from great internal shocks," the paper "*Brīvā zeme*" (The Free Land) assured its readers.[2] The campaign of lavishing praise upon the Republic of Latvia's last, authoritarian president, Kārlis Ulmanis, reached its culmination in December 1939, with celebrations marking the fortieth anniversary of his political activities. "One might be surprised at the degree to which the Latvian intelligentsia forfeited its sovereignty and allowed itself to get carried away praising its leader," remarked the historian Aivars Stranga. This was, Stranga continues, "a situation that reduced the nation's vigilance and sense of danger, and encouraged people to place overly great faith upon [Ulmanis's] leadership."[3]

One might be tempted to level this charge against the composer Jēkabs Graubiņš as well, who, in January 1940, seemed to hop aboard the Ulmanis-praising bandwagon with his song, "Priecas mācība" (The wisdom of joy), with a text assembled from lines excerpted from Ulmanis's speeches. However, this text did not in fact praise the leader. It did not promise a happy life, nor did it advocate reliance upon political cleverness. Indeed, we can sense in it a kind of

---

This essay is based on a chapter of Vizbulīte Bērziņa's recent book, *Daudz baltu dieniņu. Jēkaba Graubiņa dzīvesstāsts* (Many bright days: The life of Jēkabs Graubiņš) (Riga, 2006), 170-180. It has been translated from the Latvian by Aviva Braun and Kevin C. Karnes.

1 Edgars Andersons, *Latvijas vēsture*, (Riga, 1984), vol. 2,
2 *Brīvā Zeme* (15 September 1939).
3 Ilga Gore and Aivars Stranga, *Latvijas neatkarības mijkrēslis: Okupācija* (Riga, 1992), 250-51.

behest, like a life-raft upon which one might hope to survive the coming dangers. "If you, my people, ever let go of and lose the wisdom of joy," Ulmanis was said to have counseled, "then know that this will be your end... But if this lives, so will the nation, and so will it live forever." How did Ulmanis understand this "wisdom"? Not, obviously, as some kind of Christian doctrine, but rather as a vision of the nation's glorious and heroic future. For those of us who survived the pressures of a half-century of Soviet occupation, the meaning of these words is, perhaps, somewhat different. It is a vision of freedom regained, a vision that kept the nation alive. Unfortunately, Graubiņš's song never reached its addressee. And half a year latter, the composer's primary concern became how to hide the manuscript, rather than how to get the work performed.

At that time, Graubiņš was still passing his days working for *Brīvā Zeme*. As an official newspaper, it had to please Latvia's new strategic "partner," and thus it trumpeted fanfares for Stalin's sixty-year jubilee, for the anniversary of the October Revolution, and for the Soviet "politics of peace," which promised a radiant future for Latvia, secured by "liberation from foreign oppression" and the Republic's union with the rest of "Sovietland." In this context, Graubiņš, as music reviewer, was compelled to limit himself to commenting only upon what happened in Riga's concert halls—and only that. Thus, Graubiņš persisted in an insular little sphere of music, reminding one ever more powerfully of George Bernard Shaw's ironic comparison of the reviewer's column with the padded room in a madhouse, where one is isolated from the surrounding noise. And meanwhile, musical life itself was reaching its apex, with such highlights as the premiere of Verdi's Requiem and *The Magic Flute* under Leo Blech.[4]

At one point, however, the music reviewer felt he could bear it no longer, and he dared to leave his "padded room" to take part in broader discussions, far removed musical affairs. At the end of 1939, three of Graubiņš's essays on the Latvianization of surnames appeared. Referring to the recent repatriation of many Baltic Germans, the author rejoiced in "this positive turn of capricious fate ... those fellow citizens forced upon long ago were leaving Latvia for good. And with them went those dubious Latvians who, in those fateful days, were forced to show their true faces. This opens up a new and free vista from which to contemplate the notion of *Latvianism*."[5] Thus, Graubiņš continued, this would also be the appropriate time to "repatriate" all German surnames, and with them all Russian and Polish names as well, which had been forced on this suppressed people, and finally to free oneself from the "hated stamp of the master."

A heated discussion flared up. Some thought, that the proposed Latvianization of surnames should be postponed until more normal times arrived. Others thought that such Latvianization was wholly unnecessary, since the Latvian

---

4   The Requiem was performed on 18 December 1938, and *The Magic Flute* on 15 February 1940.
5   *Brīvā Zeme* (25 November 1939).

people, however progressive the might appear, are conservatives deep inside. Professor E. Blese even argued that foreign surnames "do the Latvians credit; we can see how the powerful foreign influence was in our country, and yet we did not succumb to it." Moerover, "German surnames have already penetrated the Latvian psyche and are fully assimilated into our social life."[6] Graubiņš, with his characteristic zeal, regarded such assimilation as a mark of laziness, indifference, and indolence.[7]

Why should a music reviewer interfere in such matters, which are so far removed from music? Graubiņš's own writings provide the answer. He wished to rescue the "tree of Latvianism from dry rot," to open up an unobstructed path toward the attainment of Latvian national self-esteem and honor.

The Soviet military occupation of 17 June 1940, tore up the "tree of Latvianism" by its roots and severely tested the national consciousness. The production of music criticism came to an end, and music itself was now harnessed to the wheels of occupation propaganda. Concerts were dedicated to commemorating the events of the Republic's "liberation": the proclamation of Soviet Latvia, the acceptance of Latvia into the Soviet Union, and so on. The Latvian Opera was opened not only to guest-performances by the outstanding artists of Moscow and Leningrad, but to also to jugglers, acrobats, accordionists, whistlers, and the like, as well as to political speechifying.

The music reviewer for *Brīvais Zemnieks* (The Free Peasant)—as *Brīvā Zeme*—was renamed—tried his best to describe this newly politicized musical life. Yet, he never shed his sense of self-respect and national conscience. In some 180 reviews that he published that year, Graubiņš managed to avoid using such expressions and vocabulary as the "radiant ideals of socialism," concerts in "honor of" those in power, *stakhanovism*, members of the Central Committee, and so forth. The only exception to this was the appearance of the word *red* in the preface to a review of a concert celebrating the October Revolution. And this was made by an alien hand, as evidence preserved in the composer's archive reveals.[8] Graubiņš tried to compensate for his political evasions by penning very long reviews, in which he mentioned by name every one of the performers, singers, dancers involved. He was holding a magnifying glass up to each and every positive detail.

Soviet authorities called for cultivating "national culture" by engaging in folklore collection and research, and Graubiņš echoed this call in the form of an appeal for national self-assertiveness. "One must do everything possible to make people… aware of the spiritual values of their own music, to teach them to

---

6 *Rīts* (14 December 1939).
7 *Brīvā Zeme* (16 December 1939).
8 Jēkabs Graubiņš archive, Rakstniecības, Teatra un Mūzikas Vēstures Muzejs (Riga). The archive is not yet cataloged. On this and other primary sources pertaining to Graubiņš's life, see Bērziņa, *Daudz baltu dieniņu*, 316-17.

honor those values and to compare them with the values of other nations. One must teach people to understand that only by refusing to adapt to some abstract international standard and by expressing the substance of our own spirit (not that of other nations)... can we Latvians justify our existence in the world."[9]

Graubiņš approached the music of Soviet composers, which now flooded the airwaves, according to those criteria he had applied to his job as a critic during pre-Soviet times. His judgments were influenced neither by the titles of authors nor by "political dedications." So, Graubiņsh ignored the generally praising tone of reviews published in the semi-official paper *Padomju Latvija* [Soviet Latvia] of the widely proclaimed performance of Ivan Dzerzhinskïy's *Tikhiy Don* (Quiet Flows the Don), with a libretto based on Mikhail Sholokhov. Latvian critics found themselves in an awkward position after the Latvian premiere of this "first Socialistic opera" on 20 December 1940. One reviewer ambiguously praised the composer for not getting "carried away with musical phrasing and not drowning in an ocean of sounds."[10] Jānis Zālītis tried to put it mildly, writing extensively about the failure of the earlier Soviet operas and expressing thanks for this "first real opera to inspire what is best in the Soviet people."[11] Volfgangs Dārziņš, in turn, noted "the proximity of the opera to the folk-drama type, the emotional musical framework, and the overcoming of old operatic traditions." And he guardedly registered a single critique, against the "occasionally somewhat naked and hollow instrumentation."[12]

In this context, Graubiņš's review in *Brīvais Zemnieks* was like a fly in the ointment. He opened with the following statement:

> Aside from its ideologically captivating story, *Tikhiy Don* is no novelty; the content of Sholokhov's libretto is stronger then the composer's gift. Although the music itself cannot be spurned (it is neither banal nor cheap), it nevertheless does not live up to the stage events, and does not characterize the dramatic situations and personalities. Critics should wonder, sometimes, at the fact that, after Tchaikovsky and Rimsky-Korsakov, the Russian operatic stage could even briefly be won by music so un-dramatic and monotonous, and by an orchestra so colorless and feeble. Only the strong, ideologically fresh and dramatically satiated libretto saved this opera from becoming a fiasco already during its first performances. Now, as we know, this opera has lost its place in the repertoire and is rarely performed today. Therefore, it is the fault of neither [conductor] Tēodors Reiters nor the performers if their endeavor yielded no significant results.[13]

---

9 *Brīvais Zemnieks* (7 August 1940).
10 *Padomju Latvia* (14 December 1940).
11 *Padomju Latvija* (22 December 1940).
12 *Darbs* (24 December 1940).
13 *Brīvais Zemnieks* (22 December 1940).

Several days later, when Shostakovich's Piano Concerto was broadcast in Riga, the *Brīvais Zemnieks* reviewer was even more impolite. The work, he wrote, gives "the impression that its composer is constantly mocking and sneering at something, sometimes good-naturedly, and other times maliciously and rudely. Even in lyrical passages... Shostakovich finds opportunities for mocking satire... This is typical of so-called *applied music*, where there is no thought, no feeling, but only a juggling with sound—ideally, in the most highly original ways—that contradicts and mocks a normal sense of beauty."[14]

It would not be fair to read this review only as a confirmation of Graubiņš's aesthetic conservatism. Even today, we cannot deny that Shostakovich's Piano Concerto was, in the overall musical context of its time, a strongly pronounced example of an anti-romantic composition. And Graubiņš was probably not far from the truth when he suggested that one hears in this music grotesque and sarcastic musical images. But at that time, of course, he could not suggest, as soviet musicologists did in the 1980s, that Shostakovich was perhaps unmasking "the philistine environment, the banalities and heartlessness" of the society in which he lived.[15]

Graubiņš did not reject the new musical trend outright, and we can believe him when he admitted elsewhere his high esteem for Shostakovich's music. When the suite from Shostakovich's *Golden Age* was broadcast in October, for instance, Graubiņš confidently proclaimed that the composer was "the most remarkable among young contemporary Russian composers; he is not afraid of drastic, brilliant, and unconventional means of expression. His music is not 'beautiful' in the usual way. It does not flatter the ear and does not ravish, nor does it seek to lull you into a sleeplike trance. Rather, it seeks to excite and to make one feel anxious—and, at times, to make one laugh and feel joyful."[16] This same benevolent attitude was seen already in 1938, when Graubiņš heard, in both the *Golden Age* suite and in Shostakovich's Fifth Symphony, "great mastership, originality, brilliant talent"—as well as matchless musical humor, splendid orchestration, great melodic skill, and dazzling colors.[17]

But now back again to the review on the Piano Concerto, in which Graubiņš also which dealt with Aram Khachaturian's *Sinfonia*. With respect to the latter work, Graubiņš did not appreciate any of Khachaturian's rich themes, based on motives from his native Armenia. They were, the critic charged, drowned in the verbosity and prolixity of the setting. He took aim at the instrumentation as well, which, he felt, focused too strongly on timbral extremities and left the middle unfilled. "This one-sided approach," he argued, "revenges itself: in spite of the

---

14 *Brīvais Zemnieks* (25 December 1940).
15 B. M. Yarustovskïy, ed., *Muzïka XX veka* (Moscow, 1980), vol 2, p. 134.
16 *Brīvais Zemnieks* (26 October 1940).
17 *Brīvā Zeme* (26 February and 19 October 1938).

colorful orchestra, it puts the audience to sleep."[18] Graubiņš voiced similar objections to works by several other Soviet composers, as evidenced in other reviews of the period.

Soon, however, enough was enough. The writings of the freethinking critic caught the attention of the upper echelons of Soviet society. On 5 January 1941, the Russian newspaper *Proletarskaya Pravda*, the official newspaper of the Central Committee, published an article entitled "On the critic Graubiņš's Personal Taste and Yielding Editor." It was signed by Vasiliy Ardamatski, a special correspondent for the Radio Broadcasting Committee and Communist Party, and sent to Riga by the *Cheka*. In his essay, Ardamatski professed tolerance for the critic's personal views, but argued that the moment such views appears in a newspaper, they cease being merely personal. That is, such views must be kept to one's self. After all, Ardamatski continued, the correct orientation for music criticism was exemplified in the all-Union press, where Shostakovich was highly praised. As for Khachaturian, one must remember that he was decorated with the "Order of Lenin" and was the author of the *Poem for Stalin*. Moreover, Ardamatski charged, Graubiņš's editor had neglected his most important duty— to assure that criticism constitutes propaganda for Soviet art, which "was silenced in Latvia or bound to the bureaucratic criticism of the administration during the years of prevailing plutocracy."[19] At the beginning of 1941 another "crime," no less grave, was added to Graubiņš's account. Retelling this story will give us a better sense of the composer's personality, and will opens up an important vista on that horrible year more generally. We must, therefore, linger a bit on this story.

The background for this incident was the feverish preparation for the Ten-Day Cultural Exhibition (*Dekāde*) in Moscow, which was to take place in the autumn of 1941. The entire second half of the "horrible year" was devoted to this event. (This fact demonstrates the great "care" that the Soviet state was taking of now "flourishing" national Latvian culture.) This exhibition was to testify to the fact that "today Moscow is the highest cultural center of modern humanity. Its spectators are the most qualified in the entire world. And among them is the greatest man of the present day, the genius of all working people, the bearer of our future: Stalin." Thus the Latvian literary historian Roberts Pelše proclaimed in *Padomju Latvija*.[20] The same degree of attention was given to other Soviet nationalities as well; the best example was the Burjat-Mongol Exhibition, which was "recently celebrated with splendor and ovations."[21] The October Revolution, it was held, finally brought culture to this recently nomadic people—a process crowned by completion of the first Mongolian opera, created

---

18 *Brīvais Zemnieks* (25 December 1940).
19 *Proletarskaya Pravda* (5 January 1941).
20 *Padomju Latvija* (1941, 26 February).
21 Jēkabs Poruks, in *Padomju Latvija* (24 November 1940).

with Moscow's help. New works were now expected from the Latvians too, works displaying the Latvians' Socialist ideals. But it was just important, in the Moscow Exhibition, that Latvia introduce the city's inhabitants to Latvian achievements of earlier times.

Long before the arrival in Riga of the requisite specialists from Moscow, Jūlijs Lācis, the Soviet Latvian People's Commissar of Education, invited Jēkabs Graubiņš to serve as his musical assistant. The latter compiled lists of participants and "classic values." At the end of the year 1940, four representatives of the Committee for Cultural Affairs of the USSR High People's Commissariat arrived in Riga to help with the planning: the theater director N. Okhlopkov, the conductor A. Hauk, the ballet master A. Yermolaev, and the head of the delegation, V. Mesheteli—a figure of obscure profession, sent "surely, for political purposes," as the composer Jānis Mediņš later wrote.[22]

We would not be lingering over this group's first meeting with Latvia's most prominent musicians if its intentions had not exceeded the bounds of friendly collaboration. Soviet musicology remained silent about this incident, and so we must listen to the accounts of those who did not keep silent: the exiled. "In the 'horrible year,' when some Latvian musicians tried to flatter the occupiers by belittling the achievements of their own national culture, Graubiņš fearlessly raised his voice to try to silence such disparaging"; so recalled the literary critic Jānis Rudzītis in his obituary for Graubiņš.[23] The composer Jānis Cīrulis also wrote about this meeting in his own short obituary for the composer: "sentenced to death by the Bolsheviks in 1919, he met them again in 1940 and spoke impudently to the Russian music-*politruk*."[24] Another account of the event is given by the composer Imants Saks in his necrology: while "some Latvian musicians, music teachers, an opera director, and a well-known 'musicologist' cowardly humbled themselves, listening to Moscow's *politruk* disparaging the retarded nature of Latvian musical life… J. Graubiņš sat silently, looking out of the window… Suddenly he jumped to his feet and began to trash the entirety of Soviet music in all of its spheres. The opera conductor started to cry on the spot, and the Moscow man—a Russian Latvian—held his breath, for never had he heard such 'un-Stalinistic' speech in his whole limited life."[25] When Arvīds Šnornieks later reproached those Latvians who "where shameless enough to defame Latvian music during the Bolshevik period," he was probably recalling this same event.[26]

Wishing to preserve for future historians a testimony about the events of the "horrible year," Graubiņš himself penned an extended account of these fatal

---

22 Jānis Mediņš, *Toni un pustoni. Mana dzīve* (Stockholm, 1964), p. 143.
23 Jānis Rudzītis, "Sarkastiskais cīnītājs," *Latvija* (13 January 1962).
24 Jānis Cīrulis, "Savā ceļā gājējs," *Latvija* (4 January 1962).
25 Imants Saks, "Redziet, kāds cilvēks!" *Latvija Amerikā* (27 January 1962).
26 Arvīds Šnornieks, in *Izglītības Menešraksts* (1943), no. 2.

days and their consequences. The reader is therefore asked to tolerate a rather long quotation from the composer's manuscript, *Mana laika sejas* (The Faces of My Time), written in November 1942:

> J. Mediņš and Tēodors Reiters began telling the Moscow men how puny our achievements were, and that we are ashamed to show them to brilliant Moscow. Latvian music and musicians were all weak and tiny… Prof. [Jāzeps] Vītols too put in a few humble words. Nobody else spoke… I started to grow exited. This groveling before the Moscow nonentities seemed to me dishonorable …I asked to speak and began to enumerate our achievements, which can compete even with those of Russia and other great peoples. I mentioned our choir-singing culture… [our] symphonic music, as well as the new operas and ballets. Unexpectedly, [Emīls] Melngailis started to speak and disputed my words about the high level of our choral music… We have no songs, he said, that can compete with the chorus from Borodin's *Prince Igor*… Then spoke Okhlopkov. He considered my words about Latvian choral culture somewhat disparaging, as if I had done Latvian musical culture a disservice. For choir singing constitutes is the lowest form of musical development; it is a form that no nation lacks. But *opera*, you see, is music's highest product and greatest achievement. Therefore, the custom of the Moscow Exhibitions is to make opera performance the main object of all efforts and concerns. I couldn't leave this unanswered. I spoke again, and said: I don't consider opera to be a musical creation as high as Okhlopkov does. There are nations with great musical cultures, like the Finns, Norwegians, Englishmen, and Belgians who cannot present one single outstanding and popular opera. But we Latvians have some ten operas, which are no worse than the new operas that other nations have. Unlike some other nations in the Soviet Union, who had their operas written by composers sent from Moscow, we do not understand the need for such help and must reject it. I asked Okhlopkov how many operas the Burjats and Mongols have, whose Exhibition-operas he praised. (I knew by then, that Moscow had helped to fabricate them!) He did not give me an answer… Then Mesheteli spoke and started to twist my words on purpose. I protested from my seat, and the chairman Jēkabs Mediņš called me to order. But I could not restrain myself. Then Melngailis spoke again. He started with himself: how he, having two classes, couldn't earn his living during the Ulmanis years, and how many positions Graubiņš was holding and what a superfluous life he led… At this moment, professor [Ādolfs] Ābele and many others protested and did not allow him to continue. Mesheteli, too, seemed to have understood what kind of a person Melngailis was, and he asked him not to speak about personal matters.[27]

However, silencing Melngailis did not mean that Graubiņš's "heavy insult to the Moscow guests" (as it was described by H. Likums, head of the Exhibition Committee of the Latvian SSR) went unnoticed. For some time, Graubiņš's participation in the discussions was still tolerated. However, sensing Mesheteli's

---

27 Jēkabs Graubiņš, *Mana laika sejas*, unpublished manuscript in private collection.

hostile attitude toward him, he suffered silently. In *Mana laika sejas*, we find such testimony as this: "the Moscow men did not discuss anything with us Latvians, having resolved, apparently, all problems on their own."[28]

But soon, having been literally expelled from these meetings in the broadcasting studio, the "founding head of the Exhibition project" was excluded from further participation. And nobody protested. "But why wonder?" Graubiņš mused in his memoir of the events. "It seems that, by then, Jūlijs Lācis, the initiator of my project, was not only no longer a minister, but was in prison, awaiting the end. . . . When reflecting on my situation at the time of the Bolsheviks, I could no longer understand why I was spared [from the mass deportations of Latvian citizens to Siberia] on July 14: compositions forbidden, decried as a blasphemous critic in *Proletarskaya Pravda*, not trusted by the Mighty Ones in Moscow—to whom would the Siberian taiga be better suited?"[29]

One might ask what significance Graubiņš's heroic act truly had. It had no effect on discussions of the Moscow Exhibition, to say nothing about the fate of the Latvian people. I also doubt that it made any of his colleagues at the meetings even the least bit ashamed. And Graubiņš did indeed reach the Siberian taiga—only ten years later than he had expected. In a sense, the practical realists were right. Graubiņš had no diplomatic tact, and he had no understanding of the political situation. Isn't stubborn self-respect and respect for one's nation during hopeless times always the province of madmen? And an honest man's deeds cannot diverge from his words.

We are now at the end of this essay, but nothing has been said about Graubiņš's musical works during the "Horrible Year." This is because, simply, he produced nothing. Aside from a choral arrangement of "Ko maza būdama" (the score is lost) and an arrangement "Kur jāsi, kur brauksi?" for solo voices and piano, he wrote no music. And if he had, where would it have been performed? Soon after some of Graubiņš's arrangements were included in the ceremonial "Friendship of Nations" concert, the censors banned his "Songs of Lāčplēsis" and, soon, other works as well. Finally, broadcasting any of Graubiņš's music became taboo.

Unambiguous testimony to the perseverance of Lativan national pride can be found in the performance—despite orders—of Graubiņš's "Nāves ēja" (The March of Death) at the historical concert "Dziesmu vara" (The Power of Songs), held on 3 March 1941, when the audience left the concert hall before the performance of the final songs on the program: "The Song of Stalin" by Revutskïy, "Mighty Broad" by Dunaevskïy, and the Soviet "International." The participants in the "Dziesmu vara" concert defied authorities not only by contravening orders pertaining to this event, but by continuing to ignore the dictates of the Moscow Exhibition committee. As one of the participants in the concert, Jānis Rudzītis,

---

28 Ibid.
29 Ibid.

recalled a quarter-century later, "It seemed that neither the conductor (Ābele) nor members of the choir were interested in going to Moscow. We did not go to the final hearing. It did not interest us. And at that time, I got the feeling that we were a people quite peculiarly united."[30]

---

30 Jānis Rudzītis, in *Contrapunct* (1953), no. 23.

Musical Instruments

Werner Bachmann

DIE SKYTISCH-SARMATISCHE HARFE AUS OLBIA
Vorbericht zur Rekonstruktion eines unveröffentlichten im Kriege verschollenen Musikinstruments

Von 1920 bis 1945 befand sich in der Antikenabteilung der Staatlichen Museen in Berlin eine Winkelharfe (Abb. 1), die leider nie Dubliziert wurde und seit Kriegsende verschollen ist. Ob sie während des Krieges vernichtet oder unmittelbar danach entwendet wurde, läst sich nicht nachweisen. Es besteht zumindest noch ein Hoffnungsschimmer, daß dieses Instrument - wie viele andere Museumsobjekte - eines Tages irgendwo wieder auftaucht.

Es handelt sich um ein außergewöhnlich kunstvolles und reich verziertes Instrument, das trotz seines hohen Alters[1] relativ gut erhalten war. Als Vergleichsobjekt zur Harfe aus dem Kurgan von Pazyryk[2] ist es von besonderem Interesse.

Bei meinen Nachforschungen in Berlin fand ich in den Archiven des Deutschen Archäologischen Instituts und der Staatlichen Museen umfangreiches, noch unveröffentlichtes Schrift- und Bildmaterial zu dieser Harfe, das detaillierte Informationen über Fundort und Fundumstände sowie über Beschaffenheit, Bauweise, Material und Maße des Instruments liefert und eine exakte Dokumentation, eventuell auch eine originalgetreue Rekonstruktion dieses einmaligen Objekts ermöglicht.

Unter der Nummer 30857 wurde die Harfe am 3. Juli 1920 in das Inventar der Antikenabteilung (damals Antiquarium genannt) der Berliner Museen aufgenommen. Aus den Eintragungen in das Inventar geht hervor, dass das Instrument 1918 in einer Grabkammer bei Olbia (sie Abb. 13) zusammen mit zahlreichen weiteren Grabbeigaben aus Gold, Silber, Eisen, Keramik, Holz und Leder gefunden wurde. Diese Objekte konnten von Theodor Wiegand für die Antikensammlung der Berliner Museen, deren Direktor er seinerzeit war, erwor-ben werden. Als Zentrum eines im 6. Jahrhundert v. Chr. gegründeten altgrie-

---

1 Nach der Chronologie der sarmatischen Kultur (3. Jh. v. Chr. bis 3. Jh. n. Chr.; ihr geht eine Frühphase voraus, die man als Kultur der Sauromaten bezeichnet) ist diese Harfe der mittel - oder spätsarmatischen Periode (1. - 3. Jh. nach Chr.) zuzuordnen.
2 Aus der umfangreichen Literatur über die Pazyryk-Harfe seien hier nur einige wichtige Arbeiten genannt: S. I. Rudenko, Vtoroj pazyrykskij kurgan, Leningrad 1948; ders., Der zweite Kurgan von Pazyryk, Berlin 1951; ders., Frozen Tombs of Sibiria, London 1970; Bo Lawergren, The Harp of the Ancient Altai People, in: Second Confrence of the ICTM Study Group on Music Archaeology, Vol. I, Stockholm, November 1986; F. M. Karomatov, V. A. Meskeris, T. S. Vyzgo, Mittelasien (Musikgeschichte in Bildern, Leipzig 1987), Bd. II, S. 50 ff.; Bo Lawergren, The Ancient Harp from Pazyryk, in: Beiträge zur allgemeinen und vergleichenden Archäologie, Bd. 9 - 10, Mainz 1990, S. 111 ff.

chischen Stadtstaates gehörte Olbia seit dem 2. Jahrhundert v. Chr. zum Herrschaftsgebiet der Skythen. Auch andere omadisierende Völkerschaften und Stammesgemeinschaften, vor allem die Sarmaten[3], lassen sich schon einige Jahrhunderte vor unserer Zeitrechnung, mit Sicherheit und in größerer Anzahl seit dem 1. Jahrhundert in dieser Gegend nachweisen. Nach Aussage antiker Autoren, wie beispielsweise Diodor von Sizilien und Plinius, sind sie iranischer Herkunft.[4] Vom Osten her - aus dem Gebiet des südlichen Ural und vom Unterlauf der Wolga - drangen die sarmatischen Stammesverbände in die Steppenzone nördlich des Schwarzen Meeres und weit in den Donauraum vor. Die seit Ende des 19. Jahrhunderts sporadisch und seit 1901 systematisch durchgeführten Grabungen in Olbia bestätigen die antiken Berichte über die Bedeutung dieser von Milet aus gegründeten griechischen Niederlassung und die engen Handelsbeziehungen zu der nomadisierenden skythisch-sarmatischen Bevölkerung.

Abb. 1

Über die Fundumstände der Harfe sind wir durch handschriftliche Aufzeichnungen Theodor Wiegands genauestens informiert. Sie befinden sich im Wiegand-Nachlaß, der im Deutschen Archäologischen Institut in Berlin aufbe-

---

3 Die Sarmaten oder Sauromaten, wie sie von griechischen Autoren ursprünglich genannt wurden, bildeten keine ethnische Einheit, sondern setzten sich aus unterschiedlichen Völkerschaften oder Stammesgemeinschaften zusammen.
4 In den antiken Schriftquellen tritt die Bezeichnung Sarmaten im 4. oder zu Beginn des 3. Jh. v. Chr. auf. Neueren Forschungen zufolge handelt es sich um Angehörige einer nordiranischen Sprachgruppe.

wahrt wird. Wiegand (1864-1936) zählt zu den bedeutendsten deutschen Archäologen. Seine besonderen Verdienste beruhen auf der Organisation und Leitung großangelegter Grabungen in Milet, Friene, Didyma und Samos. 1927 erwirkte er die Wiederaufnahme der Grabungen in Pergamon. Seiner Initiative ist auch die Gründung des 1930 eingeweihten Pergamonmuseums zu verdanken. Von 1911 bis 1931 war er Direktor der Antikenabteilung der Berliner Museen. Während der Kriegsjahre 1916 bis 1918 hielt er sich als Generalinspekteur der Altertümer des Vorderen Orients häufig in der Türkei, in Syrien und Palästina auf. Ab 1. September 1918 wurde er für drei Monate "zur Feststellung kunsthistorischer Werte" und zu Verhandlungen über deutsche Ausgrabungen in Olbia, Kertsch und Kuban in die Ukraine gesandt. Wie Wiegands Tagebuch zu entnehmen ist, fuhr er am 16. Oktober 1918 für einen Tag per Motorboot von Nikolajew nach Olbia, wo man die Ausgrabungen während des Krieges eingestellt hatte. Umsomehr waren damals illegale Grabungen durch Schatzsucher an der Tagsordnung. Diese Situation und weitere Erlebnisse, die durch die Wirren des Kriegsendes bedingt waren, schildert Wiegand seiner Frau in einem ausführlichen Brief vom 25. Oktober 1918: "Wir stellen fest," berichtet er unter anderem, "dass gerade wieder der Haupt-Raubgräber in eine neue, unberürte, anscheinend skythische Grabkammer gedrungen war und höchst merkwürdige Holzsachen gefunden hat... ."[5] Der Hinweis in dem erwähnten Brief Wiegands an seine Frau, daß er am 27. 10. nochmals nach Olbia fahren wolle, um sich diese interessanten Funde genauer anzusehen, führte mich auf eine andere Spur. Im Wiegand-Nachlaß fand ich ein Notizbuch Wiegands mit der Aufschrift "Ukraine und Krim 1918." Es enthält unter dem 27. 10. einen ausführlichen Bericht über den am Vortage von dem erwähnten Raubgräber gemachten Fund, zu dem, die uns interessierende Harfe gehört. Mit diesen an Ort und Stelle angefertigten Zeichnungen, Messungen, und Beschreibungen Wiegands besitzen wir einen mit Akribie angefertigten "Grabungsbericht" eines erfahrenen Archäologen.[6]

Wiegands Tagebucheintragungen unter den 27. 10. 1918 beginnen folgendermaßen : "Zweiter Besuch in Olbia bei dem Raubgräber Washa Krischenko. Der "Holzfund," gefunden am 26. 10., ist eine (!) Katakombe (also nicht Kurgan) 10km nördlich von Olbia, etwa 5m unter der Erde. Rechteckige Kammer mit schräger Dachflächendecke, etwa 6 x 6m, Eingang Schiebetür von Stein. Der Stein etwa 2 1/2 m hoch." Wir sehen also, dass sich Wiegand bei seinen stichwortartig formulierten Notizen der bei russischen Archäologen gebräuchlichen Unterscheidung zwischen Katakombengrab und Kurgan bedient.

---

5 Wiegand fertigte auch von seiner handschriftlichen Privatkorrespondenz Kopien an, die sich - wie alle anderen hier benutzten Dokumente im Wiegand-Nachlaß befinden, der im Deutschen Aroäologischen Institut Berlin aufbewahrt wird.
6 Er umfaßt insgesamt 22 Seiten, von denen hier nur diejenigen abgebildet wurden, auf denen Zeichnungen wiedergegeben sind, die sich auf die Harfe beziehen.

Wiegands ausführliche Beschreibung des Grabinhalts und der Grabbeigaben kann hier nur kurz zusammenfassend wiedergegeben werden: Zwei hölzerne Sarkophage standen an den beiden Seitenwänden, während die Mitte frei blieb. Die rechteckigen, kistenförmigen Särge waren aus aufrechtstehenden, miteinander verzahnten Eichenbrettern zusammengefügt (ohne Verwendung von Nägeln) und mit Leder überzogen[7]. Im linken Sarkophag lag das Skelett mit dem Kopf nach Norden, im rechten mit dem Kopf nach Süden. Beide waren auf Schilfmatten gebettet und trugen mit Tierwolle oder Pflanzenfasern gefütterte Lederjacken sowie Fausthandschuhe und Schuhe aus Leder.

Im linken Sarkophag fanden sich Reste eines Schießbogens und mehrere Pfeile. Auf der Stirn des Toten lag eine etwa 4cm breite Löwenmaske aus Gold. Am Hals des Toten fand sich ein Amulett, bestehend aus einem Zahn mit einer goldenen Fassung. An der linken Schulter lag eine flache, kreisrunde Silberschale mit einem Durchmesser von 18cm, an der drei an Ösen befestigte Ringhenkel angebracht waren, sowie ein hölzerner, 6,5 x 10cm großer Kamm. In der linken Hand hielt der Tote ein kleines Steingefäß mit zwei Henkeln in Form von Bären und Teile eines gelben Glasgefäßes, in der rechten die Reste eines Schwerts. Im rechten Sarkophag fanden sich ähnliche Grabbeigaben: Schwert, Bogen und Pfeile, am Hals des Toten mehrere Perlen einer Kette und an der linken Schulter eine Harfe.

Außerhalb der beiden Sarkophage standen in der Nähe des Grabeingans ein Holzgefäß mit Handgriff und Ausgußvorrichtung sowie eine hölzerne Schöpfkelle und schließlich eine große Tonamphore. Die Gefäße waren offensichtlich für Speisen und Getränke bestimmt, die man den Toten als letzte Zehrung auf den Weg ins Jenseits mitgab. Anlage und Ausstattung dieses Grabes unterscheiden sich deutlich von den Gräbern der stadtbewohner von Olbia. Funde und Fundumstände lassen erkennen, daß die beiden 10km von Olbia entfernt Bestatteten zu einer der in der Südukraine nomadisierenden Stammesgemeinschaften gehörten, die man unter der Bezeichnung Sarmaten bzw. Sauromaten zusammenzufassen pflegt. Die kostbaren Grabbeigaben und das Bestreben, die Grabanlage möglichst tief unter die Erde zu legen, lassen darauf schließen, daß hier Vertreter der sozialen Operschicht bestattet wurden. Viele dieser Nomaden waren in der spätsarmatischen Zeit seßhaft geworden. Dazu gehörten möglicherweise auch die beiden in Stadtnähe beerdigten Toten. Leider geht aus Wiegands Aufzeichnungen nicht hervor, ob es sich um zwei Männer oder um Mann und Frau handelt. Die Tatsache, daß beiden ein Schwert sowie Pfeile und Bogen in den Sarg beigegeben wurden, läßt keine eindeutigen Rückschlüsse auf ihr Geschlecht zu. Wie antike Schriftquellen bezeugen, galten die sarmatischen Frauen als kampferprobt. Mit Pfeil und Bogen, gelegentlich auch mit dem Schwert, griffen sie in kriegerische Aktionen ein. Diese Berichte wurden durch

---

7 Ein ähnlicher kastenförmiger Holzsarg, der aus Olbia stammt, ist bei E. H. Minns, Skythians and Greeks, Cambridge 1913, S. 322, abgebildet.

archäologische Befunde bestätigt: In frühsarmatischer Zeit betrug der Anteil der Frauengräber mit Waffenbeigaben etwa ein Fünftel aller Waffengräber, nahm später allerdings deutlich ab. Es bleibt also die Frage offen, ob es sich bei dem Toten, dem seine Harfe spielbereit in den Arm gelegt worden war, um einen Mann oder um eine Frau handelt.

Von den zahlreichen Objekten aus dem Sarmatengrab bei Olbia, die von den Berliner Museen erworben worden waren, haben leider nur wenige den Krieg überdauert: die Silberschale, der Kamm, von den Pfeilen lediglich einige der hölzernen Nocken sowie mehrere Holz- und Lederstücke, bei denen es sich wahrscheinlich um Teile der Särge und um Reste der Kleidung handelt. Sehr zu bedauern ist aber auch der Umstand, daß sich der von M. Rostovzev in seinem Buch "Skythen und der Bosporus," Band 1, Berlin 1931, auf Seite 586 geäußerte Wunsch, dieser sensationelle Fund möge recht bald publiziert werden, nie erfüllt hat. Im Zusammenhang mit der Beschreibung von skythisch-sarmatischen Gräbern gibt Rostovzev in einer Fußnote folgenden Hinweis: "Während des Krieges wurde ein anderer reicher und eigenartiger Fund desselben Charakters neben Olbia gemacht. Th. Wiegand ist es gelungen, den Fund aufzuheben und ihn nach Berlin zu Überführen, wo er jetzt im Antiquarium aufbewahrt ist. Der Publikation des Fundes, welche hoffentlich bald geschieht, möchte ich nicht vorgreifen. Vor allem merkwürdig sind in diesem Fund die Gegenstände aus Holz und Leder. Dem ganzen Charakter nach ist er den Funden im Wolgagebiet sehr ähnlich." Glücklicherweise sind im Bildarchiv der Staatlichen Museen in Berlin[8] sieben Fotos der Harfe erhalten geblieben, von denen einige hier mit freundlicher Genehmigung des Museums erstmalig veröffentlicht werden. Es handelt sich um Gesamt- und Detailaufnahmen von hervorragender Qualität, die das Instrument von allen Seiten zeigen.

Wenden wir uns nun speziell der Harfe zu, die Wiegand für das Modell eines Segelschiffes hielt, wie aus seinen Tagebuchaufzeichnungen hervorgeht. Zur Erklärung dieser Fehlinterpretation sei darauf verwiesen, daß Wiegand dieses Objekt ohne Saiten vorfand und daß es sich bei jenem Musikinstrument um das früheste Exemplar dieses Typs handelt, das jemals gefunden worden war. Nichts war damals bekannt über die Chordophone der Nomadenstämme in den riesigen Steppengebieten, die sich von Zentralasien bis Südwesteuropa Erstrekken.[9] Curt Sachs, der wohl bedeutendste Spezialist auf dem Gebiet der Musikin-

---

8 Staatliche Museen zu Berlin, Preußischer Kulturbesitz, Antikenabteilung, Berlin, Bodestraße 1 - 3. Neg.-Nr. 7174 - 7177 und 7259 - 7261. Veröffentlichung der Fotos mit freundlicher Genehmigung des Museums.
9 Dieses Thema ist bis heute nicht umfassend bearbeitet. Zu erwähnen ist allenfalls die Magisterarbeit von Cornelia Strauß zum Thema "Musikinstrumente bei Reiternomaden Eurasiens auf der Grundlage archäologischer und historisoher Quellen," Philosophische Fakultät der Universität Göttingen 1977. Sie ist leider in der Materialerfassung sehr unvollständig. Weder die Winkelharfe aus dem Sarmatengrab in Olbia, noch die Leier-

strumentenkunde, der in den zwanziger Jahren (bis 1933) in Berlin tätig war, hatte das Objekt gesehen und richtig als fünfsaitige horizontale Winkelharfe gedeutet. Unter Hinweis auf Pollux, Onomastikon IV, 60,interpretiert er das Instrument als "Pentachordon" der Skythen. Sachs bezieht sich bei seiner Deutung auf analoge Instrumente, die auf babylonischen, assyrischen und elamischen Stelen dargestellt sind und von den Musikern in horizontaler Haltung gespielt werden, wenn er auf Seite 158 seines 1929 in Berlin erschienenen Buches "Geist und Werden der Musikinstrumente" schreibt: "Die gleiche Harfe, mit nur fünf Saiten und einem Adler als Schnitzerei des aufrechten Stabes, ist aus einem sarmatischen Grab der Krim ins Berliner Antiquarium gekommen. In ihr haben wir offenbar das skythische PENTAXORDON zu sehen." Das Polluxzitat (zweite Hälfte des 2. Jh.) lautet in deutscher Übersetzung: "Das Pentachordon ist eine Erfindung der Skythen. Die Saiten werden mit einem Plektron gezupft, das aus dem Huf der Ziege hergestellt wird." Es sei dahingestellt, ob Pollux mit dem skythischen Pentachordon die horizontale Winkeharfe oder die schlanke Leier meint, die auf dem goldenen Diadem aus dem Kurgan von Sachnovka und auf einer Wandmalerei in einer Grabkammer in Neapolis Scythica abgebildet ist.[10]

Der größte Teil von Wiegands Tagebuchaufzeichnungen vom 27. 10. 1918, die den Funden und Fundumständen des Sarmatengrabes bei Olbia gewidmet sind, bezieht sich auf die von ihm als Schiffsmodell gedeutete Harfe. Er hat sie genau vermessen, fertigte eine Skizze an (Abb. 2) und lieferte eine Fülle detaillierter Angaben zu Beschaffenheit, Bauweise und Material des Objekts. Sein besonderes Interesse galt den zahlreichen Tamga-Zeichen, die an der Außenseite der Harfe eingeschnitzt beziehungsweise aufgemalt waren (Abb. 2 und 3). Unter den Spezialisten auf dem Gebiet der Tamga-Forschung gibt es keine einhellige Meinung bezüglich der Herkunft, Bedeutung und Verbreitung dieser sonderbaren Zeichen. Von einigen werden sie als religiöse Symbole mit magischer Funktion gedeutet, von anderen als Herrschaftssymbole, mit denen der Besitzer sein Eigentum kennzeichnete. Tamga-Zeichen finden sich an den Wänden von Grabkammern, auf Grabbeigaben und Grabstelen, dürften also mit dem Totenkult in Verbindung zu bringen sein. Sie lassen sich aber auch an Waffen, Gürtelschnallen und anderen Gebrauchsgegenständen nachweisen. Das Verbreitungs-

---

darstellung in einer Grabkammer in Neapolis Scythica, noch mehrere andere wichtige Funde wurden erwähnt. Die Gattung der Idiophone, die den weitaus größten Anteil am Musikinstrumentarium der Reiternomaden Eurasiens haben, blieben völlig unberücksichtigt.

10 Das skytische Golddiadem mit der Darstellung eines Leierspielers im Rahmen einer Festszene stammt aus dem 4. Jh. v. Chr. und wurde 1901in einem Kurgan bei Sachnovka, Čerkassy, ausgegraben. Es wurde häufig veröffentlicht, erstmalig in Archeologičeskaja letopis Južnoj Rossii 3, Kiev, 1901, S. 213 - 215. Die Darstellung eines Leiersplers auf der Wandmalerei in einer Grabkammer in Neapolis Scythica etwa 500 Jahre später zu datieren. Abbildung und Literaturangaben bei A. Mongait, Archaeology in the U.S.S.R., Moskau 1959, nach S. 164 und S. 183, Nr. 16.

gebiet der Funde mit Tamga-Zeichen reicht von der Wolga über die Ukraine bis nach Polen. Man hat die Ursprünge dieser Zeichen im Iran wie auch in Mittelasien vermutet, wo man ähnlichen Symbolen begegnet. Die Mehrzahl aller mit Tamga-Zeichen versehenen Objekte stammt jedoch aus dem Gebiet um Olbia und Chersones, sowie aus dem Bosporanischen Reich (Halbinsel Kertsch usw.) und sind zeitlich der mittel- und spätsarmatisehen Periode, genauer gesagt dem 1. - 3. Jahrhundert nach Chr. zuzuordnen. Damit haben wir bezüglich der Harfe einen Anhaltspunkt für deren Datierung, die sich anhand von weiteren Kriterien noch präzisieren lässt.[11] Mit grosser Wahrscheinliehkeit stammt sie aus dem 1. Jahrhundert nach Chr.

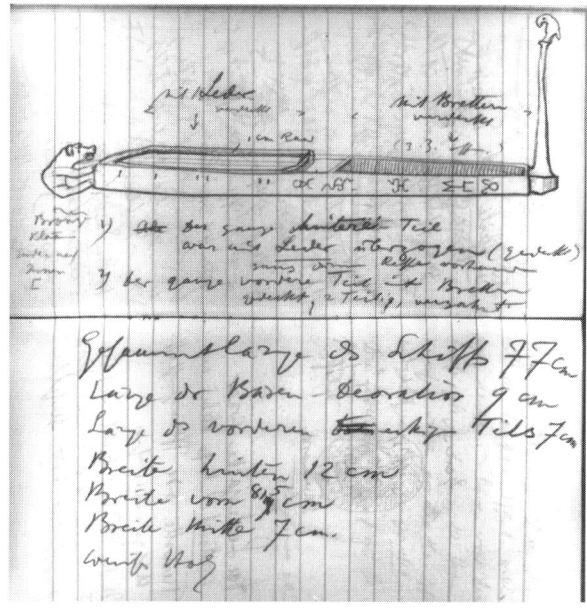

Abb. 2

---

11 Anhaltspunkte für eine Datierung in das 1. Jh. nach Chr. liefern Vergleiche der Grabbeigaben mit datierten sarmatischen Grabinventaren, vor allem die individuell aus kosbarem Material wie Gold, Silber, Glas und. edlem Gestein gefertigten Gegenstände. Nach M. Rostowzew (Skythen und der Bosporus, Bd. 1, Berlin 1931, S. 201) nimmt der Reichtum dieser Gräber, wie er noch im 1. Jh. n. Chr. anzutreffen ist, im 2. Jh. deutlich ab. Es findet sich dann fast nur noch "Marktware." Das Fehlen eines Liegebetts spricht ebenfalls dafür, daß es sich um ein Sarmatengrab aus dem 1. Jh. nach Chr. handelt. Nach Rostowzew haben die unterirdischen Grabkammern aus früher Zeit gewöhnlich keine, um die Zeitenwende nur vereinzelt und im 2. und 3. Jh. ausnahmslos derartige Liegebetten.

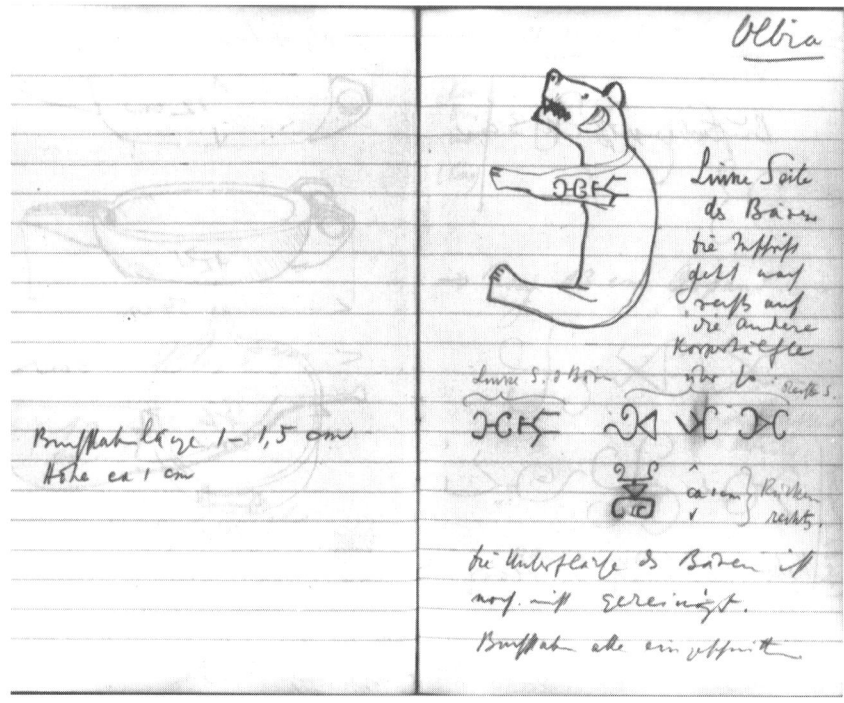

Abb. 3

Die Aufzeichnungen Wiegands ermöglichen in Verbindung mit den vorhandenen Fotos eine genaue Beschreibung des Instruments. Die mit erstaunlichem handwerklichen Können aus relativ weichem Holz geschnitzte Harfe,[12] besteht aus dem schlanken Korpus, an dessen Ende sich die Figur eines Bären anklammert, und dem stabförmigen Saitenträger, der von einer Vogelfigur bekrönt ist. Die Gesamtlänge des Korpus beträgt einschliesslich der Bärenfigur und der Halterung für den Saitenträger 77cm. Der eigentliche Resonator, das heisst der trogförmige Teil des Instruments ohne Tierfigur und Halterung, ist 61cm lang. Diese Winkelharfe ist also etwas kleiner und zierlicher als das entsprechende Instrument aus dem Kurgan II in Pazyryk, das eine Gesamtlänge von 83cm hat. Das Foto auf der Abbildung 1 zeigt das Instrument in dem Zustand, in dem es von Wiegand erworben wurde. Von der Seite gesehen weist der Resonator eine

---

12 Im Archiv der Staatlichen Museen in Berlin finden sich keinerlei Hinweise auf Materialuntersuchungen der Funde aus Olbia. So sind wir auf den Hinweis "weiches Holz" in Wiegands Tagebuch angewiesen.

leichte Krümmung auf. Er ist bootförmig ausgehöhlt und bis auf ein kleines Mittelstück oben offen (Abb. 4), was bei Wiegand zu der Deutung als Schiffsmodell führte. Die vordere Öffnung auf der Oberseite des Resonators ist etwas länger als die hintere. Der oben geschlossene Abschnitt befindet sich also nicht genau in der Mitte. Er ist 6,5cm breit und 6cm lang und hat eine Holzstärke von etwa 1cm. Es handelt sich wohlgemerkt nicht um ein aufgeleimtes oder genageltes Brettchen, sondern um einen festen Bestandteil des aus einem Stück geschnitzten Korpus der Harfe. Beim Aushöhlen des Resonators ließ man diesen Abschnitt stehen und unterhöhlte ihn von beiden Seiten bis auf die angegebene Holzstärke. Die hintere Öffnung ist durch eine hölzerne Umrandung um reichlich einen Zentimeter (bis 1,7cm) erhöht. Dieser mittels Bronzeklammern am Korpus befestigte Aufsatz war an einigen Stellen zerbrochen und hatte sich teilweise vom Korpus gelöst, da einige Klammern durch Korrosion zersetzt worden waren. Durch Zeichnungen und Beschreibungen hat Wiegand das Prinzip der Verklammerung genauestens überliefert (Abb. 5). Er weist darauf hin, daß am Rande dieses Aufsatzes noch Lederspuren erkennbar waren, was darauf schließen läßt, daß die hintere Öffnung des Resonators ursprünglich durch eine Lederdecke verschlossen war. Ob sich unter den Lederstücken aus dem Grab bei Olbia, die glücklicherweise den Krieg überdauert haben (Antikensammlung der Berliner Museen, Inv.-Nr. 30867), die Decke der Harfe befindet, bedarf noch der Nachprüfung.[13]

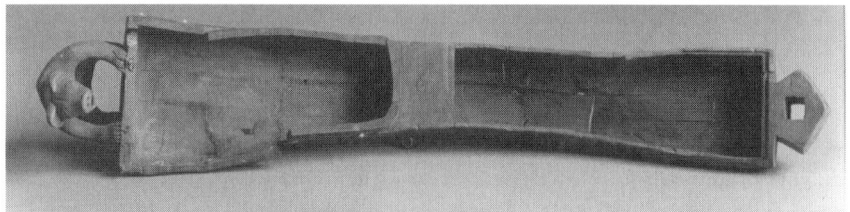

Abb. 4

---

13 Diese Lederfragmente befinden sich derzeit sämtlich im Labor des Museums für Volkerkunde in Berlin-Dahlem, wo durch eine langwierige Frostbehandlung der Schimmelbefall gestoppt werden soll. Es besteht also vorläufig keine Möglichkeit, diese Nachprüfung vorzunehmen.

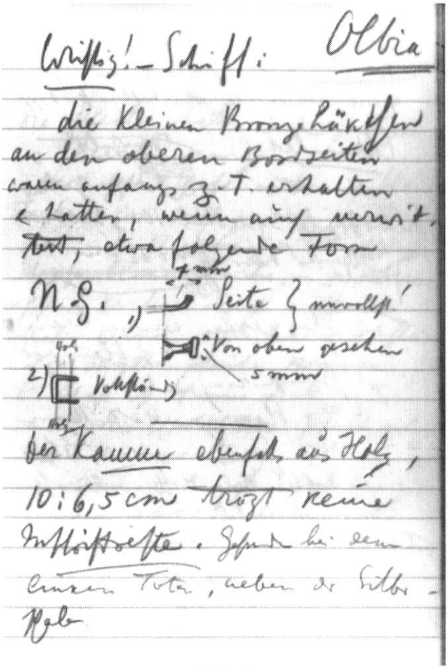

Abb. 5

Abb. 6

Der Rand der vorderen Öffnung des Resonators weist nach innen zu eine Stufe auf, die als Auflage für eine etwa 5mm starke Holzdecke dient. Wie ein Detailfoto (Abb. 6) zeigt, besteht sie aus zwei miteinander verzahnten Teilen, die in mehrere Stücke zerbrochen waren. Seitlich der Verzahnung erkennt man

Nagellöcher, die darauf schließen lassen, daß an dieser Stelle unter der zweiteilten Holzdecke ein quer verlaufendes Brettchen als deren Auflage und zugleich als stütze der dünnen Seitenwandung des Resonators eingepaßt war. Die Aufnahmen der Harfe von oben (Abb. 4) und von unten (Abb. 7) lassen erkennen, daß das Korpus hinten am breitesten und in der Mitte am schmälsten ist, also wie die Pazyryk-Harfe eine Taille aufweist, allerdings nicht, wie letztere, symmetrisch gebaut ist. Die Breite des Korpus beträgt hinten 12cm, in der Mitte 6,5 und vorn 8,5cm. Am vorderen Ende des Korpus befindet sich die Halterung für den Saitenträger, der mit dem Resonator ursprünglich einen rechten Winkel bildete.[14] Die Halterung weist eine quadratische Durchbohrung auf, in der der Vierkantteil des ansonsten runden, stabförmigen Saitenträgers steckt. An der Stelle, wo der Rundstab auf der Halterung aufsitzt, hat er seinen größten Durchmesser. Damit erhöhte man die Stabilität des Saitenträgers, der die Spannung des Saitenbezugs auszuhalten hatte. Das Originalfoto des Saitenträgers (Abb. 8) läßt in der oberen Hälfte des Stabes noch Spuren der Saitenbefestigung erkennen. Allem Anschein nach handelt es sich um Reste von schmalen Leder- oder Gewebestreifen, die man mehrfach um den Stab herumgeschlungen und mit den Saiten verknotet hatte.[15] Wie bei Leiern bildeten sie ursprünglich ringförmige Verdickungen (Abb. 12). Durch Drehen dieser Wülste ließ sich das Instrument stimmen. Möglicherweise hatten sich aber auch die Saiten selbst am Saitenträger abgezeichnet. Offenbar waren fünf Befestigungsstellen sichtbar, wie Curt Sachs bestätigt, der das Instrument seinerzeit in Augenschein genommen und als fünfsaitige Harfe bezeichnet hatte.

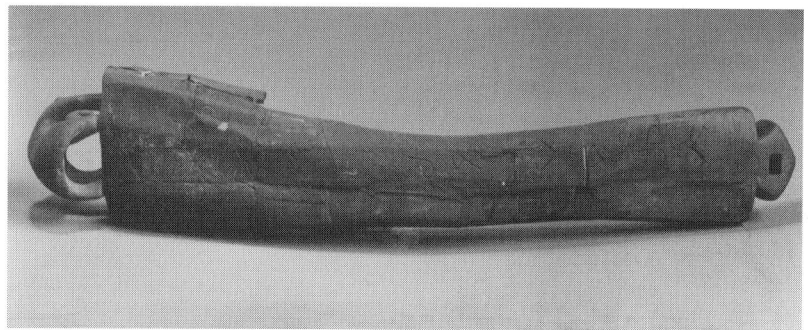

Abb. 7

---

14 Durch die Spannung der Saiten hat sich das im Laufe der Zeit etwas verändert.
15 Hinsichtlich der Befestigung der Saiten am Saitenträger sind die Harfen aus Pazyryk und aus Olbia offensichtlich identisch. Auch bei der Pazyryk-Harfe hatten die 6mm breiten Lederstreifen, an denen die Saiten befestigt waren, ursprünglich am Saitenträger fünf ringförmige Verärbungen des Holzes hinterlassen, die inzwischen verblichen sind. Beide Instrumente stimmen also auch in der Saitenzahl überein.

Dem Bericht Wiegands zufolge ist nicht auszuschließen, daß zur Harfe noch weitere Teile gehörten, die der Raubgräber achtlos beiseite geworfen hatte, beispielsweise ein Plektron und Reste von Saiten oder auch ein unter der Lederdecke des Korpus angebrachter Stab, an dem die Saitenenden befestigt waren. Bekanntlich hatte sich der nach Schätzen suchende Wascha Krischenko bereits am 26. 10.1918, also einen Tag vor dem Eintreffen Wiegands, Zugang zu der Grabkammer verschafft und das ihm wertvoll erscheinende an sich genommen. Da Wiegand die Harfe in dem ihm vorliegenden Zustand für ein Bootsmodell hielt, konnte er nicht auf den Gedanken kommen, unter dem "Abfall" des Raubgräbers nach Materialien zu suchen, die zur Harfe gehört haben könnten.

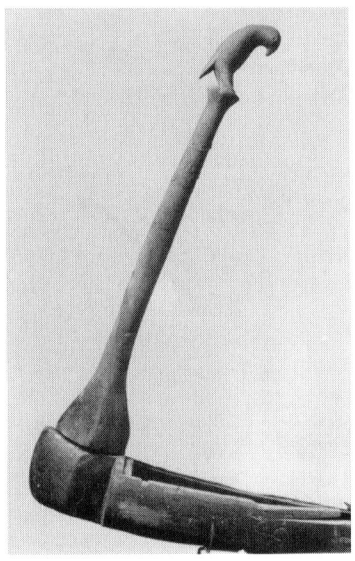

Abb. 8

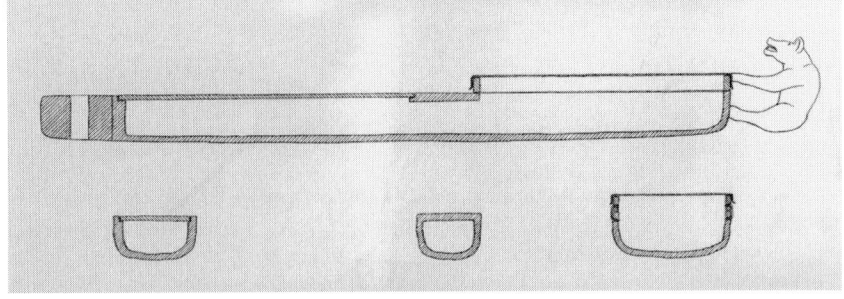

Abb. 9

Als ein erster Versuch einer Rekonstruktion des ursprünglichen Zustands der sarmatischen Harfe aus Olbia sind die maßstabgetreuen Zeichnungen zu werten, die als Abbildungen 9 bis 13 wiedergegeben sind. Der Längsschnitt des Harfenkorpus und die drei Querschnittzeichnungen vom Vorder-, Mittel- und Hinterteil (Abb. 9) zeigen den Resonator in geschlossenem Zustand. Die vordere Öffnung ist, wie oben beschrieben, durch eine dünne Holzdecke und die hintere, durch einen Aufsatzrand erhöhte Öffnung durch eine Lederdecke verschlossen. Die Aufsichtzeichnung (Abb. 10) gibt den offenen Resonator wieder. In der Annahme, daß sich das schlanke Harfenkorpus erst im Laufe der Zeit durch die ständige Saitenspannung gekrümmt hat, wurde es in der Längsschnittzeichnung, die als Rekonstruktion der ursprünglichen Form gedacht ist, gerade dargestellt (Abb. 12). Die Halterung für den Saitenträger wird auf Abb. 10 sowohl im Längsschnitt als auch in Aufsichtposition gezeigt.

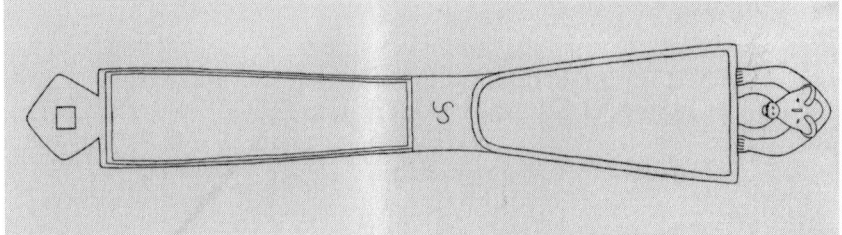

Abb. 10

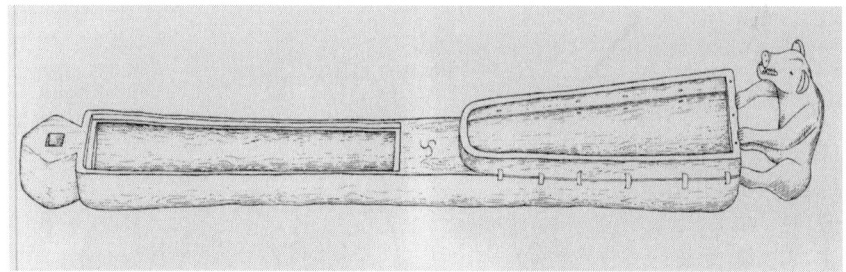

Abb. 11

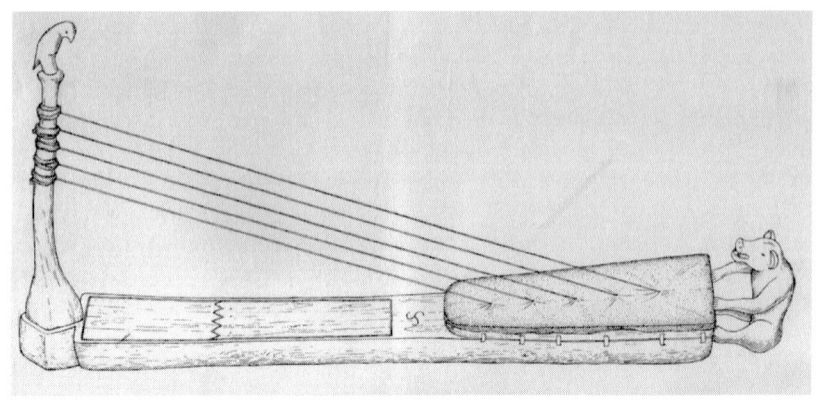

Abb. 12

Die beiden übrigen Zeichnungen bieten einen Rekonstruktionsversuch in einer Ansicht schräg von oben, einmal mit offenem Resonator (Abb. 11) und einmal komplett mit Saitenträger, Saiten und verschlossenem Resonator (Abb. 12). Bei der Zeichnung des kompletten Instruments (Abb. 13) ist zu berücksichtigen, daß bei dem gewählten Blickwinkel der nach oben ragende Saitenträger in perspektivischer Verkürzung darzustellen war.

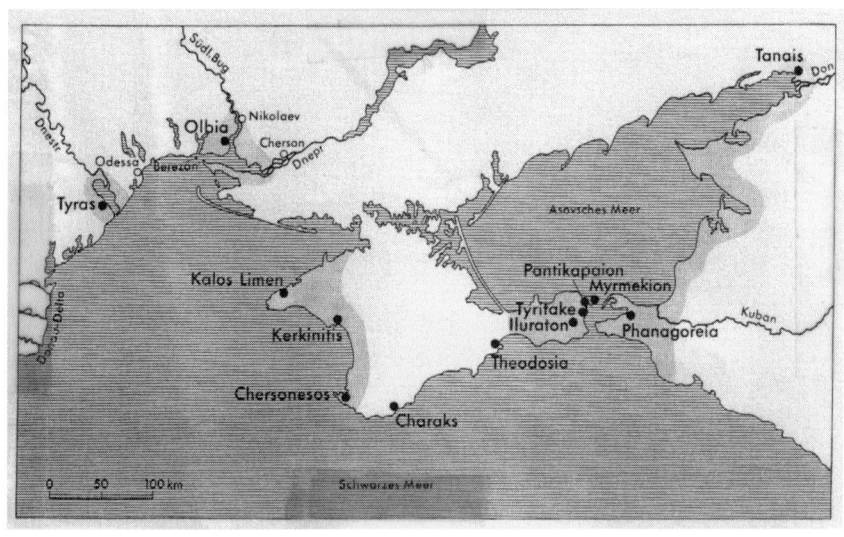

Abb. 13

Zdravko Blažeković

PERSEUS, THE HARP, AND THE SCIMITAR
Iconographic Confusion as Evidence for Early Terminology for The Harp

> On yonder side the Dragon beckons which glides between the two Bears; the Charioteer still minding his car and Bootes his wain; the heavenly gift of Ariadne's crown; Perseus, slayer of the abominable Medusa, blade yet in hand; with his wife Cepheus sacrificing his daughter Andromeda; the region of the sky where fly the Horse of stars, the Dolphin seeking to outstrip the swift Arrow, and Jupiter in swan's disguise; together with the other stars that glide at large throughout the heavens.
>
> Manilius, *Astronomica*, 5:19-26

The *Introductorium maius in astronomiam* by the Arabic astronomer Abū Ma'šar, written in Baghdad in A.H. 234 (848 A.D.), is one of the treatises that laid down the basis for Western astronomy during the Middle Ages and the Renaissance.[1] The treatise summarized the entire knowledge of astronomy at the time, incorporating elements of astrology, mythology, and science from the Chaldeans, Egyptians, Greeks, Indians, and Persians. In 1140-43 the *Introductorium* was translated into Latin by Hermann of Carinthia.[2] In the late twelfth or

---

1 Abū Maš'ar Ğaf'ar ibn Muammad ibn 'Umar al-Balhī (also known by the Latin name Albumasar) was born in or near Balkh in Khurasan, now northern Afghanistan, on 10 August A.H. 173 (787 A.D.) and died almost a centenarian in al-Wāsit, central Mesopotamia, on 8 March A.H. 272 (886 A.D.), having become the principal authority on astronomy and astrology among the Arabs.
2 Hermann of Carinthia (Hermann of Dalmatia; ca. 1110-after 26 February 1154) was both the translator and the author of an original philosophical treatise, *De essentiis*. The largest number of his translations deals with astronomy and mathematics: Ptolemy's *Planisphaera* (1143), Theodosius's *De sphaeris*, al-Khwārizmi's *Tabulae astronomicae* (ca. 1140), Euclid's *Geometria, arithmetica et stereometria* (ca. 1140, also known under the title *Elementa*), and Abū Ma'šar's *Introductorium maius in astronomiam*. With these translations he introduced the Arabic knowledge of mathematics and astronomy to the West. Several of his translations and compilations were intended for practical use, such as a compilation of two astrological works, *De occultis* and *De indagatione cordis* (after 1140), describing the planets and their influence on human life. A third group of translations includes Islamic religious texts. In 1142-43, he took part, together with Peter of Toledo and Robert of Ketton, in the earliest translation of the *Qur'an* from the Arabic into Latin, and he also translated two other texts: *De generatione Mahumet* and *Doctrina Mahumet*. Hermann's most important original work was the philosophical treatise *De essentiis* (1143), which offers an insight both into the cultural context in which these translations were made and into the period when alchemy and rational astrology were introduced

213

early thirteenth century, the otherwise unknown Georgius Zothorus Zaparus Fendulus extracted those parts of Hermann's translation of Abū Ma'šar's book that describe the constellations and the planets, and he provided them with illustrations.[3] This abridgment is essentially an illustrated encyclopedia, with seventy-six pages of images related to the three astrological systems used at the time, and to the seven planets.

There are six preserved manuscripts with Georgius's illustrated abridgment that share identical contents and structure, although they are not all preserved in their entirety. In chronological order, they are Bibliothèque Nationale de France, lat. 7330 (1220-40); the British Library, Sloane 3983 (1325-50); the Morgan Library and Museum, M. 785 (circa 1400); the Bibliothèque Nationale de France, lat. 7331 (1450-60), and lat. 7344 (shortly after 1488); and Smith-Lesouëf 8 (the end of the fifteenth century). The drawings in the six manuscripts are similar in their overall composition, and the changes introduced reflect only the new appearances of the objects, such as the clothing of figures, architectural style, or musical instruments updated to their shapes contemporaneous to the time the manuscript was produced.

Each of the manuscripts depicts a variety of instruments, many of them several times. However, with respect to present research on terminology for the harp, the most interesting source is the earliest known manuscript, lat. 7330, which is of South-Italian origin and was produced for the court of Frederick II (1194-1250), Holy Roman Emperor and King of Sicily, Cyprus, and Jerusalem.[4] Frederick's Sicilian court was a center of intellectual activity and provided a workplace for Michael Scotus, who translated some of Aristotle's treatises there; for Leonard of Pisa (Fibonacci), who introduced Arabic numerals and algebra to the West; and for several other Jewish, Christian, and Islamic scholars. The King himself was acquainted with mathematics, philosophy, and natural sciences, and was also interested in poetry, medicine, and architecture; at the time of his coronation as King of Sicily, he spoke Greek, Latin, Arabic, Provençal, and a Sicilian dialect. He was patron of a number of Arabian artists and encouraged their art in Sicily. In 1224 he founded the University in Naples, where he assembled a large collection of Arabic manuscripts and translations of Greek philosophers.

---

to the West. *De essentiis* constitutes the first notable application of Arabic astrology to Latin metaphysical speculation, merging with the neo-Platonic traditions of Chartres.

3 Knowledge of Georgius's involvement in the production of the abridgment comes from the opening line of the text: "In nomine domini pii e misericordissimi. Incipit prologus viri cognomine Georgii Zothori Zapari Fenduli. G. sacerdotis atque philosophi translatus de Persica lingua in Latinam liber Albumazaris."

4 The manuscript is fully described in François Avril, et al., *Manuscrits enluminés d'origine italienne*, vol. 2, *XIIIe siècle* (Paris: Bibliothèque Nationale, 1981-84), 160-62, pl. P, cxvi–cxviii; cf. also the facsimile edition, Marie-Thérèse Gousset and Jean-Pierre Verdet, eds., *Georgius Zothorus Zaparus Fendulus: Liber astrologie* (Paris: Herscher, 1989).

The core of Georgius's abridgment contains, in its first half, book VI, chapter 2 of Abū Ma'šar's *Introductorium maius*, entitled "De 12 signis et de figuris eorum et que stellae orientur in eis et que sunt significationes eorum," which is devoted to the twelve signs of the zodiac. Here Abū Ma'šar provided descriptions of three different astrological systems: the Greek firmament, based on the writings of Ptolemy (second century A.D.); a system of Indian decans, adopted from the Hindu astrologer Varāhamihira (sixth century A.D.); and the system codified by Teukros, an astronomer from Asia Minor (first century A.D.), who combined Egyptian with Greek and Babylonian astronomy. His presentation follows the pre-Copernican astronomical assumption that the sun revolves around the earth along the ecliptic, in the course of which appears a belt of twelve signs of the zodiac. Each sign—occupying approximately thirty degrees of the celestial ecliptic and corresponding to a thirty-day period when the sun is in that particular section of the arc—Georgius illustrated in three segments, each measuring ten degrees. Each such ten-degree arc Georgius displayed on one page, divided horizontally into three parts. The bottom third depicts Ptolemaic constellations that are visible in either the southern or the northern sky above the ten-degree arc of the ecliptic (*sphaera graecanica*). The middle section includes illustrations of the Indian system of decans (*sphaera indica*), in which each decan dominates with its astrological influences during a ten-day period. Finally, at the top of the page are illustrated constellations of the *sphaera barbarica*, which simultaneously rise to the north and to the south of the celestial equator at the time when the sun is in the corresponding ten-degree arc of the ecliptic. The manuscript is a particularly interesting source because many of the objects depicted are identified by their names in Latin.

In Georgius's representation of the sky, the constellation of Perseus appears in both the *sphaera graecanica* and the *sphaera barbarica*. The constellation is approximately twenty-eight degrees in length in the sky, which makes it one of the most extended in the heavens, stretching from the raised hand of Cassiopeia nearly to the Pleiades.[5] Since Georgius included on each page of his celestial atlas in the *sphaera graecanica*, only those elements of the constellation that appear in the sky during a particular ten-day period, parts of Perseus are extended over several decans, beginning from the middle period of Aries and spreading to the end of Taurus. In the second decan of Aries (fol. 7r) are shown Perseus's head (*caput Persei*), his hand (*finis manus*), the head of Medusa (*caput Meduse*), and a harp (*harpes Persei*) (Figure 1). Since the large number of constellations rising during this period did not leave enough space in the section usually reserved for the *sphaera barbarica* at the bottom of the page, some elements are incorporated among the elements of the *sphaera indica* in the middle band.

---

5 Cf. Richard Hinckley Allen, *Star Names: Their Lore and Meaning* (New York: Dover, 1963), 331.

Figure 1. Georgius Zothorus Zaparus Fendulus, abridgment of Abū Ma'šar's *Introduc-torium maius in astronomiam* (1220-40), showing the second decan of Aries. MS, Bibliothèque Nationale de France, lat. 7330, fol. 7r.

In the following decan, the constellation continues with the figure of Perseus shown from the waist up, holding a sword in his right hand and Medusa's head in his left (*Perseus cum manu sinistra tenens caput Meduse*) (Figure 2). In the first decan of Taurus, the left side of Perseus's body is represented; in the following decan, his right knee (*Perseus genu*); and, finally, in the third decan of Taurus, his entire figure.

Figure 2. Fendulus, abridgment of Abū Ma'šar's *Introductorium*, showing the third decan of Aries. MS, Bibliothèque Nationale de France, lat. 7330, fol. 7v.

Such features of the constellation might not be of interest for a music historian if the harp had any connection with Perseus in mythology. However, music is associated with Perseus only indirectly. In the *Metamorphosis*, Ovid mentions that, after Perseus liberated Andromeda, "incense in abundance fed the flames, garlands hung from the roof, and everywhere was heard the sound of lyres and pipes, and singing that gives happy proof of joyful hearts."[6] Thus the harp included by Georgius among the illustrations of Perseus's elements has no relationship to him in mythological terms, and the question as to why it is included here—and, moreover, unmistakably associated with him through the inscription *harpes Persei*—makes this image not only interesting but also significant for a consideration of the early terminology for the harp.

In fact, Georgius's depiction results from a misreading and misunderstanding of Hermann's Latin description of the constellation. The word *harpa* had been used during the Middle Ages for a number of objects, ranging from a harrow, a corn sieve, an instrument of torture, and a shelf for drying corn to the musical instrument itself.[7] The Latin term *harpe*, or its Greek equivalent, ἅρπη, also signified a sickle-shaped sword, the kind that Perseus received from Hermes before the fight with the Gorgon Medusa, which became one of his standard iconographic attributes in celestial atlases.[8] He is normally represented as a nude youth wearing the *talaria* (winged sandals) with a light scarf thrown around his body. In his left hand he holds the Gorgoneion (the head of Medusa) and in his right the scimitar.[9] The word *harpe* (designating this sickle-shaped sword) is used in the Greek description of the Perseus constellation in the manuscript Vatican, gr.1056 (fol. 28v),[10] and also in Hermann's translation of Abū Ma'šar. Apparently lacking sufficient familiarity with the mythology and failing to understand the text, Georgius depicted the *harpe* as a musical instrument, instead of as a scimitar.

If we were concerned with the astrological significance of the constellation of Perseus, the image of the harp would be confusing, and we might dismiss it as insignificant. In an organological context, however, it is a different matter altogether. Georgius's confusion of the harp for the scimitar indicates that he based his imagery, at this point, on the textual source. He did not, in other words, follow the established iconographic tradition surrounding the figure of Perseus.

---

6 Ovid, *Metamorphosis*, trans. by Mary M. Innes (London: Penguin, 1955), 114.
7 Cf. Martin van Schaik, *The Harp in the Middle Ages: The Symbolism of a Musical Instrument* (Amsterdam and Atlanta: Rodopi, 1992), 16.
8 Cf. Mirko Divković, *Latinsko-hrvatski rječnik za škole*, 2nd ed. (Zagreb, 1900) and the facsimile ed. (Zagreb: Naprijed, 1980), 465; and D.P. Simpson, *Cassell's Latin Dictionary* (New York: Macmillan, 1988), 272.
9 Cf. Allen, *Star Names*, 329.
10 Cf. Franz Boll, *Sphaera: Neue griechische Texte und Untersuchungen zur Geschichte der Sternbilder* (Leipzig: Teubner, 1903), 57.

The layout of his celestial atlas, representing parts of constellations within ten-day periods, was unusual, and we do not know what he used as a model for this design.[11] Indeed, errors of this kind speak in favor of the assumption that this layout might well have been entirely his own design. However, on the following page (fol. 7v), which shows the constellations of the third decan of Aries, we find a traditional representation of Perseus, holding a sword in his right hand and Medusa's head in his left (Figure 2). Since the text here calls for the entire figure of Perseus rather than just parts of the constellation, Georgius was able to return to the established iconographic tradition and to show him in his usual posture, rather than being compelled to invent a new image. Interestingly, however, the misrepresentation of the scimitar as a harp was transmitted through all later copies of the Georgius manuscripts, indicating that the artists who produced those later manuscripts did not verify the accuracy of pictures in the accompanying textual introduction, but slavishly copied them from a model.

The earliest evidence for the Latin word *harpe* being used to refer to the musical instrument is found in a poem by Valentinus Fortunatus (ca. 530–601), Bishop of Poitiers.[12] Subsequently, the word was used to signify the instrument in Latin and other European languages, but it is difficult to ascertain the identity of the instrument to which the term referred. "In the eleventh century, the terms *cithara* and *harpa* are often used synonymously. In glossaries dating from the tenth and thirteenth centuries, the term *harpa* is used for a large number of diverse musical instruments."[13] For example, Regino of Prüm, in his *Epistola de harmonica institutione* (ca. 900), included the *harpa* among the *tensibilia* (stringed instruments), but he did not provide a specific description of the instrument.[14] In the Anglo-Saxon *Vita Sancti Dunstani* (presumably written around 1000), the term "cithara" is explained to refer to the harp.[15] The word "salterium" was also interpreted as having several different meanings, one of them being the instrument today known as the harp.[16] According to Martin van Schaik, the earliest literary source indicating how the harp was played—and

---

11 The common tradition at the time followed the layout of the lavishly illustrated Carolingian manuscript the Leiden Aratea (Leiden, Bibliotheek der Rijksuniversiteit, Voss. lat. Q. 79), in which each constellation is either represented as an isolated picture or included in the planisphere, which shows all celestial phenomena at a given time.
12 "Romanusque lyra, plaudat tibi barbarus harpa, Graecus Achilliaca, crotta Britannus canat." (And may the Roman bring you homage with the lyra, the German with the harpa, the Greek sing Achilles's songs, and the Briton sound the crotta). Van Schaik, *The Harp*, 19.
13 Ibid., 36-37.
14 Ibid., 21.
15 "sumpsit secum ex more cytharam suam quam lingua paterna hearpam vocamus" (as usual took up his cithara which we call harpa in our language). Ibid., 21.
16 Cf. ibid., 21. In the Utrecht Psaltery (Utrecht, Rijksuniversiteit, MS 819), the text of Psalm 149 reads (fol. 83r): "Laudent nomen eius in choro, in tympano et psalterio psallant ei, quia bene placitum est." However, the accompanying illustrations show a harpist.

therefore positively determining the object and its name—is the anonymous German *Roudlieb* epic, datable to the period between the years 1043 and circa 1075.[17] "From the beginning of the thirteenth century," Van Schaik concludes, "the term *harp* seems to have been used consistently in poetry as the name for the musical instrument, the harp."[18]

Although the manuscript lat. 7330 does not contain the earliest iconographic source for the harp, the label that accompanies its picture in the second decan of Aries certainly makes this source a very important one. Indeed, that image can be regarded as iconographic proof of Van Schaik's argument regarding usage of the word.[19] If Georgius mistook the word *harpe* in the context of Perseus for the musical instrument, it suggests that the term was, in his environment, more commonly used to denote the musical instrument than the scimitar. We do not have any indication as to who Georgius was or where he came from, nor do we have any proof as to where he produced the prototype of his celestial atlas. But, assuming that lat. 7330 is the prototype itself, we do have, in this instance, a rare proof that the word *harp* was, by the first third of the thirteenth century, accepted in the Latin language of southern Italy to denote the same instrument that we understand today to be the harp. And, if this manuscript is a copy of an earlier Georgius prototype, the present-day meaning of the word could well have been established even earlier.

---

17 Lines 38-39 from fragment IX read: "Pulsans mox leva digitis geminis, modo dextra tangendo chordas dulces reddit nimis odas." (He played the sweetest songs, now plucking the strings with two fingers of the left hand and then again with the right hand.) Cf. ibid., 22.
18 Ibid.
19 Iconographic sources for the harp preceding and approximately contemporary to the earliest Georgius manuscript include the York Psalter, Glasgow, University Library, Hunterian MS 229, fol. 21v (ca. 1175); the Bible of St. Alban (England), The Morgan Museum and Library, M. 791, fol. 170 (1215-20); an English psalter, Morgan, G. 25, fol. 3v and 5v (1225); and a French Bible, Morgan G. 11, fol. 166 (1240). These sources, however, do not name the instrument depicted. The earliest Georgius manuscript predates, by several decades, depictions of instruments in the famous *Cantigas de Santa María* (El Escorial, MS b.I.2 E1).

Myrna Herzog

THE DIVISION VIOL
An Overview

Every viol player is familiar with the term *division viol*, widely understood as a kind of English viol described by Christopher Simpson (ca. 1602-69) in his important treatise of the same name.[1] The present article attempts to provide an overview of this instrument, compiling information available from first-hand sources. What are the instrument's roots? How and when does it appear in contemporary sources? Do we read Simpson's book accurately? Is the six-string, violin-shaped division viol that is portrayed in Simpson's book the same instrument as the six-string bass violin described in James Talbot's manuscript?[2] As we shall see, not everything one is accustomed to hearing or reading today about the division viol finds validation in the early sources.

Italian Origins

In the cultural give-and-take between nations, foreign models are absorbed and transformed, becoming new and characteristic national products. In seventeenth-century England, such process gave birth to new British genres and instruments, from out of Italian models. Since the first part of the sixteenth century, England had experienced a vogue for things Italian, especially music and poetry. Italian madrigals were translated, paraphrased and parodied, producing two important offshoots at the turn of the seventeenth century, the English madrigal and the viol fantasy, both of which evolved into genres of great individuality and vitality.

In the realm of music for solo viol, chordal practices typical of the Italian *lyra da gamba* seem to have inspired the English "lyra-way" genre of playing

---

Portions of this paper were presented at a meeting of the New York Chapter of the Viola da Gamba Society of America in January 2005. It is derived from my Ph.D. dissertation, *The Quinton and Other Viols with Violin Traits* (Bar-Ilan University, 2003), written under the guidance of Professor Joachim Braun, to whom I am indebted. My special thanks also to Eliahu Feldman, Thomas MacCracken, Ephraim Segerman, Benjamin Hebbert, Fred Lindeman, the late Dietrich Kessler, and John Topham, among many others.

1 Christopher Simpson, *The Division-Viol or The Art of Playing Extempore upon a Ground* (London, 1665; facs., London, 1965). This is the second edition of Simpson's *The Division-Violist: or an Introduction to the playing upon a ground* (London, 1659; facs., New York, 1998).
2 James Talbot, MS 1187, preserved in Christ Church Library, Oxford.

on the viol, and ultimately, the development of an instrument specifically taylored to this genre, the smaller *lyra-viol*. Another distinctive Italian style of playing the viol that appeared in England was *sonar alla bastarda*, rich in diminutions and embellishments, with a repertoire of virtuoso idiomatic instrumental compositions. The adoption of *bastarda* practices in England generated a genuinely English genre—*divisions upon a ground*—and later an instrument intended for performance of this genre, the *division viol*. In both cases, a specific musical function generated a specialized instrument to better serve it.

The "Divisions" Genre in England

The practice of improvising a descant upon a ground or foundation, usually a recurrent melody in the bass, reached England in the late sixteenth century and become a trademark of English viol playing during the seventeenth century. More than 100 sets of *divisions upon a ground* can be found in English manuscripts, by a variety of authors of varied musical statures.

Giovanni Coprario (ca. 1575-1626) was the first Englishman to address the topic of *divisions* in an organized manner, setting forth the principles of diminution and embellishment in his composition treatise, *Rules how to compose* (ca. 1610).[3] Concurrently, Angelo Notari, an Italian musician in the service of James I, published in London in 1613 a set of divisions on a madrigal by Cipriano de Rore in the *bastarda* style. The genre was aptly represented by John Jenkins (1592-1678),[4] Henry Butler (d.1652),[5] Christopher Simpson, and Daniel Norcombe (fl. 1602-41), a Brussel violist of great reputation. The writing was virtuosic, making full use of the viol's range (from the bottom string tuned down a second, up to far beyond the reach of the frets on the first string) and employing double stops, rapid passagework, and wide leaps. The intermingling of musical practices gave rise to divisions written in tablature as well,[6] to be used for variety of texture in viol consort music, as expounded in Coprario's treatise. Division writing was also present in the favorite English combination of violin, bass viol, and continuo, employed extensively by William Young (d.1671), Coprario,

---

3 See Caroline Cunningham, "John Coprario's 'Rules how to compose' and His Four-Part Fantasias: Theory & Practice Confronted," *Chelys* 23 (1994): 37-46.
4 Roger North, *The Musicall Grammarian* (1728), ed. Mary Chan and Jamie C. Kassler (Cambridge, 1990), 347: "He [Jenkins] was certainly a great master of devisions, and encouraged Sympson the devision violist by a copy of verses at the beginning, and some exemplars of devision at the latter end of his book."
5 Praised by Simpson, Butler worked at the Spanish court from 1623 until his death. Butler's Italianate style may have originated during his stay in Rome (ca. 1644-47).
6 Examples can be found in the music of Peter Leycester and Tobias Hume.

Jenkins, William Lawes, and Christopher Gibbons (1615-76) in their "setts" or fantasia-suites.[7]

As a genre, division playing suited the new spirit of music in England, and for this reason it was practiced by a number of different instruments, such as the violin, the flute, the recorder, until the 1730s.[8] Simpson stressed that "In this *Manner of Play,* a Man may show, the dexterity, and excellency, both, of his *Hand,* and *Invention*; to the *Delight,* and *Admiration,* of those that hear him."[9]

Contemporary Sources of Information on the Division Viol

The term *division-viol* was first mentioned and addressed by Simpson in his 1659 treatise, *The Division-Violist*. Three other contemporary sources also provide significant information on the instrument: John Playford's *A Brief Introduction to the Skill of Music*;[10] Thomas Mace's *Musick's Monument* (1676),[11] and James Talbot's manuscript (ca. 1690).[12] The division viol was last mentioned in contemporary sources by an enigmatic writer, "T.B.," in his 1722 work *A Compleat Musick Master.*[13]

Christopher Simpson was a brilliant instrumentalist and great improviser, a master of viol technique. He was also a teacher and a respected scholar. *The Division-Violist* was written as an instruction book for his pupils Sir John Bolles and Sir John St. Barbe. The threefold treatise—dealing with viol playing, musical composition and the manner of performing divisions,[14] and containing a few precious illustrations—is a well-constructed pedagogical tool and a valuable source of information on English musical praxis of the time.

---

7 The tradition of writing a concertante viol part in addition to the continuo seems to have been borrowed from Italy, for it "can be found throughout the Italian sonata a tre repertory from the early 17th century to Corelli and beyond." Peter Holman, "Correspondence," *Early Music* 6 (1978): 482.

8 In 1722 the division viol was still dealt with in his *Compleat Musick-Master* by "T.B." See Robert Donington, "James Talbot's Manuscript II. Bowed Strings," *Galpin Society Journal* 3 (1950): 41 and 43. Another treatise, *The Division Flute* (anonymous), was published in the same year. Apparently the final edition of Playford's *The Division Violin* was publsiehd in 1730.

9 Simpson, *The Division-Violist*, 21.

10 Published in London in successive editions and available on microfilm at the New York Public Library, New York. The first edition to mention the division viol is the 1664 one.

11 Thomas Mace, *Musick's Monument* (London, 1676; fasc., Paris, 1966).

12 See Anthony Baines, "James Talbot's Manuscript," *Galpin Society Journal* 1 (1948): 9-26; and Donington, "James Talbot's Manuscript," 27-45.

13 Quoted in Donington, "Talbot's Manuscript," 41 and 43.

14 Ted Conner, "The Groundbreaking Treatise of Christopher Simpson," *Journal of the Viola da Gamba Society* 36 (1999): 7: "This organizational framework reflects the influence of the Ciceronian model of theory, imitation, and practice typical of many pedagogical works from this period."

There has been much speculation about Simpson's identity. Part of his life is still shrouded in mystery, owing to the fact that he was a Catholic and a recusant. Margaret Urquhart[15] proposes that the mystery might be hiding the alter ego of the musician, Simpson the Jesuit, also a distinguished pedagogue, who had studied for the priesthood in Rome. This would explain the musician's intimacy with the Italian style and the European awareness evident in his works,[16] as well as the unusual translation of his treatise into Latin for the second edition, so "that it might be understood in Foreign Parts."[17]

The Jesuit's *séjour* in Rome might also be at the root of his familiarity with violin-shaped viols, which he considered to be the fittest for divisions[18]—instruments similar to the ones he might have seen there, made by great Italian masters such as Antonio (b.1540) and Girolamo (1561-1630) Amati, Giovanni Paolo Maggini (1580-ca.1630), Gasparo (1542-1609) and Francesco Bertolotti da Salò (1565-ca.1624), Pellegrino de Michelis Zanetto (ca. 1522-1615), and others.[19] The Church was traditionally a client of viol makers, and Jesuits, in particular, owned and used viols for performance during the Mass and celebrations.[20] It is significant that in the second edition of his treatise, alongside other updates such as removing his own hat from his portrait, Simpson *renamed* his book *The Division-Viol* (formerly *The Division-Violist*), moving the focus from the player to the instrument itself.

The second key author to address the division viol was John Playford (1623-86), in his best-selling book (first printed in 1654) *A Breefe Introduction to the Skill of Music for Song and Violl*. Between 1654 and 1730 Playford's book went through seventeen or eighteen editions and twenty-two reprints. It was repeatedly revised and its sections were enlarged or excised according to new demands. In this way, the treatise became a showcase for the latest fashions, trends, and developments in English musical life. Playford's *Breefe Introduction* is a reliable indicator of *what* came into use and *when* it came into use.

The first edition of Playford's book (1654) addresses only treble, tenor and bass viols, while the second edition (1655), to which "Mr. Christoph. Sympson" is listed as a contributor, mentions also the *Lyra viol* and introduces a small, new section on the Violin, "now an instrument much in request, & suits best to the Musick of this Age," and a paragraph on the Bass Violin, tuned a–d–G–C.[21] The

---

15 Margaret Urquhart, "Was Christopher Simpson a Jesuit?" *Chelys* 21 (1992): 3-26.
16 Ibid., 14-15.
17 Simpson, *The Division-Viol*, second unnumbered page of The Epistle Dedicatory.
18 Ibid., 1-2.
19 For detailed information and pictures of viols with violins by these makers see Myrna Herzog, *The Quinton and Other Viols with Violin Traits*," vol. 2.
20 See Iukimi Kambe, "Viols in Japan in the Sixteenth and Early Seventeenth Centuries," *Journal of the Viola da Gamba Society* 37 (2000): 68.
21 John Playford, *An Introduction to the Skill of Music* (London, 1655), 54-5.

third edition (1658) introduces a significant novelty: In addition to the usual "*Directions* for the Playing on the *Viol de Gambo*" we read "also on the *Treble-Violin*, a cheerful and sprightly instrument, and much practiced of late."[22]

The following editions of Playford's book, "The Third Edition, Enlarged" (1660) and the fourth edition of 1662, both acknowledge Simpson's treatise, but still refer only to "The *Viol de Gambo* or *Consort Viol*," of which there are three sizes (treble, tenor, and bass) played from regular musical notation, and to the *Lyra-viol*, played from Tablature.[23] Technical directions are omitted, "it being already done and lately published by a more Able and Knowing Master on this Instrument, *viz* Mr. *Chr. Simpson*, in his excellent book, entitled, *The Division Violist*." It was not until the 1664 edition that Playford distinguished between "three Sorts of *Basse Viols*, as there is three manner of ways in playing" - consort, divisions, and lyra-way, each genre having its own medium.[24] Over the next ten years the viol section of Playford's book remained largely unchanged, while the violin section was progressively enlarged.

The division viol is also addressed by Thomas Mace (1612-1706), a player of the lute and viol and a clerk at Trinity College, Cambridge. Mace's *Musick's Monument,* published in 1676, is one of the most important sources on seventeenth-century English music and performance practices. It is a nostalgic book, an homage to the musicians and the music of former days. Listing Christopher Simpson among "our Best Authors deceased, English and Italian,"[25] Mace's treatise turns to the past as much as Simpson's turned to the future.

Our final source of information on the division viol comes from James Talbot (1664-1708), a friend of the composer Henry Purcell (1659-95), who was a fellow and Regius Professor of Hebrew (1689-1704) at Trinity College, Cambridge.[26] During the years 1692-95, Talbot engaged himself in the preparation of a treatise on musical instruments, addressing their histories, descriptions, dimensions, tablatures, and tunings. Talbot's manuscript was never completed, but his manuscript annotations, recorded into a set of unbound papers, has became one of the most important sources on English organology. It is preserved at Oxford's Christ Church Library as Music MS 1187.

Talbot acquired his information from books and from prominent London musicians. This seems to be the cause of some conflicting data on viols in the manuscript, for it is possible that "there were two different sets of instruments

---

22 Playford, *A Brief Introduction to the Skill of Musick for Song and Viol* (London, 1658), 79.
23 Playford, *A Brief Introduction the the Skill of Musick* (London, 1660), 75 and 78.
24 Playford, *A Brief Introduction the the Skill of Musick* (London, 1664), 88-91.
25 Mace, *Musick's Monument*, 234.
26 See Robert Unwin, "'An English Writer on Music': James Talbot, 1664-1708," *Galpin Society Journal* 40 (1987): 59.

with information probably given by different informants."[27] Some of the names of informants on string instruments are revealed, among them James Paisible and Edward Lewis for the Bass violin, and Gottfried Finger for the treble and tenor viols, the double-bass, and the enigmatic *Viol di Corunna* (would it be the baryton, known also as *Viola Bordone, Paraton, Pardon*?). The informant on the division viol is unidentified. Of all the seventeenth-century sources presently known to us, Talbot's manuscript is by far the richest in organological matters, giving actual measurements in great detail.

Characteristics of the Division Viol

In England, as mentioned above, divisions were performed on various instruments, including viols. In the second half of the seventeenth century, a specific kind of viol became identified as the ideal medium to fulfil this musical function. It was called *division-viol*,[28] and it had a special character: It was a soloistic instrument apt for highly virtuosic playing.

Simpson's treatise depicts viols of two different shapes, both of which are described as apt for the performance of divisions (see Figure 1).

Although Simpson himself is depicted in portrait playing on a viol of the second ("viol-") shape, the author advocates the first, "violin-shaped" viol as better suited for the purpose of divisions, being more resonant and having a livelier, faster sound ("like a violin"). This is clearly stated in the section of his text entitled "*What kind of viol is fittest for Division*": "The Sound [of that kind of viol] should be quick, and sprightly, like a Violin; and Viols of that shape ["violin-shaped"] (the Bellyes being digged out of the Plank) do commonly render such a Sound."[29] Preferably, division viols should have carved fronts like violins, in place of the bent fronts customary in English viol building.[30] The caption of the illustration of the two types of viols (Figure 1) confirms the superior reso-

---

27 Personal communication with Ephraim Segerman, January 2001. See also Segerman, "The Sizes of English Viols and Talbot's Measurements," *Galpin Society Journal* 48 (1995): 33-45. Talbot's accuracy of measurements is discussed by Darryl Martin, "The Talbot Manuscript—Better As It Is Than the Book It Never Was?" (paper presented at a postgraduate seminar, University of Edinburgh Department of Music, 2005). Martin's paper is available online at http://www.darryl-martin.co.uk/talmanbetter.htm (accessed 19 May 2009).
28 Simpson, *Division-Violist*, 1.
29 Simpson, *The Division-Viol*, 1.
30 Bent fronts were made out of strips of spruce that were joined, bent, and then slightly carved. See Segerman, "A Note on the Belly Construction of Early English Viols," *FoMRHI Quarterly* 20 (1980): 25; and Michael Fleming, "Viol-Making in England c. 1580-1660" (doctoral diss., The Open University, 2001), 1:10.

nance of the violin-shaped viol: "Either of the two viol shapes is suitable for divisions, but the first is more resonant."[31]

Figure 1.   Viols in Simpson's *Division-Violist*: (a) "violin-shaped"; (b) "viol-shaped"

The back of the division viol is neither discussed nor depicted by Simpson. Our source of information on this part of the instrument is Talbot, whose measurements, according to Ephraim Segerman, imply that it had an arched back as well as front. Analyzing the data in the Talbot's manuscript, Segerman concludes that "The difference between the depth under the bridge and the depth at the sides, which should be the arching height, is twice as great as we would expect... . This could be the result of the back being arched as well as the belly. His Division Viol may then be one of the type preferred by Simpson with 'the Bel-

---

31 "Forma Chelyos utravis Minuritonibus apta, Sed Prima resonantior." Simpson, *The Division-Viol*, caption of illustration facing page 1.

lyes being digged out of the Plank' (and back as well) in a violin type of construction."[32] According to Segerman, Talbot's measurements for the division viol also imply that the arched back had an upper cant, in the *Amati-fashion*, "because the body depth at the neck was 1 5/8" less than elsewhere along the edge (there is no such entry for the bass violin)."[33]

The presence of a cant together with the arched back is a feature characteristic of the Cremonese school of viol construction: of viols made by the Amati Brothers, such as the 1597 bass (preserved at the Smithsonian Institution, Washington, DC), and the 1611 tenor (in the Russian State Collection, Moscow) and bass (in the Ashmolean Museum, Oxford) made for the Medicis.[34] This kind of construction found its way to Britain in the second half of the seventeenth century, and it can be seen in most of the surviving violin-shaped English viols of the period 1660-1730, made by a maker of "the Richard Meares School," ca. 1680[35]: by William Baker, 1682; Edward Lewis I, ca. 1685 and c.1690; Barak Norman, 1708; and Edward Lewis II, ca. 1720.[36] All of these instruments were transformed into celli at some point after viols fell from fashion. But still, the presence of the cant on their arched backs identifies them as former viols, as we can infer from a note taken from the diary of Alfred Hill:

> Miss Helen McGregor, the rather attractive little Scottish violinist... is taking up, for teaching purposes, the cello, and we have recently sold her an interesting instrument of small dimensions made by Barak Norman in 1708, which is a curious blend of Gamba and cello—the back, although modeled, cants off at the top like that of a Gamba. The price we are getting for this cello is £40, payment to be made by installments!"[37]

Makers would go to considerable pains to insert cants in viols with arched backs, cants with no practical function as in flat-backed viols,[38] because, I believe, as Hill points out, the cant functioned as a viol trademark. It is interesting to note that arched backs with upper cants appear solely on violin-shaped viols like Simpson's, possibly to further mark them as viols (Figure 2).

---

32 Segerman, "Sizes of English Viols," 38. See also Segerman, "On Talbot's Measurements of Viols," *FoMRHI Quarterly* 25 (1981): 56.
33 Segerman, personal comunication (March 2009).
34 See Herzog, "Violin Traits in Italian Viol Building, Rule or Exception?" in *The Italian Viola da Gamba: Proceedings of the International Symposium on the Italian Viola da Gamba, Magnano, Italy, 29 April-1 May 2000*, ed. Susan Orlando (Solignac and Turin, 2002), 160.
35 Sotheby's Catalogue, 3/03/85, lot 73.
36 All of these instruments can be seen in Herzog, *The Quinton and Other Viols*," vol. 2.
37 As noted in the diary of Alfred Hill (currently in private collection), on 22 February 1919; courtesy of Charles Beare.
38 The cant became a part of viol construction during the sixteenth century.

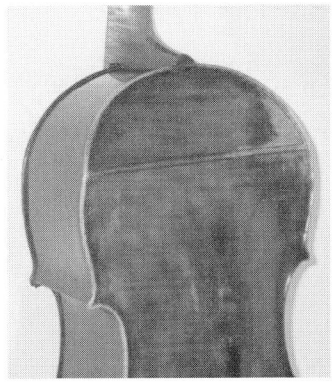

Figure 2. Arched backs with upper cants on two viols by Edward Lewis ca. 1685

To my knowledge, all of the surviving violin-shaped English viols of the period have arched backs with cants, with two exceptions: an instrument with flat back and a cant by Thomas Cole, 1678; and an instrument with an arched back without cant by Barak Norman, ca. 1722.[39] All of the viols with arched backs also display the overlapping edges of table and back that are typical of the violin family, which seem to be present in Simpson's picture of the violin-shaped division viol as well. (The flat-backed 1678 viol by Thomas Cole (fl. 1660-90) has flush edges.) Cole's viol is one of the instruments that most closely resemble that depicted in Simpson's illustration, with pointed corners, rounded shoulders, and double purfling on front and back.[40]

Christopher Simpson addresses the size of a division viol in relation to other viols as follows: "I would have a *Division-Viol* to be of something a shorter *size* than a *Consort-Basse*... The *Strings*, a little bigger than those of a *Lyra-Viol*."[41] This same ratio is confirmed in John Playford's book:

> There are three Sorts of *Basse Viols*, as there is three manner of ways in playing. First, a *Basse Viol* for *Consort* must be one of the largest Size, and the strings proportionable. Secondly, a *Basse viol* for *Divisions* must be of a lesse Size, and the strings according. Thirdly, a *Basse viol* to Play *Lyra way* which is by *Tablature*, must be somewhat lesse then the two former, and strung proportionable.[42]

---

39 For details, see Herzog, *The Quinton and Other Viols*, vol 2.
40 Cole also made instruments with so-called viol-shaped bodies (personal communication with Thomas MacCracken).
41 Simpson, *The Division-Violist*, 1-2.
42 Playford, *Brief Introduction* (1664), 88.

In his viol classification scheme,[43] James Talbot also describes the division viol as an intermediate size between the consort bass and the lyra viol. The measurements given by Talbot agree with proportions given by others, although there are discrepancies between the measurements of individual viols. Ephraim Segerman notes that the discrepancies are too numerous to ascribe them to measuring or scribal error, although Talbot did make occasional errors in individual measurements. He suggests instead that it is likely that measurments were taken from two different sets of viols.[44] Viol measurements were never absolute; they varied according to maker, the needs of the client, and within each size of viol, although the sequence of sizes (from the smallest to the largest: tenor, lyra, division, consort) was typically largely followed. An instrument at the outer limit of its size-range could be used as a substitute for the instrument in the category just above or below it, as exemplified by Thomas Mace's advice to use the bigger lyra viols as division viols: "Add to all *These* 3 *Full-Siz'd Lyro-Viols...* Let *Them* be *Lusty, Smart-speaking Viols*; ... They will serve likewise for *Division-Viols* very properly.[45]

On the actual dimensions of the division viol, Simpson writes: "I would have a *Division-Viol* to be of something a shorter *size* than a *Consort-Basse*, that so the *Hand* may better command it; more or less short, according to reach of his fingers who is to use it: but the ordinary size, such as may carry a String of thirty Inches from the Bridge (duely placed) to the Nutt."[46] Simpson refers to the ordinary division viol as having a string length of thirty inches (76.14 cm), allowing some variation to accommodate the needs of the individual violist. Such string length was reiterated in 1722 by "T.B." (who might be simply reproducing Simpson) in his *Compleat Musick-Master*.[47] Talbot's string length for the division viol is 27 inches (68.52 cm), which is comfortable for all but the smallest of hands. But Simpson's string length of 30 inches (76.14cm), given in both editions of his treatise, leaves it abundantly clear there is no reason to call the division viol a "*small* bass viol," as some writers do.[48] On the contrary, Simpson's division viol was very large, from a modern perspective.

Perhaps Simpson and Talbot used inches of different lengths? The answer to this question is no. In the period between 1658 and 1824, England used one single standard, the Queen Elizabeth Yard. The original yardstick that defined this

---

43 Cited in in Donington, "Talbot's Manuscript," 28.
44 Segerman, personal communication (March 2009).
45 Mace, *Musick's Monument*, 246.
46 Simpson, *The Division-Violist*, 1-2.
47 "T.B.," quoted in Donington, "Talbot's Manuscript," 41 and 43.
48 According to Ian Woodfield, "Two small bass instruments called 'lyra' and 'division' viols were used in the performance of solo music in England." See Woodfield, "Viol," in *The New Grove Dictionary of Music and Musicians*, 2nd ed., ed. Stanley Sadie (London, 2001), 26:663.

standard survives but has been broken, so it cannot be measured accurately; another one, from 1659, "has been measured to give a foot length of 304.563 mm," and the inch as 2.538 cm instead of the modern 2.54 cm. But even if Simpson had used the earlier standard from 1497, the difference would have been negligible, for the earlier foot was only slightly shorter, at 304.49 mm.[49]

Talbot also gives us other figures for his division viol: body length of 69.16 cm, body widths of 35.53, 25.38 and 40.60 cm respectively, neck length of 39.34 cm, fingerboard length of 46.95 cm, and tailpiece length of 27.92 cm.

Hoping to have at least a rough idea of the other dimensions of Simpson's violin-shaped division, I asked Ephraim Segerman to project those dimensions by scaling Simpson's drawing based on the measurements provided by the author. He kindly did so, using as departure point the distance between hair fixings on the bow, given by Simpson as 27 inches.[50] This factor (measured as 9.7 cm) produced a body length of 30.1 inches (76.4 cm), a neck length of 14.2 inches (36.1 cm), a fingerboard length of 20.7 inches (52.7 cm), and a projected string stop of 29.4 inches (74.6 cm), which "corrected for the angle of the strings, leads very close to the 30-inch string stop that Simpson reported."[51]

Now, in order to compare these figures with Talbot's, it is necessary first to address what seems to be a mistake in Talbot's figures for the division viol: his total sum of *nut to tailpiece via bridge* figure of 104.70 cm does not correspond to his total sum of *neck and body lengths* figure of 108.50 cm, as it should.[52] The mistake seems to lie in the disproportionately large figure given for the *neck length*.[53] It does not make sense for the division viol, classified by Talbot as *smaller* than the consort bass and the double bass, to have a neck *longer* than both—especially taking into account the fact that Talbot offers a second set of measurements where the division viol is smaller than the consort bass and the double bass in *every* parameter.

It is possible to correct Talbot's mistake with the help of his own data: One takes his "nut to tailpiece end via bridge" figure (104.70 cm), deducts 2% to account for the increase caused by the angle (arriving at 102.61 cm) and then subtracts the instrument's body length. The result is a figure of 33.44 cm for the neck-length, consistent with the 32.57 cm arrived at by scaling down Simpson's figures. Translated into inches, this means that the neck-length recorded by Tal-

---

49 Martin, "Talbot's Manuscript."
50 Simpson, *The Division-Violist*, 2 (referring to a picture on page 1).
51 Segerman, personal communication, 2001.
52 The first figure should in fact be greater than the second, "because of the longer route caused by the angle over the bridge." See Segerman, "Sizes of English Viols," 37.
53 This is a hypothesis considered but dismissed by Segerman. He suggests that the problem derives from the fingerboard length figure of 1 foot, 6 inches, 4 lignes—which should have been bigger (1 foot, 9 inches, 4 lignes), thus matching "the string stop specified by Simpson and T.B." See Segerman, "Talbot's Measurements," 58-9.

bot of 1 foot 3 inches 4 lignes should have been 1 foot 0 inches 4 lignes—i.e., three inches shorter.[54] Segerman acknowledges the possibility that the mistake might be in the neck-length figure, observing that this "also provides a satisfactory solution. It has the attraction, when compared with the longer-fingerboard solution [which he prefers], that the proportion of the neck with respect to other parameters is more like that of the other viols."[55]

Once the mistake in Talbot's neck-length figure has been corrected, and once we have projected Simpson's division viol, it is possible to make a rough comparison between these two instruments. This is done in Table 1.[56] Simpson's viol has been scaled down to Talbot's string length, and Talbot's viol has been scaled up to Simpson's string length, so that by having viols of the same string length side by side, it is easier to compare the other parameters. The Table 1 shows us that Talbot's measurements for the division viol are surprisingly close to the measurements inferred from Simpson's drawing. The main differences are due to the profiles of the viols: Simpson's is proportionally narrower in its upper part and waist, and wider in its lower part.

Table 1. Dimensions of viols given by Simpson and Talbot (with figures in cm)

	Simpson	Talbot scaled to Simpson (factor 1,1112084)	Simpson scaled to Talbot (factor 0,8999212)	**Talbot**
Body length	*76.40*	76.85	*68.75*	69.16
Body width upper	*33.9*	39.48	*30.50*	35.53
Body width middle	*24.7*	28.20	*22.22*	25.38
Body width lower	*47.4*	45.11	*42.65*	40.60
Neck length	*36.10*	37.16	*32.48*	*33.44*
Fingerboard length	*52.70*	52.17	*47.42*	46.95
Tailpiece length	*29.69*	31.02	*26.71*	27.92
String length	76.14	76.14	68.52	68.52

---

54 I am indebted to Ephraim Segerman for his help in this calculation.
55 Segerman, "Talbot's Measurements," 58.
56 Figures in italics are deduced from other statements. The body- and neck-length of Simpson's viol are deduced by Segerman from Simpson's drawing, using the bow hair and string length as scaling factors; its body widths and fingerboard length were measured and calculated by myself using Segerman's factor. They are approximations. The scaling factor is 7.07 full-scale millimeter = 1 picture millimeter.

It is important to note that the sizes of Simpson's and Talbot's division viols represent only a *range* of acceptable sizes for the instrument. The division viol, with a body length varying from Talbot's 69.16 cm to Simpson's projected 76.40 cm, would fit just below the consort bass (usually considered to range between 60 and 80 cm in length) in a general taxonomy of bass viols.

Type of Finial

Finial is the generic name for the end of the peg-box of an instrument, made in an ornamental way. The finials of viols were usually formed in the shape of a carved head, an open scroll, or a full-fledged scroll like that commonly seen on violins. In Simpson's illustration of two viols (Figure 1), we see two kinds of finial: The viol-shaped instrument has a carved head, while the violin-shaped one has a scroll. The scroll is shown with one broad turn visible, suggestive of the open scroll commonly associated with viols. Talbot mentions a carved head only in his measurements for the double-bass viol.

Type of Tailpiece

Talbot's manuscript describes two kinds of tailpiece attachment: one usually associated with viols, with the tailpiece resting "on [a] square piece of wood called *term* [hookbar]"; and another typical of violins, with the tailpiece attached to a button (which he names *breech*)[57] with gut or even iron wire. In Simpson's engraving (Figure 1), both tailpieces seem to rest on a *term*. The tailpieces of Talbot's tenor, lyra, and consort bass viols rest on a *term*, unlike the tailpiece of his double bass viol, which is attached to a *breech* by tail gut or wire. Segerman observes that "in Talbot's list of measurements [for the division viol], there is an entry 'From the end of the Tailpiece to the bottom of the Belly' which is crossed out, and no measurements are filled in. This entry tells us that there was no *term*."[58] The presence of a *term* or hookbar implies a projection of the tailpiece beyond the bottom of the instrument, producing what is called *tailpiece excess*, expressed in a figure deducted by Talbot from the whole length.[59] The fact that this deduction is absent in his division viol measurements indicates that, in Talbot's division viol, the tailpiece attachment was of a violin type. It is possible, therefore, that either type of tailpiece attachment was used in division viols.

---

57 Cited in Donington, "Talbot's Manuscript," 31 and 34.
58 Segerman, personal communication (January 2001).
59 Cited in Donington, "Talbot's Manuscript," 31.

Bridge, Nut, and Soundpost

The bridge for a division viol described by Talbot has a height of 8.25 cm and a breadth of 9.20 cm at the top and 8.88 cm at the bottom. Talbot's measurements for viol bridges increase proportionally in height relative to the size of the instrument. The bridge of Simpson's division viol is depicted in the his illustration of the two viols (Figure 1), and it seems to be in scale with them. If we project its dimensions by scaling to the same factor used before, we get a height of 9.89 cm at the center and a breadth of 10.60 cm at the top (from both the isolated bridge and the bridge on the violin-shaped viol) and 11.31 cm at the bottom.

Since the bridge curvature is set according to the viol's function (viols destined to play chordal music were usually equipped with a flatter bridge than those intended to play melodic lines, jumps and runs), Simpson recommended that that the *Bridge*, as round as that of a *Consort-Basse*, that so each several String may be hit with a bolder touch of the Bow. One presumes from this statement that the lyra had a comparatively flatter bridge, more suitable for playing chords. Nevertheless, the height of the nut should be similar on both viols (lyra and division), "for ease and convenience of Stopping."[60] Fingerboard and bridge should match their curve, causing the strings to stand at a uniform distance from the fingerboard: "The *Strings,* a little bigger than those of a *Lyra-Viol,* which must be laid at the like nearness to the Finger-board, for ease and convenience of Stopping.... . *The Plate* or *Finger-board...* must also be of a *proportionate* roundness to the Bridge, so that each String may lie at an equal nearness to it."[61]

Thomas Mace comments on the *due place* of the bridge, alluded to by Simpson: "The *Best Place* for the *Bridge*, is to stand *just* in the 3 *Quarter Dividing* of the *Open Cuts Below*; though *Most, most erroneously* suffer them much to stand too *High*, which is a *Fault.*"[62] This placement of the bridge, present in many viol iconography sources, is lower than today's standards. Talbot, writing two decades later, advocates placing the bridge close to its location on the violin: "Place bridge even with Notch or the 'f' of the Sounding holes."[63] Talbot also refers to two possibilities for the placement of the soundpost, the first being just opposite the foot of the bridge, an old practice referred to in treatises by Bagatella and Galeazzi in the eighteenth century and employed by nineteenth-century Mirecourt builders,[64] and the second being the modern one, slightly away from the foot of the bridge.

---

60 Ibid.
61 Ibid.
62 Mace, *Musick's Monument*, 246.
63 Cited in Donington, "Talbot's Manuscript," 30.
64 Luc Breton, "The Physical Problems of Barring and the Function of the Bridge" (paper presented at the International Symposium on the Italian Viola da Gamba, Magnano, April-

The Bow

According to Simpson, "A *Viol-Bow* for *Division*, should be stiff, but not heavy. Its *Length*, (betwixt the two places where the Haires are fastned at each end) about 27 inches [68.52 cm]. The *Nutt*, short. The *Height* of it, about a Fingers bredth, or little more."[65] The bow in James Talbot's manuscript seems to be described in terms its total length: 30 inches [76.14 cm] for the lyra and division viols.[66] The total length of Simpson's bow, scaled from the drawing, is roughly 31 inches [78.7 cm]—i.e., slightly longer than Talbot's.

Strings, Frets, and Temperaments

According to Simpson, the division viol has seven frets tied to its neck and six strings tuned as on a bass viol, D–G–c–e–a–d'. Addressing their relative gauge, he writes: "It must be *accommodated* with six Strings; and seven Frets, like those of a *Lute*, but somthing thicker. The *Strings*, a little bigger than those of a *Lyra-Viol*."[67] Playford refers to the division viol as a "Sort of Basse Viol" with the same number of strings, tuning, and number of frets.[68]

The number and tuning of the strings of the division viol is not mentioned by Talbot. In his manuscript, the staff allocated for this purpose is left blank, and Talbot reports only that the instrument's lowest string is a D.[69] In a partially illegible note (the words in brackets are uncertain), he informs us that the lowest strings of the viol and bass violin could be overspun (wound with metal), a fairly recent novelty that had an impact on the sizes of bowed instruments, as this new technology enabled to the instrument to produce lower pitches: "In low[est] Basses [mixed] with Copper or [Silver] Wire in lowest [*illegible*] of Bass Violin or Viol."[70] Talbot documents the presence of movable frets, arranged in a variable way according to the temperament chosen by the player: "The Division Viol has 7 Frets placed at the discretion of the Master."[71]

We now have a picture of the instrument. However, there are still some questions to be answered.

May 2000); and Breton, "The System and Proportions of Barring on Viols," *The Italian Viola da Gamba*, ed. Orlando, 187.
65 Simpson, *The Division-Violist*, 2
66 Cited in Donignton, "Talbot's Manuscript," 43.
67 Simpson, *The Division-Violist*, 4.
68 Playford, *Brief Introduction* (1664), 88.
69 See John R. Catch, "James Talbot's Viols," *Chelys* 17 (1988): 34.
70 Catch, "Talbot's Viols," 37.
71 Cited in Donington, "Talbot's Manuscript," 32.

The Violin-Shaped Division Viol

Although he depicted division viols of two shapes, one traditionally associated with violins and the other with viols, Simpson advocated the latter for the performance of divisions rather than the violin-shaped instrument What was the background of Simpson's preference, what do we know about violin-shaped viols in England?

Since the beginning of their history, viols had been built in diverse shapes, some or them resembling contemporary plucked and bowed instruments like the violin, lyra, and guitar. Violin-shaped viols were present all over Europe, including England, from the sixteenth through the eighteenth centuries.[72] The earliest known extant painting of a viol in England is possibly that of a violin-shaped viol, with six strings and frets, depicted in a wall painting from a modest domestic dwelling in an Oxfordshire village. As Michael Fleming observes, "The source for this cello-shaped viol is probably a Netherlandish print from the third quarter of the sixteenth century rather than a local instrument, but it is typical of the images that viol-makers would have in mind when deciding what their viols should look like."[73]

The incidence of viols with violin traits in sixteenth- and seventeenth-century British iconography is surprisingly high, considering the fact that depictions of viols are rare in British painting. Fleming suggests that the form of those English instruments could have been influenced by imported Continental paintings and prints, so that "viols based on these designs would be dominated by 'cello-shaped' instruments, the sort favored by Christopher Simpson."[74] And, he adds, "This helps to explain the mass disappearance of English viols, because instruments of this shape are most easily transformed into violins and cellos." Such viols could also have been imported to England, as was common at least until 1660.[75] Harvey notes that English makers flourishing at this time "must have been heavily influenced by the instruments then coming from northern Italy, not least those of the well-established Amati family."[76]

When, in 1659, Simpson selected a violin-shaped viol as the ideal (but not the sole) medium for playing divisions, the coexistence of different viol shapes was clearly established in England. In Figure 3, a contemporary English etching, viol-shaped viols with C-holes are displayed side by side with violin-shaped vi-

---

72 See Herzog, *The Quinton and Other Viols*.
73 See Fleming, *Viol-Making in England*, 1: 81, 88-89.
74 Fleming, *Viol-Making in England*, 1:114.
75 Guy F. Oldham, "Import and Export Duties on Musical Instruments in 1660," *Galpin Society Journal* 9 (1957): 97-9.
76 Brian W. Harvey, *The Violin Family and its Makers in the British Isles: An Illustrated History and Directory* (Oxford, 1995), 27.

ols with F-holes, all apparently double-purfled, bearing carved heads or scrolls and tailpiece-attachments of the hook-bar type.

Figure 3.   English etching ca. 1660[77]

Simpson's *Division-Violist* was printed just before the Restoration of the Monarchy in England in 1660, a time of transformation in the musical scene, with an increased interest in violin music,[78] Italian monody, and solo writing:

> [U]pon the Restauration of King Charles [II], the old way of consorts were layd aside at court, and the King made an establishment, after a French model

---

77 Cover of *Chelys* 19 (1990).
78 While Italian solo violin music had been sold since the 1630s, the arrival of German virtuoso Thomas Baltzar around 1656 certainly made an impact. See Peter Walls, "The Influence of the Italian Violin School in 17th-century England," *Early Music* 18, no. 4 (1990): 577 and 579.

of 24 violins, and the style of musick was accordingly. So that became the ordinary music of the Court, Theaters, and such as courted the violin...This French manner of instrumentall musick did not gather so fast as to make a revolution all at once, but during the greatest part of the King's reigne the old musick was used in the countrys and in many meetings and societys in London: but the treble viol was discarded, and the violin took its place.[79]

The imbalance between the ordinary consort bass viol and the new-fangled "scoulding" violin could probably be felt at the "many meetings and societys in London" dedicated to the performance of chamber music, where violins and viols played together. In order to solve the problem and improve the dialogue with the violin, some partisans of "the Noble Base Viol"[80] decided to employ the more resonant and powerful division-viol in place of the ordinary and "weak-sounding" consort viol, as documented by "T.B." in 1722 (by that time, the word *consort* had come to denote an ensemble with violins): "A Viol of Division size ... may serve to play in Consort or a single Lesson, or both as you will have it strung."[81] So, in addition to its obvious use by soloists performing divisions upon a ground, the division viol could also fulfil the role of an appropriate bass for a violin consort. This passage tells us that the instrument should, in principle, be strung differently for each of its functions (possibly more heavily when providing the bass for violins), although compromise stringing could be done as well.

In this way, the viol, an instrument favoured by gentlemen, would find its place anew in the private corners of English society—in music meetings and in the exclusive gatherings of music societies, like the weekly concerts organized by Thomas Britton since 1678, well into the eighteenth century.[82]

The Six-String Violin-Shaped Division Viol and Talbot's Six-String Bass Violin

One final question remains, concerning Talbot's manuscript report of a six-string bass violin, tuned D–G–c–e–a–d' like a division viol. What would be the difference between those two violin-shaped instruments, a bass violin and a viol, both with six strings, tuned in the same way, considering the possibly that not every violin-shaped viol would have the distinctive Amati-inspired round back with a fold?

Given the violin-like construction of the division viol, it has been proposed that "Talbot's division viol *was* a converted bass violin"[83] (or a small violone[84]),

---

79 North, *Musicall Grammarian*, 349 and 351.
80 Ibid., 227.
81 "T.B.," *Musick-Master* (1722); cited in Donington, "Talbot's Manuscript," 43.
82 See Sir John Hawkins, *A General History of the Science and Practice of Music* (London, 1853; repr., New York, 1963), 2:763, 790, and 805-806.
83 Segerman, "Talbot's Measurements," 56 (emphasis in original).

and also that Simpson's viol was "a fretted six-string form of the bass-violin."[85] However, it seems logical to assume that Talbot knew *exactly* what he was writing when he described the six-string bass violin and the six-string division-viol as *two different instruments*. I would also consider information given by Simpson on this matter to be both accurate and reliable.

To my mind, the one obvious physical difference between viols and violins lies in the length of their necks relative to their bodies,[86] *not* in the shapes of their bodies, because viols can be built in at least four different shapes (guitar, violin, festoon, and the so-called viol-shape). The neck length is crucial in establishing the string length, and therefore the string gauge, of a bowed instrument. In a bass instrument, a short string length calls for thick strings in order to be effective at all; and the contrary is true for a long string length. Early cello necks are short, viol necks are long. Together with the number and tuning of strings, neck length is a decisive factor defining the sound output, nature and character of a bowed instrument.

Talbot's manuscript mentions bass violins with four strings (referred to as English), five strings (referred to as French), and six strings.[87] Compared to his division viol, Talbot's four-string bass violin has a larger body and a shorter neck. Its body length is 71.06 cm, longer than that of his division viol with a length of 69.16 cm, and its neck length is 25.38 cm, shorter than that of the division viol with a neck of 39.34 cm, if we use the seemingly mistaken original figure, or 33.44 cm in the corrected measurement.

Five-string bass violins are described by Talbot as French; such instruments were indeed used extensively in France, as part of the *basse continue* section of the orchestra of the Parisian Opera. In particular, they were associated with the music of Jean-Baptiste Lully. They were bulky, larger than the modern cello, and tuned C–G–d–a–d′, with an added top string to expand the limited range and compensate for the lack of agility of the four-string instrument.[88] In England, French five-string bass violins were also employed for performances of music "in the Babtist [Lully] way," and in "a society of gentlemen of good esteem" (see Figure 4).[89]

---

84 Donington, "Talbot's Manuscript," 40; Catch, "Talbot's Viols," 36-7.
85 Benjamin Hebbert, "A Catalogue of Surviving Instruments by, or Ascribed to, Barak Norman," *Galpin Society Journal* 54 (2001): 287.
86 This issue has been tackled in Herzog, "Italian Viol Building," 147; and Herzog, *The Quinton and Other Viols*, 1:62-65.
87 Cited in Donington, "Talbot's Manuscript," 28.
88 See Mary Cyr, "Basses and *basse continue* in the Orchestra of the Paris Opéra," *Early Music* 10, no. 2 (1982): 158.
89 North, c. 1726, "on Music", 304; NORTH, *Musicall Grammarian*, 352.

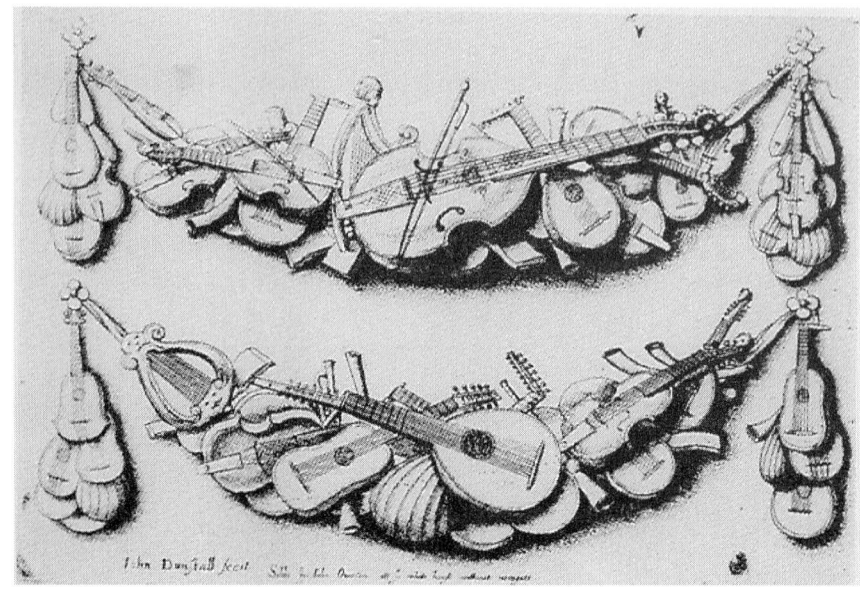

Figure 4. Simpson's Division Viol and a five-string cello depicted in Theodor Matham's Vanitas (1622), Gemeentearchief, Haarlem. Note the relative proportions of body length to neck length.

The six-string bass violin described by Talbot would have been an attractive alternative for viol players performing French music, and they also would have provided a more solid foundation to the violin ensemble. The tuning of the strings would remain the same, as would the underhand bow-grip, which was not uncommon for cellists until quite late in the eighteenth century.[90] This could be the functional background for the special six-string bass violin made by Edward Lewis the father (1651-1717[91]) for Lord Abergenny, as reported by Talbot in a passage that has given rise to a great deal of controversy (see Figure 5):[92] "Lewis has a Bass Violin (made for Lord Abergenny) which has 6 strings: its neck is somewhat shorter than that of usual Violin [in order] to bear a Pitch: he

---

90 See Mark Smith, "The Cello Bow Held the Viol Way; Once Common, but Now Forgotten," *Chelys* 24 (1995): 47-61.
91 My thanks to Benjamin Hebbert and John Topham for these dates.
92 See Donington, "Talbot's Manuscript," 40; Catch, "Talbot's Viols," 36-7; Segerman, "Sizes of English Viols," 33-45; Segerman, "Late 17th century English bass violins, and catlin highest pitches," *FoMRHI Quarterly* 92 (1998): 28-9; Catch, "Talbot's 'Usual' Bass Violin," *Galpin Society Journal* 51 (1998): 271; and Segerman, "On Talbot's 'Usual' Bass Violin," *Galpin Society Journal* 52 (1999): 389-90.

says the treble string is of the same sound and size with the 3d of Bass Violin (or Viol) ... And tuned B. Viol way.[93]

Figure 5.   From the James Talbot manuscript

Lewis was an important maker with clients from the upper segments of society. His work today "stands in high repute, though extremely rare ... his originals passed off as Italian ... Lewis is one of a group of distinguished English makers the absence of whose better work from any museum in Britain is a national tragedy."[94] Lewis's special instrument would have been louder than a viol or an ordinary bass violin; it would have been strung with very thick strings, tuned like a bass viol. And if, in Talbot's manuscript, the four-string bass violin had a larger body and a shorter neck than the division viol, this proportion would have been even more strongly marked in the case of Lewis's six-string bass violin, its neck being "somewhat shorter than that of usual B. Violin."[95]

---

93 Cited in Donington, "Talbot's Manuscript," 30.
94 Harvey, *The Violin Family*, 78-79.
95 Cited in Donington, "Talbot's Manuscript," 30.

Ephraim Segerman was the one to open the path to a full understanding of this passage,[96] pointing out that Lewis's six-string bass violin top string could only be of "the same sound and size" (i.e., of the same pitch and gauge) as "the 3d [string] of B. Violin or B. Viol" if the bass violin were tuned to the high pitch standard of the violin band (described by Talbot as *Chappell Pitch*),[97] which was a tone higher than that of the viols (Consort Pitch). In this case, the third string of the bass violin would have a nominal pitch D equivalent in "sound and size [gauge]" to the third string of the bass viol, which has the nominal pitch E.

So, the passage can be summarized as follows. Edward Lewis made a special six-string bass violin for Lord Abergenny.[98] The instrument was intended to produce a powerful sound, to be louder than both the bass viol and the usual bass violin. This was achieved by giving the instrument a very short neck, even "shorter than that of the usual B. Violin," which would enable it to hold a special D–G–c–e–a–d' stringing with very thick strings (the top d' string being of the same gauge of a common viol third string) at high tension.

There was, therefore, a clear distinction between the six-string, long-necked, violin-shaped division viol and the six-string, short-necked, bass violin in the late seventeenth and early eighteenth centuries. Today, however, nearly all the surviving instruments of both kinds have been converted into four-string celli, which means that their original necks are gone—and with them, most of our chances to distinguish between the two instruments. Of those violin-shaped instruments, only the viols with an Amati-like back can still be identified. The true identity of the other violin-shaped six-string instruments, stripped of their original necks, will probably be never known.

---

96 See Segerman, "Bass Violins and Catlin Pitches," 28-29.
97 See Segerman, "Early 18th Century English Pitches ... ," *FoMRHI Quarterly* 67 (1992): 54-56.
98 Abergenny was possibly a viol player, as were many aristocrats. Curiously, *Abergenny* is also the name of a tune in Playford's *The Dancing Master* (London, 1698); and it also appears in *The Compleat Country Dancing-Master* (London, 1731).

Free Historical Subjects

Levon Hakobian

OCTOËCHOS AS AN IDEA
On the Example of Medieval Armenian Sacred Hymnody

From a modern point of view, the category of *echos*—a central one for all medieval Christian sacred music, irrespective of confessional differences—appears rather vague, leaving room for ambiguous interpretations. In modern scholarship, *echos* is usually treated as a combination of two mutually complementary aspects: a modal scale and a collection of stable melodic formulae. It is not always clear, however, which melodic configurations have to be treated as formulae, where the boundaries between different formulae lie, what distinguishes formulae proper from intermediary or linking material, to what extent a formula may be changed or varied, and so forth. In terms of known musical-theoretical categories, the notion of *formula* itself still appears largely abstract, the principles of differentiation of formulae remaining essentially unverifiable. Some scholars prefer to discuss only the "scale" aspect of *echoi*, especially since no known medieval source provides a description of anything resembling the modern notion of a melodic formula (in other words, the "formula" aspect of *echos* seems to have been conceptualized in relatively recent times).

In this paper I will discuss the nature of *echos* as evinced by the example of medieval Armenian sacred hymns, known as *šarakans*. For a number of reasons, *Šaraknoc^c*—the collection of *šarakans*, codified in the thirteenth century and since then remaining unchanged—is a convenient object for a typological study of archaic chant. First, the *šarakans* belonging to various stages of the genre's historical development clearly differ from each other as regards both their poetic style and the structure of their tunes. In other words, the evolution of the genre appears in the *Šaraknoc^c* more or less manifestly. Second, though the genre of *šarakan* developed independently of its Syrian, Byzantine and other counterparts, it originated from the same source as these latter—hence, the conclusions drawn from the study of *šarakans* may be valid for early non-Armenian sacred chant. Third, *Šaraknoc^c* has been preserved in the form of a sufficiently reliable bilingua: its traditional version, with *xaz* (neumatic) notation, was supplemented in the nineteenth century by a version in which the tunes were notated by means of a specially invented system of signs, easily convertible into European staff notation.[1] My main hypothesis consists in the following: The nature of *echos* is based on the primordial ("syncretic") unity of four aspects of *šarakan* as both

---

[1] For more details on *Šaraknocc*, see my earlier book, *Analiz glubinnoy strukturï muzïkal'nogo teksta* (Moscow, 1995), chapter 2.

poetic form and melodic configuration. The aspects in question are syntax, prosody, rhythm, and mode.²

As an illustration, let us examine a stanza from the *šarakan* to All the Apostles, belonging to the archaic stratum of Armenian hymnody (traditionally dated to the fifth through the seventh centuries). As with virtually all archaic *šarakans*, this text is free from syllabic or accentual versification. The stanza consists of three sentences of unequal length with irregular distribution of stresses; in the original, the sentences are separated with the punctuation sign *mijakēt* ("middle stop"), which normally serves for demarcation of more or less finished syntactical units and is roughly equivalent to a semicolon, colon, or comma. For convenience, let us write the stanza in three lines, each line corresponding to a sentence:

(1) Ōrk^c aṙik^c išxanut^{c}iwn i veray azgi mardkan;
(2) kapel ew arjakel i yerkins ew i yerkri;
(3) arjakec^{c}ēk^c əzmez i kapanac^c mełac^c meroc^c.

The stanza's interlinear translation runs:

(1) You, who took the power over humankind,
(2) to bind and to unbind in the earth and in heaven;
(3) unbind us from the fetters of our sins.

Such three-phrase stanzas are the most common structural units of *šarakan* texts. As a rule, they divide into two unequal parts according to the scheme (1+2), 3. The stanza's first part, consisting of its first and second phrases, can be called the *narrative* part, while the second part is *doctrinal*. In the narrative part, the *šarakan*'s topic is developed in more or less concrete terms, while the doctrinal part appears as a rather generalized formula, which, according to the hymn's function in the liturgy, is addressed to saints (in this case to the apostles), God, the faithful, etc. In contrast to the narrative part, the doctrinal part, possibly with some variations, may pass from one hymn to another and is often used as a refrain.

The Example 1 shows this same stanza in a version written down around 1875 by means of so-called new Armenian notation. Devised by H. Limončean specially to record monodic chant, this system of signs can easily be transcribed into staff notation (to be sure, the latter is not adapted to discern non-tempered intervals, but this is unimportant for our purposes).³ The *šarakan* in question belongs to the third *jayn* (*echos*) of the Armenian system of eight modes (*ut^c-jayn*

---

2   The latter term is used in the sense of melodic or scale type, synonymously with the Russian word *lad*.
3   Quoted from *Jaynagreal Šarakan hogewor ergocc* (Sharakan [*sic*]: Hymns of the Armenian Apostolic Church) (Yerevan, 1997), vol. 1, 464-65 (in ancient Armenian).

= octoëchos). In the conventional terms of the theory of medieval chant, the third *jayn* has the following parameters: ambitus *(f)g-f'*; tenor and finalis (full cadence tone) *c'*; "half cadence" tone *g'*; and its distinctive interval is the augmented second between second and third degrees from the "half cadence" tone (*a* flat-*b* natural). The choice of a *šarakan* of the third *jayn* is, in this case, arbitrary; in the theoretical system advanced here, the differences between parameters of *echoi* are merely of surface nature and do not affect the primordial and fundamental unity.

Example 1

As we see in this example, both sentences of the stanza's narrative part are sung essentially to the same tune. Minor differences are conditioned by the unequal length of the two phrases, and by irregular distribution of stresses. The first phrase has a disyllabic anacrusis *g-as*, with each of these two tones corresponding to one metric unit (quarter-note); when the voice reaches tenor on the third metric unit, this coincides with the phrase's first stressed syllable. The second phrase's anacrusis is monosyllabic; the unstressed first syllable is sung on two metric units, while the stressed second syllable also falls on tenor.[4] In the middle of both the first phrase (after the word *išxanut͡ʿiwn*, power) and the second (after *arjakel*, unbind) there are semantic and syntactic caesuras ("minor" caesuras); in the example they are, for convenience, marked with bar lines. According to the rules of Armenian prosody, the last syllable of a word is always stressed; hence, both caesuras are immediately preceded by stressed syllables. In the melody, these syllables correspond to *c'* (in the first phrase, the closing syllable is enlarged due to a kind of "fermata" with neighbor note); both closing syllables are preceded by identical melodic turns. Even more similar are the

---

4 In *šarakans* of the third *jayn*, the turn between A-flat and C is more common for monosyllabic anacruses.

closing segments of both phrases of the narrative part before the "major" semantic and syntactic caesuras (i.e., those caesuras marked by *mijakēt* in the original text). The closing (stressed) syllables of both phrases coincide with the "middle stop" note *g*, reached via downward motion.

Thus, in terms of melodic configuration, each phrase is more or less arch-like: the ascending movement towards the first stressed syllable in the beginning of the phrase is complemented by descending movement towards the phrase's final syllable, just before the "major" caesura. The "minor" caesura occurs in the middle of the "arch." In Example 1, the arch-like shape is more obvious in the first phrase, while in the second its left-hand segment is considerably truncated (its monosyllabic anacrusis is rather atypical for the Armenian language, which abounds in polysyllables). In other *šarakans* the details may vary, but the general principle of an arch-like configuration (usually with "minor" caesura in the middle) remains fundamental. Let me underline once more that the length of the arch's left-hand, ascending segment depends upon the length of anacrusis, while the right-hand, descending segment's configuration is rather stable.[5]

Now we can proceed to a functional differentiation of key points and zones that form the structural framework of a phrase of a *šarakan*'s narrative part and, hence, define the rhythm of its unfolding. The phrase's key points are its first stressed syllable (coinciding, in Example 1, with c' reached in upward motion), the stressed syllable immediately preceding the "minor" caesura (and coinciding with the same note), and the stressed syllable immediately preceding the "major" caesura (and coinciding with *g* reached in downward motion). The key zones correspond to several (most often three) syllables on the left of the "minor" caesura, and to several (most often five) syllables on the left of the "major" caesura. In these zones, stable melodic turns are formed. They pass, essentially unchanged, from one *šarakan* tune to another. In contrast to such stable zones, those zones in between, as well as the turns corresponding to the anacruses, are variable.

Thus, the *rhythm* of unfolding within the stanza's narrative part depends upon both *prosody* (the distribution of principal stressed syllables) and *syntax* (the relationship of "minor" and "major" caesuras that segment the text into relatively finished syntactic units). The category of *mode* fits into this syncretic system. The framework of the mode is composed of the closing tones of the minor and major syntactic units, i.e., in the case of the third *jayn*, of *g* and *c'*. Though in other *echoi* the identities of these basic tones are not the same, the "minor" caesura is, in principle, always preceded by the higher basic tone, while the "major" caesura is preceded by the lower one. In different *echoi*, the spans between these basic tones are filled in by different tone collections, imparting to each

---

5 In *šarakans* with melismatic or richly ornamented textures, this regularity is "camouflaged" by adornments, but it can nonetheless be easily revealed through a simple technique of reduction. For details, see Hakobian, *Analiz glubinnoy strukturï*.

echos its specific identity (in the case of the third *echos*, such identity is provided especially by the characteristic interval of the augmented second).

With regard to the doctrinal part of a *šarakan*, that part that completes the stanza's rhetorical disposition, the melodic configuration is different. The only substantial similarity between the doctrinal and narrative parts concerns the ascending formula for the anacrusis (in Example 1, the anacrusis is trisyllabic, and hence the corresponding melodic turn is one metric unit longer than at the beginning of the piece). The doctrinal part as a whole is a relatively long phrase not divided into lesser syntactic units; in other words, it does not contain an inner semantic and syntactic caesura. In the doctrinal part, the element of melodic "standardization" is pronounced more strongly than in the narrative part.[6] Hence, the function of the doctrinal part as the "summary" of the stanza—which, essentially, can be regarded as a kind of miniature sermon—is stressed.[7] Needless to say, the melodic configurations of such doctrinal parts are based upon similar principles in all eight *echoi* of the Armenian *octoëchos*.

The structural scheme presented here is valid for the vast majority of archaic *šarakans*, as well as for a number of more recent ones dated to the eleventh through the thirteenth centuries. Though the scheme is fairly strict, it does not exclude a certain amount of entropy. First, the narrative part can be limited to one sentence, or—more rarely—it can consist of three sentences. Second, the length of variable zones, depending upon the length of the text, may fluctuate within more or less considerable limits. Third, longer phrases often contain additional "minor" caesuras, while in shorter phrases inner caesuras may be absent. Fourth, the structure of the poetic phrase—and, accordingly, the location of a caesura—can be treated in different ways; this sometimes results in discrepancies between the two editions of *Šaraknocʿ* recorded in Limončean's notation.[8] Fifth, in those hymns sung in a slow tempo, the monody's structural framework is often "camouflaged" by ornaments, passing tones, and neighbor tones.[9] Be that as it may, a general structural model exists, and it "works" efficiently in a great number of *šarakans*. To substantiate this point, I would need to adduce numerous examples, perhaps accompanied by extended commentary. Here, however, I will confine myself to a few stanzas drawn from a single source and

---

6 In many *šarakans* of the third *echos*, the concluding phrase is almost identical with this one, save minor variations conditioned by differences in the number of syllables and distribution of stresses.

7 The doctrinal part's special importance is additionally emphasized by prolongations of some syllables, especially the final one.

8 Both were written down in the 1870s, independently of each other, by two equally competent specialists, N. Tcaščean and E. Tntesean. Our example is from Tcaščean's edition.

9 Some relevant examples are given in my above-mentioned book, *Analiz glubinnoi struktury*.

representing the first, the second, the second "lateral,"[10] and the fourth *echoi*, as shown in Examples 2-5. (Note that in those stanzas shown in Examples 2, 3 and 5, the narrative part consists of a single sentence.) The reader will notice structural similarities between all of these examples, despite their surface differences.

---

10 In the Armenian *octoëchos*, the *echoi* are divided into four "main" and four "lateral" *echoi*. This division seems to be purely formal; structurally, the "lateral" *echoi* are independent units rather than derivatives (in contrast to plagal modes of the Western system).

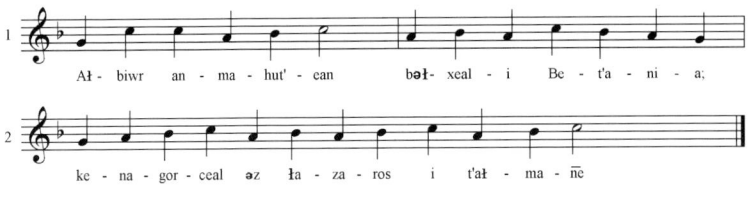

Example 5

The existence of such a model proves that the notion of "melodic formulae" and, perhaps, some other notions of a similar kind (for instance, the Russian *popevka*), intended to characterize the category of *echos* (in Russian, *glas*), are fruits of a somewhat anachronistic rationalization. With respect to formulae, the syncretic unity of the aforementioned categories of syntax, prosody, rhythm, and mode is ontologically more important. The system of eight *echoi* appears as a totality of such unities conditioned by a common rhetorical disposition (to put it somewhat metaphorically, as a group of variations on the same ontological model), or else as an "unity of unities" brought together under the sacred number eight.[11] And it may well be that the same ontology is valid for other regional versions of *octoëchos* as well.

The structural uniformity of archaic *šarakans*, irrespective of their *echoi*, is reflected in the patterns of their *xaz* (neumatic) notation. Any discussion of *xaz* notation inevitably involves a great deal of preliminary explanation and technical detail. Here, I will have to skip over such things and limit myself to a simple assertion: in *xaz*-notated sources, the arch-like configuration of the narrative part is graphically outlined in terms of an opposition between the "ascending" sign *šešt* (/) above the first syllable, and the "descending" sign *but^c* (\) above the last syllable, while the doctrinal part has a different arrangement of *xaz* signs and invariably ends with the sign *erkar* (~), indicating a fermata-like prolongation of the syllable.

In the ninth or tenth century, the orderly syncretic system described here began to break down. New, structurally "looser" models emerged, including the so-called *darjvack^c* or "mutant" tunes, which are essentially independent of the *octoëchos* system though formally attached to some of the eight "canonic" *echoi*. In its definitive form, which took shape around the twelfth century, the Armenian *octoëchos*, though formally still based upon the sacred number eight,

---

11 On the archetypical and sacral meaning of the number eight in connection with *octoëchos*, see Eric Werner, *The Sacred Bridge: The Interdependence of Liturgy and Music in Synagogue and Church during the First Millennium* (New York and London, 1959), 367 ff.

includes some forty to fifty melodic models, many of which bear the stamp of individual authorship.[12]

The idea of *octoëchos* in Armenian hymnody evolved in the same manner as the rest of the genre's essential parameters, including the versification of *šarakan* hymns and the method of representing theological propositions in *šarakans*.[13] The analysis of all of these parameters, embraced in their totality, results in a sufficiently orderly picture. The latter reflects the general typology of the passage from a medieval mentality to one characteristic of more recent epoch, when canonical art was being gradually replaced by individual creation.

---

12 See article, "Šaraknocci ergeriełanaknerə ew nrancc storabažanumnerə" (The Tunes of Armenian Medieval Sacred Hymns [*Šarakan*] and Their Variants"), *Echmiadzin* 49, nos. 4-5 (1992): 63-86; repr. in Manrusum, *Hogewor eražštutcyan patmutcyan, tesutcyan ew gełagitutcyan harccer* (Problems of History, Theory, and Aesthetics of Sacred Music) (Yerevan, 2005), vol. 2, 109-134.

13 See my essay "The Versification of the *Šarakan* Hymns," *Revue des études arméniennes* 24 (1993): 113-27; and "Miǰnadarean šarakanə mšakutcabanakan tesankiwniсс" ("The Medieval *Šarakan* from a Perspective of Cultural History"), *Ganjasar* 4 (1993): 324-33.

Dagmar Hoffmann-Axthelm

SIMONE MARTINI'S *INVESTITURE OF ST. MARTIN*
An Iconographical Approach

The fresco of the investiture of St Martin forms part of the cycle depicting St. Martin's life in the chapel of St. Martin in the lower church of S. Francesco in Assisi. It is attributed to Simone Martini (1284-1344). Of particular interest to organologists is the group of musicians it portrays, and above all the minstrel playing the double recorder. He uses a playing technique seen only rarely in medieval art (Figure 1).[1]

Figure 1. Simone Martini, St Martin's *Investiture* as a Knight

Furthermore, Martini made this minstrel the focal point of the composition, although his rank and the picture's subject would seem to demand that he occupy a marginal place. Minstrels were at the bottom of medieval society, and the

---

This essay is an English revision of my "Kithara und Aulos im Streit. Zur ikonologischen Deutung des Freskos *L'Investitura a Cavaliere di San Martino* von Simone Martini," *Imago Musicae* 3 (1986): 31-50. It has been translated from the German by Roger Harmon.

1 Figures 1-11 are reproduced by permission of the Archivio fototgrafico e copyright Sacro Convento, I – 06082 Assisi.

253

main figure of the fresco—one would like to think—is St. Martin. The recorder player's prominence, therefore, may well come to us as a surprise. In the world of scholarship, however, this picture has evoked not so much surprise as admiration. Nearly every art history textbook, nearly every historical study of costumes contains a reproduction of it. But it seems that not a single publication has interpreted the picture beyond observing that it is a genre-painting of an investiture with musical accompaniment.

Nor do musicologists know what to make of the recorders and the ensemble. Some see the entire group of musicians as a source for the instrumentation of *trecento* music: voice, recorder, and *chitarra* would perhaps be appropriate for a three-voice song of Landini. David Munrow, himself a recorder player, is sceptical, however. "The Pied Piper figure in Simone Martini's *L'investitura di San Martino*," he writes, "looks in great difficulties: he seems to have more finger-holes than he can cope with and some balance problems too, since the right-hand little finger is being used to support the instrument" (Figure 2).[2] Going beyond purely organological discussion of the picture, Munrow continues by observing that the position of the two recorders recalls the *aulos*. This is an observation to which we must return.[3]

Figure 2. Detail of the musicians

But the significance of the ensemble cannot be inferred from the instruments alone. The situation surrounding the minstrel and his two recorders can be fully understood only when we consider the entire fresco (that is, the other persons portrayed in it), and when we view the picture in its larger thematic and metaphorical

---

2 David Munrow, *Instruments of the Middle Ages and the Renaissance* (London, 1976), 12.
3 Ibid.

context. The principal concern here will be neither the organology nor the performance practice of the double-recorder, but rather the prerequisites to such studies.

We must first examine the entire cycle as it appears in St Martin's chapel. Then, we will focus on the *Investiture*, starting with a description of its contents. Only after that, using a contemporary book of legends and drawing on the history of medieval culture and religion, may we attempt to describe the picture's deeper contextual significance. Once that is done, the answers to several questions regarding performance practice will become apparent. In other words, my remarks to come will have more to do with saints and heathens, evil spirits, sorcerers, devils, and demons than with music as sonorous experience.

Let us start at the beginning. Decorating the chapel of St. Martin, the cycle tells the story of the saint's life. Eight of the chapel's original ten frescos are very well preserved. They cover the walls to the right and left of the altar and are divided into three levels. The lower part of the wall bears two frescos on each side of the altar, as does the middle part. The uppermost part of the wall has one fresco on each side.

The thematic arrangement seems to be related to the level at which the fresco is hung: On the lower level to the left of the entrance is the famous scene in which Martin shares his cloak, and the dream-scene in which Christ appears to him, a Roman Gentile (Figures 3 and 4).

Figure 3. Martin shares his cloak   Figure 4. Martin's dream

On the lower right appears the *Investiture* (see Figure 1), and at its side the renunciation of the sword and acceptance of the cross (Figure 5).

Figure 5. The renunciation of the sword and acceptance of the cross

On the middle left a child is raised from the dead. Alongside, St. Ambrose falls into trance and sees St. Martin ascend into heaven (Figures 6 and 7).

Figure 6. A child is raised from the dead

Figure 7. St Ambrose falls into trance and sees St Martin ascend into heaven

On the middle right we see the miraculous mass in which an angel covers St. Martin's naked arms with gold and jewels. Next to it, St. Martin is shown with the Emperor Valentinian, whose throne begins to burn when he refuses to listen to the saint (Figures 8 and 9).

Figure 8. The miraculous mass   Figure 9. St Martin with the Emperor Valentinian

Finally, on the uppermost level we see a depiction of the saint's death on the left, and his requiem mass on the right (Figures 10 and 11).

Figure 10. The death of St Martin   Figure 11. The requiem mass

The three spatial levels therefore stand both for three periods in the saint's life, as well as for three corresponding qualities. The lower level signifies the world of sin: The heathen knight is shown among heathens, searching for God and Christ. The middle level depicts the world as imitation of Christ: Martin appears as a wonder-working ascetic and bishop. The uppermost level is also qualitatively the highest: The dead saint is transfigured in God's proximity.

Musicians appear in two of the tableaux—once at the very bottom, on the worldly, heathen level, where the recorder player is shown; and once at the very top, in the sphere of God's proximity. There, at the saint's deathbed, two monks sing and piously raise their eyes. Heathen music versus divine: Already on this superficial level, a duality is established. Later I shall examine this in detail.

The Investiture

So much for the place of the *Investiture* in the fresco-cycle; now we shall turn to the *Investiture* itself. In the middle, St Martin—distinguished by his halo—stands with his hands raised. Another man, shown by a laurel wreath to be a Roman ruler, girds him with a sword. A group of men stands to the left, one of whom holds a helmet, another a falcon. On the right, somewhat in the background, are placed the musicians: the recorder player, another instrumentalist, and two singers.

The title *The Investiture of St. Martin* must refer to an event in the fourth century (the saint's dates being 316–97 CE), but Martini stages the event as a medieval dubbing as practiced in his own day. Why did Simone Martini choose to portray St. Martin as a novice knight? The answer requires a brief digression into late-medieval chivalry.

According to medieval ideals, the task of the knight (Latin *miles*) was to guarantee justice, order, and security for the population with his sword. According to one twelfth-century cleric, knights were furthermore obliged "to defend the Church, to battle unbelievers, to honor the clergy, to protect the rights of the poor, to pacify the countryside, to shed their blood for their brothers, and, if necessary, to lay down their lives." "God's high praise," continues this source, "comes from their mouths; they hold the double-edged sword in their hands . . . in order to carry out the judgement whose execution they have sworn, whereby no one acts of his own will, but rather in obedience to the well-considered decision of God, the angels, and mankind in accordance with justice and the common good."[4] Thus, the ideal knight is a guardian soldier in the service of God and of the world. From this, Bernard of Clairvaux and others derived the knight's obligation as that of a Knight of Christ (*miles Christi*), in service of the

---

4 Cited in Sidney Painter, "Die Ideen des Rittertums," in *Das Rittertum im Mittelalter*, ed. Arno Borst (Darmstadt, 1976), 34-35.

Church militant (*ecclesia militans*), marching eastward to liberate Jerusalem from the infidel.[5]

The knight's double task—to fight for God and for the world—is reflected in the dubbing ritual. According to a late-medieval account, a novice preparing himself for investiture is shaved and bathed. Then he is dressed in a long, hooded robe for the vigil he is to hold before the ceremony. To music and the accompaniment of knights and pages, he proceeds to a chapel and spends the night there in prayer. The next morning, he proceeds to the king's throne-room, where two of the noblest knights fasten spurs to his heels.

> Then the king girds him with the sword, and as he holds his arms high over his head, the king embraces his neck with both hands, hits him on the nape of the neck with his right hand, and says: "Be a good knight." Then they proceed once again to the chapel, where the young knight lays his hands upon the altar and swears to protect the Church. Then he gives his sword to the priest to bless.[6]

This ceremony is obviously pervaded with elements reflecting both the sacred and the secular components of chivalry. This is also the case when medieval authors turn their sights on earlier times. For example, in another late-medieval treatise describing investiture in Julius Caesar's day, one reads that, after bathing, the novices put on a red cloak "as a sign that they ought not to hesitate to shed their blood for the common good; they pray the whole night in an oratory sacred to Mars and are then girded by Caesar with the sword."[7] Our fresco appears to illustrate these treatises.

In Martini's painting, chivalric, Christian, and antique elements are mingled. The main pattern of the scene is chivalric: the girding, the attaching of spurs, the hooded cloak worn by the novice, his raised arms; also, the presence of the men on the left, identifiable as knights by the chivalric attributes of the helmet and falcon. Chivalric too are the minstrels accompanying the ceremony, just as specified in the literary sources and as seen in other investiture pictures. Christianity is represented by the saint's halo, and perhaps by the meekness radiated by the singers as well, foreshadowing the two monks who sing the saint's requiem mass. The singers' attitude stands in direct contrast to the proud posture and forthright gaze of the recorder player. Antiquity is represented by the figure of the ruler, whose head seems to be modeled on a Roman medallion; it may also be intended by the *aulos*-like position of the recorders.

---

5 S. Bernardus Abbas, *De laude novae militiae* (Paris, 1854), 921-940.
6 Cited in Dietrich Sandberger, "Die Aufnahme in den Ritterstand in England," in *Das Rittertum im Mittelalter*, 87-88.
7 Ibid., 100.

The Golden Legend

We have the good fortune to know the literary prototype of the painter's program: namely, the Golden Legend (*Legenda aurea*) by Jacobus de Voragine, a Dominican monk who, after long years of itinerant evangelizing in Italy, died as Archbishop of Genoa in 1298. The *Legenda sanctorum*, as the author originally entitled his work, narrates in popular style the life-stories of the saints of the ecclesiastical year. For Jacobus, it is not so much a matter of communicating historical facts. Rather, he fascinates the reader with miracles and adventures, thus rendering him devout and predisposed. Its readily understandable style guaranteed the work's success. The Golden Legend was translated into all western languages and was continually expanded. The earliest surviving manuscript, of 1288, has 182 chapters; the first printed edition, of 1470, has 448.

The chapter on St. Martin is called "De sancto Martino episcopo" or "St. Martin the Bishop." Here are a few episodes from the saint's youth:

> Saint Martin, bishop: Martinus is like *Martem tenens*, one who makes war, namely, against vice and sin. . . . Martin was born in the town of Sabaria in Pannonia but grew up in Pavia, Italy, with his father, who was a military officer. Martin served in the army under the Caesars Constantine and Julian, but a military career was not his own choice. Even in childhood he was inspired by God. . . . Then the caesars decreed that the sons of veterans should take their fathers' places in the legions. Martin was pressed into service at the age of fifteen. . . . Once, in the wintertime, he was passing through the city gate of Amiens when a poor man, almost naked, confronted him. No one had given him alms, and Martin understood that this man had been kept for him, so he drew his sword and cut the cloak he was wearing into two halves, giving one haf to the beggar and wrapping himself in the other. The following night he had a vision of Christ wearing the part of his cloak with which he had covered the beggar, and he heard Christ say to the angels who surrounded him: "Martin, while still a *catachumen*, gave me this to cover me." The holy man saw this not as a reason for pride, but as evidence of God's kindness, and he had himself baptized at the age of eighteen. . . . At that time, the barbarians were breaking through the empire's frontiers, and Emperor Julian offered money to soldiers who would stay and fight them. Martin had had enough of soldiering and refused the proffered bonus, saying to the emperor: "I am a soldier of Christ, and I am forbidden to fight." Julian was indignant and charged that Martin was refusing not for motives of religion but because he was afraid of fighting in a war. Martin, who knew no fear, retorted: "If my refusal is attributed not to faith but to cowardice, I will stand forth tomorrow morning at the line of battle, unarmed, and, in the name of Christ, protected not by shield or helmet but by the sign of the cross, I shall walk safely through the enemy's line." He was put under guard immediately to ensure that he would face the barbarians unarmed, as he had said that he would. But the next day the enemy

sent legates to convey their surrender of all men and materials, so there can be no doubt that this bloodless victory was due to the holy man's merit.[8]

Obviously the painter followed his literary prototype, but it is also clear that Martini used the leeway granted him by the expressive possibilities of painting versus language. How, for example, should a dream be depicted? In painting, unlike in language, is it not easy to depict two levels of existence, the external reality of the sleeping dreamer and the inner reality of the vision. Martini solved this problem, like many painters of his time, by joining the two levels in one scene. Thus, it might appear as if Christ and the angel appear at the bedside of a sleeping, sick, or dead saint. But in Martini's time, every observer would have known the story and would have recognized that both inner experience and external appearance were being portrayed simultaneously in the painting.

The "miles Christi"

It has often been stated that, among all ten frescos in the cycle, the *Investiture* alone has no literary prototype, either in the Golden Legend or in any other source concerning Martin's life. But is that really the case? Jacobus de Voragine's chapter on St. Martin begins "Martin means *Martem tenens*"—that is, "he who wages war against vice and sin." There is also Martin's response to the emperor Julian: *Christi ego miles sum*—"I am a soldier of Christ." We might also consider earlier comments on chivalry, and in particular descriptions of knightly investiture in Roman times. According to one late-medieval author, investitures took place at the altar of Mars, the god of war. The historical Martin was a heathen who stood under the command of a Roman military leader. At the beginning of his career, he was also a Roman knight. But the saint whose legendary career Jacobus de Voragine narrates fought not against men but, in Jacobus's words, *contra vitia et peccata*, "against vice and sin." Here, it is already clear that Martin's identity is seen in terms neither of Roman knighthood nor of chivalry in the Church militant, which was fulfilled in the Crusades. St. Martin's weapon, as Martini shows, is the cross, not the sword. The heathens are not his enemies. His enemy is evil, in the form of vice and sin.

Thus Martini chose the sphere of chivalry as the framework for our fresco because he wanted to elucidate something that had been essential to Jacobus de Voragine's legend: that Martin was a knight of Christ, who, in the imitation of Christ, fought against evil and for good. His enemies, vice and sin, are by no means abstractions in the painting. Martini integrates them graphically into the

---

8 Cited in Th. Graesse, *Jacobi a Voragine Legenda aurea, vulgo Historia lombardica dicta* (Breslau 1890; repr., 1969), 741-42. For an alternate English translation, see Jacobus de Voragine, *The Golden Legend*, trans. William G. Ryan (Princeton, 1993), 2:292.

picture, specifically in the figure of St. Martin's counterpart, the Roman ruler, who Jacobus de Voragine identifies the emperor Julian.

Sin and Vice: Emperor Iulianus Apostata

The historical Flavius Claudius Iulianus Augustus (331–63 CE) was a nephew of Constantine the Great, founder of the Christian state-church in Rome. Concerning his biography, suffice it to say that he was made Caesar in 355, and that he fought in Gaul, won Cologne from the Franks in 356, was proclaimed Augustus in 360, and, in 361, left the Christian church in favor of a religion characterized by neo-platonic ideals. For the story of Martin's departure from military service, the Golden Legend drew on the earlier Life of St. Martin by Sulpitius Severus (ca. 360-ca. 420), who specifically states that he gathered his information from St. Martin in person, and moreover that the military leader concerned was indeed the Emperor Julian.

The Emperor Julian's return to the religion of his fathers earned him, among Christians, the epithet *Apostate*, "the recreant." He thus entered the annals of Christianity as the epitome of everything evil, forbidding, and cruel. This view is also present in the Golden Legend, for as far as Jacobus de Voragine is concerned, the Emperor Julian was possessed by demons. In the legend of "St Julian," a namesake of the emperor, Julian the Apostate's life is portrayed, in counterpoint to that of the saint, as a heap of wickedness and devilry. "There was another Julian," so begins the legend, "but, far from being a saint, he was one of the most evil of all men."[9] Jacobus explains that Julian the Apostate started out as a monk, but even as a child was acquainted with black magic. He was a great sorcerer who owed his power to commerce with devils and evil spirits. His apostasy and subsequent persecution of Christians derived from his need to keep the demons satisfied, "because otherwise the demons would scarcely obey him," Jacobus reports.[10]

According to the Early Fathers of the Church, Julian committed the mortal sin of *contemptus dei*, the conscious and deliberate revolt against God for the sake of worldly ends. For this act of conscious renunciation of God there could be no mercy, according to medieval belief. Hence, the Golden Legend outdoes itself in its description of the cruel deeds of this emperor; they serve to illustrate the misery and depravity of his existence. This sketch alone allows us to make out the prototype of the heathen emperor's character and way of life. It was the devil who posed for this portrait, that fallen angel who was once a child of God just as Julian was once a monk, yet who renounced God and now reigns as Lord of Darkness over the depths of Evil, supported by a throng of demons.

---

9 Graesse, *Jacobi a Voragine Legenda*, 143.
10 Ibid.

In Christianity, the devil is Christ's evil counterpart who tries to diminish Christ's power derived from love and faith. But he succumbs to Christ and will receive his last, decisive defeat on Judgement Day. Until then, however, the devil will stop at nothing to practice his dark craft upon mankind. He constitutes a perpetual threat to the faithful trying to lead their lives in imitation of Christ. The Christian must remain conscious of this threat and know how to counteract it. St. Paul expresses this in his letter to the Ephesians, as follows:

> Put on the whole armor of God, that you may be able to stand against the wiles of the devil. For we are not contending against flesh and blood, but against the principalities, against the powers, against the world rulers of this present darkness, against the spiritual hosts of wickedness in the heavenly places. Therefore take the whole armor of God, that you may be able to withstand in the evil day, and having done all, to stand. Stand therefore, having girded your loins with truth, and having put on the breastplate of righteousness, and having shod your feet with the equipment of the gospel of peace; above all taking the shield of faith, with which you can quench all the flaming darts of the evil one. And take the helmet of salvation, and the sword of the Spirit, which is the word of God. (Ephesians 6:11-17)

What Paul sketches here is the archetype of the *miles Christi*, the knight of Christ, who goes out to fight against the dark power of evil. In light of this background, Martini's opposition of Martin and Julian at the moment of investiture acquires deeper significance: Martin, the knight and vassal of Christ, stands face to face with Julian, lord of the world and devil's vassal. The picture shows, therefore, an existential moment of confrontation between good and evil. The knight hears the seductive message of evil, promising power and glory. Martini has captured Martin at that juncture of the imitation of Christ corresponding to Christ's temptation in the wilderness, when the devil offered Him authority over the kingdoms of the world. And just as Christ stood firm, so will Martin resist the devil in the Emperor Julian. He will forgo a brilliant military career, will forgo power, honor, and luxury, in order to become an ascetic preacher. It is not the proffered way of heathen chivalry that he will choose, but rather the difficult struggle of the Christian knight.

The Musicians

From here we may now turn to the double-recorder player. As we saw, the chivalric ambiance of the fresco is asserted by the *miles Christi* motive. But for the musicians there is no explicit literary source, unless we follow the typical view that they simply belonged to the *Investiture* genre. As correct as this may be, however, it obscures precisely the atypical details in this group of musicians: the recorder player's overly-rich clothing; the unusual double recorder and its distorted perspective, in which the openness of the holes vis-à-vis the viewer lends them a demonstrative quality; the diversity of the musicians' facial expressions and postures (here pride, there humility); and finally the combination of an unusual double recorder with a by-no-means unusual lute-type instrument probably called a *chitarra* in fourteenth-century Italy. Not all of these questions can be answered definitively. However, an iconographic approach to the character of the musicians allows them to be understood more deeply.

Our point of departure is their clothing. In the Middle Ages, clothing meant more than cover and ornament; it indicated the social class of the wearer. What one could or could not wear was fixed by law. Members of each social class had to wear clothes appropriate to their station. A peasant could not go around dressed like a burgher, nor a burgher like a knight.[11] From this viewpoint, the recorder player's clothing is markedly distinguished from that of all other persons present, and especially from that of the other musicians.

For headgear, the singers wear simple caps, while the *chitarra* player's cap has a peak that hangs down. This kind of cap was widely worn and belonged to the clothing of the lower classes. Nor are the *chitarra* player's and singers' robes unusual. The *mi-parti*, where each robe-half is of a different material and color, was favored by musicians in those days (in our picture, the knights wear it too). The hair of the singers and the *chitarra* player is also styled in the fashion of the time; it is short and curled in at the neck. Their postures, the singers' upward gaze, the proximity of mouths and ears, the hand of one on the shoulder of the other (presumably to beat time), and the *chitarra* player's introspective look: All of these things unite the three and identify them as belonging to a group. Each musician seems to be listening both to himself and to the others.

The man in the background, on the other hand, gives the impression of being a stranger. He is often counted among the singers. This is wrong, however, for, as a close look shows, his mouth is closed. Furthermore, the height of his hat and the direction of his gaze link him with the piper, who stands apart from the persons already described. Whereas the emperor, the knights, and the musicians are rather modestly dressed, the recorder player's costume is fashioned with every finesse. The robe artistically combines three different materials, but that is not all: It is partially pleated, ornamented with gold lace, and has long, train-like sleeves. A belt adds to the effect. A tall, stiff hat, whose decoration answers that of the robe, contributes to making this figure the actual focal point of the picture.

Why did Martini dress this musician so splendidly? Hats, rare in the late middle ages, were worn only by knights. Likewise, medieval sumptuary laws indicate that pleated shirts and gold lace also were reserved for knights. Caught wearing such apparel, a burgher of the imperial free city of Nuremberg, for ex-

---

11 Catherine Kovesi Killerby, *Sumptuary Law in Italy, 1200-1500* (Oxford, 2002), 38 and 137.

ample, would have had to pay a fine of three guilders. The wearing of long, pleated sleeves by burghers was also prohibited by fine.[12]

Thus, the recorder player's dress goes far beyond a costume appropriate to his class. The meaning of this can be inferred when one bears the following point in mind: Literary works of the fourteenth century castigated the wearing of elegant clothing as soul- and character-corrupting, and it did so in such a consistent manner that the idea became a *topos*. Namely, exaggeratedly luxurious clothing stood for corruption of the soul.[13] Applying this *topos* to the recorder player, we see that his elegant apparel puts him in the sphere of spiritual corruption and ungodliness. His posture too, as mentioned earlier, betrays not a trace of meekness: He alone is depicted frontally, and he alone is not turning inward, toward the other musicians. His sinister eyes directly confront the viewer's gaze. Unlike the others, who have curled hair, the recorder player's hair hangs straight.

Finally, we must consider his playing technique. It is unusual, to say the least. Only a few fourteenth-century references to this method of playing two recorders are known. While those few references might suffice to account for our picture, what are we to make of the following facts? Martini depicted the *chitarra* player's fingers true-to-life, for lutenists confirm that their position is accurate. Recorder players, however, declare that Martini's depiction of the little finger to support the instrument may be idiomatic, but that the open-hole fingering shown here can give no positive sonorous result. Since Martini did not work intuitively, relying instead, as we have seen, upon literary sources and contemporary commonplaces, we may assume that the recorder player's fingering reflects not so much ignorance of performance practice as a carefully executed, precise idea. In sum, it may be said that the recorder player breaks the mold of this picture. Dressed with knightly vanity, his face barbaric, his recorder fingering patently absurd, to questioning the meaning of so much apparent nonsense is inevitable.

The Demon

The picture shows St. Martin face to face with his life's task, the struggle against evil. At the same time, it shows him at a crossroads, confronted with the choice between God and the world, between chivalry as *miles Christi* and that as a vassal of Satan, in the person of the Emperor Julian. Now is the time to recall the role of itinerant minstrelsy in the medieval church's value system. Simply put, the minstrel was considered to be the servant of the devil. His purposes were

---

12 Gertrud Hampel-Kallbrunner, *Beiträge zur Geschichte der Kleiderordnungen mit besonderer Berücksichtigung Österreichs* (Vienna, 1962), 21-22.
13 Lieselotte C. Eisenbart, *Kleiderordnungen der deutschen Städte zwischen 1350 und 1700* (Göttingen, 1962), 150.

evil, his task to seduce the souls of the faithful to vice and sin in the devil's struggle for power against God and Christ. Ecclesiastics damned minstrels as *ministri Satanae*, servants of the devil. They were excluded from the holy sacraments and, according to Augustine, it was an "abominable vice" to give them alms. They are possessed by devils and forfeited to Satan, without hope of redemption.[14]

In many discussions of the minstrels' salvation, or rather perdition, they are named in one breath with magicians. Minstrels, in other words, were suspected of sorcery. This is self-evident, for, as we have learned from Jacobus de Voragine, magicians and minstrels belong to the same family—namely, that of the devil. In the Golden Legend the Emperor Julian Apostate is described as a great sorcerer and magician, who from early childhood onward communed with demons and derived his superhuman power from this dark source. This gives rise to the suspicion that there is a deeper affinity between the emperor-sorcerer and the devilish minstrel in our picture.

Before pursuing this possibility further, I would like to turn to the actual mediators of evil, whom Jacobus de Voragine called demons. Medieval demonology fuses antique and Christian elements in a manner difficult for laymen to understand. According to the Bible and the Apocrypha, demons are fallen angels who, in service of the devil, take up residence in such persons as cannot or will not defend themselves, in order to seduce them to devilry. In passing, they were made responsible for the relapse of Christians back into the world of heathen gods, for the erection and worship of graven images, and for the cruel and evil heathen way of life led by relapsed Christians.[15] St. Paul forcefully asserts the connection between demons and idols. In the first letter to the Corinthians he warns the congregation against idolatrous sacrifice and the devouring of flesh sacrificed in an idolatrous manner, for "You cannot drink the cup of the Lord and the cup of demons. You cannot partake of the table of the Lord and the table of demons. Shall we provoke the Lord to jealousy? Are we stronger than he?" (I Corinthians 10:14-21).

Thus, demons are responsible for Julian the Apostate's mortal sin of *contemptus dei*, revolt against God in favor of idolatry. Interesting here is the question of how the middle ages imagined demons to look. In the late middle ages, demons were not portrayed as animals or monsters, as in Romanesque art, but rather in human form. Thus, according to one conception of demonic appearance, an evil spirit assumes the form of the person it possesses. Correspondingly, in a monastery the abbot is possessed by an abbot-demon, the prior by a prior-demon, and the cantor by a cantor-demon. From this we can infer that

---

14 Cf. Reinhold Hammerstein, *Diabolus in Musica* (Bern, 1974).
15 Paul Rießer, ed., *Altjüdisches Schrifttum außerhalb der Bibel* (Augsburg 1928), 570.

there existed in the notion that, externally, men could not be distinguished from demons.[16]

An example of such a man-demon in representational art is offered by an Umbrian psalter of circa 1330, a source from Martini's immediate temporal and geographic vicinity. Here, a demon blows the poisonous substance of his devilish soul, via creepers and blossoms, into the world, while, in the initial, King David, advocate of good, serenely goes about playing his psaltry (Figure 12). Not only does the duality of good and evil, of David and demon in this miniature recall the duality in our fresco of saint and idolator (consider the axiality of the demon's facial features, his wild hair, his tall hat, and—of course—the motive of "blowing" on double pipes), but all of this establishes the fraternal kinship of the demon in the miniature with our recorder player.

Figure 12. Initial to Psalm 80, *Exultate Deo* (Perugia, Biblioteca Comunale Augusta, MS 3272n.2, fol. 1v)

To summarize our position thus far:

1. In the pictorial program of St. Martin's chapel, the *Investiture* appears on the lowest level; below, Satan's kingdom; above, God's.
2. The saint is depicted as *miles Christi*, as warrior against sin and vice. Sin and vice are the work of heathen demons.

---

16 Karl Beth, "Dämonen," in *Handwörterbuch des deutschen Aberglaubens* (Berlin, 1929), 2:159.

3. The Emperor Julian is a sorcerer and a student of black magic.
4. Because he revolted against God and obeys heathen demons, the Emperor Julian is the epitome of evil.
5. Demons can look like human beings.
6. Minstrels can be servants of the devil and magicians.
7. The piper neither looks nor behaves like a normal minstrel.
8. As exemplified by his depiction of Martin's dream, Martini depicts internal and external reality as a continuum.

Any interpretation of the picture must therefore begin with the premise that the recorder player is not to be seen as a real minstrel. On the contrary, his prominent position in the picture, his splendid costume, the imperiously-set tall hat, the somehow idolatrous axial posture, and his two recorders identify him as the demon by which the Emperor Julian is possessed. He represents, as it were, the demonic corporeality of the emperor. Let the viewer not be deceived by the nobility of the emperor's external appearance. In Julian the Apostate there hides an evil spirit. And, in order to make this clear to all, the painter refers to this invisible inner truth with externally visible sign of the demonic recorder player. This demon looks the viewer directly in the eyes, just as the emperor looks St. Martin in the eyes. In both cases, the intent is to deter. The picture's message to the faithful visitor of St. Martin's chapel is the following: Be as steadfast in the face of evil as St. Martin was when he faced the emperor.

Aulos and Chitarra

In light of this hypothesis, interpreting the instruments no longer poses major problems. The interpretation according to which the two recorders represent, via late-medieval means, the *aulos*, appears to be manifestly correct. The recorder, as frequently observed in the literature, is one of the devil's favorite instruments. Both demons and the devil play the recorder (sometimes together with a drum), and we know of fabulous creatures who played on their trunks as on a recorder. The recorder is also the favorite instrument of those minstrels who serve the devil—that is, of itinerant conjurers and sorcerers. The recorder is therefore well suited to be the instrument of an evil spirit. We have only to clarify the apparently absurd blowing into pipes whose un-idiomatically open holes are turned demonstratively toward the viewer.

In the Bible, blowing is an act of singular importance and holiness. God gave men breath and souls by breathing upon them. As the book of Genesis reports: "Then the Lord God formed man of dust from the ground, and breathed into his nostrils the breath of life; and man became a living being" (Genesis 2:7). A soul permeated by the pure breath of God does good. But a soul permeated by the breath of evil brings harm into the world. The *aulos*-recorders of Martini's minstrel are therefore an objectively perceptible expression of the breath that motivates an evil, heathen soul. And the open holes demonstrate the path taken by the breath of sin in order to reach the outside world and seduce and corrupt devout viewers. The painter thus uses recorder-holes as a way of giving pictorial expression to something that is invisible.

The same is true in reverse for the *chitarra* player. Just as the emperor has helpers in evil, the saint has his own helpers in good. In support of this, it is perhaps enough to mention that the *chitarra* is second only to the psaltery in its use by the Early Fathers of the Church to symbolize Christian salvation.[17] More important for us, however, are two other segments of the *chitarra*'s rich iconographic spectrum. Firstly, it was by playing what the Vulgate called "cithara" that the young David succeeded in driving the evil spirit out of Saul: "And whenever the evil spirit from God was upon Saul, David took the lyre and played it with his hand; so Saul was refreshed, and was well, and the evil spirit departed from him" (I Samuel 16:23). The *chitarra* therefore assumes the function of an instrument of exorcism, and in this sense was described in medieval music treatises. For example, in the *Summa Musicae* of Lambertus, we read the following verses (later re-used by Johannes Tinctoris in his *Complexus Effectuum Musices*):

> Sic David in Saule sedavit daemonis iram,
> Ostendens citharae virtutem carmine miram.
>
> Thus David calmed the ire of the demon in Saul,
> Showing in song the wondrous virtue of the cithara.[18]

In the *Investiture* ensemble, the *chitarra* can thus be interpreted as symbolizing a power protecting St. Martin from the influence of evil spirits.

Secondly, the *chitarra* as depicted by Martini has seven frets. This corresponds to the organological tradition in which certain musical instruments reflect the artistic idea of cosmic order, and the place of human beings in a universe ordered by God according to measure, number, and weight. The impure, evil, heathen soul of the *aulos* stands in contrast to the pure, ordered, Christian soul of the *chitarra*.

As far as the other persons on the right half of the picture are concerned, they reflect the extension from one spiritual sphere or the other. The man in the background merges with the demon by virtue of his tall hat and the direction of his gaze. By contrast, the singers form an ensemble with the *chitarra* player by

---

17 Cf. Hugo Steger, *David rex et propheta* (Nuremberg, 1961), 68-71; and Reinhold Hammerstein, *Die Musik der Engel* (Bern, 1962), 196-97.
18 Cf. Dagmar Hoffmann-Axthelm, "David und Saul – über die tröstende Wirkung der Musik," *Basler Jahrbuch für Historische Musikpraxis* 20 (1996): 146-47.

virtue of their facial expressions and postures. In its turn, this ensemble no doubt reflects actual *trecento* performance practice. But that the painter intended to depict an ensemble consisting of double recorder, *chitarra*, and voice, even on the concrete level of an investiture scene, is out of the question. On a deep, existential level of interpretation, the *Investiture* allows good to shine through in its struggle with evil. *Aulos* and *chitarra* can thus be seen as means by which two elementarily opposed powers are released from abstraction and given pictorial expression.

Fabio Carboni e Agostino Ziino

UNA RACCOLTA DI MOTTETTI PER LEONE X
Una Scoperta E Nuove Osservazioni

Nella sede staccata di Collemaggio della Biblioteca Provinciale "Salvatore Tommasi" di L'Aquila si conservano tre fogli appartanenti ad una finora sconosciuta parte di *Bassus* di un *Liber Secundus* di mottetti, stampato con caratteri intagliati forse da Andrea Antico.[1] Il primo foglio, ripiegato verticalmente, è stato cucito sul bordo del frontespizio del volume intitolato *I quattro libri delle prediche del reverendissimo mons. Cornelio Musso, vescovo di Bitonto . . . In Torino, appresso gl'heredi del Bevilacqua. MDLXXIX.*[2] Allo stesso modo il secondo e il terzo foglio sono stati cuciti sul bordo del frontespizio e dell'ultima pagina di un secondo volume che comprende gli altri due libri delle prediche.[3] I due volumi provengono dal monastero francescano di Rocca Calasci,[4] come si desume dalle note d'uso apposte sui rispettivi frontespizi: "Ad usum fratris Archangeli de Rocca Calascij ordinis minorum de osservantia" e dall'ulteriore nota di possesso sul primo: "Frater Franciscus Valeri ab Ofena."

I fogli, che misurano circa mm. 425 x 152, non sono stati tagliati orizzontalmente al fine di confezionare il relativo libro-parte, ovviamente di formato oblungo. Non sappiamo per quale motivo essi siano rimasti inutilizzati, ma le due ipotesi più percorribili sono che si tratti di prove di stampa oppure di fogli lasciati in deposito per essere utilizzati eventualmente nella confezione di libri-parte su richiesta. Di questa parte di *Bassus* finora sono venuti alla luce solo tre duerni (per un totale di undici pezzi) indicati con il *Registrum*, stampato in basso a destra: Q Q_{II}, R R_{II}, S S_{II}: il primo va da c. 1r a c. 4v e corrisponde al primo foglio (r/v); il secondo va da c. 5r a c. 8v e corrisponde alle otto facciate impresse

---
1 Ringraziamo in modo particolare Laura Zonetti, coartefice del ritrovamento di questi preziosi fogli e costante punto di riferimento e di informazioni, e Francesco Zimei, da sempre complice di scorribande archivistiche aquilane, che ha lasciato a noi il piacere di studiare queste carte. Ringraziamo per la generosa collaborazione e per i preziosi suggerimenti Bianca Maria Antolini, Bonnie Blackburn, Massimo Ceresa, Paolo Cherubini, Fabrizio Colitta, Anthony Cummings, Elisabeth Dunkl, Marcello Eynard, Teresa M. Gialdroni, Siegfried Gmeinwieser, Klaus Pietschman, Domenico Rocciolo, Licia Sirch, Christine Streubuehr, Barbara Ventura, Roberto Versaci, Alfredo Vitolo.
2 Il volume, però, comprende solo il primo e il secondo libro di prediche.
3 I due volumi hanno la collocazione *Cinq B 163/1A* e *Cinq B 136*.
4 Si tratta di una frazione di poche case intorno al convento, che si trovano non lontano da Ofèna, piccolo centro abitato a 50 km. dall'Aquila. Il convento, o meglio quello che ne resta, è diventato famoso recentemente, essendo servito per alcune riprese esterne del film *Il nome della Rosa*, tratto dal famoso romanzo di Umberto Eco.

nel secondo foglio (r/v); il terzo va da c. 9r a c. 12v e corrisponde all'ultimo, sempre r/v (si veda la Tavola e le fotoriproduzioni allegate). Dal momento che nella *Tabula* sono elencati sedici pezzi per un totale di diciotto carte (ovvero sei duerni), si può dedurre che mancano gli ultimi tre fogli (due duerni corrispondenti alle cc. 13r-20v), con i cinque pezzi residui più il colophon, che avranno avuto il *Registrum* T T_{II}, U U_{II}.

Sopra al primo pentagramma del terzo duerno (c. 9r) è ripetuto il termine *Bassus*, indicazione, utilizzata a mo' di richiamo, che serviva al legatore per confezionare correttamente il libro-parte. Questo particolare potrebbe indicare che nella stamperia erano contemporaneamente presenti anche i fogli degli altri libri-parte della stessa antologia, in previsione, come detto, del confezionamento dei relativi volumetti. Sul frontespizio si osserva una lettera iniziale maiuscola ornata, raffigurante la "B," sopra la quale è impresso in capitale maiuscola: "BASSUS LIBER SECUNDUS"; sul *verso* figura in *gothica rotunda*, con paginazione progressiva in cifre romane, l'indice degli autori e degli incipit testuali. Sopra all'indice si legge, sempre in capitale maiuscola: "TABULA LIBRO SECUNDO." Tutti i brani sono preceduti dal nome dell'autore stampato al centro, sopra il primo pentagramma, sono scritti in *gothica rotunda italica* e iniziano con un capolettera ornato. La marca della filigrana è un mano con una M sul palmo e un grande fiore sopra le dita, che non è stata riscontrata in alcuno dei repertori d'uso. La fogliazione, a differenza della *Tabula*, che come abbiamo visto è espressa in cifre romane, utilizza i numeri arabi: incomincia dal numero "2" e si interrompe al numero "12."

A nostro parere, la parte mutila di *Bassus*, oggetto di questo articolo, è da collegare a quella completa dell'*Altus liber secundus*, in *unicum* nel Museo Internazionale e Biblioteca della Musica di Bologna con la collocazione *R 141.1*, noto come "*RISM* [1521][4]," anche se questo accostamento non prova che si tratta della stessa edizione. Il *Bassus* aquilano e l'*Altus* bolognese sono comunque assimilabili sia per la sequenza dei compositori e dei brani, sia per i caratteri di stampa, sia, infine, per la marca della filigrana, che è la stessa. Anche la successione del *Registrum*, stampato ugualmente in basso a destra, collega coerentemente i due libri-parte: *Altus* L L_{II}, M M_{II}, N N_{II}, O O_{II}, P P_{II}; *Bassus* Q Q_{II}, R R_{II}, S S_{II}, [T T_{II}, U U_{II}]; coincide perfino la fogliazione che inizia in entrambe le parti con il numero "2" e prosegue regolarmente fino al numero "20" nel primo e fino al numero "12," come detto, nel secondo. La particolarità di ricominciare la fogliazione dall'inizio in ogni libro-parte si riscontra anche nei *Motetti libro primo* di Antico e Torresani (Venezia 1521), ma è l'unico dei quattro libri di mottetti pubblicati da Antico a presentare questa caratteristica, perché negli altri tre la fogliazione continua progressivamente dal *Superius* al *Bassus*. L'unica divergenza significativa tra questi due libri-parte, escludendo gli errori di stampa, riguarda il numero dei pezzi riportati nelle due *Tabulae*: quindici nell'*Altus* e sedici nel *Bassus*, in quanto alla fine della *Tabula* di quest'ultimo è aggiunto, ma senza il nome dell'autore, l'incipit del brano italiano *Viva el Sol e chi l'adora*. Di questo componimento, però, non è possibile sapere di più, sia perché si sarebbe dovuto trovare in una delle carte mancanti (c. 18), sia perché non è stato trovato nei repertori di incipit di lirica italiana già pubblicati o in preparazione.

Il fatto che i fogli aquilani possano essere una prova di stampa troverebbe conferma anche nella presenza di varianti testuali errate in rapporto all'*Altus*. Nel mottetto *Christus vincit* si legge *universalis* contro il più corretto *et universali* e più avanti per due volte *illos* in luogo di *illum*; in *Philomena praevia* si legge *terporis* per *temporis*, *avis prudentissima* per *avis predulcissima*[5] e *enim avis* in luogo di *enim aves*; *Virgo carens* nel *Bassus* diventa *Virgo carena* e nella conclusione si legge *locet cum gaudio* invece di *locet eos cum gaudio*; infine in *De ore prudentis* figura *in sermone eius* al posto di *in sermone oris illius*.[6] Inoltre la presenza di un solo componimento in italiano sembra essere molto improbabile in una raccolta di mottetti latini e quindi si può pensare che sia stato inserito per errore: non sono esclusi, però, anche altri possibili esiti, come si vedrà in seguito.

La mancanza delle due carte finali del *Bassus*, nell'ultima delle quali di solito era stampato il colophon, non permette di conoscere né il nome dell'editore, né la città, né l'anno di impressione. Le ipotesi finora formulate si basavano sulla conoscenza del solo libro-parte dell'*Altus* che notoriamente non presenta il colophon. Se il ritrovamento di queste carte non consente di dare una risposta esaustiva a tali quesiti, permette però di formulare qualche nuova ipotesi e delineare meglio i contorni e il contesto di questo *Liber secundus*.

– – –

A nostra conoscenza il primo a descrivere dettagliatamente la parte dell'*Altus liber secundus* è stato nel 1949 Walter Rubsamen. Egli già da allora aveva supposto che "may possibly be the second book of motets published by A. Antiquis in 1521," aggiungendo, però, "as his Motetti Lib. I and IV (*Eit. Bibl.* Nachtrag 1521 and 1521a) also contain 15 motets each, and there are no concordances between the three collections. But the printing of the tabulae differs somewhat, hence no positive identification is feasible at this time."[7]

---

5 Anche se gli editori degli *Analecta Hymnica Medii Aevii* (vol. 50, pp. 602-603, n° 398), preferiscono la lezione *prudentissima*.
6 D'altro canto in tre casi il *Bassus* è più corretto dell'*Altus*: *et comparavit* contro *et comperavit* (*Simile est regnum*) *pasca nostrum* contro *pasca nostris* (*De ore prudentis*) e *et pro cunctis* contro *ut pro cunctis* (*Virgo carens*), errori questi ultimi già segnalati da Winfried Kirsch nel *CMM* 49, alle pp. XIV e XVI.
7 Cfr. Walter H. Rubsamen, "Music Research in Italian Libraries," in *Notes* VIII (March.-Sept. 1949; Dec. 1950), p. 89; ristampato con il titolo *Music Research in Italian Libraries. An Anecdotal Account of Obstacles and Discoveries*, Los Angeles, California 1951, p. 61.

François Lesure nel 1960 nel repertorio da lui curato, nel quadro delle collane del *RISM*, sembra accettare l'ipotesi avanzata da Rubsamen, datando la raccolta al 1521, pur se indica l'anno tra parentesi quadrata: "[1521][4] [Motetti Libro secondo] [4 v.] - [Venezia, A. Antico, 1521]. 4 voll. in 8° obl 20 f."[8]

È solo, però, nel 1964, quando appare il primo studio ampio e sistematico su Andrea Antico, ovvero la "dissertation" harvardiana di Catherine Weeks Chapman, che viene esclusa l'ipotesi che la parte dell'*Altus* sia da ascrivere all'editore istriano. La studiosa afferma infatti che "although woodcuts were used, the book does not resemble Antico's work in other details. Moreover, it contains two concordances with Antico's motet books of 1520."[9] Essa ritiene inoltre che questa parte di *Altus*, appartenente a un non meglio specificato "Libro secundo" (o *"Liber secundus"*), "can probably be identified"[10] con i *Motetti libro secondo*, pubblicati a Roma nel 1521, una copia dei quali fu acquistata a Roma da Hernando Colón, figlio di Cristoforo Colombo, e da lui registrata nel *Supplementum Musica* del suo *Abecedarium B*, (col. 850, n° 68) con la seguente segnatura: "Moteti li[br]°. 2°. n[umer]°. 16. diversorum autorum. p[rimu]^s. Jo[hannes]. Mouton Ulti[mu]^s. anton de viti. 6215. R. 1521. 8."[11] In effetti la parte di *Altus* in questione inizia con un mottetto di Mouton e termina con uno di Divitis, ma contiene 15 pezzi (contro i 16 indicati da Colombo); la parte del *Bassus*, invece, ne riporta 16, ma si chiude, come detto, con il brano *Viva el Sol e chi l'adora*, dopo il mottetto di Divitis. Grazie a questa differenza tra l'*Altus* bolognese e l'edizione acquistata da Colombo, la Chapman può concludere che "this discrepancy precludes an absolutely certain identification of the surviving part book [dell'*Altus*] with the entry."[12] Essa tuttavia non esclude che possa trattarsi di un banale errore di conteggio da parte di Colombo: a noi questa ipotesi sembra molto remota, data la precisione con la quale egli ha redatto i suoi registri. La Chapman formula, comunque, anche altre soluzioni, tra le quali quella che la parte di *Altus* "belongs to a different edition of the same book,"[13] assunto che sembra anche a noi plausibile, specialmente dopo la scoperta del *Bassus*.[14]

---

8 Cfr. *Requeils Imprimés XVIe-XVIIe Siècles. Liste chronologique,* Henle Verlag, München-Duisburg 1960, p. 101.
9 Cfr. Catherine Weeks Chapman, *Andrea Antico,* Ph.D. diss. Harvard University 1964, p. 113. I due mottetti in comune sono *Philomena praevia* di Richafort, presente anche nei *Motetti novi libro secondo,* Venezia, Andrea Antico 1520, e *Salve, Mater Salvatoris* di Jean Mouton, che figura già nei *Motetti novi libro tertio,* Venezia, Andrea Antico 1520.
10 Cfr. Chapman, *Andrea Antico,* p. 112.
11 Cfr. Catherine Weeks Chapman, "Printed Collections of Polyphonic Music Owned by Ferdinand Columbus," in *Journal of the American Musicological Society,* XXI (1968), pp. 34-84: 50, 71 n° 68, e Plate IV.
12 Cfr. Chapman, *Andrea Antico,* p. 112.
13 Cfr. Chapman, *Andrea Antico,* ibid.
14 Difatti potrebbe trattarsi, nel caso della raccolta acquistata dal figlio di Cristoforo Colombo, di una ristampa con 16 pezzi invece di 15, nella quale l'ultimo, *Viva el Sol e chi*

Scartata quindi la possibibilità di assegnare con certezza la parte di *Altus* all'edizione del 1521, acquistata da Ferdinando Colombo, la Chapman, sulla base di alcuni elementi, ipotizza che l'intagliatore delle matrici possa essere lo stesso che ha curato i *Motetti e canzone libro primo* del 1520[15] e le parti in questione (*Altus* e *Bassus*) ne costituirebbero la prosecuzione, ovvero il "*Libro secundo*." Difatti, come osserva la studiosa, se da una parte "there are no concordances between the two books," dall'altra "De Silva, C. Festa, Mouton, Molu (as it is spelled in both *tabulae*), and Richafort are represented in each."[16] Tra gli aspetti materiali comuni ad ambedue le stampe, ovvero "the layout, typography, and general physical appaerance," la Chapman indica i seguenti: „The decorative capitals and the large "A's" on the title pages of the part books are similar. The tables of contents are both consecutively arranged and include composers' names, then titles of the compositions, then, although foliation is arabic, folio numbers in small Roman numerals. Four staves per page are used in both."[17] Come sempre, però, alle somiglianze si appaiano le differenze e alcune di esse sono messe in particolare evidenza dalla Chapman: "While Gothic rotunda type is used for the texts, the same font did not supply the types for both books. New pieces begin on the next staff in the 1520 print, whereas in the 1521 print they begin either on a fresh page or after a blank staff. The *Motetti e canzone* is collated in large gatherings, one to each part book; the *Altus liber secundus* contains five *duerni*, each of which bears above the music on its first folio the word 'Altus.' "[18]

L'accostamento proposto tra i *Motetti e canzone libro primo* del 1520 e questo ancora oscuro *Libro secundo* (o *Liber secundus*) potrebbe forse trovare un'ulteriore conferma nella presenza del pezzo italiano, probabilmente profano, *Viva el Sol e chi l'adora*. Forse l'anonimo editore aveva progettato inizialmente una raccolta contenente sia mottetti che "canzone," ma, accortosi che non disponeva di un numero sufficiente di brani profani, ha successivamente cambiato idea. Questo potrebbe spiegare quindi anche il mancato utilizzo dei tre fogli con il *Bassus*, rimasti pertanto solo una prova di stampa. Se questo fosse vero sarebbe allora legittimo identificare la parte del *Bassus* con l'edizione acquistata

---

l'adora, inserito per errore nella parte del *Bassus* (rimasta, quindi, inutilizzata), è stato eliminato e sostituito con un mottetto latino, ma non nella stessa posizione (finale) del brano italiano.
15 Cfr. Chapman, *Andrea Antico*, p. 113: „we tentatively suggest attribution of the music to the unknown woodcutter of the *Motetti e Canzone* of 1520."
16 Cfr. Chapman, *Andrea Antico*, ibid. Purtroppo, non avendo a disposizione l'unico esemplare finora conosciuto della raccolta *Motetti e canzoni libro primo*, conservato alla Pierpont Morgan Library di New York, non possiamo controllare se anche la lettera maiuscola ornata "B" impressa sul frontespizio dei due libri-parte del *Bassus* è la stessa in ambedue le stampe, come si osserva per la lettera "A" dell'*Altus*.
17 Cfr. Chapman, *Andrea Antico*, pp. 113-114.
18 Cfr. Chapman, *Andrea Antico*, p. 114.

da Fernando Colombo, che conteneva appunto 16 brani. L'apparente discrepanza tra la descrizione di quest'ultimo e la parte di *Altus*, registrata dalla Chapman, troverebbe in questo caso la sua soluzione: difatti egli avrebbe contato proprio 16 pezzi, quanti sono realmente nella parte del *Bassus* ed avrebbe considerato Divitis, o come ultimo reale compositore presente nella raccolta, o come autore anche dell'anonimo *Viva el Sol*, dal momento che esso è collocato subito dopo un suo mottetto. A questo punto allora la parte dell'*Altus* potrebbe appartenere ad una ristampa riveduta e corretta dell'antologia, in considerazione anche degli errori presenti nell'ipotizzata "prima" edizione, che sarebbe testimoniata dalla parte del *Bassus* appena ritrovata e dalla descrizione lasciataci da Colombo.

Sulla scorta di Alfred Einstein, che attribuiva ipoteticamente i *Motetti e canzone libro primo* a Jacopo Giunta,[19] Edward E. Lowinsky nel 1957, nel suo primo articolo sul "Medici Codex" ipotizzava che egli potesse essere stato anche l'editore della parte di *Altus liber secundus*.[20] Partendo da questa considerazione la Chapman così conclude: "Giunta's participation would not shed any light on the identity of the woodcutter. What the Roman prints of 1520 and 1521 do reveal is that, after Antico left Rome, the woodcut method which he was the first to use in printing collections of polyphonic music was similarly employed by at least one other craftsman."[21] Lo stesso Lowinsky, però, nella sua monumentale edizione del "Medici Codex" del 1968, sembra accettare la proposta del *RISM* e assegna la parte dell'*Altus* a Andrea Antico tra parentesi quadre.[22]

---

19 Cfr. Alfred Einstein, "A Supplement; an Old Music Print at the J. P. Morgan Library in New York," in *The Musical Quarterly*, XXV (1939), pp. 507-509; cf. anche Chapman, *Andrea Antico*, pp. 110-112, che in particolare scrive: "Einstein, in his brief study of this print, reasons that it is not Antico's because it contains not five but four staves to the page, notes different in shape from those used by Antico, and Moulu's motet 'In omni tribulatione,' which Antico would soon include in another collection. He suggests Jacopo Giunta as a possible printer. While we are in substantial agreement with Einstein, we must make a few revervations and additions" (p. 110). A nostro parere invece la *gothica rotunda* dei *Motetti e canzone* del 1520 e dei *Motetti libro primo*, pubblicati da Antico e Torresano nel 1521, è sostanzialmente la stessa e il fatto che le capitali decorate "differ in detail" non ci sembra elemento sufficiente a inficiare l'assunto. Ne consegue che le due collezioni potrebbero essere attribuite entrambe ad Antico.
20 Cfr. Edward E. Lowinsky, "The Medici Codex," in *Annales Musicologiques*, V (1957), pp. 61-178: 122. Lo studioso estende questa ipotesi anche ad altre due parti, sempre di *Altus*, unite alla prima e conservate al Museo internazionale e Biblioteca della Musica di Bologna con l'unica collocazione: "R. 141."
21 Cfr. Chapman, *Andrea Antico*, p. 114.
22 Cfr. *The Medici Codex of 1518. A Choirbook of Motets Dedicated to Lorenzo de' Medici, Duke of Urbino*, 2 Vols., ed. Edward E. Lowinsky, Chicago & London, The University of Chicago Press – Toronto, The University of Toronto Press, 1968 ("Monuments of Renaissance Music," Vols. III-IV), Vol. III, p. 111. Anche in Harry B. Lincoln, *The Latin Motet: Indexes tu printed Collections, 1500-1600* (Ottawa, The Institute of Mediaeval Music, 1993) il libro-parte dell'*Altus* è registrato secondo le indicazioni del *RISM*.

Da ultimo, Martin Picker esclude invece, anche sulla scorta della Chapman, che Antico possa essere stato "as either engraver or publisher of the edition," principalmente per il fatto che questa ipotetica stampa romana del 1521 del *Liber Secundus* ha con le due stampe veneziane del 1520 (*Motetti novi libro secondo* e *Motetti novi libro tertio*) due mottetti in comune, *Philomena previa* di Richafort e *Salve Mater Salvatoris* di Mouton, mentre l'editore istriano „customarily does not print the same composition in different collections."[23] D'altra parte, però, lo stesso Picker nella voce su Andrea Antico del *New Grove*[24] inserisce la parte di *Altus liber secundus* tra le opere "doubtful," opinione confermata con la locuzione "zweifelhaft" anche nella nuova edizione dell'enciclopedia *Die Musik in Geschichte und Gegenwart*[25]. Sulla stessa scia si allinea anche Licia Sirch nella "voce" da lei redatta per il *Dizionario degli Editori musicali italiani 1500-1750.*[26]

Non è tuttavia da escludere che questo incompleto *Liber secundus* del 1521 faccia seguito al *Liber primus*, pubblicato nel 1518, ora perduto, e ristampato nell'agosto del '21. A questo *Liber secundus* avrebbero fatto seguito il *tertius* ed il *quartus* (dei quali, però, manca il terzo) formando così una serie unitaria, non solo nell'intitolazione, ma anche nel numero dei mottetti tramandati (15). Ora, dato che il libro-parte del *Bassus*, testé ritrovato, ne contiene 16, dobbiamo ritenere che esso rappresenti una fase preliminare, o comunque antecedente, rispetto all'*Altus* che rappresenterebbe l'edizione definitiva, dal momento che contiene 15 mottetti, esattamente come il primo e il quarto. Martin Picker, invece, aveva considerato come serie unitaria le raccolte del 1520 intitolate *Motetti novi libro secondo* e *libro tertio*, fatte in collaborazione con Luca Antonio Giunta e quelle del 1521 intitolate *Motetti libro primo* e *libro quarto*, fatte in collaborazione con Andrea Torresano. Inoltre, per quanto concerne la diversità delle due intitolazioni, Picker ritiene che "the title *Motetti novi* itself, may be credited more to Giunta than to Antico, who appears to have left the verbal matter to his printer-collaborators while he executed the musical plates. Giunta may well

---

23 Cfr. Martin Picker, "The Motet Anthologies of Andrea Antico," in *A Musical Offering. Essais in Honor of Martin Bernstein*, Ed. by Edward H. Clinkscale and Claire Brook, New York, Pendragon Press 1977, pp. 211-237: 214. Il testo di *Philomena praevia* da Raby è attribuito a John Peckham, morto nel 1292 (cf. Frederic J. E. Raby, *A History of Christian-Latin Poetry from the Beginnings to the Close of the Middle Ages*, Clarendon Press, Oxford 1926, pp. 425-26. Il testo è edito anche in *Analecta Hymnica Medii Aevi*, 50, pp. 602-603, n° 398.
24 Cfr. *The New Grove Dictionary of Music and Musicians*, Vol. 1, 1980, pp. 467-469 e *The New Grove Dictionary of Music and Musicians, Second Edition*, edited by Stanley Sadie, MacMillan, London, 2002, Vol. 1, pp. 731-733.
25 Cfr. *Die Musik in Geschichte und Gegenwart*, ed. Ludwig Finscher, Bärenreiter, Kassel, Personenteil, Bd. 1 (2003), coll. 779-783: 780.
26 L'opera, a cura di Biancamaria Antolini, è in corso di stampa per la Società Italiana di Musicologia.

have looked upon 'his' three books of *Motetti novi* as a series, but Antico as musical editor must have seen them quite differently."²⁷

— — —

Aldilà della descrizione materiale dei libri-parte e dei loro rapporti con le altre stampe musicali coeve, dei problemi relativi all'identificazione dello stampatore e della data di impressione, elementi ricavabili con certezza solo dal colophon (che purtroppo, come detto, manca), riteniamo utile in questa sede evidenziare il significato della raccolta e il contesto storico che l'ha promossa.

L'antologia è stata indubitabilmente concepita in onore di Leone X, come dimostra il fatto che comincia con il mottetto *Christus vincit* di Jean Mouton, nel quale si invoca Cristo affinché protegga il papa e il suo clero:

> Christus vincit, Christus regnat, Christus imperat
> Exaudi, Christe.
> Leoni, Summo Pontifici et Universali Pape
> Salvator mundi
> Sancte Petre, Sancte Paule
> Decano Cappellano et omni clero sibi commisso
> Sancta Maria, Sancta Barbara
> Vita et salus perpetua
> Tu illum adiuva
> Tu illum adiuva
> Pax et vita et salus perpetua
> Tu illos adiuva.

Se questa intepretazione della raccolta è corretta, allora potremmo anche indicare come significativa alla fine del libro-parte del *Bassus* la presenza del componimento italiano *Viva el Sol*, che verrebbe letto come un'altra esplicita allusione al Pontefice, paragonato al Sole che tutto e tutti illumina e vivifica.

Il brano di apertura secondo Lowinsky sarebbe stato "undoubtedly written to celebrate the election of Pope Leo X" avvenuta il 2 marzo del 1513,[28] ma in realtà possono essere prese in considerazione anche altre occasioni, tra cui la più significativa potrebbe essere l'elezione dei 31 cardinali avvenuta il 1 luglio del 1517. Le motivazioni di questa nostra ipotesi si basano sul fatto che nel 1513 Jean Mouton non era ancora entrato in contatto con Leone X, essendo al servizio di Francesco I, a quell'epoca suo fiero oppositore.[29] Il musicista conobbe perso-

---

27 Cfr. Picker, "The Motet Anthology," p. 216.
28 Cfr. Lowinsky, "The Medici Codex," pp. 109-110: "The text of this motet undoubtedly written to celebrate the election of Pope Leo X"; vedi ancora Lowinsky, *The Medici Codex of 1518*, Vol. III, pp. 39-40.
29 Anche Howard Mayer Brown nella voce "Mouton" del *The New Grove* (Vol. 12, 1980, pp. 656-660: 657) scrive che "Mouton doubtless composed *Christus vincit* in honour of

nalmente il papa solo tra l'11 e il 15 dicembre 1515 mentre si trovava a Bologna al seguito del re, insieme ad altri componenti della *Chapelle royale*, allor quando i due grandi personaggi si incontrarono per siglare la pace, dopo la battaglia di Marignano (13-14 sett. 1515).[30] Leone X, che evidentemente già da tempo teneva Mouton in grande considerazione, pochissimi giorni dopo averlo conosciuto (il 17 dicembre) gli concesse la grande onoreficenza di Protonotaro apostolico.[31] Sembra quindi più probabile che Mouton abbia composto questo mottetto per una occasione veramente eccezionale come l'elezione dei 31 cardinali, piuttosto che per una elevazione al Soglio già avvenuta.[32] L'ipotesi che il brano sia stato scritto in occasione dell'elezione dei 31 porporati è ancora più convincente se si pensa che essa rappresentò un evento eccezionale, il primo del genere per l'alto numero degli eletti, e che ebbe vastissima eco in tutto il mondo, dando luogo ad una lunga serie di indimenticabili festeggiamenti, tant'è che dopo più di quaranta anni Vasari ancora sente la necessità di immortalare la nomina dei cardinali con un grandioso e famoso affresco, realizzato a Palazzo Vecchio tra il 1556 e il 1562. D'altra parte sappiamo che il mottetto *Christus vincit* non era cantato solo per le incoronazioni dei re[33] e dei papi, ma poteva essere utilizzato anche in

---

Leo X's election as pope in 1513," ma nella seconda edizione (aggiornata da Thomas G. MacCracken), più cautamente si afferma che "The Pope's acquaintance with Mouton's music may well have antedated their meeting in 1515, if the motet *Christus vincit* was indeed written in honour of Leo's election as pope in 1513" (*The New Grove..., Second Edition*, 2002, Vol. 17, pp. 239-251: 240). Anche Ludwig Finscher nella voce "Mouton" a proposito di *Christus vincit* afferma "vielleicht auf dessen (Leo X) Inthronisation 1513" (Cf. *Die Musik in Geschichte und Gegenwart*, ed. Ludwig Finscher, Bärenreiter, Kassel, Personenteil, Bd. 12 (2004), coll. 558-574: 560).

30 Il cerimoniale di questo incontro è illustrato in Lowinsky, *The Medici Codex of 1518*, p. 73.
31 Per la carica di Mouton cf. Herman-Walther Frey *ad vocem* "Leo X," in *Die Musik in Geschichte und Gegenwart*, Band 8 (1960), coll. 619-622: 620.
32 Ciò non esclude che possa trattarsi di un mottetto composto in Francia per l'elevazione al trono di Leone X, nella segreta speranza di ottenerne qualche favore. Ricordiamo che per lo stesso avvenimento o per il primo ritorno di Giovanni de' Medici a Firenze da papa, Andrea de Silva aveva composto il mottetto *Gaude felix Florentia* (cf. Edward E. Lowinsky, "A Newly Discovered Sixteenth-Century Motet Manuscript at the Biblioteca Vallicelliana in Rome," in *Journal of the American Musicological Society*, III (1950), pp. 173-232: 175-176 e 201-202; cf. anche David Maulsby Gehrenbeck, *Motetti de la corona: A Study of Ottaviano Petrucci's four Last-known Motet Prints (Fossombrone, 1514, 1519)*, voll. 4, Ph.D. diss., Union Theological Seminary in the City of New York, 1970 (UMI, 1971), p. 333). La presenza nel *Liber secundus* del *De profundis* a 5 voci di Josquin, composto probabilmente per la morte di Luigi XII, avvenuta nel gennaio del 1515, due anni dopo l'elezione di Leone X, potrebbe contribuire a spostare in avanti la datazione dell'antologia in oggetto (per la datazione del *De profundis* cf. *Das Chorwerk*, vol. 57, ed. Helmuth Osthoff, Möseler Verlag, Wolfenbüttel 1955, p. IV; Helmuth Osthoff, *Josquin Desprez*, Schneider, Tutzing 1962-65, voll. 2: I, 47).
33 Anche Gascogne scrisse il mottetto *Christus vincit*, probabilmente per l'incoronazione di Francesco I, avvenuta nel 1515.

molte altre occasioni solenni e importanti presenziate dal pontefice o da un alto porporato in sua rappresentanza.

Continuando nell'analisi di questo primo mottetto, che a nostro parere è emblematico e aiuta a comprendere l'intero progetto tipografico del *Liber secundus*, notiamo che, nonostante il linguaggio strettamente formulare desunto dalle *laudes regiae*, è data grande rilevanza al "Decano Cappellano et omni Clero sibi commisso" che per Lowinsky è il Decano della Cappella papale, mentre da parte nostra non si esclude che possa trattarsi anche del Decano del Sacro Collegio. Solo facendo riferimento ad un organismo così importante e complesso sul piano politico e religioso, si può comprendere che, mentre per il papa si implora la "vita et salus perpetua," per il Decano cappellano e per tutti coloro che sono a lui collegati si augura anche la "pax." Questo inoltre potrebbe spiegare anche la presenza di Santa Barbara,[34] già da tempo considerata salvaguardia dalle morti improvvise e protettrice delle guardie pontificie e dei "bombardini di Castello,"[35] che a loro volta garantivano l'incolumità del papa e del Sacro collegio. A questo proposito non è forse casuale che Ottaviano Petrucci abbia aperto il primo libro dei *Motetti de la Corona* (1514) proprio con il brano di Mouton *Gaude Barbara beata*, "a favorite intercessor of men facing combat, as did Louis and his armis."[36] D'altra parte nel nostro *Liber Secundus* figura anche un altro mottetto dedicato a s. Barbara, *Intercessio quaesumus, Domine* di Adriano Willaert,[37] nel quale si implora la sua protezione ("nos protegat"). È interessante anche il fatto che testo di questo mottetto coincide quasi interamente con quello presente in un Libro d'Ore di Philippe Pigouchet, stampato a Parigi da Simon Vostre nel 1497.[38] Inoltre la circostanza che questo pezzo si trovi sia nel "Medici-Codix," sia nei due libri-parte di questo *Liber secundus*, induce a pensare che essa, similmente ai *Motetti de la Corona*, sia stata concepita come un'opera a carattere fondamentalmente celebrativo. Infine il collegamento del mottetto *Christus vincit* all'elezione dei 31 cardinali nel '17 permette di ipotizzare che questo *Liber secundus* sia stato programmato subito dopo l'avvenimento, ma che sia stato effettivamente pubblicato solo nel '21, subito dopo la ristampa del *Liber primus*, risalente al 1518.

Anche la circostanza che nel *Liber secundus* figurino in prevalenza brani di compositori presenti, o anche solo in repertorio, in quegli anni nella Cappella di Leone X, fa riflettere sul fatto che questa antologia non sia stata concepita unicamente come omaggio al papa, ma bensì, come detto, a tutta la sua corte, a par-

---

34 Nel codice A 17 della Biblioteca Capitolare di Padova il nome "Barbara" è sostituito con "Giustina."
35 Questo è l'appellativo dei soldati posti a difesa di Castel Sant'Angelo.
36 Cfr. Gehrenbeck, *Motetti de la corona*, p. 338.
37 Questo musicista, già allievo di Mouton, è autore anche di una *Missa Gaude Barbara*, forse in omaggio al suo vecchio maestro.
38 Cfr. Lowinsky, *The Medici Codex of 1518*, p. 165.

tire dalla Cappella musicale,[39] come suggerisce la presenza del *Decano cappellano*, se non addirittura dal Sacro Collegio. Il committente della raccolta, o perfino lo stesso stampatore, doveva essere quindi una persona in contatto con le alte sfere ecclesiastiche e che aveva interesse a produrre un omaggio tanto importante. Il primo personaggio a cui pensare è ovviamente Andrea Antico, o qualche stampatore a lui vicino, a iniziare da Jacopo Giunta, senza escludere, però, neppure Ottaviano Petrucci, proprio in quegli anni a Roma. Comunque questo tipografo, chiunque egli sia, vuole attuare un preciso progetto editoriale, iniziato forse già con uno scomparso *Liber primus* di mottetti o, come suggerisce la Chapman, con il meno probabile *Motetti e canzone liber primus*.

D'altro canto i musicisti presenti nell'antologia godono tutti di ampia fama, tanto che, come accennato, operano per un certo periodo a Roma, specialmente presso la Cappella papale (Costanzo Festa, Josquin, Richafort, Carpentras, De Silva, Compère e forse Willaert) o presso la *Chapelle royale* di Luigi XII e successivamente di Francesco I (Mouton, Divitis, Gascogne, Moulu).[40] A questo proposito è bene osservare che buona parte delle raccolte a stampa e dei manoscritti musicali esemplati in Italia nel primo quarto del Cinquecento tramanda composizioni di autori operanti quasi esclusivamente in queste due cappelle, certamente le più importanti del periodo. Anche Catherine Chapman, a proposito dei quattro libri di mottetti pubblicati da Andrea Antico nel 1520 e 1521, osserva: "Antico's four motet books are among a closely related group of sources concentrated in time chiefly between 1518 and 1522. During those years, we have, in approximate chronological order, the *Medici Codex* and *Q 19* (1518), Petrucci's second, third, and fourth books of *Motetti de la Corona* (1519), Antico's *Motetti novi* II and III and the *Motetti e canzone libro primo* No. 45, (1520), Antico's *Motetti* I and IV and the *Altus liber secundus* No. 46 (1521), and the Padua manuscript *A 17* (1522). Undated but more or less contemporaneous sources are the 'Motetti et carmina gallica' (No. 43) probably printed in Venice in 1524, and Ms. St. Gall *463*. All of these collections ore de-

---

39 A tale proposito osserviamo che in alcuni mottetti si invoca la protezione divina anche per i cantori. Ricordiamo *Omnium bonorum plena* di Compère, tràdito dai codici B 80 dell'Archivio s. Pietro, ff. 27v-30 e dal cod. 91 del Castello del Buon Consiglio di Trento, ai ff. 33v-35; *Mater floreat* di Moulu, composto intorno al 1515. A questi si deve aggiungere il mottetto di Mouton *Sancti Dei omnes*, presente a ff. 11v-15r del cod. 42 della Cappella Sistina, databile tra il 1503 e il 1512 (cf. Jeffrey Dean, "Listening to sacred polyphony c. 1500," in *Early Music*, 25 (1997), pp. 611-636: 624-626). Su *Mater floreat* cf. anche Lowinsky *The Medici Codex of 1518*, pp. 73-74.
40 Sulla Cappella musicale francese cf. J. T. Brobeck, *The Motet at the Court of Francis I*, Ph.D. diss. University of Pennsylvania, Philadelphia 1991; Id., "Musical Patronage in the Royal Chapel of France under Francis I (r. 1515-1547)," in *Journal of the American Musicological Society*, 48 (1995), pp. 187-239.

voted largely to the works of composers associated with the papal chapel, the French Royal Chapel under Louis XII and Francois I, or both."[41]

Prendendo spunto proprio dalle parole della Chapman e sulla base delle concordanze individuate, anche se non complete (se ne veda l'elenco più avanti), possiamo ritenere che il compilatore di questo *Liber secundus* dovette conoscere molto bene non solo l'ambiente musicale romano, gravitante intorno al papa,[42] ma anche quello "oltramontano," legato alle cappelle di Luigi XII e di Francesco I. Sembra inoltre sembra molto probabile che egli attingesse a fonti privilegiate e di prima mano, come lascerebbero supporre varie circostanze, tra le quali, innanzitutto, il fatto che il mottetto di Mouton *Christus vincit* sembra essere, per quanto ne sappiamo, un *unicum*,[43] così come *Oremus pro cunctis fidelibus* di Pierre Moulu.[44] In secondo luogo, per i mottetti *Dignare me laudare* di Gascogne[45] e per il *De profundis clamavi* (a 5 voci) di Josquin,[46] questo ora non più tanto fantomatico *Liber secundus* risulterebbe il più antico testimone italiano.[47] Questo potrebbe valere anche per il mottetto *Intercessio quaesumus* di Willaert, qualora fosse accertata la nostra ipotesi che questo secondo libro sia stato programmato già nel 1518. In terzo luogo, limitandoci ai soli testimoni italiani, c'è da osservare che esso sembra essere una delle fonti più antiche, relativa-

---

41 Chapman, *Andrea Antico*, p. 308.
42 Sui musicisti alla corte di Leone X esiste una vasta bibliografia: in questa sede ricordiamo i lavori più recenti: Rainar Heyink, "Zur Wiederentdeckund der Motu proprio-Erlasse Papst Leos X. an Jean Mouton und weitere Mitglieder der französischen Hofkapelle," in *Kirchenmusikalisches Jahrbuch*, 1992, pp. 45-58; Dean, "Listening to sacred polyphony c. 1500," cit.; Adalbert Roth, "Französische Musiker und Komponisten am päpstlichen Hof unter Leo X" in *Der Medici-Papst Leo X. und Franlreich*, edd. Götz-Rüdiger Tewes e Michael Rohlmann, Mohr Siebeck, Tübingen 2002, pp. 529-545; Klaus Pietschmann, *ad vocem* "Leo X," in *Die Musik in Geschichte und Gegenwart*, ed. Ludwig Finscher, Bärenreiter, Kassel 2003, Personenteil, Bd. 10, coll. 1580-1581.
43 Il fatto era stato già evidenziato da Lowinsky: "It is interesting that this motet should be preserved only in one print which we ascribe to Giunta in Rome of which, unfortunately, only one voice part has survived. Nevertheless, it furnishes valuable confirmation of the relations between the Pope and the director of the French Royal Chapel, Jean Mouton" (cfr. Lowinsky, "The Medici Codex," p. 110).
44 Cfr. James Glien Chapman, *The Works of Pierre Moulu: a stlylistic Analysis*, voll. 2, Ph.D. diss., New York University, 1964, I: p. 24.
45 Per la descrizione del codice München, Art. 401, l'altro testimone del mottetto di Gascogne, cfr. Lowinsky *The Medici Codex of 1518*, III, pp. 118-119.
46 Difatti il codice 38 della Cappella Sistina che tramanda il *De profundis* (a 5 voci) è del 1563.
47 Per quanto riguarda *Philomena praevia* di Richafort, osserviamo che il mottetto è stato pubblicato pressoché contemporaneamente da Antico nel 1520 (*Motetti novi libro secondo*) e dall'anonimo compilatore del *Liber secundus*, oggetto di questo studio. Tale circostanza rafforza sempre di più l'ipotesi che l'editore di quest'ultimo sia stato un persona molto vicina aa Andrea Antico quando questi operava a Roma e che abbia pubblicato un progetto editoriale già da lui predisposto.

mente al repertorio in esse contenuto, insieme al cosiddetto "Medici Codex" (1518), al manoscritto Q 19 di Bologna (1518),[48] ai quattro libri di mottetti di Andrea Antico (1520 e 1521), al manoscritto A 17 della Cattedrale di Padova (1522), al codice P della Biblioteca capitolare di Casale Monferrato (1521-1526) e infine al manoscritto 1209 della Biblioteca Comunale di Bergamo, esemplato tra il 1542 e il 1545.[49] Non è quindi un caso se le concordanze più numerose sono proprio con queste fonti: otto con il codice di Padova, quattro con quello di Bergamo e tre rispettivamente con il "Medici Codex," con il Q 19 e con il manoscritto D di Casale Monferrato. Infine, è anche molto significativo che i mottetti *Per lignum* di Divitis, composto quasi certamente in onore del suo maestro Mouton, e *Regina coeli laetare* di Willaert, anch'egli allievo del grande compositore francese, siano gli unici pezzi di questi autori presenti nel nostro *Liber secundus* e nel "Medici Codex."

Tavola delle concordanze

1. Jean Mouton, *Christus vincit*
UNICUM

2. Pierre Moulu, *Oremus pro cunctis fidelibus*
UNICUM

3. Costanzo Festa, *Felix Anna quaedam matrona*
Mss: **I-Pc 17**, ff. 115v-116, n° 76; **I-BGc 1209**, ff. 13v-14r (12v-13r). Cf. *RISM* B IV^5, p. 314.
Ed.: *CMM* 25, V, pp. XVII, 63-65, n° 48.

4. Jean Mouton, *Salve, Mater Salvatoris*
Mss: **I-Pc 17**, ff. 74v-75, n° 47; **I-Fn 232**, ff. 153v-154, n° 48; **CH-SGs 463**, n° 91; **GB-Lbl, Add. 35087**, ff. 83v-84. Cf. *RISM* B IV^5, pp. 207, 313.
Stampe: **Antico 1520.3**; **Glareanus 1547**, III, 464-465
Ed.: **Shine**, 768-770; **Picker**, 214, n° 15.

5. Jean Mouton, *Ave Maria, gratia plena*
Mss: **I-Bc 19**, ff. 43v-44, n° 30; **I-Bc 142**, ff. 11-11v, n° 10. Cf. *RISM* B IV^5, pp. 52, 73.
Ed.: **Shine**, 66-68; **Sherr** 102-104.

6. Adrian Willaert, *Intercessio quaesumus, Domine*
Mss: **I-Fl 666**, ff. 70v-72, n° 25; **I-Pc 17**, ff. 155v-156, n° 103; **I-MOe F.2.29**, p. 23; **I-MOe C 313**, p. 8; **GB-Lrc 2037**, ff. 69v-70, n° 46; **GB-Lbl Add. 19583**, ff. 29v-30. Cf. *RISM* B IV^5, pp. 140, 316.
Stampe: **Attaingnant 1534^3**; **Gardane 1545**.
Ed.: *CMM* 3, II, 93-96, n° 17; **Lowinsky**, III, pp. 165-166, n° 25; IV, pp. 180-185, n° 25.

---

48 Su questo codice si veda anche Rainer Heyink, *Der Gonzaga-Kodex Bologna Q 19*, Paderborn 1994 (in particolare le pp.: 247, *Ave Maria*; 252, *Simile est*; 255, *Per lignum*).
49 Per una descrizione del codice cfr. David Crawford and Scott Messing, *Gaspar de Albertis Sixteenth-Century Choirbooks at Bergamo*, American Institute of Musicology, Hänssler-Verlag, 1994, pp. 21-25.

7. Andrea de Silva, *De ore prudentis*
Mss: **I-Pc 17**, ff. 55v-57, n° 33; **I-CMac D (F)**, ff. 28v-30, n° 13. Cf. *RISM* B IV⁵, pp. 101, 312
Ed.: ***CMM* 49**, I, 24-28, n° 7.

8. Mathieu Gascogne, *Dignare me, laudare te*
Mss: **D-Mub 4° Art. 401**, n° 34 e n° 35
Stampe: **Attaingnant 1534³**

9. Carpentras, *Simile est regnun coelorum*
Mss: **I-Bc 19**, ff. 75v-76, n° 48; **I-Bc 20**, f. 27v, n° 20; **I-CMac D (F)**, ff. 48v-49, n° 25; **I-CFm 59**, ff. 73v-74, n° 35; **I-PC 17**, ff. 106v-107, n° 69; **D-Rp 211-215**, ff. 31r-32r; **D-LEu 49**, ff. 192v-194r. Cf. *RISM* B IV⁵, pp. 53, 58, 102, 115, 314
Ed.: ***CMM* 58**, V, pp. 13, 111-113, n° 12.

10. Jean Richafort, *Philumena praevia*
Mss: **F-CA 125-128**, ff. 35v-36; **B-Lbu 163**, f. 54r-v; **D-Rp 772**, ff. 220v-226; **P-C 48**, f. 45r-v. Stampe: **Antico 1520.2**, n° 14; **Attaingnant 1528²**, n° 3; **LeRoy-Ballard**, f. 4r-v n° 4
Ed.: ***CMM* 81**, II, pp. 147-152, n° 21; **Picker**, p. 206, n° 14.

11. Andrea de Silva, *Virgo carens criminibus*
Mss: **I-Pc 17**, ff. 60[bis]v-61, n° 37; **I-BGc 1209 D**, ff. 75v-76r (80v-81r). Cf. *RISM* B IV⁵, p. 312.
Stampe: **Attaingnant 1534⁶**
Ed.: ***CMM* 49**, I, pp. 59-61, n° 15.

12. Loyset Compère, *Paranimphus salutat Virginem*
Mss: **I-Pc 17**, ff. 112v-113, n° 74; **I-BGc 1209**, ff. 76v-78r (81v-83r); **GB-Lrc 1070**, pp. 156-159, n° 24. Cf. *RISM* B IV⁵, p. 314
Ed.: ***CMM* 15**, IV, pp. 39-40.

13. Adrian Willaert, *Regina coeli laetare*
Mss: **I-Bc 23**, ff. 14v-15; **I-Bc 71**, pp. 209-210, n° 2; **I-Fl 666**, ff. 47v-49, n° 15; **I-MOcap IX**, ff. 29v-31, n° 14; **I-MOe N. 1.2**, ff. 188v-190, n° 22; **GB-Lrc 2037**, ff. 86v-87, n° 58 (solo *T* e *B*). Cf. *RISM* B IV⁵, pp. 71, 139, 266, 291
Ed. ***CMM* 3**, II, pp. 112-115, n° 20; **Lowinsky**, III, pp. 152-154, n° 15; IV, pp. 114-119, n° 15.

14. Josquin, *De profundis clamavi* (a 5 voci)
Mss: **BAV CS 38**, ff. 109-110 (106v-107); **D-Kl 24**, n° 66; **D-Dlb 1270**, n° 4 Ed.: **Osthoff**, 26-32, n° 3.

15. Antonius Divitis, *Per lignum salvi facti sumus* (a 5 voci)
Mss: **I-Bc 19**, ff. 83v-84, n° 54; **I-Fl 666**, ff. 98v-100, n° 39; **I-Pc 17**, ff. 109v-110, n° 72; **I-BGc 1209**, ff. 103v-104r (96v-97r); **BAV CS 54**, ff. 121v-123r. Cf. *RISM* B IV⁵, pp. 54, 140, 314 Ed.: **Shine**, 673-675; **Lowinsky**, III, n° 39, pp. 188-193; IV, n° 39, pp. 255-260.

Siglario delle edizioni a stampa

***CMM* 15** = Loyset Compère, *Opera Omnia*, edidit Ludwig Finscher, voll. 4 (Corpus Mensurabilis Musicae, 15), American Institute of Musicology, 1961 (IV: pp. 39-40 s.n. *Paranimphus*).

***CMM* 25** = Costanzo Festa, *Opera Omnia*, edidit Albertus Seay, voll. 5 (Corpus Mensurabilis Musicae, 25), American Institute of Musicology, Hänssler- Verlag 1979. (V: xvii e pp. 63-65 n° 48 *Felix Anna*).

***CMM* 3** = Adriani Willaert, *Opera Omnia*, edidit Hermannus Zenck, voll. 2 (Corpus Mensurabilis Musicae, 3), American Institute of Musicology in Rome, V. Biagiotti Firenze 1950. (II: pp. 93-96 n° 17 *Intercessio*; e 112-115 n° 20 *Regina coeli*).

***CMM* 49** = Andreas de Silva, *Opera Omnia*, edidit Winfried Kirsch, voll. 2 (Corpus Mensurabilis Musicae, 49), American Institute of Musicology, 1970 (I: pp. xiii-xiv e xvi; n° 7 pp. 24-28 *De ore prudentis*; n° 15 pp. 59-61 *Virgo carens*).

***CMM* 58** = Elziarii Geneti (Carpentras), *Opera Omnia*, edidit Albertus Seay, voll. 5, (Corpus Mensurabilis Musicae, 58), American Institute of Musicology, 1973. (V: xiii e 111-113 n° 12 *Simile est regnum*).

***CMM* 81** = Johannes Richafort, *Opera Omnia*, edidit Harry Elzinga, voll. 2 (Corpus Mensurabilis Musicae, 81), American Institute of Musicology, Hänssler- Verlag 1999 (II: pp. 147-152 n° 21 *Philomena*).

Lowinsky = *The Medici Codex of 1518. A Choirbook of Motets dedicated to Lorenzo De' Medici, Duke of Urbino*. Historical Introduction and Commentary by Edward E. Lowinsky, voll. 2, Chicago and London, The University of Chicago Press, 1968. (III, pp. 152-154 n° 15 e musica IV pp. 114-119 *Regina Coeli laetare*; III, pp. 165-166 n° 25 e musica IV pp. 180-185 *Intercessio*; III, pp. 188-193 n° 39 e musica IV, 255-260 *Per lignum*).

Osthoff = *Das Chorwerk*, vol. 57, ed. Helmuth Osthoff, Möseler Verlag, Wolfenbüttel 1955 (pp. 26-32, n° 14 *De profundis*).

Picker = *The Motet Books of Andrea Antico*, Edited with an Introduction by Martin Picker, Chicago end London, The University of Chicago Press, 1987. (p. 214 n° 15 *Salve mater*; p. 206 n° 14 *Philomena*).

Sherr = Richard Sherr, *Selections from Bologna, Civico Museo Bibliografico Musicale, MS Q 19 ("Rusconi Codex"), The Sixteenth-Century Motet, VI-VII*, New York & London, 1989. (VI, pp. 102-104 n° 5 *Ave Maria*).

Shine = *The Motets of Jean Mouton* by Josephine M. Shine, voll. 3, New York University, 1953 (pp. 66-68 *Ave Maria*; 673-675 *Per lignum*; 768-770 *Salve Mater*).

Sigle dei manoscritti e delle stampe

Attaingnant 1528[2] = *Motetz nouvellement composez*, Paris, P. Attaingnant 1528: n° 10

Attaingnant 1534[3] = *Liber primus quinque et viginti musicales quatuor vocum motetos complectitur...*, Paris, P. Attaingnant 1534: n° 10

Attaingnant 1534[6] = *Liber quartus XXIX musicales quatuor vel quinque parium vocum modulos habet...*, Paris, P. Attaingnant 1534: n° 11

Antico 1520.2 = *Motetti novi libro secondo*, Venezia, Andrea Antico 1520: n° 10

Antico 1520.3 = *Motetti novi libro tertio*, Venezia, Andrea Antico 1520: n° 4

BAV CS 38 = Città del Vaticano, Biblioteca Apostolica Vaticana, Cappella Sistina, ms. 38: n° 14

BAV CS 54 = Città del Vaticano, Biblioteca Apostolica Vaticana, Cappella Sistina, ms. 54: n° 15

B-Lbu 163 = Leuven, Bibliothèque de l'Université, ms. 163 (distrutto nel 1914): n° 10

CH-SGs 463 = St. Gallen, Stiftsbibliothrk, ms. 463 (Tschudi's Liederbuch): n° 4

D-Dlb 1270 = Dresden, Landesbibliothek, ms. Mus. 1270: n° 14

D-Kl 24 = Kassel, Landesbibliothek, ms. Mus. 24: n° 14

D-LEu 49 = Leipzig, Universitäts Bibliothek, ms. Thomaskirche 49/50: n° 9

D-Mub Art. 401 = München, Universitäts Bibliothek, ms.4° Art. 401,1-4 (*olim* Cim. 44i): n° 8

D-Rp 772 = Regensburg, Bischöfliche Zentralbibliothek, Sammlung Proske, ms. A. R. 772 (*olim* C. 99), n° 10

D-Rp 211-215 = Regensburg, Bischöfliche Zentralbibliothek, Sammlung Proske, ms. B 211-215: n° 9

F-CA 125-128 = Cambrai, Bibliothèque municipale, mss. 125-128 (*olim* 124): n° 10

Gardane 1545 = Adriano Willaert, *Musica Quatuor Vocum...Liber Secundus*, Gardane, Venezia 1545: n° 6

GB-Lbl Add. 35087 = London, British Library, ms. Additional, 35087: n° 4

GB-Lbl Add. 19583 = London, British Library, ms. Additional, 19583: n° 6

GB-Lrc 1070 = London, Royal College, ms. 1070: n° 12

GB-Lrc 2037 = London, Royal College, ms. 2037: nn^i 6, 13

Glareanus 1547 = Henricus Glareanus, *Dodecachordon*, Basilea 1547: n° 4

I-Bc 142 = Bologna, Museo Internazionale e Biblioteca della Musica, ms. R 142: n° 5

I-Bc 19 = Bologna, Museo Internazionale e Biblioteca della Musica, ms. Q 19: nn^i 5, 9, 15

I-Bc 20 = Bologna, Museo Internazionale e Biblioteca della Musica, ms. Q 20: n° 9

I-Bc 23 = Bologna, Museo Internazionale e Biblioteca della Musica, ms. Q 23: n° 13

I-Bc 71 = Bologna, Museo Internazionale e Biblioteca della Musica, ms. A 71: n° 13

I-BGc 1209 D = Bergamo, Biblioteca Civica, ms. 1209 D (*olim* Archivio Santa Maria Maggiore): nn^i 3, 11, 12, 15

I-CFm 59 = Cividale del Friuli, Museo Archeologico Nazionale, ms. LIX: n°9

I-CMac D (F) = Casale Monferrato, Archivio Capitolare, ms. D (F): nn^i 7, 8, 9

I-Fl 666 = Firenze, Biblioteca Medicea-Laurenziana, Acquisti e Doni, ms. 666 (*alias* "*Codice Medici*"): nn^i 6, 13, 15

I-Fn 232 = Firenze, Biblioteca Nazionale Centrale, ms. II I 232 (Magl. XIX 58): n° 4

I-MOcap IX = Modena, Archivio Capitolare, ms. IX: n° 13

I-MOe C 313 = Modena, Biblioteca Estense, ms. C. 313: n° 6

I-MOe F.2.29 = Modena, Biblioteca Estense, ms. α. F. 2. 29 (*olim* lat. 1232): n° 6 (solo framm. del *Tenor*)

I-MOe N. 1.2 = Modena, Biblioteca Estense, ms. α. N. 1. 2 (*olim* lat. 452, *ex* V. H. 2.): n° 13

I-Pc 17 = Padova, Biblioteca Capitolare, ms. A. 17: nn^i 3, 4, 6, 7, 9, 11, 12, 15

LeRoy-Ballard = Joannis Richafort, *Modulorum quatuor quinque & sex vocum, liber primus*, Paris, LeRoy & Ballard 1556: n° 10

P-C 48 = Coimbra, Biblioteca Geral da Universidade, ms. Mus. 48: 10

TAVOLA

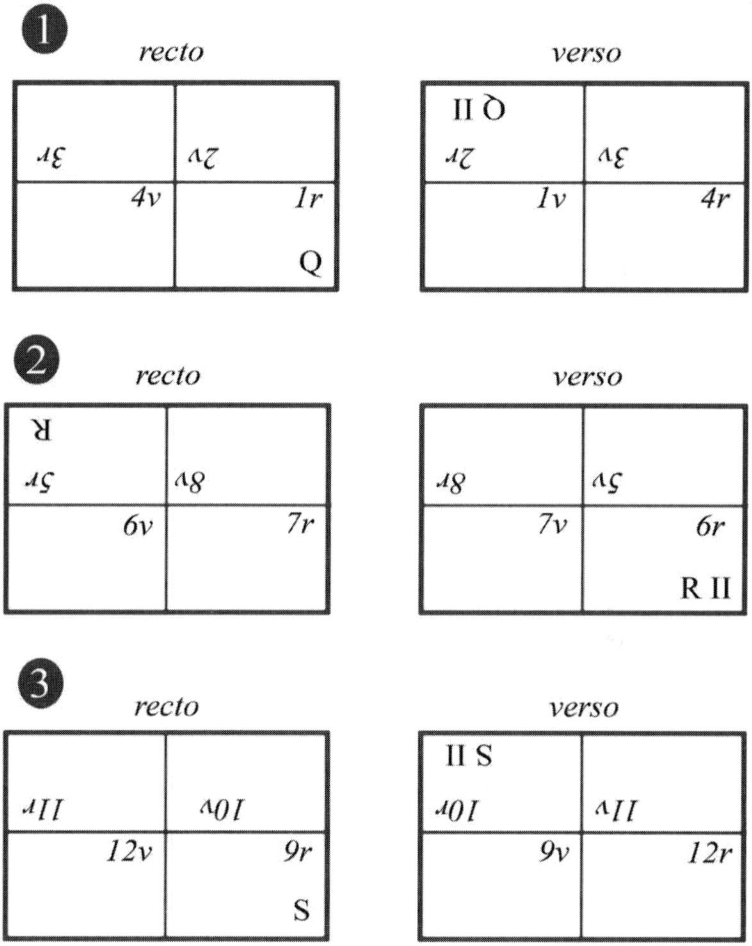

❶

recto

ʌƐ	ʌᄀ
4v	1r Q

verso

II Q	
ʌᄀ	ʌƐ
1v	4r

❷

recto

ꓤ	
ʌϚ	ʌ8
6v	7r

verso

ʌ8	ʌϚ
7v	6r R II

❸

recto

ʌII	ʌ0I
12v	9r S

verso

II S	
ʌ0I	ʌII
9v	12r

Figure 1. L'Aquila, Biblioteca Provinciale "Salvatore Tommasi", Volume segnato: Cinq B 163/1°, foglio n° 1. Lato sinistro: *Bassus Liber secundus*, c. [1r] (in alto) e c. 2v (in basso). Lato destro: Cornelio Musso, *I quattro libri delle prediche*, Torino 1579, Frontespizio

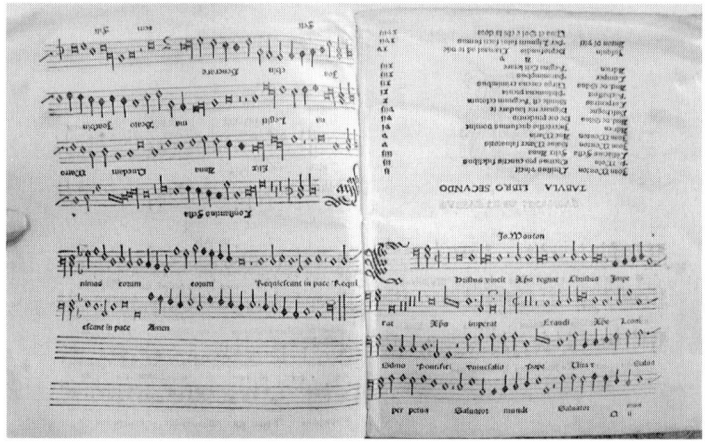

Figure 2. L'Aquila, Biblioteca Provinciale "Salvatore Tommasi", Volume segnato: Cinq B 163/1°, foglio n° 1. Lato sinistro: Bassus Liber secundus, c, 4r (in alto) c. 3v (in basso). Lato destro: Bassus Liber secundus, c. [1v] (in alto) e c. 2r (in basso)

Figure 3. L'Aquila, Biblioteca Provinciale "Salvatore Tommasi", Volume segnato: Cinq B 136, foglio n° 2. Lato sinistro: Bassus Liber secundus, c. 8r (in alto) e c. 7v (in basso). Lato destro: Bassus Liber secundus, c. 5v (in alto) e c. 6r (in basso)

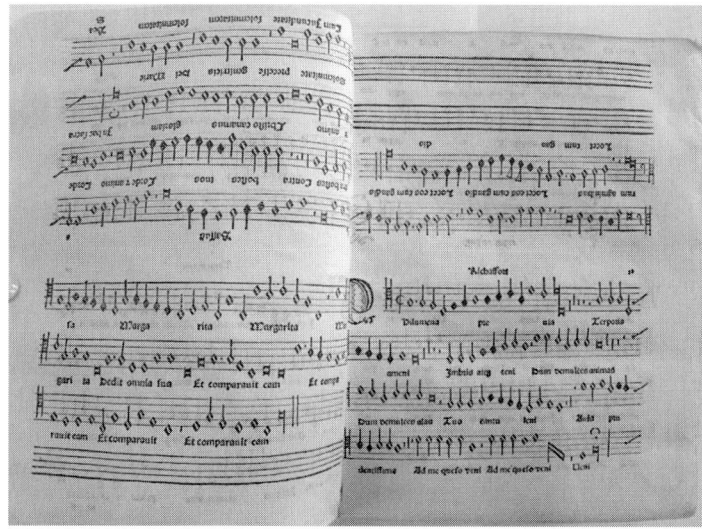

Figure 4. L'Aquila, Biblioteca Provinciale "Salvatore Tommasi", Volume segnato: Cinq B 136, foglio n° 3. Lato sinistro: Bassus Liber secundus, c. 9r (in alto) e c. 10v (in basso). Lato destro: Bassus Liber secundus, c. 12v (in alto) e c. 11r (in basso)

Levi Sheptovitsky

TWO CHROMATIC FANTASIAS BY JOHN DOWLAND
Were They Composed as a Pair?

"The crown jewel of the lute repertoire," "the most remarkable of all Dowland's solo works for the lute," "the highest peak in the whole repertoire of the solo lute": Expressions such as these are typical in descriptions of *Farewell* and *Forlorn Hope*, two chromatic fantasias by John Dowland.[1] These works, well known masterpieces of lute music, have drawn the attention of modern musicologists, and a number of important studies of Renaissance music have discussed the possible influence of the fantasias on contemporary keyboard music.[2]

The obvious relationship between the two fantasias has been noted by researchers of Dowland's heritage: Poulton discussed the two pieces side by side and published them in succession, placing *Farewell* after *Forlorn Hope*.[3] And they are mentioned together by Lowinsky, Rooley, Williams and other musicologists,[4] none of whom, however, has raised one key question: "Are the fantasias a pair?" Only Taylor has suggested that the appearance of the two fantasias in the Cracow Lute Tablature[5] "reinforces that *Farewell* and *Forlorn Hope* are a pair."[6] Unfortunately, however, Taylor does not substantiate his assumption. The present study, to the best of my knowledge, offers, for the first time, a discussion of the two compositions as a pair.

---

1 See, for instance, Gustave Reese, *Music in the Renaissance* (New York, 1959), 847; David Stanley Tayler, "The Solo Lute Music of John Dowland" (Ph.D. diss., University of California, Berkeley, 1992), 123-34; and Anthony Rooley, record liner notes to *John Dowland: Complete Lute Music* (Decca D 187D5), p. 7.
2 See especially Alan Curtis, *Sweelinck's Keyboard Music*, 3rd ed. (Leiden, 1987), 140-44.
3 Diana Poulton, *John Dowland* (London, 1972), 114-15; Diana Poulton and Basil Lam, eds., *The Collected Lute Music of John Dowland* (London, 1974), 13-19.
4 Edward E. Lowinsky, *Tonality and Atonality in Sixteenth-Century Music* (Berkeley and Los Angeles, 1961), 54-61; Rooley, liner notes to *John Dowland: Complete Lute Music*, p. 7; Peter F. Williams, *The Chromatic Fourth During Four Centuries of Music* (Oxford and New York, 1997), 28-30; Curtis, *Sweelinck's Keyboard Music*, 140-44.
5 Lvov State Ivan Franco University, MS 1400/1 (ca. 1553 to no earlier than the first decade of the seventeenth century). For more on this manuscript, see Levi Sheptovitsky, "The Cracow Lute Tablature (Second Half of the 16th Century): Discussion and Catalogue," *Musica Disciplina* 48 (1994): 69-97; and Sheptovitsky, "The Cracow Lute Tablature (CLT): Study of the Manuscript and Critical Edition" (Ph.D diss., Université Paris-Sorbonne, 2003).
6 Tayler, "The Solo Lute Music of John Dowland," 130.

The idea that *Farewell* and *Forlorn Hope* constitute a pair of fantasias is interesting but controversial. In the instrumental music of Dowland's period, pairs and larger groups of dances created out of the same material were common.[7] In these and similar cases two or more pieces were grouped by their authors. In the case of *Farewell* and *Forlorn Hope*, the situation is different. They do not occur together in the main sources (Cambridge D5, D9 and Glasgow G), and even in the Cracow Lute Tablature, which incorporates both fantasias, they do not appear in succession. Furthermore, in this latter manuscript another Dowland *Fantasia* and *Farewell* follow one another in succession (fols. 47v-51r), but *Forlorn Hope* appears separately (fols. 62v-64r). In Mertel's *Hortus Musicalis* (1615), *Forlorn Hope* is published as an independent composition and *Farewell* does not appear at all. We have no references by the composer to this matter, and none of the known sources of the fantasias contains any indication that would permit a positive answer to the question: Did Dowland in fact compose the fantasias as a pair?

Nevertheless, one cannot ignore the evident relationship between the two pieces. Indeed, Dowland himself does not disguise it, as would appear from the semantic connection between the titles "Farewell" and "Forlorn Hope,"[8] and also from the employment of mutual variants of the same theme in both compositions.

The titles are invaluable as Dowland's "instructions" for the emotional character of these works, which can serve as examples of "program-music" in the Baroque sense. The turn of the sixteenth century, a possible date of composition of the two fantasias,[9] falls within the transitional period from the late Renaissance to the Baroque, and comprises one of the most interesting periods in the history of music. During this musical epoch, the "program" was realized not by a development of dramatic events, as in the post-Beethovenian period, but by a comprehensive description of one *Affekt*. This trait was common to composers

---

7 Sheptovitsky, "Tripartite Dance 'La Verlata' for Solo Lute by Giovanni Pacoloni," *Lute News Quarterly* (December 2004): 12-17.
8 Only three of Dowland's fantasias bear titles: the two chromatic fantasias and another Farewell. The latter is not related to the chromatic fantasia of the same name and is an entirely different piece, which is, in fact, an *In nomine* composed on *Gloria tibi Trinitas*. See Poulton and Lam, *The Collected Lute Music of John Dowland*, 20-23.
9 We can date the principal sources of the fantasias as follows. *Farewell*: MS.Dd.5.78.(III), fols. 43v-44r, ca.1600, another dating ca. 1595-1600. *Forlorn Hope*: MS.Dd.9.33, fols. 16v-17r, 28 February 1600, another dating before 1597 to after 1603. Tayler suggests 1597 and 1603-04 as likely lower and upper limits for the date of composition of the chromatic fantasias; see Tayler, "The Solo Lute Music of John Dowland," 7 and 126-27.

of the new musical style, who were struggling to find musical means for the expression of states of the soul or *affections*.[10]

Without doubt, the titles express a sorrowful emotion, which is common to the two pieces and connects them through the same expressive content.[11] The musical expression of the *Affekt* is not through imitation of natural sounds and movements, but by means of melodic, harmonic, and rhythmic formulas or the *musical-rhetorical figures*, which, together with the departure from the diatonic, symbolism, and numerology drawn from Greek culture, were signs of the new musical lexicon.[12]

Both fantasias are built on the same musical-rhetorical figure—the *passus duriusculus* (hard/harsh step/passage) in its familiar and widely used form—with the chromatic fourth (also called the "chromatic tetrachord" or "chromatic hexachord")[13] placed in ascending order in *Farewell* and descending order in *Forlorn Hope* (Example 1).

Example 1. *Passus duriusculus* in *Farewell* and *Forlorn Hope*

The *passus duriusculus* is found in both vocal and instrumental compositions as a musical effect expressing emotions such as sadness, penitence, melancholy, devotion, sorrow, and so forth. The expressive content of this musical-rhetorical figure has been explored by many great composers. Peter Williams, in his book entirely devoted to the chromatic fourth, gives numerous examples from the vocal pieces at the turn of the century, which prove the close connection between this melodic figure and words expressing the above-mentioned

---

10 See Sheptovitsky, "Mastery of Sorrow and Melancholy: Expressivity in Two Chromatic Fantasias by John Dowland," *Lute News Quarterly* (April, 2007): 20-32.

11 In 1594, Dowland's application for the post of court lutenist to Queen Elizabeth was rejected and he left England for travels abroad. Tayler assumes that *Farewell* and *Forlorn Hope* reflect this major disappointment in the composer's life; see Tayler, "The Solo Lute Music of John Dowland," 129-30.

12 Gregory G. Butler, "Music and Rhetoric in Early Seventeenth-Century English Sources," *Musical Quarterly* 66, no. 1 (1980), 53.

13 Dietrich Bartel, *Musica Poetica: Musical-Rhetorical Figures in German Baroque Music* (Lincoln, NE, and London, 1997), 357. This musical-rhetorical figure has been the focus of musicological attention from the middle of the last century to the present time. See, for instance, J. Müller-Blattau, *Die Kompositionslehre H. Schütz in der Fassung seines Schülers Chr. Bernard* (Kassel, 1963); Olga Zakharova, *Ritorika i zapadnoevropejskaja muzïka XVII – pervoy polovinï XVIII veka: printsipï, priyomï* (Moskow, 1983), 25; Raymond Monelle, *The Sense of Music. Semiotic Essays* (Princeton, NJ, 2000), 73-77.

emotions.[14] Dowland himself provides examples that demonstrate the expressive content of the *passus duriusculus*. For example, in the song "All ye whom love or fortune hath betraide," he uses this melodic figure for the words "Lend ears and tears to me, most hapless man." The consciousness of these associations is evidenced also by a great resemblance between sections in *Farewell* (mm. 40-43)[15] and in this song (mm. 11-15). It is not known which of these is the earlier work. However, in each case the intentions of the composer are clear (Example 2).

Example 2.   Text setting and the *passus duriusculus*

Nothing could more powerfully confirm the association of the chromatic fourth with sadness, sorrow, melancholy, disappointment, or even heavy foreboding than the titles of the fantasias.

Side by side with the *passus duriusculus*, other musical-rhetorical figures support the *Affekt* and the concept of the relationship between the two fantasias. One of the most important motives in both pieces is a three-note melodic figure consisting of a falling second with repetition of one of the notes in the rhythmic figure of the *corta* (Example 3).

Example 3.   Melodic figure common to *Farewell* and *Forlorn Hope*

---

14 Williams, *The Chromatic Fourth*, 25-28.
15 Measure numbers in the transcriptions of *Farewell* and *Forlorn Hope* refer to bars in the tablature, where one bar is equal to a whole note in the transcription.

This motive is elaborated throughout the compositions and also appears in altered forms (in *Farewell*, mm. 10, 31-33, 44, and 49-51; in *Forlorn Hope*, mm. 4-7, 10, 21, 26, and 31).[16] The most expressive effect of sadness is achieved when the motive is built on a falling semitone (in *Farewell*, mm. 10, 20, and 32; in *Forlorn Hope*, m.7) (Example 4).

Example 4. Melodic figures based on a semitone

In both fantasias, four-note motives related to the *corta* are introduced. One of them (in *Farewell*) represents an ascending stepwise figure, and another (in *Forlorn Hope*) includes descending chromatic semitones derived from the theme (Example 5).

Example 5. Motives derived from the *corta*

At the end of *Farewell* the two motives are fused (Example 6).

Example 6. Fusion of the motives

---

16 See the complete transcription of the fantasias at the end of the present essay.

Moreover, combinations of the *corta* with this new motive, employed in both *Farewell* and *Forlorn Hope*, contribute to the melodic unity of the two compositions (Example 7).

Example 7.   Combinations of motives

A successive performance of the fantasias in the order *Farewell – Forlorn Hope* provides additional arguments in favor of pairing the two pieces. The logic of this order of succession is shown in the following analysis. Each fantasia falls into three sections (indicated as SI, SII, and SIII in Example 8), divided according to the treatment of the thematic material. The sections can be defined as Exposition – Middle Section – Final Section.

Farewell

SI (mm.1-21)	SII (mm.21-39)	SIII (mm.39-53)
20½	18	14½

Forlorn Hope

SI (mm.1-12)	SII (mm.12-27)	SIII (mm.27-36)
11½	15	9½

Example 8.   Formal structure of *Farewell* and *Forlorn Hope*

Each opening section consists of seven entrances of the theme, in which the order of the entrances is opposed to the direction of the melodic movement of the theme, i.e., the ascending theme of *Farewell* enters in the exposition in descending form; and, conversely, the descending theme of *Forlorn Hope* enters in ascending form. In both compositions the appearance of the theme in the lowest register marks the end of the exposition. Example 9 demonstrates the mirror resemblance of the opening sections in the fantasias:

Farewell

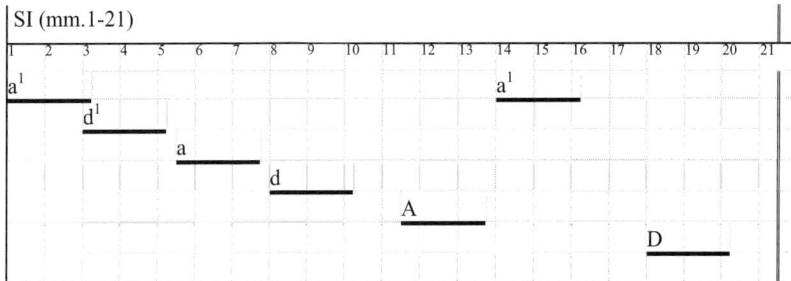

Forlorn Hope

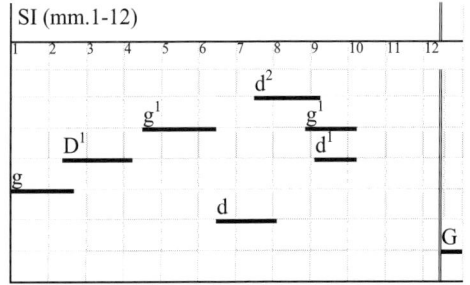

Example 9. Structure of expositions: *Farewell* and *Forlorn Hope*

Considering the fantasias within the pair, the mirror resemblance becomes apparent in the "symmetrical" sections (as we will see in Example 12). The outer sections of the pair, namely the opening section of *Farewell* and the concluding section of *Forlorn Hope*, use the same compositional technique, in which melodic variations are set against another part composed of statements of the theme presented in succession. In *Farewell*, the length of each variation is for the most part determined by the length of a phrase in the bass (Example 10).

297

Example 10. Variations in *Farewell*

In contrast, *Forlorn Hope* features melodic variations moving in rapid notes, which develop freely throughout the section (Example 11).

Example 11. Melodic variations in *Forlorn Hope*

The inner sections of the pair—namely, the concluding section of *Farewell* and the opening section of *Forlorn Hope*, together with the first half of the latter's middle section (mm. 12-21)—are imitative throughout. Dowland explores the same contrapuntal devices in both fantasias, such as diminution, truncation, *stretti* and the highly original combination of two statements of the theme on d^1, creating a long, continuous line in the range of an octave (*Farewell*, m. 39-42; *Forlorn Hope*, mm.17-20).

The middle section of *Farewell* and the second half of the middle section of *Forlorn Hope* are mostly set in free counterpoint. The above-described mirror resemblance of the fantasias within the pair can be depicted as shown in Example 12.

Variations on the theme	Free counterpoint	Intensive imitation, *stretti*		Free counterpoint	Variations on the theme
SI	SII	SIII	SI	SII	SIII
Farewell			*Forlorn Hope*		

Example 12. Mirror relationships in the fantasias

This symmetry reflects the dissimilar functional meanings of each fantasia within the pair, dissimilarities that become especially clear in the inner and concluding sections. According to the basic formal principles of grouping two pieces, in the inner sections (where *Farewell* ends and *Forlorn Hope* begins), a logical transition between the two compositions should be provided, and the concluding section of *Forlorn Hope* should serve as the common final of the pair.

Along these lines, it is noteworthy that the end of *Farewell* and the beginning of *Forlorn Hope* meet precisely at the point of the so-called "golden section" of the pair.[17] At this point, the fantasias could be coupled in the manner of *conjunct* combination of the themes in *Forlorn Hope* (mm. 17-20 and 32-33),[18] where the last note of one is also the first note of the other—i.e., the note G is both the cadence tone of *Farewell* and the starting-point of *Forlorn Hope*. Marked by the ornamented authentic cadence and prolonged in the form of a rhythmically divided pedal point to the end of *Farewell* (mm. 51-53), the note G could serve as a clasp that fastens the two compositions together. This smooth connection between *Farewell* and *Forlorn Hope* would contribute to the expression of lowly and negative images; the musical-rhetorical figure *descensus* or *catabasis*[19] at the end of *Farewell* (mm. 49-51) continues the descent through the *passus duriusculus* at the beginning of *Forlorn Hope*, increasing the *Affekt*.

The intensive imitative development and the employment of the *corta*-motives in the inner sections of the pair provide melodic and emotional continuity in the two compositions. From m. 49 to the end of *Farewell*, this musical emblem becomes the principal means of conveying the emotional message of the whole. The *corta*-motives reappear in *Forlorn Hope* and are reworked intensively until the final section (mm. 5-7, 10, 12, 16, 21-22, 25-26). Thus, in a successive performance of the two compositions, *Forlorn Hope* sounds like a natural continuance of *Farewell*, which would not be so if the order were reversed (Example 13).

---

17 A ratio, observed especially in the fine arts, between the two dimensions of a plane figure or the two divisions of a line such that the ratio of the smaller to the larger is equal to the ratio of the larger to the sum of smaller and larger—a ratio of roughly three to five.
18 For more on conjunct and disjunct combinations of the themes, see below.
19 A fall by step in successive repetitions of the motive. See Bartel, *Musica Poetica*, 214.

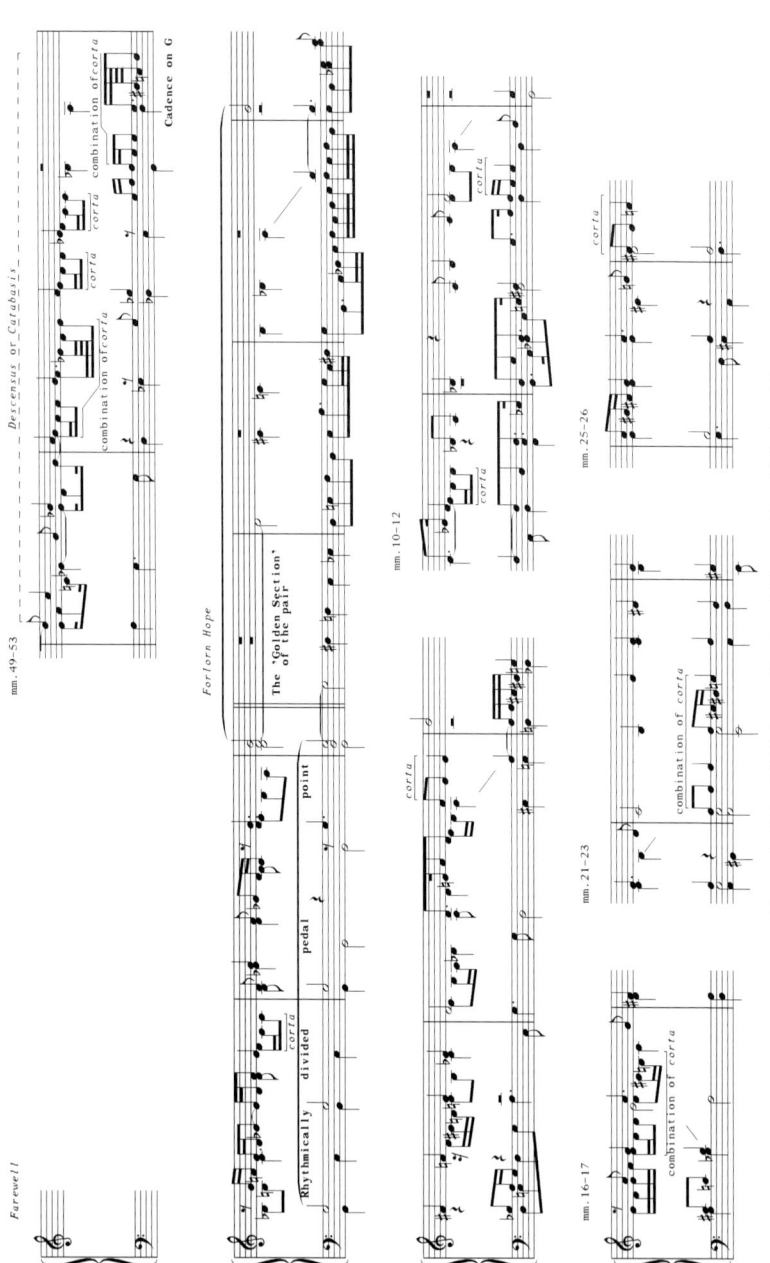

Example 13. Motivic continuity of *Farewell* and *Forlorn Hope*

As a logical conclusion, the final section of *Forlorn Hope* bears features of the *reprisa* and *coda* of the whole pair. Although the *reprisa* in this case does adhere strictly to the classical meaning of the term, several thematic references clearly indicate a reprise: the return of the thematic material and the main key of the pair, the order of entrances of the theme from high to low (as in the opening section of *Farewell*), and the gradually increasing number of parts.

The ascending theme in *Farewell* and the descending theme in *Forlorn Hope* emphasize the dissimilar functional meaning of each fantasia in the pair. When the themes are considered in succession, a melodic wave is created (Example 14).

Example 14. Melodic contour of *Farewell* and *Forlorn Hope* themes

This wave refers, in turn, refers to its own larger variant, which appears in the concluding section of *Forlorn Hope*. This latter large wave begins with the ascending diatonic scale $d^1 - d^2$ (mm. 27-29), which comes to be identified with the combination of the two statements of the theme in *Farewell* (mm. 39-42, also at the beginning of the concluding section!), thereby creating a long, continuous line exactly in the same range (Example 15).

Example 15. Melodic waves in *Farewell* and *Forlorn Hope*

In *Forlorn Hope* this scalar ascending motion reaches d^2 and then changes direction, pursuing a descending "diagonal" that nearly crosses the entire section (mm. 29-33; Example 16).

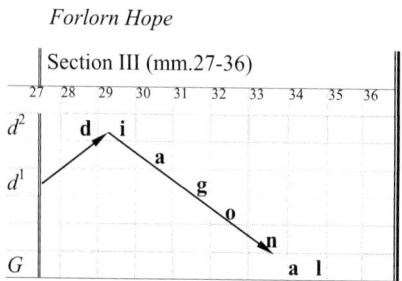

Example 16: Melodic "diagonal" in *Forlorn Hope*

The diagonal appears as an important succession of events that first occurred in the previous sections of both fantasias, and thus it constitutes the reprise. This two-and-a-half octave descent is made up of disjunct and conjunct themes (alluding to the two ways of combining tetrachords in the Greek "Greater Perfect System"). The same disjunct combination of the themes (mm. 29-31), featuring a whole tone between two chromatic fourths following one another in succession, can also be identified in the concluding section of *Farewell* (mm. 39-42) and is an inversion of the latter. The *conjunct* chromatic tetrachords (mm. 32-33) clearly refer to the combination of the themes in the middle section of *Forlorn Hope* (mm. 17-20), where the last note of one is also the first note of the next. This combination, which, in the middle section, was sounded at the level of the "dominant," here recurs at the level of the tonic scale degree (mm. 32-33).

In the midpoint of the section, the disjunct and conjunct combinations of the theme are bridged by the diatonically filled descending fifth between the fifth and tonic scale degrees (mm. 31-32). This melodic figure bears evident relation to the form and location of the diatonic inversion of the theme in *Farewell*: Both appear in exactly the same rhythmic form, on D, at the midpoint of the section, and, surprisingly, at the same distance from the beginning of the fantasia at mm. 31-32! (Do these numbers have numerological importance?) Another appearance of this melodic figure in *Forlorn Hope* (m. 26) also refers to the diatonic inversion of the theme in *Farewell*; in both cases, they are found in the middle sections in the lower part on D (Example 17).

Example 17. Thematic relationships in *Farewell* and *Forlorn Hope*

Thus, the concluding section of *Forlorn Hope* contains elements from both fantasias, creating a condensed summary of the essential components of the pair. To be more precise, this combination of events should be referred to as "synthetic recapitulation."

Side by side with the *reprisa* traits, we should also consider some obvious features of the coda. The concluding section of *Forlorn Hope* contrasts sharply with the other sections of the fantasias in almost all of its compositional components, such as sound, counterpoint, and rhythm. The cessation of intensively imitative development and the shift to active diminutions in SIII of *Forlorn Hope* display the principle of the final change before the end of the composition. Dowland maintains a constant drive toward the final climactic cadence through the abrupt change of surface rhythm from slow to fast, with the intensive *crescendo* achieved by the gradual increase of the number of parts, from two at the beginning of the section to six at the end. This, along with the compressed form of the last section, provides for a wild finale and recalls the virtuosic codas of instrumental compositions from later periods. Combining the two fantasias into a pair, the final section of *Forlorn Hope* can serve as a "common ending" for both pieces and naturally places *Forlorn Hope* after *Farewell*. Therefore, if the fantasias are performed together, *Farewell* should be followed by *Forlorn Hope*.

Clearly, the lack of any indication by the composer himself or any evidence of contemporary performance of the two pieces together thwarts an unequivocal identification of the fantasias as a pair. However, the modern musicologist or performer must note the fact that the performance of the two fantasias in succession makes their common traits even clearer, and leads to the tentative conclusion that they are indeed a pair, together providing mutual variants that supplement one another. The same expressive content and thematic unity of the two pieces create an overall unity of a higher level than in the suite form, thereby anticipating another combination of compositions based on variants of the same theme: J.S.Bach's *The Art of Fugue*.

— — —

The above reassessment of the fantasias has also lead me to a reconsideration of editing principles. The following is my transcription of *Farewell* and *Forlorn Hope* from a little known manuscript, the Cracow Lute Tablature, in which both fantasias are preserved.[1] The present rendition differs from the transcription of the fantasias in *The Collected Lute Music of John Dowland*.[2] My transcription takes musical-rhetorical figures into consideration; and the barring, I believe, mirrors the natural movement of the music.

The original tablature is mostly preserved, representing the version of the fantasias from the Cracow Lute Tablature without additions from other sources. Obvious errors have been corrected and all changes are enumerated in the accompanying editorial notes, which give the original reading. My own additions to the original tablature are placed in square brackets. In cases where bar lines have been regularized, the position of the original bar line is indicated by an asterisk (*), and that of the editor's bar line by two asterisks (**) below the tablature.

---

1 Three fantasias by Dowland preserved in the Cracow Lute Tablature, including *Farewell* and *Forlorn Hope*, have no titles and do not indicate the name of the composer. During a study of the manuscript in the Lvov University library in 1980, I identified these pieces independently.
2 Poulton and Lam, *The Collected Lute Music of John Dowland*, 13-19.

FANTASIA
[Farewell]

John Dowland

fols.49ᵛ-51

FANTASIA
[Forlorn Hope Fancy]

fols. 62V-64

310

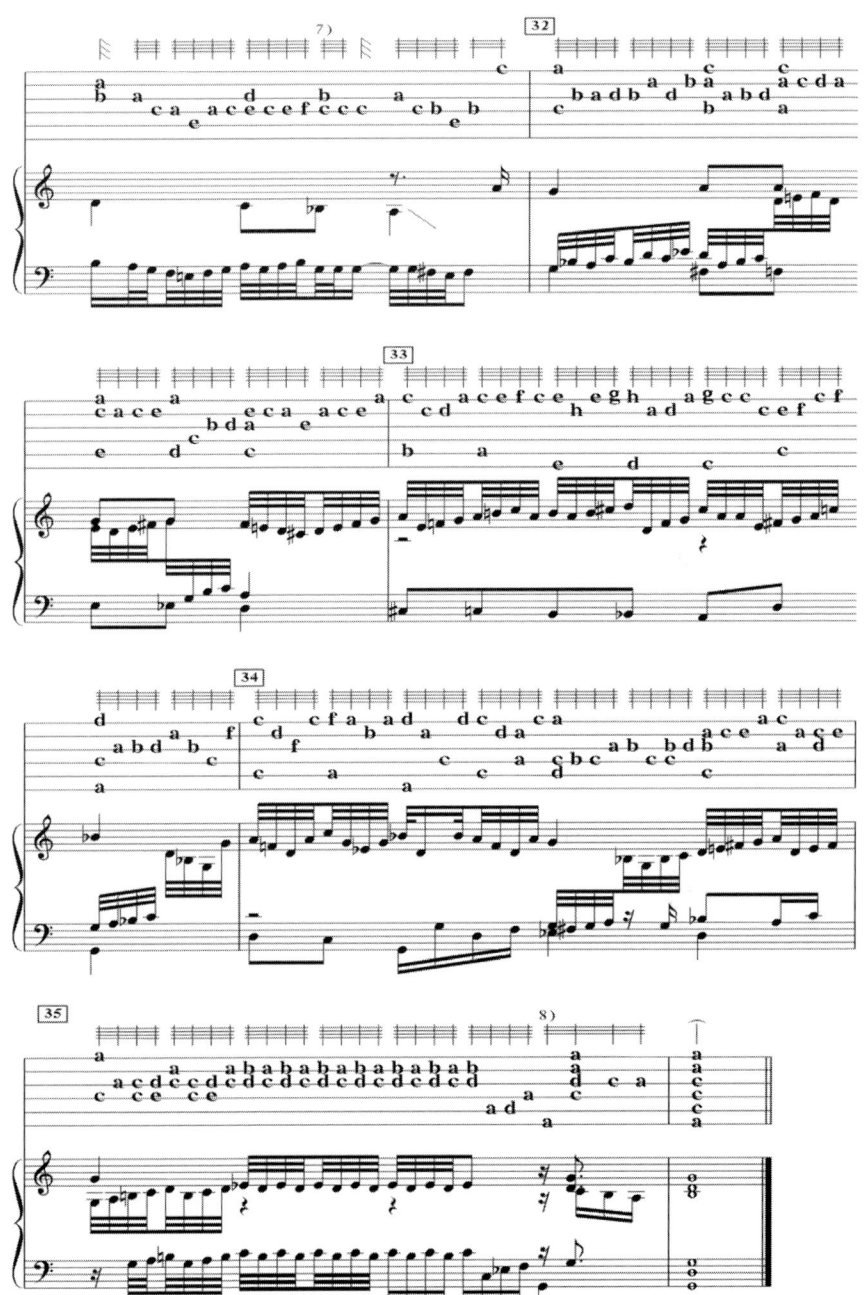

EDITORIAL NOTES

FANTASIA (FAREWELL)

1) orig.:
2) orig.:
3) orig.:
4) orig.:
5) orig.:
6) orig.:
7) Letter 'e' instead of letter 'i' in original.
8) orig.:
9) orig.:
10) orig.:
11) orig.:
12) orig.:
13) orig.:
14) orig.:
15) orig.:
16) orig.:
17) orig.:

FANTASIA (FORLORN HOPE)

1) orig.:
2) orig.:
3) orig.:
4) orig.:
5) orig.:
6) orig.:
7) orig.:
8) orig.:

Wolfgang Ruf

RELIGIÖSE MUSIK UND POLITIK
Die Aufführung von Händels "Messias" in Berlin 1786

Die berühmte Berliner Aufführung des *Messias* im Jahre 1786 durch Johann Adam Hiller ist mehrfach beschrieben und als wichtige Station der Rezeptionsgeschichte Händels auf dem europäischen Kontinent gewürdigt worden.[1] Sie war bekanntlich nicht die erste Präsentation des Werks auf deutschem Boden; vorausgegangen waren mehrere halböffentliche oder höfisch-exklusive Aufführungen, so in Hamburg durch Michael Arne (1772, in Englisch) und Carl Philipp Emanuel Bach (1775, in deutscher Übersetzung von Friedrich Gottlieb Klopstock und Christoph Daniel Ebeling), sowie in Mannheim durch Georg Joseph Vogler (1777, in Italienisch), in Schwerin (1780, deutsche Übersetzung von Klopstock/Ebeling) und in Weimar durch Ernst Wilhelm Wolf (1780/81, deutsche Übersetzung von Johann Gottfried Herder). Händels *Messias* erfreute sich vor allem unter norddeutschen Musikkennern in den 1780er Jahren einiger Bekanntheit, wie zuvor schon das *Alexanderfest*, mit dessen privater Berliner Aufführung im Jahre 1766 durch Christian Gottfried Krause die Rezeption der oratorischen Werke Händels auf dem Kontinent eingesetzt hatte.[2] Doch von allen frühen Darbietungen Händelscher Werke auf deutschem Boden war die Berliner Aufführung die bei weitem spektakulärste, aufwendigste und folgenreichste. Sie war es, die den Anstoß gegeben hat, dass Händel als deutscher Komponist im Land seiner Herkunft einer breiten Öffentlichkeit bekannt und zu einer Figur nationaler Bedeutung und zum "kanonisirten

---

1 Walther Siegmund-Schultze: Über die ersten Messias-Aufführungen in Deutschland, in: Händel-Jahrbuch 1960, S. 51-109; Gudrun Busch: Das "Händel-Dreieck" Braunschweig – Berlin – Hamburg in der Eschenburg-Nicolai-Korrespondenz 1770 bis 1779, in: Göttinger Händel-Beiträge VI, 1996, S. 236-253; Annette Monheim: Die Londoner Gedächtnisfeiern und ihre Auswirkung auf Deutschland am Beispiel von Johann Adam Hiller und Johann Friedrich Reichardt, in: Händel-Jahrbuch 1978, S. 15-33; Gudrun Busch: Zwischen Berliner Musikliebhabern und Berliner Anglophilie, Aufklärung und Empfindsamkeit: Zur Genese der frühesten Berliner Händel-Rezeption 1748-1771, in: Laurenz Lütteken (Hrsg.): Händel-Rezeption der frühen Goethe-Zeit, = Marburger Beiträge zur Musikwissenschaft IX, Kassel 2000, S. 81-134; Hartmut Grimm: Johann Adam Hillers Berliner "Messias"-Aufführung im Kontext seines Schrifttums, in: dass., S. 187-207.
2 Daten zur Rezeptionsgeschichte des Messias bei Donald Burrows: Handel "Messiah," Cambridge 1991, S. 47-54; Hans Joachim Marx: Leben und Werk, in: Siegbert Rampe (Hrsg.): Georg Friedrich Händel und seine Zeit, Laaber 2009, S. 162-167.

Tonmeister" (Christian Daniel Schubart)³ erhoben wurde. Im Folgenden werden einige personelle und funktionale Aspekte des außerordentlichen Ereignisses beleuchtet, deren komplexer Zusammenhang von der bisherigen Literatur nicht ausreichend beachtet worden ist.

Die Initiatoren

Das Verdienst, den *Messias* in Berlin erstmals öffentlich aufgeführt zu haben, wird gewöhnlich dem Dirigenten, Johann Adam Hiller, zugesprochen. Durch seinen gedruckten, fünf Tage nach dem Konzert datierten und dem preußischen Kronprinzen Friedrich Wilhelm gewidmeten Bericht hat er nicht unerheblich zum eigenen Ruhm als Propagator Händels beigetragen.⁴ Die Initiative ging jedoch nicht von ihm aus, sondern es waren nach Hillers Aussage "einige Berliner Musikfreunde," die den Prinzen für den Plan der Aufführung begeistern konnten. Wer waren diese ungenannten Musikfreunde? In erster Linie ist hier an den Buchhändler, Verleger und Schriftsteller Friedrich Nicolai (1733-1811) zu denken. Er hatte im bürgerlichen Kulturleben Berlins die Fäden in der Hand und beste Beziehungen zum Hof. In Berlin war er ein angesehener, einflussreicher Mann; er zählte mit Johann Georg Sulzer (1720-1779), Gotthold Ephraim Lessing (1729-1781) und Moses Mendelssohn (1729-1786) zu den Anführern der bürgerlichen Intelligenz.⁵ Nicolai war theologisch gebildet, ein kritischer Protestant, daneben zeitweise Mitglied einer Freimaurer-Loge. Ferner war er die treibende Kraft in den beiden wichtigsten Berliner Intellektuellen-Clubs, dem eher geselligen und schöngeistigen "Montags-Club," dem auch Musiker angehörten, und der strikt im Geheimen wirkenden, aus Akademikern und leitenden Beamten bestehenden "Mittwochs-Gesellschaft"; sie betrieb die Auseinandersetzung mit aufklärerischem Gedankengut und mit Ideen einer Reformierung der erstarrenden und als rückständig empfundenen friderizianischen Gesellschaft - trotz Loyalität zum preußischen König und Staat. Mitglieder der Mittwochs-Gesellschaft standen in enger Beziehung zur *Berlinischen Monatsschrift*, einem der bedeutendsten Publikationsorgane der deutschen Aufklärung.⁶ Nicolai war ausgesprochen anglophil – einer der Shakespeare, Milton und Shaftesbury in der Originalsprache las und Alexander

---

3 Ludwig Finscher: "gleichsam ein kanonisirter Tonmeister." Zur deutschen Händel-Rezeption im 18. Jahrhundert, in: Aleida Assmann/Jan Assmann (Hrsg.): Kanon und Zensur. Archäologie der literarischen Kommunikation II, München 1987, S. 271-283.
4 Johann Adam Hiller: Nachricht von der Aufführung des Händelschen Messias, in der Domkirche zu Berlin, den 19. May 1786, Berlin 1786.
5 Zu Nicolai siehe Johan van der Zande: Popular Philosophy and Absolute Monarchy, in: Hans Blom/John Christian Laursen/Luisa Simonutti: Monarchisms in the Age of Enlightenment: Liberty, Patriotism and the Common Good, Toronto 2007, S. 203-206.
6 Rudolf Vierhaus: Friedrich Nicolai und die Berliner Gesellschaft, in: Bernhard Fabian (Hrsg.): Friedrich Nicolai 1733-1811. Essays zum 250. Geburtstag, Berlin 1983, S. 89.

Popes Gesamtwerk verlegte. Er teilte die Anglomanie zahlreicher Landsleute, die England entdeckt hatten "*als den einzigen Sitz der Freyheit, der Toleranz und der Grossmuth.*"[7] Schließlich war Nicolai im ganzen deutsch-sprachigen Raum bekannt durch sein kritisches, nicht unumstrittenes Journal *Allgemeine deutsche Bibliothek*, dem führenden nationalen Anzeigen- und Rezensionsorgan für alle Wissenschaften von der Philosophie und der Musik bis zur Mathematik und Kriegswissenschaft.

Nicolai war auch organisatorisch der Dreh- und Angelpunkt des Berliner Musiklebens. Er war ein begeisterter Liebhaber der Tonkunst, der Hauskonzerte veranstaltete und im "Concert der Musikliebhaber" den Ton angab. In einem Brief an Johann Joachim Eschenburg in Braunschweig hatte er bereits im Sept. 1771, also Monate vor den Hamburger *Messiah*-Aufführungen durch Michael Arne, die "*complette Partitur des Händelschen Meßias, worin alle Chöre stehen*" erbeten.[8] Offenbar war in Berlin nur die unvollständige Ausgabe mit den Arien zugänglich; Eschenburg hingegen war glücklicher Besitzer der Partituren von *Messiah* und *Judas Maccabaeus*. Vermutlich war Nicolai durch den Auftritt Michael Arnes in Deutschland und durch dessen Präsentation von *Alexander's Feast* in Hamburg angeregt worden, sich mit Händels *Messiah* zu befassen. Nicolais Wunsch einer öffentlichen Darbietung dürfte bestärkt worden sein durch den Aufenthalt von Charles Burney in Berlin und Potsdam im Herbst 1772, der in Burneys Tagebuch ausführlich beschrieben und in der Korrespondenz von James Harris jr. mehrfach bezeugt ist.[9] Burneys Hausbesuch im gastlichen Hause des angesehenen Musikexperten Nicolai war eine Selbstverständlichkeit, nicht aber die ehrenvolle Einladung zur Tafel des Kronprinzen und seiner Gemahlin in Potsdam.[10] - Eschenburg ließ Nicolai erst nach längerem Zögern im Dezember 1772 die Partitur von *Messiah* zukommen, und zwar auf dem Umweg über den Hofkapellmeister Johann Friedrich Agricola.[11] Daraus ist zu schließen, dass die Königlich-preußische Hofkapelle sehr früh vomin das Projekt der öffentlichen Aufführung in der Hauptstadt eingeweiht war. Wieweit die Kapelle in die vom Kronprinzen veranlasste, exklusive (Teil-) Aufführung in der Katholischen Kirche von Potsdam im Jahre 1781[12] impliziert war, ist nicht bekannt. Warum die öffentliche Darbietung des

---

7 Bernhard Fabian: Nicolai und England, in: Friedrich Nicolai 1733-1811 (vgl. Anm. 3), S. 178.
8 G. Busch: Das "Händel-Dreieck" (vgl. Anm. 1), S. 241.
9 Carl Burney's der Musik Doctors Tagebuch seiner musikalischen Reise, übers. von Christoph Daniel Ebeling, 3. Band, Hamburg 1773, S. 55-176; Donald Burrows/ Rosemary Dunhill: Music and Theatre in Handel's World. The Family Papers of James Harris 1732-1780, Oxford 2002, S. 678-691.
10 Carl Burney's... Tagebuch (vgl. Anm. 9), S. 147-149.
11 G. Busch: Das "Händel-Dreieck" (vgl. Anm. 1), S. 245.
12 Hinweis auf Ort und Jahr bei Hans Joachim Marx: Händels Oratorien, Oden und Serenaden. Ein Kompendium, Göttingen 1998, S. 157. Zelter berichtet in seinen

Werks dann mehrere Jahre aufgeschoben wurde, wissen wir gleichfalls nicht. Nicht auszuschließen ist, dass sich König Friedrich II., ohnehin kein Freund figuraler Kirchenmusik, gegen eine öffentliche, vom Hof unterstützte Präsentation ausgesprochen hat.

Ort und Zeitpunkt

Es bedurfte offensichtlich erst des Anstoßes durch die monumentale, mehrtägige Londoner Zentenar-Feier des Jahres 1784, die sowohl an das Geburtsjahr (1685) als auch an den Tod Händels vor einem Vierteljahrhundert (1759) erinnerte und 1785 wiederholt wurde, damit das Berliner *Messias*-Projekt erneut in Angriff genommen wurde. Nicolai brachte 1785 eine Übersetzung von Burneys Bericht ("Account") unter dem Titel *Nachricht von Georg Friedrich Händel's Lebensumständen und der ihm zu London im Mai und Jun.1784 angestellten Gedächtnißfeyer*, ins Deutsche übertragen von Johann Joachim Eschenburg, heraus. Da zuvor schon Besprechungen des Ereignisses in der deutschen Fachpresse erschienen waren[13] und Friedrich Reichardt in Berlin die kleine anekdotische Biographie *George Friedrich Händel's Jugend* veröffentlicht hatte, waren die Musikkenner auf die *Messias*-Aufführung des kommenden Frühjahrs bestens eingestimmt.

Ort der Veranstaltung zu Berlin am 19. Mai 1786 war die barocke Domkirche, die man, laut Hillers Bericht, wegen ihrer Größe und günstigen Lage beim königlichen Schloss anderen Kirchenräumen und dem Opernhaus vorgezogen hatte. Die Wahl dieses repräsentativen Ortes lag nahe, nicht nur wegen der extensiven Besetzung an Sängern und Instrumentalisten, des zu erwartenden großen Publikums und des Wunschs nach großer akustischer Wirkung; es dürften auch religiöse und politische Motive eine Rolle gespielt haben. Denn die reformierte Domkirche war die Hofkirche und Grablege der brandenburgischen Kurfürsten und des preußischen Königshauses – ein Ort von starker Symbolkraft in der Hauptstadt eines noch jungen Staates, der sich anschickte, eine Großmacht europäischen Ranges zu werden und die Führung unter den norddeutschen, protestantischen Ländern zu übernehmen.

Doch die Domkirche war keine Heimstätte großer Kirchenmusik. Friedrich II. hatte eine Abneigung gegen Kirchenmusik und gestattete im Berliner Dom nur den in reformierten Gemeinden üblichen Psalmen- und Liedgesang, der durch die Knaben der Gymnasien auszuführen war;[14] bestallte Kirchenmusiker gab es außer dem Domorganisten nicht. Große Aufführungen mit Chor und

---

Selbstbiographien von dieser ihn begeisternden Auffführung (Carl Friedrich Zelters Darstellungen seines Lebens, hrsg. von Johann-Wolfgang Schottländer, = Schriften der Goethe-Gesellschaft XLIV, Weimar 1931, S. 147 und S. 255).
13 Belege bei A. Monheim: Die Londoner Gedächtnisfeiern (vgl. Anm. 1), S. 17.
14 Ingeborg Allihn: Berlin, Musikstädte der Welt, Laaber 1991, S. 44 und 67.

Orchester wie die der Passionskantate *Der Tod Jesu* von Carl Heinrich Graun durch die bürgerliche *Musikausübende Gesellschaft*, die von der Schwester des Königs, Prinzessin Anna Amalia, angeregt worden war und seit 1755 jährlich am Karfreitag gegeben wurde, blieben die Ausnahme. Dem musikalisch einseitigen und konservativen Monarchen bedeuteten die Kompositionen Händels nichts, aber es ist durchaus denkbar, dass seine an geistlicher Musik stark interessierte und einst selbst Choräle, Kantaten und Kirchenlieder komponierende Schwester, die gealterte und kränkelnde Anna Amalie, eine verschwiegene Befürworterin der *Messias*-Aufführung war. Eine Darbietung des geistlichen Oratoriums außerhalb einer Kirche kam nicht in Betracht, übrigens auch nicht im königlichen Opernhaus, das unter Friedrich II. nur für exklusive repräsentative Veranstaltungen zugänglich war. Denn anders als in England war geistliche, auch die nichtliturgische Musik in Deutschland bislang dem Kirchenraum vorbehalten; sie gelangte nur selten, etwa bei Darbietungen im privaten oder höfischen Zirkel oder in geschlossenen Gesellschaften mit spiritueller Orientierung, wie bei den Freimaurern, in profane Räume.

Ein merkwürdiger Umstand ist die Eile, mit der die Aufführung zustande kam. Binnen von vier Wochen mussten das Konzert mittels Rundschreiben und in den Lokalzeitungen angezeigt, die Musiker zur freiwilligen Mitwirkung gewonnen, Sänger und Instrumentalisten ausgewählt, die Proben durchgeführt, die Subskription aufgelegt und die Eintrittsbillette verkauft werden. Innerhalb von zwei Tagen wurde der Kirchenraum mit einem hölzernen Podium für das Orchester und mit Tribünen für den Chor ausgestattet, damit das Konzert an einem Freitag, der in Berlin üblicherweise dem Opernbesuch vorbehalten war, stattfinden konnte. Hauptverantwortlich für die von langer Hand geplante und nur generalstabsmäßig zu meisternde Organisation war der Rittmeister des Kürassier-Eliteregiments Gens d'armes Valentin von Massow, ein Adliger von hohem Ansehen, der einen Sinn für Kunst und für Musik hatte, Sohn des früheren Staatsministers gleichen Namens und Vertrauensperson des Kronprinzen.[15] Vermutlich sah der Kronprinz im plötzlich (seit April 1786) verschlechterten, bald zum Tode führenden Gesundheitszustand Friedrichs II. und in seiner faktischen Übernahme der repräsentativen Geschäfte eine seltene Chance, Händels Werk in aller Pracht zum Erklingen zu bringen – zum Gedenken an Händel, zum Ruhme Preußens und nicht zuletzt zur eigenen Gloire des designierten Thronfolgers. Der bis zum Geiz sparsame, im Alter allem Glanz und Ritual abholde und todkranke Autokrat konnte den horrenden Aufwand für das singuläre geistliche Musikereignis nicht gutheißen, aber unterbunden hat er die Aufführung des Oratoriums immerhin nicht.

---

15 Wilhelm von Massow: Die Massows, Halle 1931, S. 228-230.

Die Ausführenden

Das Orchester hatte eine bislang in Deutschland unbekannte Dimension und eine in der Mischung von professionellen Musikern und Amateuren ungewöhnliche Zusammensetzung: Es bestand aus 185 Instrumentalisten, davon etwa zwei Drittel Musiker der Königlichen Kapelle und der Kapelle der Kronprinzen, ferner Militärmusiker verschiedener Regimenter, Stadtmusikanten und freischaffende Künstler, sowie ein Drittel dilettierende Liebhaber. Die ersten Violinen waren prominent besetzt: an der Spitze standen der neue königliche Konzertmeister Joseph Benda und als Gäste die Geiger Ignaz Fränzl und dessen Sohn Ferdinand aus Mannheim sowie Carl Stamitz aus Straßburg. Die Cellisten wurden von Jean Pierre Duport angeführt. Am Cembalo saß Carl Friedrich Fasch, der spätere Gründer der Berliner Singakademie. Zu den Dilettanten unter den Violinisten, die jeweils mit einem Berufsmusiker an einem Pult standen, zählte Carl Friedrich Zelter, Goethes späterer Freund. Die Gesangssolisten und ein Teil des ca. 120 Personen umfassenden Chors waren Berufssänger und -sängerinnen der italienischen Oper, an der Spitze der Kastrat Carlo Concialini; er war seit seinem Debüt in Agricolas *Achille in Sciro* (1765, zur Hochzeit von Friedrich Wilhelm) einer der gefeierten Stars des Königlichen Operhauses. Ergänzt wurde der Chor durch Laiensänger und durch Berliner und Potsdamer Schulchöre. Die Einstudierung erfolgte durch die Schulkantoren unter der Oberleitung des rührigen städtischen Musikdirektors Lehmann, der für die Kirchenmusik der Berliner Nikolai- und der Petrikirche zuständig war. Gesungen wurde in italienischer Sprache (übersetzt von Dirceo Gasparini), gewiss nicht nur mit Rücksicht auf die italienischen Sänger, denen man eine deutsch- oder englischsprachige Aufführung nicht zumuten wollte, sondern auch wegen der Teilnahme der Hofkreise, für die Italienisch die gewohnte Sprache der vokalen Kunstmusik war. Dass nicht alle Mitwirkenden und Zuhörer den fremden Wortlaut der gesungenen Bibeltexte verstanden, nahm man in Kauf.

Der Dirigent der Berliner Aufführung, der 57jährige Johann Adam Hiller, war ein respektabler, vielseitiger Mann, deutschlandweit bekannt als Komponist von Singspielen und Liedern, als Musikdirektor und Gesangspädagoge, als viel gelesener Musikschriftsteller und Herausgeber; er war Gründer und Leiter musikalischer Gesellschaften und Konzertreihen. Für das Leipziger "Große Concert" hatte er bereits in den 1760er Jahren die beiden damals berühmtesten deutschen Sängerinnen, Corona Schröter und Elisabeth Schmeling, engagiert. Schmeling war 1771 die erste deutsche Primadonna der Berliner Hofoper geworden und feierte später unter dem Namen Mara in Paris und London triumphale Erfolge, auch bei der Händel-Commemoration von 1784 hatte sie geglänzt. Hiller und Nicolai kannten sich persönlich aus Leipzig, wo sich Nicolai jährlich wegen der Buchmesse mehrere Wochen aufhielt. Bereits 1767 hatte Nicolai versucht, Hiller eine Anstellung in Berlin schmackhaft zu machen;[16] vielleicht suchte man in Berlin einen Ersatz für Carl Philipp Emanuel Bach, der damals im Begriff war, nach Hamburg zu wechseln und Nachfolger Telemanns zu werden. Hiller lehnte ab, da er das erfolgreiche Wirken in der ruhigeren Messestadt Leipzig dem Dienst in der Residenzstadt Berlin und unterm Diktat des autoritären Königs vorzog. Vergeblich war auch 1778 der Versuch Reichardts gewesen, Hiller als Musikdirektor der Berliner Hauptkirchen zu gewinnen.

1786 jedoch war die Situation eine gänzlich andere: Der gealterte und vereinsamte König hatte seit dem Ende des die Kräfte erschöpfenden Bayerischen Erbfolgekriegs (1779) die Freude an Musik und Theater verloren und hielt sich von den nicht staatsnotwendigen Dingen des Hoflebens fern. Die einst exzellente Hofkapelle hatte ihre besten Köpfe durch Tod oder Weggang verloren, und der seit 1775 als Nachfolger von Johann Friedrich Agricola tätige Hofkapellmeister Johann Friedrich Reichardt hatte es nicht vermocht, sie wieder auf das einstige Niveau zu bringen und den uneingeschränkten Beifall seines kritischen Dienstherrn zu erhalten. Er verlegte sich ab 1783 immer mehr auf das Reisen und weilte im Frühjahr 1786 in Paris.[17] Als im März 1786 auch der Konzertmeister Franz Benda verstarb, waren die Königliche Kapelle und die Hofoper ohne herausragende leitende Persönlichkeit. Es lag daher nahe, für die Leitung des *Messias*-Projekts als Gast einen auswärtigen Künstler von Rang nach Berlin zu rufen. Hiller, der inzwischen aus Leipzig wegstrebte und das Amt eines Herzoglich Curländischen Kapellmeisters angenommenen hatte, war zweifellos die erste und die beste Wahl. Er hatte sich zuletzt als Direktor des Leipziger Gewandhauses und als Musikdirektor der Neuen Kirche hervorgetan und seine praktische Vertrautheit auch mit geistlicher Musik und mit Händels Werken unter Beweis gestellt. Zudem hatte er das *Utrechter Te Deum* ediert und eine Kurzbiographie Händels verfasst.[18]

Hillers Bearbeitung

Die Direktionspartitur der Berliner Aufführung ist verschollen. Es steht jedoch außer Zweifel, dass die Partitur erheblich gekürzt wurde, um eine Gesamtdauer der Aufführung von zwei Stunden nicht zu überschreiten. Hiller hat glücklicherweise in seiner *Nachricht* einige der vorgenommenen Streichungen von Arien

---

16 Brief an Friedrich Nicolai vom 5. Dez. 1767, in: Mark Lehmstedt (Hrsg.): Johann Adam Hiller: Mein Leben. Autobiographie, Briefe und Nekrologe, Leipzig 2004, S. 33-35.
17 Walter Salmen: Johann Friedrich Reichardt. Komponist, Schriftsteller, Kapellmeister und Verwaltungsbeamter der Goethezeit, 2. Aufl., Hildesheim 2002, S. 61 f.
18 Georg Friedrich Händel: Te Deum laudamus, zur Utrechter Friedensfeyer ehemals in Englischer Sprache componirt, und nun mit dem bekannten lateinischen Texte, Leipzig o. J. (1780); Händel (George Friedrich), in: Johann Adam Hiller: Lebensbeschreibungen berühmter Musikgelehrten und Tonkünstler neuerer Zeit, Leipzig 1784.

und Chören benannt und zudem aus Anlass der zweiten Leipziger Nachfolgeaufführung des Jahres 1787 allgemeine "Betrachtungen"[19] zum *Messias* angestellt, so dass sich einige Beweggründe seiner Auslassungen und nicht unerheblichen Eingriffe in die Musik Händels nachvollziehen lassen. Hartmut Grimm verweist auf den bewussten Verzicht auf musikalisch allzu expressive oder pathetische, dem Ideal edler Simplizität widersprechender Stücke, ferner auf solche, deren Text und Vertonung ein zur Zeit der Spätaufklärung theologisch anfechtbares Bild vom alttestamentarischen, strafenden Gott im zornigen Affekt vermitteln. Als Beispiel einer in Augen Hillers wohl übertriebenen Expressivität nennt Grimm die als koloraturenreiche Rachearie gestaltete Bassarie *Why do the nations so furiously rage together* mit dem anschließenden fugierten Chor *Let us break their bonds asunder*, während die Worte der folgenden Tenorarie *Thou shalt break them with a rod of iron* für die anachronistische Gottesauffassung stehen. Dass für die Streichung dieses großräumigen, dramatisch gesteigerten Komplexes vor dem mitreißenden Hallelujah-Chor am Schluss des zweiten Teils des Oratoriums außer den ästhetischen und religiösen Motiven auch politische Rücksichten in Frage kommen, sollte zumindest erwogen werden. Denn Charles Jennens vom zweiten Psalm abgeleiteter Text der beiden Arien und des sie verbindenden Chorsatzes über die wild mit- und gegeneinander tobenden Nationen und die wider den Höchsten aufbegehrenden Könige und Fürsten (Bassarie), mit dem Aufruf an die Völker, das zwingende Joch abzuwerfen (Chor) und der Androhung des Gottesgerichts (Tenorarie), war für deutsche Ohren heikel. Es wundert daher nicht, dass alle zeitgenössischen Übersetzer (Klopstock/Ebeling, Hiller, Herder) mit dem Vorwurf der Missachtung des Gottesfriedens durch die Herrscher ihre Probleme hatten und dass, nach dem Befund der Partitur aus dem Klopstock-Nachlass, in der sprachlich so behutsam und empfindsam modernisierenden Übertragung von Klopstock und Ebeling der Appell zum Aufbegehren der Unterdrückten und die Vision vom Strafgericht nicht enthalten sind.[20] Schon gar nicht passten die Textpartien zur Geisteshaltung einer sich zwar christlich-tolerant gebenden, aber nach wie vor die Untertanen gängelnden und den Krieg bedenkenlos als legitimes Mittel des Machtstrebens und Machterhalts sanktionierenden absolutistischen Monarchie. Die Tilgung war jedenfalls wohl überlegt, gleichgültig, ob für sie letztlich der

---

19 Johann Adam Hiller: Der Messias, nach den Worten der heiligen Schrift, in Musik gesetzt von George Friedrich Händel. Nebst angehängten Betrachtungen darüber, zur Ankündigung einer zweyten Aufführung, in der Paulanerkirche zu Leipzig. Freytags den 11. May, 1787, Leipzig o. J. [1787]. – Hiller führte den Messias in Leipzig am 3. Nov. 1786 und am 11. Mai 1787 sowie in Breslau am 30. Mai 1788, jeweils in seiner eigenen deutschen Übertragung, auf.

20 Magda Marx Weber/Hans Joachim Marx: Der deutsche Text zu Händels »Messias« in der Fassung von Klopstock und Ebeling, in: Rainer Cadenbach/Helmut Loos (Hrsg.): Beiträge zur Geschichte des Oratoriums seit Händel. Festschrift für Günther Massenkeil zum 60. Geburtstag, Bonn 1986, S. 30 f. und S. 50 f.

Werkbearbeiter Hiller, der italienische Librettist, ein pflichteifriger preußischer Zensor oder eine andere Person verantwortlich war.

Staatspolitik und Konfessionspolitik

Das glanzvolle Berliner Konzert am 19. Mai 1786 stand unter der Schirmherrschaft des Kronprinzen Friedrich Wilhelm; es wurde jedoch durchgeführt als gemeinschaftliche Veranstaltung des Preußischen Hofes und der Berliner und Potsdamer Bevölkerung. Die demonstrative Gemeinsamkeit von Monarchie, Aristokratie und Volk, letzteres vertreten durch höhere Beamte, Offiziere und gebildete Bürger, war im friderizianischen Staat, in dem streng hierarchisches Denken und ein ausgeprägtes Ständebewusstsein vorherrschten, etwas Einmaliges. Der egalitäre Schulterschluss auf dem unverfänglichen Terrain geistlicher Musikausübung folgte einerseits dem Vorbild der Londoner Zentenar-Feier. Andererseits entsprach er einem in den 1780er Jahren sich abzeichnenden Trend der preußischen Monarchie, die Untertanen ungeachtet ihres Standes und sozialen Rangs als Gleiche zu behandeln, zumindest juristisch vor dem Gesetz sowie in den Belangen des religiösen Glaubens. 1785 war des hundertsten Jahrestags des Toleranzedikts von Potsdam gedacht und der Grundsatz der Religionsfreiheit bekräftigt worden. Der berühmte Satz des aufgeklärten Königs Friedrich II. aus dem Jahre 1749: *"Ein jeder kann bei mir glauben, was er will, wenn er nur ehrlich ist,"* war längst zum festen Staatsprinzip erhoben worden, aber nicht aus Achtung der Gewissensfreiheit der Menschen, sondern aus kühlem Kalkül, das Lutheraner, Pietisten, Reformierte und Katholiken gleichermaßen an Krone und Staat band und auch die jüdischen Mitbürger zumindest so weit respektierte, wie es die Staatsräson gebot.[21] Die prinzipielle Duldung freier Religionsausübung stand freilich einer sich gegen Ende der Regierungszeit Friedrichs II. auf Druck der protestantischen Geistlichkeit allmählich wandelnden Konfessionspolitik entgegen; sie wird alsbald dem Luthertum als der Glaubensrichtung der überwiegenden Mehrheit der Einwohner Brandenburg-Preußens mehr Gewicht einräumen als den anderen Bekenntnissen, trotz der fortbestehenden grundsätzlichen Akzeptanz aller Religionen.[22] Der Staat begann sich innerhalb des Deutschen Reichs, vor allem gegenüber Österreich und dem Kaiser Joseph II., als Schutzmacht des Protestantismus zu profilieren. Der preußische Patriotismus, der bereits seit dem Siebenjährigen Krieg von den kirchlichen Kanzeln herab gepredigt worden

---

21 Zur Zweckorientierung der Toleranzpolitik siehe Christian Graf von Krockow: Friedrich der Große. Ein Lebensbild, München 1993, 5/1998, S. 135-143, und Gerd Heinrich: Religionstoleranz in Brandenburg-Preußen. Idee und Wirklichkeit, in: Manfred Schlenke (Hrsg.): Preussen. Politik, Kultur, Gesellschaft, Bd. 1, Hamburg 1986, S. 83-102.

22 Michael Sauter: The Prussian Monarchy and the Practices of Enlightenment, in: H. Blom/J. Christian Laursen/L. Simonutti (Hrsg.): Monarchisms (vgl. Anm. 5), S. 217-239.

war,[23] bestärkte zunehmend den protestantischen Charakter des Staatswesens führte allmählich zu dessen latenter Sakralisierung. Sie stand im krassen Widerspruch zur säkularen Staatsauffassung des Spätabsolutismus und suchte Monarchie und Untertanen unter dem Begriff "Vaterland" zur auserwählten, gottbegnadeten Schicksalsgemeinschaft zusammenzuschweißen. Hinzu kam eine neue, gleichfalls als Gegengewicht zur Macht der Habsburger geplante außenpolitische Orientierung, in Verfolgung der von Friedrich II. konsequent verfolgten Hegemonialpolitik. Sie bewog Preußen zur Annäherung an andere deutsche Fürstentümer, vor allem an das Kurfürstentum von Hannover. Zu Hannover und wegen dessen Personalunion zu Großbritannien bestanden nicht nur enge verwandtschaftliche Beziehungen und Empfindungen geistiger Verbundenheit, sondern Gemeinsamkeiten in den realen Interessen der Reichspolitik und der europäischen Politik. Sie waren jüngst im Juli 1785 beim sogenannten "Fürstenbund" mit Hannover und Sachsen besiegelt worden.[24] Die Wiedergabe des schon in England prunkvoll gefeierten Sakralwerks eines Komponisten lutherischen Glaubens, von deutscher Herkunft und mit englisch-hannoveraner Bindung, bei vergleichbaren Bedingungen: unter höfischer Protektion, in der Hauptkirche der Monarchie, als imposante Großveranstaltung, zum Benefiz bedürftiger Witwen und Waisen, bei Verzicht der Aktiven auf Honorierung, mit der Teilnahme von Spitzenmusikern und Amateuren sowie vor einem Publikum, das Adel und Bürger, Christen und Juden einträchtig umfasste. Diese Beschwörung einer idealen königstreuen und toleranten Volksgemeinschaft war zum einen die bewusste Nachahmung der monumentalen Londoner Händel-Commemoration von 1784. Zum anderen war die *Messias*-Aufführung das unausgesprochene Bekenntnis zur Gleichgesinntheit und Gleichgestimmtheit mit der englischen Nation, was freilich Zwischentöne des machtpolitischen Konkurrierens nicht ausschloss. Darüber hinaus schien sie geeignet, in Preußen und im ganzen nördlichen Deutschland die Solidarisierung der Bürger und die nationale Selbstfindung zu fördern. Die Berliner Aufführung war gewiss nicht zuletzt eine große Feier zur spirituellen Erbauung der Gläubigen mit religiöser Musik des überragenden Komponisten Händel, aber vor allem war sie ein spektakuläres preußisch-deutsches Politikum.

Nachwirkungen

Symbolische Wirkungen repräsentativer Akte wirken untergründig; sie lassen sich eher erahnen als nachmessen. Dennoch gibt es konkrete Anhaltspunkte für

---

23 Christopher Clark: Preußen Aufstieg und Niedergang 1600-1947, München 2007, S. 261-274.
24 Theodor Schieder: Friedrich der Große. Ein Königtum der Widersprüche, München 1983, ²2002, S. 278f.; Johannes Kunisch: Friedrich der Große. Der König und seine Zeit, München 2004, S. 520-523.

die Folgen der Berliner Aufführung. Hans Joachim Marx sprach vom "Aufbruchssignal" der Zentenarfeier in der Westminster Abbey.[25] Wir können ergänzend anfügen: Das Signal fand ein starkes Echo im Dom zu Berlin und strahlte weiter aus in verschiedenste Richtungen. Erstens gab es das Zeichen für andere öffentliche, orchestral und chorisch groß besetzte Aufführungen des *Messias* in deutschen Städten wie Leipzig (1786 und 1787)[26] und Breslau (1788). 1789 folgte dann die Aufführung in der Bearbeitung Mozarts in der Kapitale des Deutschen Reichs, in Wien. – Zweitens kündete es noch vor dem Tode König Friedrichs II. eine einschneidende Wende der Musikkultur in der Hauptstadt Preußens an. Der zukünftige König Friedrich Wilhelm demonstrierte in spektakulärer Weise seine Entschlossenheit, Berlin zum Brennpunkt deutscher Musik, Literatur und Kunst wieder aufblühen zu lassen. Er wird den Bann brechen für die Pflege von Stilarten erhabener oder dramatischer Musik, die zur Zeit Friedrichs des Großen entweder als modernistisch oder als anachronistisch verpönt waren. In den weltlichen und geistlichen Hofkonzerten treten von jetzt an die Stelle von Werken Grauns, Hasses oder Agricolas die vokalen Kompositionen von Händel, C. Ph. E. Bach, Fasch, Pergolesi, Gluck, Haydn und alsbald auch Palestrina, Werke, die alsbald zum bevorzugten Repertoire der bürgerlichen Laienchöre werden. – Drittens wird fortan in Berlin das Benefizkonzert in den Dimensionen einer Massenveranstaltung, bei der Künstler und Dilettanten freiwillig und ohne Entlohnung für ein gemischtes, zahlendes Publikum zugunsten Not leidender Bevölkerungsgruppen musizieren, zum beliebten Spezialtypus des Konzerts. Die *"große Musik zum Besten der Wittwen und Waysen verstorbner Tonkünstler"* mit über 400 Mitwirkenden, die im September 1786 in der Berliner Garnisonkirche mit Reichardts Trauerkantate *Cantus lugubris* auf Friedrich II. und einem Te Deum gegeben wurde, war nur das nächste der sich fortsetzenden Reihe öffentlicher Wohltätigkeitskonzerte der Königlichen Kapelle und später der Berliner Singakademie.[27] – Viertens war die *Messias*-Aufführung für Carl Friedrich Fasch nach seinen Erfahrungen mit der missglückten Darbietung seiner 16stimmigen Messe der Anlass, fortan im Verein von Gesangsschülern und Berufssängern regelmäßige Chorproben zum Einstudieren großer geistlicher Werke der Vergangenheit abzuhalten. Daraus entstand 1791 die Berliner Sing-akademie zur Pflege der 'wahren Kirchenmusik' alten wie neueren Stils mit Wirkung weit über Berlin und Preußen hinaus. – Fünftens ist die Berliner Aufführung das Initial für die noch

---

25 H. J. Marx: Händels Oratorien (vgl. Anm. 12, S. 157.
26 Annette Monheim: "Unternehmen Händel." Johann Adam Hillers "Messias"-Aufführungen in Leipzig in den Jahren 1786 bis 1787, in: Händel-Jahrbuch 2001, S. 351-268.
27 Christoph Henzel: Die italienische Hofoper in Berlin um 1800. Vincenzo Righini als preußischer Hofkapellmeister, Stuttgart u. Weimar 1994, S. 36, 87 und 277 f.; Gottfried Eberle: 200 Jahre Sing-Akademie zu Berlin: "Ein Kunstverein für die heilige Musik," Berlin 1991, S. 17 f.

intensivere musikpraktische und ästhetische Befassung mit *Messiah* und mit anderen oratorischen Werken Händels. Sie ist hinreichend belegt durch die Bearbeitungen Mozarts (1789-90) und durch bedeutende musikpoetische Texte wie diejenigen von Herder, Wackenroder, Heinse oder Kleist[28]. – Und schließlich – dies ist musikgeschichtlich wohl das Nachhaltigste – wird jene nicht-liturgische religiöse Vokalmusik fortan gesell-schaftsfähig und ideologisch allseits akzeptiert, die, weil ihr Text poetisch gestaltet oder (durch paraphrasierende Übersetzung) umgeformt ist, sich nicht mehr streng an das Wort der Bibel hält. Geistliche Musik tritt mit Entschieden-heit aus der konfessionell beschränkten Sphäre der Kirchen heraus in die offene säkulare Welt einer übergemeindlichen, allgemein-menschlichen Geistigkeit.[29] Sie eint nicht bloß Gläubige durch die gesungene Verkündigung, sondern bildet allumfassende Gemeinschaft und erzeugt das Zusammengehörigkeitsgefühl der Rezipienten durch die verbindende und bezwingende Macht der Musik. – Als Fazit kann festgehalten werden: Die Berliner *Messias*-Aufführung von 1786 war ein politisches und gesellschaftliches Ereignis von vielschichtiger Bedeutung und nationalem Rang. Seine Nachwirkung auf die deutsche Kultur und die Musikauffassung am Übergang zur bürgerlichen Romantik kann nicht hoch genug eingeschätzt werden.

---

28 Johann Gottfried Herder: Cäcilia (1793), Händel (in Adrastea, 1802); Wilhelm Heinrich Wackenroder: Das merkwürdige musikalische Leben des Tonkünstlers Joseph Berglinger (1793); Wilhelm Heinse: Hildegard von Hohenthal (1796); Heinrich von Kleist: Die Heilige Cäcilie oder die Gewalt der Musik (1810).
29 Hierzu Hans Joachim Kreutzer: Von Händels "Messiah" zum deutschen "Messias." Das Libretto, seine Übersetzungen und die deutsche Händel-Rezeption des 18. Jahrhunderts, in: Deutsche Vierteljahrsschrift für Literaturwissenschaft und Geistesgeschichte LXVII (1993), S. 77-100.

Bathia Churgin

BEETHOVEN AND THE NEW DEVELOPMENT-THEME IN SONATA-FORM MOVEMENTS

A well-known feature of the development section in Beethoven's *Eroica* Symphony, first movement, is the prominent new theme. This was not a novel effect, however, for in Classic music the introduction of a new theme in the development, or, more accurately, new developmental material is an old device. What is new about the *Eroica's* new theme is its dramatic and dissonant preparation, the extremely remote key in which it first appears—e minor, enharmonically the minor Neapolitan of the tonic E♭ major—and the five-fold repetition of the theme.[1] Three presentations occur in the development, each beginning in a different key—e minor, a minor, and e♭ minor, and two near the start of the long coda, in the keys of f minor—the normal second degree—and again in e♭ minor (the theme begins in mm. 284, 292, 322, 581, and 589). This quintessential example of a new development-theme will be our paradigm against which we can measure other such examples.

If we examine the tradition in which Beethoven composed, we find that new themes, phrases, motives, and figurations (which I will designate as N) occur in the development section of sonata-form movements from the earliest phase of the Classic period onward. For example, such ideas appear before 1740 in many movements of early symphonies by G. B. Sammartini and Antonio Brioschi. In first movements of two Sammartini symphonies, J-C 7 and 65, the composer introduces distinctive themes, the more significant ones in one of the earliest and best Sammartini symphonies, J-C 7 in C major, probably composed by 1730 (Example 1).[2]

This article was published in *The Journal of Musicology*, Vol. 16, No. 3, New Perspectives on Beethoven Sources and Style (Summer, 1998), pp. 323-343. Published by: University of California Press.

1 Because of the many references to keys in this survey, major keys are indicated by capital letters and minor keys by lower-case letters. Lower-case Roman numerals stand for minor chords or key relationships.

2 For the score and analysis of J-C 7, see my edition, Giovanni Battista Sammartini, *Ten Symphonies,* "The Symphony, 1720-1840," ed. Barry S. Brook, Series A, vol. 2 (New York and London, 1984), Score 1. The Symphony J-C 65 (dated before 1738) is published in my edition, *The Symphonies of G. B. Sammartini. Volume I: The Early Symphonies* (Cambridge, MA, 1968), No. 16 in the volume). For new developmental material in all three movements of Brioschi's symphony in G, Fonds Blancheton 32 (dated before October 1733), see my edition and analysis in "The Symphony, 1720-1840," Series A, vol. 3 (1985), Score 1.

Here, two new themes are placed in the key of the mediant—e minor—a fairly remote key for Sammartini. 1N is 18 mm. long and 2N 8 mm. Like many later N themes, these themes contain both new and derived elements, the second theme also related to the first. In 1N, a derived motive (here, a bass motive) accompanies the theme as well, a technique later found in some Beethoven N themes (see Example 5). The bass motive returns at the start of the recapitulation combined with the cadential (K) theme, from which it most closely derives. In addition, 2N comes back in the recapitulation in the tonic minor. The recurrence of a new theme or idea in the recapitulation thus has a long history.

Example 1. G. B. Sammartini, Symphony in C Major, J-C 7/I: cadential theme (K) and start of the development with 1N.

The use of new material in the development may reflect the influence of the B section of the da capo aria, as Leonard Ratner suggests.[3] Recall of such material in the recapitulation may well stem from a similar procedure found in late Baroque concerto movements in ritornello form, which often incorporate ideas presented later in the movement in a final recapitulation section.[4]

That the development can contain new material should not surprise us since Classic sonata form is basically a tonal, not a thematic plan. New material in this section has many functions, such as contrast, surprise, enrichment, intensification, and structural articulation. Obviously, each example of new material must be studied individually in order to comprehend fully its role in the movement's structure.

Theorists like Koch, Galeazzi, Reicha, and Czerny all mention the possibility of introducing a new theme or idea, first of all at the opening of Part II of a sonata-form movement. Galeazzi (1796) specifies such new themes as one of the standard options at this point in the structure,[5] while Koch (1793) states that the device is common only in the concerto.[6] Much later, Czerny (1848?) broadens the possibility and observes that in the first section of Part II "the ideas of the first part must be displayed, developed, worked up, and necessarily augmented with new ones."[7] Reicha's remarks (c. 1825) are both more far reaching and more specific. He indicates that at the start of Part II, a new theme can be 8-16 mm. long and be developed together with earlier ideas. New ideas can be further introduced in Part II and especially in the coda.[8]

After about 1740, new themes in symphonic allegros, especially first movements, usually occur at the beginning of Part II, as described much later by the theorists. Such themes are often cantabile and piano, providing lyrical and

---

3 Leonard G. Ratner, *Classic Music: Expression, Form, and Style* (New York, 1980), 229, 233.
4 Examples can be found in Antonio Vivaldi's Concerto, Op. 3 No. 8/III (pub. 1711), where a variant of the modulatory Solo 2 moving from a to e (mm. 35-50) returns in the tonic near the end of the movement (mm. 132-41); and in J. S. Bach's Italian Concerto/III (1735), where new material in F-B♭ (mm. 77-84) returns in the reprise section in B♭-C-F (mm. 155-66).
5 See my article, "Francesco Galeazzi's Description (1796) of Sonata Form," *Journal of the American Musicological Society* XXI (1968), 195. Galeazzi recommends that the N theme "for greatest surprise ... be in some related key [not the secondary key], but separated and unexpected."
6 See Heinrich Christoph Koch, *Versuch einer Anleitung zur Composition*, vol. 3 (Leipzig, 1793), par. 150, 395-96n.
7 Carl Czerny, *Practical School of Composition*, Op. 600, trans. John Bishop, vol. 1 (London, 1848?), Ch. VI, "Of the Sonata," 35.
8 Antoine Reicha, *Traité e haut composition musicale*, vol. 2 (Paris, c. 1825), 298 ("De la seconde partie de la grand coup binaire"). Beethoven's codas also introduce N ideas, as Reicha recommends, the most famous examples perhaps being the N ideas in the codas of the Ninth Symphony, movements I and III.

broader rhythmic contrasts otherwise lacking in the movement. These themes may also be imitative, or feature the winds; they may remain in the second key or be modulatory; and they may have some derived material or figures. In all such cases, the change in theme, rhythm, dynamics, texture, orchestration, and expression strongly articulate the start of Part II and what we call the development section.[9] Sometimes new themes also end the section, functioning as the retransition. Many early Classic modulation sections offer largely or entirely new material, a feature of many Mozart developments even into the early 1780s.[10] Perhaps the most famous N theme besides the *Eroica* theme is the minuet-like lyrical interlude closing the development of Haydn's Symphony No. 45 (the "Farewell"), first movement (1772), recently the subject of detailed analysis and debate.[11]

When we consider Beethoven's exploitation of this long-standing device, we discover that he both follows and departs from traditional usage. I have focused this survey on the piano, violin, and cello sonatas, the string quartets, the String Quintet Op. 29, the concertos, and the symphonies, a total of 80 works. Of these, 40—one-half—incorporate significant new material in the development sections of sonata-form movements. This high percentage comes as a surprise since the emphasis of analysts has been on Beethoven's use of derived material rather than new material in the development section. The survey shows the employment of new material is a major Beethoven technique that requires further study.

Though N material appears in music composed throughout Beethoven's life, the most striking and frequent examples are especially characteristic of the early period and the early middle period through 1806. They disappear from the piano sonatas after Op. 14/1 (written in 1798) except for the two special finales of Opp. 54 and 57 (dated 1804-06). Rather than the symphonies and sonatas, it is in the string quartets that the procedure is most tenacious, occurring in almost all of the Op. 18 and Op. 59 quartets and four of the last five quartets (1824-26), including the second finale of Op. 130, Beethoven's last completed movement.[12] (See the list of works containing N material in Table 1.)

---

9 Such N themes appear in one or two sonata-form movements in all the middle and late symphonies by Sammartini in my Garland volume, the symphonies dating from the 1740s to 1772.

10 A late example is the development in Mozart's Piano Sonata in C, K. 330/I, now dated 1781-83.

11 See Judith L. Schwartz, "Periodicity and Passion in the First Movement of Haydn's 'Farewell' Symphony," and James Webster, "The D Major Interlude in the First Movement of Haydn's 'Farewell' Symphony," in *Studies in Musical Sources and Style. Essays in Honor of Jan LaRue*, ed. Eugene K. Wolf and Edward H. Roesner (Madison, WI, 1990), 293-338 and 339-80.

12 All references to Op. 130/VI are to the second finale of the quartet.

Table 1   Overview of New Material in Sonata-Form Developments Found in Beethoven's Piano, Violin, and Cello Sonatas, String Quartets, String Quintet Op. 29, Concertos, and Symphonies

EARLY PERIOD: c. 1793-1800
Piano Sonatas, c. 1793-98: Op. 2/1/IV and 3/I; Op. 7/I; Op. io/ /I, 2/I, 3/II; Op. 14/1/I; Op. 49/1/I
Violin Sonatas, 1797-1800: Op. 12/3/I, Op. 23/I
Cello Sonatas, 1796: Op. 5/1/I, 2/I
String Quartets, 1798-1800: Op. 18/1/II; 2/I, IV; 3/IV; 6/I
Concertos, 1795? (rev. 1800), 1800?: Piano Concertos No. i Op. 15/I; No. 3 Op. 37/I

MIDDLE PERIOD: 1801-09
Piano Sonatas, 1804-06: Op. 54/II, Op. 57/III
Violin Sonatas, 1801-02: Op. 30/2/I, Op. 47/III
String Quartets, 1806: Op. 59/1, III; 2/II; 3/I, II, IV
String Quintet, 1801: Op. 29/11, IV 328
Concertos, ca. 1803-09: Piano Concertos No. 4 Op. 58/I; No. 5 Op. 73/I; Violin Concerto Op. 61/I; Triple Concerto Op. 56/I
Symphonies 1801-08: No. 2 Op. 36/I; No. 3 Op. 55/I; No. 4, Op. 6o/I; No. 6 Op. 68/II

LATE PERIOD: 1815-26
Cello Sonatas, 1815: Op. 102/1/II, 2/I
String Quartets, 1824-26: Op. 127/I; Op. 130/I, III, VI (2nd finale); Op. 131/VII; Op. 135/I

Beethoven also occasionally introduces two or more N themes or ideas in the development, like the two lyrical N themes in the Violin Sonata Op. 23/I, the two contrapuntal ideas in the Quartet Op. 131/ VII, or the long, episode-like N section of the Quartet Op. 130/VI, enriched by four distinctive themes (see Example 2). Beethoven's awareness of this device is illustrated by his well-known remark after a sketch for the beginning of Part II of the Piano Sonata Op. 14/1/I: "ohne das The[ma] durchzufuhren"— "without developing the theme."[13]

---

13 See Ludwig van Beethoven, *Autograph Miscellany From circa 1786 to 1799*, British Museum Additional Manuscript 29801, ff. 39-162 (The "Kafka Sketchbook"), ed. Joseph Kerman, vol. 2, Transcription (London, 1970), 28.

Example 2. Beethoven, String Quartet, Op. 130/VI, development: episode-like N section.

Example 2. (continued)

The works analyzed embody several types of new ideas. The largest categories consist of the traditional lyrical theme, which is the most common type, and contrapuntal ideas. Examples of the lyrical type occur in 24 movements. Many are modulating, and start or remain in the minor mode, as in the *Eroica*. Besides the *Eroica* theme, there are memorable, often long lyrical themes in such works as the Piano Sonatas Op. 2/1/IV, Op. 10/l/I, Op. 14/1/I; the first movements of the Violin Sonatas Op. 23 and Op. 30/2; the Third Piano Concerto and the Violin Concerto (see Example 5); and the Quartet Op. 59/1/III.

A special type of lyrical N resembles a rondo episode and occurs at or near the start of the development of three finales that synthesize sonata and rondo procedures without actually being sonata-rondos. The movements involved are in the Piano Sonatas Op. 2/1 and Op. 57, and the Quartet Op. 130. These themes, as usual in the rondo style, feature largely symmetrical units of four and eight measures. Two themes, in Op. 2/1 and Op. 130, are extremely long. The N unit in Op. 2/1 is 50½ measures (mm. 59-109) and organized in rounded binary form with varied repeats. It appears in A♭ major, the relative major of the tonic f minor, a key Beethoven studiously avoids in an exposition that moves to the dominant minor instead. In Op. 130, a lyrical and contrapuntal section of 47 measures also appears in A♭, here the key of ♭VII (mm. 109-55; see Ex. 2). The key of A♭ and the melodic line in 3N relate to the *Grosse Fuge*, the original finale of the quartet, and lyricism is otherwise lacking in the movement. Unlike the other examples, the entire episode returns in the coda in the subdominant and tonic keys by way of recapitulation (mm. 353-99).

The contrapuntal category of N ideas comprises new subjects for fugal or quasi-fugal and imitative passages, and new countersubjects against derived ideas. New fugue subjects are explored in the Quintet Op. 29/IV (Ex. 3) and in the first movements of the Quartets Op. 18/2, Op. 59/1, and Op. 135; and new countersubjects and cantus-firmus-like material in the Quintet Op. 29/IV, and the Quartets Op. 18/3/IV, Op. 59/2/II, Op. 127/I, and Op. 131/VII. Other categories involve motivic ideas, like the stormy countermotive in the Quartet Op. 18/1/II (see Ex. 4); new figural material, especially in the Piano Concertos Nos. One Op. 15 and Five Op. 73, first movements; chromatic passages, as in the Piano Sonatas Op. 2/3/I and Op. 54/II, and the Cello Sonata Op. 5/1/I; and humorous but formal melody in the Quintet Op. 29/IV.

Moreover, Beethoven varies the placement of his N material, which can be located at any point in the development. The traditional lyrical theme starting Part II, however, is less favored and occurs in only six 329 movements—the Piano Sonatas Op. 2/1/IV and Op. 10/3/II, the Quintet Op. 29/II, the Violin Sonata Op. 30/2/I, the Triple Concerto Op. 56/I, and the Quartet Op. 130/VI—in addition to four examples of significant motives and phrases in the Quartet Op. 18/1/II, the Sixth Symphony Op. 68/II (goldfinch motive),[14] and the Cello Sonatas Op. 102/1/II and Op. 102/2/I. Three of these follow brief transitions to the development proper, such as the fugal section in Op. 29/IV. Other themes or new material come fairly close to the opening of the development, after a citation or development of the primary or other themes, as in the Piano Sonatas Op. 2/3/I and Op. 10/1/I, the Third Piano Concerto Op. 37/I, the Fourth Symphony Op. 60/I, and the Quartets Op. 130/I and Op. 131/VII. A group of N themes enters toward the middle or second part of the development, like the *Eroica* theme, as in the Cello Sonata Op. 5/2/I, the Quartet Op. 59/1/I, III, the Violin Concerto Op. 61/I, or the second countersubject in the Quartet Op. 131/VII. On the other hand, some material emerges dramatically near or at the end of the development usually functioning as the retransition. Such striking examples are the N units in the Cello Sonata Op. 5/1/I, the Violin Sonatas Op. 12/3/I and Op. 23/I, and the Quintet Op. 29/IV; only in the case of Op. 29 does the N theme, in a distant key, require a brief retransition to the recapitulation.

---

14 For the identification of the bird as a goldfinch rather than a yellow hammer, see Owen Jander, "The Prophetic Conversation in Beethoven's ‚Scene by the Brook,' " The *Musical Quarterly* LXXVII (1993), 518-21.

In most cases N themes possess a distinctive outline and character, though they may incorporate some derived elements. Thus the *Eroica* theme takes the dotted rhythm from the first secondary theme (which is emphasized in the buildup to the N theme), and many analysts have tried to prove its triadic connection to the primary theme.[15] The fugue subject in the Quartet Op. 59/1/I features a rising sixth, also found in the two primary themes, while in the Quartet Op. 130/VI, 1N utilizes a neighbor-note figure appearing in the primary and transitional themes. Nevertheless, N ideas may bring material for which little or no derivation can be discovered—like the thirty-second note pattern of the countermotive in the Quartet Op. 18/1/II, or the dotted, march-like rhythm of the fugue subject and the syncopation of its countersubject in the Quintet Op. 29/IV. Both ideas assume a new $\frac{2}{4}$ meter versus the $\frac{6}{8}$ meter of the movement that continues in other voices (Example 3). In this case, the dotted rhythm links the fugue with the humorous third N theme ending the development in a slower tempo, the Andante con moto e scherzoso, in yet another meter—$\frac{3}{4}$.[16]

Example 3.   Beethoven, String Quintet, Op. 29/IV, development: new fugue subject (1N) and countersubject (2N).

---

15 See the example in Lawrence Earp, "Tovey's, ‚Cloud' in the First Movement of the *Eroica*. An Analysis Based on the Sketches for the Development and Coda," *Beethoven Forum* II (1993), 74, and references in n. io to such an interpretation by August Halm, "Die fremdkörper im ersten Satz der *Eroica*," *Die Musik* XXI (1928/29), 481-85; Heinrich Schenker, "Beethovens Dritte Sinfonie zum erstenmal in ihrem wahren Inhalt dargestellt," in *Das Meisterwerk in der Musik III* (Munich, 1930), 50, fig. 24 and Bild 1; and David Epstein, *Beyond Orpheus: Studies in Musical Structure* (Cambridge, MA, 1979), 116.

16 The interpolation of a new section in a slower tempo is an influence of the da capo overture. See my article, "The Italian Symphonic Background to Haydn's Early Symphonies and Opera Overtures," in *Haydn Studies, Proceedings of the International Haydn Conference, Washington, D.C., .1975*, ed. Jens Peter Larsen, Howard Serwer, and James Webster (New York and London, 1981), 331-32; and the revised reprint in *Orbis Musicae* XII (1998), 75-76, and n. 12.

Example 3. (continued)

Some N ideas are borderline cases and analysts may prefer to consider them transformations or derivations rather than N ideas. This may be the case, for example, regarding the lyrical 2N in the Fourth Piano Concerto Op. 58/I (mm. 231-35). The phrase can be thought of as a transformation of the introductory descending scale idea that dominates the first part of the development (mm. 196-215), though 2N is preceded not by that idea directly but by a brilliant, cadential 1N unit that establishes the tritone key of c♯ minor in which the lyrical 2N arrives.[17]

Another, remarkable transformation marks the development of the Fourth Symphony Op. 60/I (mm. 221-40), where the new lyrical phrase is actually a

---

17 Another borderline case is the cantus-firmus-like descending tetrachord and its extension in the Quartet Op. 127/I, first found in mm. 89-93, with a balancing phrase, mm. 93, beat 3-97, beat 1. The descending line is closely related to the similar bass line and melodic outline, moving in parallel tenths, in the first phrase of the primary theme (mm. 7-10), where the fourth note, however, moves up by step. The descending tetrachord itself appears in the melodic outline of the second phrase (mm. 11-14). Yet, this N idea has an identity of its own, and it returns in the coda as well, at its start (mm. 241-44), its climax (mm. 267-71), and its end (viola mm. 275-82).

variation of the assertive, cantus-firmus-like phrase of the second transitional period (starting in m. 81).[18] Nevertheless, this remains a characteristic N idea that introduces a notable contrast in the section.

Table 2   Distant Keys for the Start of N (in Relation to the Tonic Key)

♭ii	Op. 55, Op. 59/3/IV
♭II	Op. 131 (2N)
II	Op. 54 (PNh—new accompaniment to the primary theme)
♭III	Op. 2/3, Op. 15, Op. 102/1
III	Op. 60, Op. 127, Op. 130/I
iv	Op. 61
tritone	Op. 7, Op. 54 (4N), Op. 58, Op. 59/2, Op. 59/3/II
♭VI	Op. 12/3, Op. 18/2/I, Op. 54 (3N)
VI	Op. 29/IV, Op. 68/II
♭VII	Op. 130/VI
♭vii	Op. 59/1/I
vii	Op. 29/11

As in the *Eroica*, Beethoven presents 24 N themes in remote keys, thus pairing the concept of new material with distance in tonality (see Table 2). In c.1795-1801, seven such examples show the way to the *Eroica* (which is dated essentially in 1803), with N material appearing or starting in the keys of ♭III (Op. 2/3/I), the tritone (Op. 7/I) ♭VI (Op. 5/1/I, Op. 12/3/I, Op. 18/2/I), major VI (Op. 29/IV, 3N), and minor vii (Op. 29/II). The *Eroica* N theme also focuses our attention on the Neapolitan key relation, a favorite with Beethoven. The minor Neapolitan recurs only once for the key of N, in the finale of the Quartet Op. 59/3 (C-c♯=d♭, dated 1806, and the normal Neapolitan is the key of 2N in the finale of the Quartet Op. 131, dated 1826 (c♯-D). Both examples are post-*Eroica*. However, 2N in the Violin Sonata Op. 23/I, dated 1800, though first heard in the tonic key of a minor after a 334 false retransition, ends up in the Neapolitan key of B♭ major (mm. 152-57) before the tonic is restored to usher in the recapitulation.

In fact, this N theme shares another rare feature with the *Eroica* theme—it receives special emphasis by means of extensive repetition. Like the *Eroica* theme it is heard three times in the development, with two full presentations in the tonic and subdominant, together with a partial repetition in the Neapolitan key just mentioned. Further, the theme's initial phrase returns in the coda, where

---

18 See Ludwig Misch, "Ein unbemerkter thematischer Zusammenhang in Beethovens IV. Symphonie," *Die Musikforschung* V (1962), 375-77.

it is again heard three times, twice in the subdominant and tonic, and a third time in the tonic, with an extension leading to the primary theme that ends the movement.

Table 3   Recall of N Material in the Recapitulation and/or Coda (in the Tonic Key Unless Otherwise Specified)

Op. 2/3:	coda, N variant (♭VI-I)
Op. 10/3:	coda
Op. 18/1:	recap and coda
Op. 23:	coda, 2N (iv-i)
Op. 29/II:	coda, 1N, 2N (iv-I); mvt. IV, coda, 3N
Op. 30/2:	coda (I)
Op. 54	recap, 1N (i), 3N (I-mod.-I), replacing S and K
Op. 55:	coda (ii-i)
Op. 68:	recap
Op. 102/1/II:	coda (♭VI-IV-♭II)
Op. 127:	coda
Op. 130/III:	coda (IV-I-V^7/IV); mvt. VI, coda (IV-I)
Op. 131:	recap, 2N (iv-♭II); coda, 1N, 2N

The recurrence of N in the recapitulation and/or the coda can be found in 15 movements by Beethoven, including this violin sonata and the *Eroica* (see Table 3).[19] Such recurrence, of course, integrates the new material into the larger structure and expressive world of the movement. Two of these examples recall N in the recapitulation and eleven in the coda; two Quartets, Op. 18/1/II and Op. 131/VII, refer to N ideas in both sections. How this material is recalled differs in each example. In the Quartet Op. 18/1 (see Example 4), two variants of the development countermotive to the primary theme combine with the primary theme in the recapitulation (I have labeled them N^1 and N^2), and both return in the coda

---

[19] Donald Francis Tovey, article "Sonata Forms," in *Musical Articles from the Encyclopaedia Britannica* (London, 1943), 215-16, mentions examples of a new theme in the development, which he calls an "episode," and he also refers to the possibility of the re-turn of the "episode" in the coda. In the article by Joseph Kerman, "Notes on Beethoven's Codas," in *Beethoven Studies* III, ed. Alan Tyson (Cambridge, 1982), 141-59, and the chapter on the coda in Charles Rosen, *Sonata Forms*, rev. ed. (New York, 1988), 297-352, no mention is made of the return of new material in Beethoven's codas beyond a passing reference to the *Eroica* theme by Kerman (152). Nor is the return of material mentioned in Robert G. Hopkins, "When a Coda is More than a Coda: Reflections on Beethoven," in *Explorations in Music, the Arts, and Ideas. Essays in Honor of Leonard B. Meyer*, ed. Eugene Narmour and Ruth A. Solie (Stuyvesant, NY, 1988), 393-410.

together with the original version, which itself leads to the shattering climax of the movement—a most dramatic elaboration of the idea.

In the Quintet Op. 29, coda returns occur in both the slow and final movements, the entire Andante section of the finale coming back in the tonic, a recapitulatory effect, as in Op. 130/VI. Six of the works recalling themes in the coda were composed before the *Eroica* and can thus be viewed as significant precedents for this procedure in the symphony (these are Op. 2/3/I, Op. 10/3/II, Op. 18/1/II, Op. 23/I, Op. 29/11, IV, Op. 30/2/I).

Example 4 Beethoven, String Quartet, Op. 18, no. i/II: (a) development, with N countermotive; (b) recapitulation with N1 and N2; (c) coda, with all three N forms.

Example 4 (continued)

Example 4. (continued)

While Beethoven's models for these recurrences need considerable research, some immediate models can be found in compositions by Mozart, as cited by Kerman and Rosen.[20] Indeed, Mozart's extensive use of N material furnishes a significant background for Beethoven. Kerman notes the returns of motivic N

---

20 See Kerman, "Notes on Beethoven's Codas," 142, and Rosen, *Sonata Forms*, 321-22.

ideas in the first-movement codas of Mozart's String Quartets K. 458 (the "Hunt"; 1784), and K. 590 (1790). We may add that both ideas conclude the movement, and in K. 590 N first appears in the distant key of ♭VII. We should remember, however, that Haydn's earlier interlude in the "Farewell" symphony is also set in a distant key—D major, a third-relationship with the tonic, f♯ minor. Rosen points to the lyrical N theme found at the start of Part II in the Piano Sonata in C major, K 330/I (1781-83), which also rounds off the movement; and to the chromatic N theme that dominates the development and coda of the Two-Piano Sonata in D, K. 448 (1781). Neither author, however, mentions the themes in the finale of Mozart's A-major Quartet, K. 464 (1785), a work that Beethoven admired and even copied into score.[21] Here, brief new counterpoints to the primary theme return in the recapitulation and coda, again ending the movement. In addition, Mozart presents a new theme in the middle of the development as a total surprise, a mysterious chorale-like melody in long notes and chordal setting, which is given contrapuntal and developmental expansion.

In conclusion, let us consider the lyrical N theme in Beethoven's Violin Concerto in D major, first movement. The theme comes in the second part of the development after an intensive reworking of the last five notes of the primary theme's initial phrase, a reworking that takes place in the orchestra with figuration in the violin. Thus, the N theme provides relief from the motivic development and deepens the lyricism of the movement, while shifting the spotlight to the soloist. It is certainly one of the great moments in the concerto (see Example 5 for the start of the theme).

In examining this theme, we should notice the following:

1. Though I call it a theme, like many N ideas it is really an N area lasting 26 measures (mm. 331-56), in which a new theme is introduced, extended, varied, and fragmented.
2. The N theme is accompanied throughout in the orchestra by the pervasive tapping motive of the movement. Embedded in the preceding development of those five notes, the motive eventually repeats without pause as tension increases toward the retransition.
3. As many of Beethoven's N themes, the theme enters in minor, here g minor, the same key as the lyrical N theme in the rondo finale. The subdominant key in general acts like the secondary key of the entire work, G major also being the key of the slow movement, and it is associated with most of the intensely lyrical portions of the concerto.
4. The theme, like many N themes, is modulatory, moving from g minor to E♭ major, again the Neapolitan key, and from there to d minor, used as a foil for the brilliant return to the recapitulation in D major.

---

21 Only Beethoven's copy of the second movement has survived. Dated c. 1800, it is housed in Stockholm, Stiftelsen Musikkulturens främjande, Collection of Captain Rudolf Nydahl.

5. Though the theme seems new, like most N themes it contains some links with earlier material. The rhythmic pattern of its first two measures (mm. 331-32) duplicates the pattern found in the first transition theme (mm. 18-19); the prominent half steps stem perhaps from the third secondary theme (mm. 65-68); and the poignant sigh motives echo such motives in the primary theme itself.

Example 5. Beethoven, Violin Concerto, Op. 61/I, development: start of the N area.

Example 5. (continued)

This theme validates the device of new development material in every aspect.

Frans C. Lemaire

DIMITRI CHOSTAKOVITCH: RESTER ET RÉSISTER

Lorsqu'un artiste, un intellectuel ou un opposant politique se trouve confronté à un régime totalitaire impitoyable, peu de possibilités s'offrent à lui:

- rester et se soumettre ou bien disparaître, au mieux dans le silence, au pire dans un camp ou la mort;

- quitter et résister de l'une ou l'autre façon, ne fut-ce que par le seul fait d'avoir rompu et pris les risques de l'exil. C'est ce qu'ont choisi après la Révolution de 1917 la plupart des musiciens russes jouissant d'une certaine notoriété internationale: Stravinsky, Prokofiev, Rachmaninov, Medtner, Koussevitski, Lourié, les Tchérépnine et même Glazounov en 1928. Beaucoup d'autres comme Wyschnegradski, Obouhov resteront largement méconnus

Chostakovitch n'avait que onze ans en 1917 et la mort prématurée de son père en 1922 l'a obligé, comme aîné de sa famille, à gagner sa vie très tôt. Mineur, il était trop jeune pour émigrer et par la suite l'obtention d'un visa deviendra quasi impossible. Toute la carrière de Chostakovitch s'est donc déroulée en Union soviétique et il est devenu ainsi le musicien le plus représentatif de la musique soviétique. Lorsqu'il meurt le samedi 9 août 1975, le Comité Central a besoin de deux jours de réflexion pour rédiger, approuver et faire publier dans la *Pravda* du mardi suivant, l'annonce de sa mort et l'hommage nécrologique qui convenait, saluant d'abord "le fils fidèle du Parti communiste, l'important fonctionnaire de l'État et le digne représentant de la vie publique" l'artiste, enfin "qui a consacré sa vie au développement de la musique soviétique, à la consolidation des idéaux d'humanisme et d'internationalisme socialistes et au combat pour la paix et l'amitié des peuples." Et la musique dans tout cela? Ce que retenait le Comité Central de plus de 150 partitions se limitait essentiellement à quatre symphonies sur quinze et aux œuvres "consacrées à la Révolution et à la grande figure de Lénine." On citait abondamment ses nombreux titres et prix officiels, autre façon de rappeler que c'était bien le grand artiste soviétique et le meilleur des communistes que l'on enterrait au cimetière de Novodevitche.[1]

Quatre ans plus tard, en 1979, paraissait à New York un ouvrage intitulé *Testimony. The Memoirs of Shostakovich as related to and edited by Solomon Volkov,* auteur qui prétendait avoir été mandaté par le compositeur pour publier,

---

1 *Pravda* (11 août 1975).

après sa mort, des *Mémoires* donnant une image totalement opposée de sa vie, celle d'un musicien...antisoviétique.[2] En réalité, c'était un habile montage à la première personne d'informations et de documents d'origines diverses, par quelqu'un qui les connaissait bien puisque avant son émigration en 1974, Volkov avait été rédacteur de *Sovietskaya Muzïka,* l'organe officiel de l'Union des compositeurs. A ce titre, il avait sollicité et obtenu plusieurs interviews de Chostakovitch et il avait fait parapher, selon l'usage, la transcription de ses propos avant leur publication. Plus tard, en Amérique, il présentera ces feuillets comme des pages des "Mémoires" comme preuves de son mandat. Le subterfuge fut dénoncé un an plus tard dans *The Russian Review* par une universitaire américaine Laurel Fay qui voyageait beaucoup en URSS et avait ses entrées à l'Union des compositeurs où son secrétaire général Tikhon Krennikov n'avait été que trop heureux d'aider à discréditer Volkov dans une revue américaine avec des arguments meilleurs que les "traître, juif ennemi du peuple ou punaise" utilisés par la presse soviétique. Malgré cela, des émigrés notoires comme Rostropovitch et Galina Vischnevskaya, le chef d'orchestre Kyrill Kondrachine, le pianiste Vladimir Ashkenazy et en 1981, le propre fils de Chostakovitch, Maxime, qui avait demandé asile en Allemagne, confirmèrent que, même si les Mémoires n'étaient pas authentiques ("ce n'est pas un livre de mon père mais sur mon père" a déclaré Maxime Chostakovitch), ce qui était raconté reflétait largement la condition de l'artiste en Union soviétique, telle qu'eux-mêmes l'avaient connue.[3]

Au départ de ce travail révélateur et de son succès international, (le cinéaste Tony Palmer en a même fait un film en 1987 avec Ben Kingsley dans le rôle de Chostakovitch) certains se sont mis à faire de chaque partition de Chostakovitch y compris les plus apparemment conformes aux vœux du régime, des œuvres antistaliniennes, transformant ainsi Chostakovitch en une sorte de héros ou de martyr perpétuel, ou comme on dit en Russe, de *yurodivie,* l'innocent, le fou de Dieu qui ose dire la vérité face au tyran. Ces excès révisionnistes ont irrité certains musicologues comme Richard Taruskin de l'université de Californie (Berkeley) qui en a pris le contre-pied en s'efforçant de montrer que Chostakovitch n'a pas eu le courage qu'on lui prêtait mais avait été essentiellement soumis et obéissant. Taruskin alla jusqu'à écrire dans la revue américaine *The New Republic* du 20 mars 1989: "*Shostakovitch was even perhaps Soviet Russia's most loyal musical son.*"[4] On remarquera l'utilisation des mots "*even perhaps,*" "même peut-être," qui relève plus du journalisme d'insinuation en quête de sensation que de la rigueur académique. Quelques semaines à peine avant cet article

---

2 Solomon Volkov, *Testimony: The Memoirs of Solomon Volkov*, traduit par Antonina W. Bouis (New York, 1979).
3 Pour témoignage trouvé par Fay et par les autres, voir Malcolm Hamrick Brown, ed., *A Shostakovich Casebook* (Bloomington, IN, 2004).
4 Richard Taruskin, "The Opera and the Dictator: The peculiar martyrdom of Dmitri Shostakovich," *The New Republic* (20 mars 1989): 34-40.

avait eu lieu à Washington la première audition sous la direction de Rostropovitch de la cantate "antiformaliste" *Rayok* de Chostakovitch restée longtemps cachée dans laquelle il parodiait le débat de 1948 sur le formalisme en ridiculisant Staline, Jdanov et certains de leurs collaborateurs. Malgré cette preuve évidente de la rébellion de Chostakovitch, Taruskin a continué à attaquer les révisionnistes,[5] suscitant de nombreuses réactions, dont en 1998, un ouvrage préfacé par Vladimir Ashkénazy intitulé *Shostakovich reconsidered* qui réunit des commentateurs de niveau variable, la plupart non universitaires, si bien qu'ils s'efforcent d'attaquer le monument de culture et d'arrogance académique qu'est Richard Taruskin, avec ses propres armes: 800 pages de texte et 1430 notes de bas de page! Cette *"Chostakovitchologie"* essentiellement anglo-saxonne est donc faite, au départ, d'un conflit personnel Taruskin-Volkov et de considérations idéologiques qui, en dehors du contexte particulier de quelques œuvres, oublient largement la musique alors que Chostakovitch a, selon certains auteurs, exprimé la priorité qui lui revenait: "Les mots ne sont pas mon fort, mais en musique je ne mens jamais" ou encore "c'est ma musique et non mes paroles qu'il faut écouter."

Toue interprétation idéologique d'une musique purement instrumentale est aléatoire, comment savoir si elle exprime ou pas, rejette ou pas un tel contenu? Les seules oeuvres qui échappent à cette ambiguïté sont celles qui renferment des textes chantés. Bien que Chostakovitch ait écrit 18 cycles totalisant une centaine de mélodies, cette partie de son œuvre, comme celle plus personnelle et intime des quatuors n'a été véritablement découverte qu'au cours des deux décennies succédant à la perestroïka. Même les livres de Volkov et de Taruskin présentent cette énorme lacune d'ignorer les trois quarts des 15 quatuors et, à une exception près, la totalité des 18 cycles mélodiques. Donc ils se disputent sur ce qu'il faut penser de l'homme et de sa musique, en ignorant ce à quoi il attachait le plus d'importance à la fin de sa vie. Ils mènent une bataille en se trompant de terrain et de munitions, le terrain c'est sa musique et non le livre de Volkov, les munitions ce sont les partitions les plus explicites et les plus personnelles et non quelques pages énigmatiques permettant des interprétations contradictoires qui font tantôt de Chostakovitch un artiste dissident, tantôt "un fils loyal du Parti."

Le but de cette étude est de montrer comment Chostakovitch a développé peu à peu une résistance qui, restée secrète ou "intérieure" au début, a dépassé progressivement le cercle intime en déjouant la censure et a fini en 1962 par déboucher sur ce que l'on peut véritablement appeler une dissidence. L'analyse des textes et de leur musique permet ainsi de renvoyer dos à dos Volkov, Taruskin et leurs querelles devenues aujourd'hui sans intérêt.

---

5 Même huit ans après la révélation de *Rayok,* Taruskin continue à ignorer cette pièce essentielle du dossier dans son ouvrage *Defining Russia Musically: Historical and Hermeneutical Essays* (Princeton, NJ, 1997).

Né en 1906, Chostakovitch devint célèbre dès l'âge de 20 ans avec une *1e Symphonie* dirigée aussitôt dans le monde entier. L'Union soviétique en avait bien besoin après avoir vu tous ses compositeurs importants choisir l'émigration au cours des années précédentes.

Fort de ce succès, Chostakovitch écrivit alors deux opéras en cinq ans, le second *La Lady Macbeth du district de Mzensk* récoltant un véritable triomphe en 1934 et 1935 avec quelque 170 représentations, au point que le Bolchoï décida de monter le spectacle à son tour. C'est là que Staline le vit avec, comme conséquence la condamnation bien connue dans la *Pravda* du 26 janvier 1936. Terrorisé, réduit au silence, Chostakovitch, dit-on, ne reprit la plume que le 18 avril 1937, 15 mois plus tard, pour écrire une nouvelle *Symphonie* dont le langage simplifié, clair, accessible, populaire est présenté par la presse du régime comme la "réponse créative de l'artiste aux justes critiques du Parti." Le fils prodigue rentre ainsi au bercail du socialisme, tout comme un an auparavant, un autre fils encore bien plus prodigue, Prokofiev, était rentré en URSS après 18 années passées en Occident. Victoire complète du Parti qui met ainsi au pas ses deux plus grands compositeurs qui en succédant à la génération des traîtres Stravinsky et Rachmaninov, vont ouvrir l'âge d'or de la musique au service du réalisme socialiste, un âge d'or dont la *5e Symphonie* de Chostakovitch est devenue le symbole. En réalité, contrairement à ce que l'on raconte d'ordinaire, il n'avait pas cessé de composer: quelques mois seulement après sa condamnation, il avait bel et bien entamé une œuvre nouvelle mais elle restera pratiquement inconnue jusqu'à aujourd'hui même dans les biographies récentes. Il est vrai que le régime avait tout fait pour qu'il en soit ainsi.

Chostakovitch avait pensé que le centenaire de la mort de Pouchkine en 1937 lui donnerait une occasion de revenir sur la scène musicale en présentant un cycle de 12 mélodies sur des textes du célèbre poète national mais il abandonna son projet après quelques unes seulement , se rendant sans doute compte que cette œuvre n'avait aucune chance d'être exécutée car il restait en disgrâce et, en outre, humilié et blessé, il n'avait pu résister à la tentation de retenir des textes qui reflétaient l'amertume et la rancune du poète, victime comme lui de la bêtise du pouvoir.

Intitulé *Renaissance* le premier poème raconte qu'une main barbare a noirci de traits insensés la toile d'un peintre de génie mais avec les années, cette couche indigne s'écaillera et l'œuvre originale réapparaîtra devant nous dans toute sa splendeur. Et le poème conclut, "les désillusions disparaîtront de mon âme tourmentée… ." N'est-ce pas là une parfaite allégorie de la censure barbare qui a chassé *Lady Macbeth* de la scène et de la situation de Chostakovitch confronté désormais au dilemme: se soumettre ou résister? Ce dilemme est reflété dans la troisième mélodie qui dit: "Une fois encore de sombres nuages se sont accumulés…Une fois encore le destin envieux me menace de ses malheurs. Vais-je défier ma destinée en lui opposant l'inflexibilité de ma fière jeunesse?"

L'impact de cette oeuvre comme acte de résistance a été évidemment nul: Elle ne fut exécutée qu'en 1940 et tomba ensuite dans l'oubli n'étant pas éditée avant 1960 ni enregistrée avant 1973 (à Prague). Cela n'en reste pas moins un premier témoignage d'une attitude très différente de celle d'un fils loyal répondant sagement à de justes critiques.

N'osant plus écrire d'opéra, fort du succès de sa 5e *Symphonie,* Chostakovitch ne pouvait que poursuivre dans cette voie et avant même sa 40e année, il achève sa 9e *Symphonie*. Mais en dehors de la 5e et de la 7e *de Leningrad,* ses symphonies ne plurent guère et, en 1948, il fut violemment attaqué par Andreï Jdanov, le responsable de l'idéologie, soutenu par la meute des collègues médiocres. Le 10 février, un décret du Comité central le condamna officiellement pour formalisme avec cinq autres compositeurs. Relevé de ses postes de professeur, il tombe presque sans revenus car la plupart des salles de concerts n'osent plus programmer la musique d'un "ennemi du peuple," même pas les trois symphonies sur neuf qui restent pratiquement autorisées. Pour vivre, Chostakovitch écrit des musiques de film, une cantate sur le reboisement des forêts mais, comme en 1936, il continue à composer, une autre musique, sa vraie musique qu'il tient cachée dans l'attente de temps meilleurs. Ceux-ci finissent par arriver : Staline meurt le 5 mars 1953 et à partir de 1955 les œuvres composées six ou sept ans plus tôt comme le 1er *Concerto pour violon,* un cycle vocal sur des poésies juives et le 4e *Quatuor* sont finalement exécutés. En réalité, toutes ces partitions renferment des mélodies juives. Elles ont été écrites au moment où commençait avec l'assassinat de Solomon Mikhoels, la persécution de la communauté juive et on en trouve d'autres exemples jusqu'à la protestation ouverte en 1962 de la symphonie *Babi Yar*.[6]

Nous sommes donc en présence d'une protestation mais seule la communauté juive la perçoit véritablement. L'hostilité de Chostakovitch vis-à-vis du régime ne deviendra véritablement évidente que lorsque sera révélée en 1989 l'existence d'une autre partition composée en 1948, la *Cantate "Rayok" sur la lutte contre le formalisme* qui en reprenant des phrases des discours officiels en fait une satire féroce de ce qui s'est passé à ce moment avec, en particulier, trois personnages. Grâce à l'analyse de Manashir Yakubov,[7] on peut les identifier

---

6 Les œuvres d'inspiration juive débutent avec le Trio, op.67 de 1944. Les éléments juifs dans la musique de Chostakovitch ont fait l'objet des études pionnières du Professeur Joachim Braun dès la fin des années 70. L'ensemble de ces travaux ont été repris dans un ouvrage récent: Joachim Braun, *On Jewish Music: Past and Present* (Frankfurt am Main, 2006).

7 En russe dans la partition publiée en 1995 par Izdatelstvo "DSCH," en anglais dans Rosamund Bartlett, ed., *Shostakovich in Context* (Oxford and New York, 2000). Manashir Yakubov dirige les archives Chostakovitch à Moscou.

ainsi que leurs collaborateurs et mesurer l'ampleur des sentiments que le compositeur ressentait à l'époque au point de courir le risque de composer une telle oeuvre.

Edinitsii c'est-à-dire en russe, le premier, l'unique, c'est évidemment Staline, *Dvoïkin*, le deuxième est naturellement Jdanov. Chostakovitch fait ainsi chanter Staline sur la chanson géorgienne qu'il préférait, *Souliko,* Jdanov sur une danse géorgienne, la *lezhingka*, allusion à l'opéra du compositeur géorgien Muradeli qui a été à l'origine des condamnations de 1948. Staline donne ainsi une leçon sur ce que la bonne musique doit être, écrite par des compositeurs populaires (*narodnïy kompositori*), tandis que les auteurs *formalisticheskuyu muzïku* sont *antinarodnïy* c'est-à-dire des ennemis du peuple.

Les quelques intimes auxquelles Chostakovitch montra cette cantate en 1948 lui conseillèrent de la détruire au plus tôt mais il n'en fit rien. Révélée en 1989, elle a permis de décrypter d'autres œuvres en confirmant ce que l'on soupçonnait ou ce que certains comme Volkov avaient suggéré. On retrouve en effet les premières notes de *Souliko* dans d'autres œuvres de Chostakovitch, comme un signal, en particulier dans sa *10ᵉ Symphonie* écrite précisément au lendemain de la mort de Staline. Un tel signal est subtil car la mélodie de *Souliko* comporte en réalité 35 notes et Chostakovitch ne retient que les cinq premières mais l'usage d'une brutalité inouïe qu'il en fait dans le deuxième mouvement ne laisse aucun doute sur sa signification. Celle-ci a d'ailleurs été confirmée par Rostropovitch qui a raconté qu'après avoir joué en 1959 dans la datcha du compositeur le *1ᵉʳ Concerto pour violoncelle* qui renferme également ces cinq notes, Chostakovitch avait bien précisé qu'il s'agissait de *Souliko*.[8]

Chostakovitch a ajouté, sans doute ultérieurement, le troisième personnage appelé *Troikin* de sa *Cantate Rayok* car c'est Dmitri Chepilov qui, Ministre de la Culture en 1957 avait fait à l'Union des compositeurs un discours citant en exemple les grands musiciens d'autrefois dont les compositeurs soviétiques devraient s'inspirer pour écrire de la musique agréable et harmonieuse, Glinka-Tchaikovski et Rimski-Korsakov, mais cette prononciation de Korsakov trahit son incompétence. C'est ce détail qui a permis de l'identifier. En outre, Chostakovitch le fait chanter sur un air d'une musique de film de Tikhon Khrennikov, le tout puissant secrétaire général de l'Union des compositeurs. Il fustige ainsi ensemble les deux ténors du 2ᵉ Congrès général de l'Union des compositeurs et leurs recommandations d'écrire de la musique facile et plaisante pour le peuple[9].

Chepilov avait la réputation de boire facilement, aussi dans son discours se met-il à bafouiller et à confondre Glinka, Dzerzhinka et Tishinka or Dzerzhinka est le nom de la place où se trouvait le siège du KGB et Tishinka celui de celle où se trouvait la prison de transit vers le goulag, Chepilov passe ainsi des re-

---

8 Anecdote rapportée et commentée par Elizabeth Wilson dans *Shostakovich: A Life Remembered* (New York, 1994), 322-23 et 477-79.
9 Wilson, *Shostakovich*, 298-99.

commandations aux menaces que les fonctionnaires reprennent en chœur en chantant sur une musique d'Offenbach: "ceux qui se laissent encore influencer (sous entendu par le formalisme) un camp de travail les attend pour un long séjour."

Cette partition extraordinaire est accompagnée d'une soi-disant *Préface de l'éditeur* dans laquelle Chostakovitch règle ses comptes avec quatre *apparatchiki* de niveau moins élevé mais qui reçoivent un traitement vraiment spécial. L'éditeur raconte, en effet, que le camarade Opostylov a trouvé le manuscrit de la cantate dans une poubelle, l'a nettoyé, analysé et commenté, malheureusement son travail est resté inachevé car au cours d'une mission du "Service de la Sécurité musicale du Ministère de la Pureté idéologique," Opostylov est tombé dans une bouche d'égout. Appelés aussitôt, les services de vidange ne retrouvèrent que quelques excréments; "c'est normal expliqua le vidangeur en chef, il y a des gens comme çà, entre eux et leurs excréments on ne peut pas voir la différence."[10]

Comme dans son texte, Chostakovitch donne les initiales des prénoms et patronymes des personnages qu'il vise, on reconnaît sans peine dans le camarade P.I. Opostylov, Pavel Ivanovitch Apostolov, un spécialiste de la musique militaire que le Comité Central envoyait aux répétitions des œuvres nouvelles de Chostakovitch pour voir si elles convenaient; c'est ainsi qu'il était encore présent, vingt ans plus tard, lors d'une répétition de la *14e Symphonie* mais il eut un infarctus et mourut quelques semaines plus tard. On a raconté – mais sans doute l'anecdote est-elle apocryphe – que Chostakovitch commenta l'événement en disant: "Que voulez-vous? ma musique est bien trop sombre pour qu'un membre aussi élevé du Parti puisse y survivre."[11]

Un autre agent du comité central, Boris Mikhailovitch Yaroustovski avait été envoyé à Léningrad à la fin de 1937 pour enquêter sur le sens de l'ovation interminable qui avait accueilli la création de la *5e Symphonie,* afin de s'assurer avant de la jouer à Moscou que ce n'était pas là une sorte de manifestation de sympathie envers Chostakovitch désapprouvant sa condamnation antérieure. Dans la Préface de *Rayok*, il devient B.M.Ya*srou*stovski en glissant un "s" supplémentaire dans son nom, or *Ya srou* en argot russe veut dire *je chie* et Chostakovitch fait la même chose avec deux autres noms de bureaucrates de l'idéologie

---

10 Dmitri Shostakovich, *Anti-Formalist RAYOK for four basses and mixed choir accompanied by piano and narrator*; introduction "From the Publisher" (text par le compositeur); Izdatelstvo "DSCH" (Moscow, 1995) (textes uniquement en russe). Le texte de la *Préface de l'éditeur* a été publié en français (pp. 12-15) et anglais (pp. 16-19) dans la notice accompagnant l'enregistrement de *Rayok* par M. Rostropovitch (1ère version sans chœur) paru en CD *Chant du Monde* (ECD 75571).

11 Les biographies qui racontent l'anecdote font mourir Apostolov sur place, ce qui est inexact.

qui commencent en Ru et deviennent ainsi ***Sriou***mine et ***Sriou***rikov. C'est donc une façon de dire clairement à quel point il les…emmerde!

Le professeur de Berkeley aurait donc mieux fait de parler de Chostakovitch comme étant non pas le plus loyal mais le plus scatologique des fils musicaux de la Russie soviétique. Ceci correspond d'ailleurs à une tradition russe que nous retrouvons même chez Pouchkine grâce à une autre œuvre de Chostakovitch. L'année 1966 étant celle de son 60e anniversaire, le régime annonça qu'il allait entreprendre une grande édition de ses œuvres complètes et il demanda au compositeur d'en écrire lui-même la Préface. La réaction de Chostakovitch fut, ici aussi, significative: Il écrivit en un jour, le 2 mars 1966, une mélodie pour basse et piano d'à peine trois minutes intitulée : *Préface à l'édition complète de mes œuvres et brève réflexion sur cette préface, op. 123. Paroles de D. Chostakovitch.*

En réalité, si la réflexion est bien de lui, les paroles de la Préface sont, en réalité, de Pouchkine dont Chostakovitch reprend, sans le dire, une épigramme, c'est-à-dire un petit poème – genre quatrain – qui épingle littéralement un personnage en évoquant un trait caractéristique que la chute, le dernier vers, tourne en ridicule. La victime de cet épigramme est un officier supérieur d'Alexandre 1er, le Comte Dimitri Khvostov auquel Pouchkine avait déjà fait allusion, non sans ironie, dans la célèbre nouvelle, *Le Cavalier de bronze*: "Le Comte Khvostov, poète aimé des dieux, a chanté dans des vers immortels les infortunes des rives de la Neva" mais avant cela, le jeune Pouchkine avait déjà épinglé Khvostov dans une épigramme adressée au tsar Alexandre 1er dans un ton familier qui finira par lui coûter cher:

> *Votre postérieur dodu, vous le torchez avec du calicot*
> *Moi plutôt que de cajoler mon cul délicat comme celui d'un enfant*
> *Je le frotte avec les odes rugueuses de Khvostov*

C'est la version russe du *Misanthrope* mettant le sonnet d'Alceste au cabinet mais Pouchkine aura sans doute médité sur les dangers de ce genre de plaisanterie durant ses années d'exil dans le Caucase.

Poète prolifique, le Comte Khvostov était aussi appelé le roi des graphomanes, et c'est sans doute parce que cela reflétait sa propre situation que Chostakovitch l'a choisi car il disait parfois de lui-même lorsqu'il composait trop vite: je deviens un véritable graphomane.

Chostakovitch a donc repris une autre épigramme de Pouchkine sur Khvostov, l'a mise à la première personne après avoir permuté les deux premiers vers, ce qui donne:

> *Je noircis toute une feuille d'un seul trait*
> *Mon oreille entraînée en perçoit les grattements*
> *Ensuite je fais souffrir les oreilles du monde entier*
> *Ensuite on me publie mais c'est pour m'oublier aussitôt après!*

Donc au lieu d'exprimer de la satisfaction ou de la gratitude pour un tel projet, Chostakovitch montre ici son amertume pour avoir si souvent vu ses œuvres majeures publiées mais non jouées :

- son opéra avant-gardiste *Le Nez* n'est plus représenté après 1931 et le restera durant 43 ans ;
- son autre opéra, *Lady Macbeth*, a attendu 26 ans pour être autorisé à nouveau ;
- l'extraordinaire *4e Symphonie,* achevée en 1936, n'a pu être créée qu'en 1961, soit après 25 ans ;
- la condamnation de 1948 a été accompagnée d'une mise à l'index d'autres œuvres comme les *8e* et *9e Symphonies.*

Dans *la brève réflexion* qui suit la Préface, Chostakovitch ajoute: "Une telle préface conviendrait non seulement à mes œuvres complètes mais à celles de beaucoup d'autres compositeurs, soviétiques et étrangers."[12] Il proteste donc ouvertement contre la censure qui a empêché l'exécution en URSS de nombreuses musiques et pas seulement les siennes. Pour bien marquer qu'il prend la responsabilité de cette protestation, il ajoute: "Et je signe: Dimitri Chostakovitch," l'énoncé de son nom étant accompagné du célèbre monogramme musical DSCH formé des notes *Ré – Mi bémol – Do – Si*. Il fait suivre cette signature musicale d'une énumération ironique de ses titres officiels: "Artiste du peuple de l'SSSR, Premier secrétaire de l'Union des compositeurs de la Fédération SSR, secrétaire de l'Union des compositeurs de l'SSSR, et porteur d'autres nombreux titres, charges et fonctions" soulignant ainsi le ridicule d'une situation qui le couvre d'honneur mais a souvent empêché que l'on joue ses meilleures œuvres.

Chostakovitch ne verra jamais cette édition de ses oeuvres complètes, même pas le premier volume car il ne paraîtra finalement qu'en 1977, deux ans après sa mort. Sa *Préface* n'y figurait évidemment pas mais comme on ne pouvait l'ignorer totalement, on la glissa discrètement en 1984 avec sa commentaire en russe dans le 33e volume, non en tête mais à la page 62, parmi d'autres mélodies diverses.

C'est évidemment une page mineure mais elle met en évidence les sentiments profonds de frustration de Chostakovitch, mais comme les mélodies de Pouchkine de 1936 ou la cantate *Rayok* de 1948, cette protestation resta pratiquement inconnue du public soviétique. L'image de Chostakovitch, compositeur célèbre, personnage officiel, restait donc bien celle d'un artiste soumis au régime. Seul un cercle intime et quelques auditeurs plus perspicaces pouvaient per-

---

12 Texte en russe dans le volume 33 des *Oeuvres complètes*, Edition "Muzïka" (Moscou, 1984), 62. Traduction anglaise dans : Christopher Norris, ed., *Shostakovich. The man and his music* (London, 1989), 135.

cevoir la différence. Pour qu'on puisse véritablement parler de dissidence, il faut que la contradiction devienne publique et durable, entraînant un véritable débat.

La situation restait d'autant plus ambiguë qu'au printemps 1960, un émissaire du Kremlin était venu informer Chostakovitch que Khrouchtchev souhaitait qu'il se fasse membre du Parti. Ceci va le tourmenter beaucoup et on en trouve l'écho dans un cycle de mélodies achevé à cette époque. Intitulées *Satires*, il met en musique des poésies de Sacha Tchorny dont on venait d'éditer une anthologie après un demi siècle d'oubli (de son vrai nom Alexandre Glikberg, Tchorny était un poète juif de l'époque tsariste). On y trouve une mélodie, intitulée *Les descendants* ou *La progéniture,* qui dénonce la répétition à chaque génération des mêmes promesses pour demain d'un bonheur qui n'arrive jamais alors que les sacrifices demandés pour sa réalisation sont eux bien présents. Comme une critique aussi transparente risquait d'être interdite, Chostakovitch sous-titra ce cycle "*Images du passé*" sur la recommandation de Galina Vischnevskaïa qui le créa ainsi sans problèmes puisque c'était du temps du tsar. Tout le monde ne fut pas dupe pour autant et lorsque le cycle fut inscrit dans un programme de la télévision, on demanda de supprimer cette première mélodie ce que les interprètes, G.Vischnevskaïa et M.Rostropovitch refusèrent et le cycle ne fut pas donné. Ce n'est qu'en 1976 à Paris, après leur exil, qu'ils purent en faire un enregistrement. En 1980, un élève de Chostakovitch, le compositeur Boris Tichtchenko en réalisa une version orchestrale du cycle qui accentue encore le caractère satirique des mélodies en particulier celle des *Descendants* dont la musique adopte un rythme de valse, la valse étant chez Chostakovitch une sorte d'archétype du bonheur socialiste. On danse mais c'est en ricanant. "C'est pour moi que je voudrais un peu de bonheur, tant que je suis vivant. Les descendants n'ont qu'à se débrouiller tout seuls" conclut la mélodie. Avec cette oeuvre, Chostakovitch passait de la protestation clandestine à une première tentative de critique publique.

Un mois après le cycle *Satires,* Chostakovitch écrit son *8e Quatuor,* une œuvre particulièrement sombre et dramatique mais le Parti s'en empara en prétendant qu'elle était dédiée aux victimes de la guerre et du fascisme et l'utilisa dans ses manifestations pacifistes en racontant qu'elle avait été composée à la vue des ruines de Dresde, la ville sauvagement détruite à la fin de la guerre par les impérialistes anglo-américains. Il faudra attendre la publication en 1993 d'une lettre de Chostakovitch du 19 juillet 1960 pour qu'on réalise que l'un et l'autre sont faux. Le *8e Quatuor* a été composé dans une station thermale que Chostakovitch décrit comme un endroit rêvé pour composer. Quant au contenu, il est entièrement autobiographique, ce que l'on pouvait déjà soupçonner puisque le motif DSCH y revient 88 fois.

En septembre 1961, Chostakovitch découvre dans la *Literaturnaya Gazeta* le poème *Babi Yar* d'Evgueni Evtouchenko qui dénonce l'attitude soviétique officielle d'ignorer le martyre juif, en particulier les massacres qui ont eu lieu en Ukraine. Non seulement il le met aussitôt en musique mais afin d'en faire une symphonie entière, sa *13ᵉ*, il y ajoute d'autres poèmes d'Evtouchenko, tout aussi critiques puisqu'ils dénoncent l'incapacité des dirigeants à comprendre l'humour, le sort de la femme soviétique entre le dur travail et les files devant les magasins, enfin la peur, la peur de parler, la peur d'être dénoncé, la peur quand on frappe à la porte. Le dernier mouvement, intitulé *Carrière* évoque à travers Galilée le drame du savant qui pour protéger sa famille et faire carrière doit trahir son propre idéal, ne peut pas rester fidèle à lui-même. Cette partition devient ainsi une véritable symphonie du malheur russe.

Apprenant les intentions de Chostakovitch, le régime lui déconseille d'utiliser le texte de *Babi Yar*. Lorsque la partition est achevée, Mravinski qui devait diriger la première à la Philharmonie de Leningrad, se désiste ainsi que la basse prévue. La seconde basse à laquelle on avait fait appel, reçoit l'ordre le matin même de la création de faire un remplacement au Bolchoï, tandis que le ministre de la culture téléphone personnellement au chef d'orchestre K. Kondrachine pour qu'il renonce, mais celui-ci tint bon et la création eut lieu comme prévue avec une troisième basse. C'était la première fois en Union soviétique que des artistes avaient le dernier mot, qu'une protestation, qu'une dissidence pouvait, malgré l'opposition du régime, s'exprimer publiquement et finalement, quatorze ans plus tard, un monument fut élevé à Babi Yar, énorme, grandiose, dix-sept mètres de hauteur mais sans mention de victimes autres que soviétiques et il faudra encore attendre 16 ans et la chute du régime pour qu'un monument payé par Israël commémore aussi les 33 717 victimes juives des nazis et de leurs nombreux collaborateurs ukrainiens. Chostakovitch, compositeur non juif, est ainsi l'auteur de l'œuvre musicale commémorative de la Shoah la plus jouée dans le monde.

Après beaucoup d'hésitation et encore plus de vodka, selon Isaak Glikman, Chostakovitch avait finalement signé à la fin de l'été 1960 une demande d'adhésion au Parti. Peu après, il fait une chute et se fracture la jambe gauche. A son ami Glikman qui vient le visiter à l'hôpital, il dit ironiquement: "ce doit être Dieu qui me punit pour mon adhésion au Parti."[13] Ce n'est malheureusement que le premier d'une longue série d'accidents de santé qui vont le mener 14 fois à l'hôpital et parfois longuement, mais Chostakovitch va utiliser ses problèmes de santé pour se libérer de la plupart des obligations officielles. Son âge et sa position font qu'on n'ose plus l'attaquer. Abandonnant totalement la symphonie comme grand-messe de la musique soviétique, il écrit entre 1960 et 1975, 8 quatuors et 8 cycles vocaux dont la moitié des textes ont un caractère protestataire évident, comme les poèmes de Marina Tsvetaeva qui évoquent le destin de Pouchkine: *Le poète et le tsar* (allégorie de Chostakovitch et Staline) et *Njet, njet baraban, Non,non le tambour* qui met en scène les funérailles de Pouchkine où les premières places sont occupées non par ses amis mais par ceux qui l'ont

---

13 Dimitri Chostakovitch, *Lettres à un ami. Correspondance avec Isaac Glikman* (Paris, 1994), 162 (commentaire de la lettre de Chostakovitch du 19 juillet 1960).

persécuté, allégorie prophétique de ce que seront les funérailles de Chostakovitch à peine deux ans plus tard. On y retrouve les reproches de la *Préface des œuvres complètes* sur les honneurs dont on couvre hypocritement ceux-là mêmes que l'on a si souvent humiliés.

Dans le tout dernier cycle composé un an avant sa mort, en 1974, la *Suite sur des vers de Michel-Ange, op.145,* Chostakovitch donne aux 6e et 7e mélodies, les titres *Dante* et *À l'exilé* faisant ainsi clairement allusion au sort semblable réservé au même moment à Soljénitzyne : "On ne dira jamais de lui tout ce que l'on devrait en dire, son éclat était trop puissant pour les aveugles que nous sommes…Jamais il n'y eut d'exil plus indigne que le sien… ."

Une fois membre du Parti, Chostakovitch a bénéficié d'une influence et d'une immunité qui ont certainement contribué a rendre possible l'exécution d'oeuvres comme sa *4e Symphonie* de 1936, la *Symphonie "Babi Yar"* et, après 26 ans, son opéra *Lady Macbeth.* Déjà proposée après la mort de Staline, la reprise de celui-ci avait été jugée idéologiquement inopportune par une commission dont deux des trois membres étaient Khrennikov et Kabalevski, ceux-là mêmes dont les opéras occupaient d'abondance les scènes soviétiques. Ce n'est finalement qu'en janvier 1963 que le chef-d'oeuvre de Chostakovitch revit la scène dans une version modifiée baptisée du nom de l'héroïne, *Katerina Ismailova,* ce qui a été interprété comme une édulcoration de son œuvre pour répondre aux exigences du Parti.

Ici encore il n'en est rien, car la plupart des modifications se trouvent déjà dans la réduction pour piano de *Lady Macbeth* que Chostakovitch avait établie en 1935, donc avant sa condamnation. Qui plus est, l'extrême fin est modifiée dans un sens nettement accusateur et que l'on peut interpréter comme une allusion à son propre destin. Dans la version originale de *Lady Macbeth,* le chœur des bagnards chante à la fin de l'opéra:

> *Chemins de Sibérie, chemins creusés par les chaînes,*
> *Semés d'ossements, imbibés de sueurs et de sang,*
> *Ô steppes immenses, jours et nuits sans fin,*
> *Comme nos pensées sont tristes, nos gardes sans pitié.*

Dans la version soi-disant édulcorée de *Katerina Ismailova*, le dramatisme est, au contraire, fortement accentué par un vieux bagnard qui chante sur un rythme de marche funèbre:

> *Pourquoi avons-nous une vie si sombre et si terrible*
> *Est-ce pour connaître un tel destin que nous devons venir sur la terre?*

La version originale *Lady Macbeth* a été à ce point mythologisée comme la meilleure, parce que condamnée par Staline, que c'est la seule qui est jouée aujourd'hui sur toutes les scènes du monde. Elle est plus crue ou, si l'on veut, plus forte sur le plan érotique, ce qui convient sans doute à notre modernité ou postmodernité mais sur le plan éthique, par contre, *Katerina Ismaïlova* transforme en une protestation de caractère général les lamentations des bagnards de *Lady Macbeth*.

Quelles conclusions tirer de tout cela?

Après la chute du régime, un ami et collègue de Chostakovitch au Conservatoire de Saint-Pétersbourg, le théâtrologue Isaac Glikman a publié les 288 lettres que Chostakovitch lui avait adressées entre 1941 et 1974 et qu'il avait précieusement conservées. Dans la 233e datée du 24 septembre 1968, c'est-à-dire à la veille de son anniversaire, Chostakovitch lui avait écrit: "Demain, j'aurai 62 ans. Les gens de mon âge, à la question "Si c'était à recommencer?" répondent souvent par coquetterie: "Oui, bien sûr, il y a eu des échecs, des chagrins, mais *grosso modo,* j'aurais passé ces 62 années de la même manière." Eh bien moi, si on me posait cette question, je répondrais "Non! mille fois non!"[14]

C'est de ce "Non!" que beaucoup de partitions renvoient l'écho et parfois le cri, faisant de son œuvre un grand témoignage de résistance, c'est-à-dire de dignité, dans un siècle qui en a tant manqué.

---

14 Ibid., 244 (lettre du 24 septembre 1968 de Chostakovicth à Isaac Glikman).

Tatiana Kurysheva

MUSIC CRITICISM AS AN ART OF PERCEPTION

Musical perception is a creative act. It was made such by the lengthy history of human musical activity, over the course of which the listener was gradually transformed into a self-sufficient, autonomous figure. In the historical evolution of musical practice, the transferring of attention from the musical *activity*—the serving ritual, the ceremony, the leisure-time entertainment—to the musical *composition* has essentially changed the alignment of forces. The center of the cultural process became the *homo audiens*, the listening human being.

"In my opinion, the ability to hear is, to a considerable degree, a form of art that is no less difficult than the ability to compose music"; thus asserts Gennady Rozhdestvensky, a musician who has spent his life creating music in the concert hall.[1] In these words of the famous conductor, musical perception is presented as a special talent, with which the listener must be endowed. Among such gifted listeners are, first and foremost, music critics, ideally the most responsive and experienced of all listeners. The basic energy that drives the critic's musical thought is evaluative in its basic nature.

Notwithstanding the differences between the object of understanding, which pertains to literature, for example, or to painting, theater, or music, the process of artistic perception is the same for all forms of art. The essential commonality is manifest in what is most important: the subjective character of perception and the possibility of an infinite multitude of individual approaches. This suggests yet another commonality that is especially important for the activities of the critic; namely, that the critical utterance is necessarily *personified*.

The issue in this case is not particular to the formal side of analysis, pertaining to questions about how and by whom a text was written. Rather, it pertains to the essential side, addressing the very character of the utterance. Critical judgment is capable of convincing or arousing opposing viewpoints on the part of the reader only when it distinctly shows the personality of the speaker. Only a personalized approach—a living, direct expression of an intrinsic "point of view"—can make an impression and actively affect those to whom the statement is addressed. The writer's way of thinking, his position, his peculiarity of viewpoint and his temperament—all of these are of importance to the reader who seeks value in a critical text. More often than not, a scholarly text aspires to downgrade the individuality of the author, hiding it under the traditional "we"

---

[1] Gennady Rozhdestvensky and Alfred Schnittke, "Sem' not v mazhore i minore," *Literaturnaya gazeta* (3 March 1989): 8.

and emphasizing the objective, seemingly depersonalized character of the viewpoint presented. In contrast, the artistic, critical text always carries in itself the "I," even if this pronoun is not used overtly. Even the great Russian writer Nicolai Gogol has stated that "criticism based on high taste and a lofty mind, criticism endowed with a high degree of talent, is of equal merit with any original work of art: it shows the author under examination, but it spotlights to an even greater degree the examiner himself."[2] The act carried out by the "examiner" pertains not to creation but to comprehension. The reader is affected the *art of perception* imprinted in the critic's words. The mechanism of artistic perception, which works upon contact with an art-object, is comprised of four basic components that are indispensable and sufficient for absorption of artistic information. They are: personality traits, taste, acquired habits of perception, and attitudes.

Personality traits are the individual—innate or acquired—features of the perceiver. Here the question is one regarding the most common of human traits: namely, temperament and predilections about the world, personal ideals, and the psychological aspects of personality (for instance, about the correlation between the emotional and the rational). Here one must include the system of acquired knowledge, of both general and specific types, as well as a critic's life experience, which is directly reflected in the inner life of the human being. Bright, inimitable qualities of personality and a clearly expressed individuality in thinking and in perception constitute the most important preconditions for profound and substantial critical activities in the sphere of art. However, the practice of music criticism requires that we add a number of important details to this position. Thus, all the merits of the specific music critic do not always lead to a "fair" evaluation of an artistic phenomenon. And, one of the specific characteristics of a personal approach to any artistic entity turns out to be a *kinship of the inner worlds* of the creator and the perceiver. It is a kindred spirit that enables the perceiver's approach to the essence of a work of art. This is apparently what Robert Schumann had in mind when, in his famous article "Neue Bahnen," he stated that "in all times there existed a certain hidden union of kindred souls" (*Es waltet in jeder Zeit ein geheimes Bündnis verwandter Geister*).[3] This statement is also of much relevance to music criticism.

Such a kinship of world-view, of artistic ideals or of other inner personal qualities allows one to immerse oneself in an artwork on an intuitive, subconscious level, and to depths that are unfathomable to others. Also, the differences between psychic constitutions of people who are inwardly distant from each other are capable of setting up impassable barriers to fathoming a dissimilar artistic world. It is precisely here that we must search for the roots of "great mis-

---

2 Nikolai Gogol, "O dvizhenii zhurnal'noy literaturï v 1834/35 godu," in *Sobranie sochineniy v 6 tomakh* (Moscow, 1953), 6:106.

3 Robert Schumann. "Neue Bahnen," in *Gesammelte Schriften über Musik und Musiker* (Leipzig, 1883), 375.

understandings" that can go as far as total rejections. These sorts of misunderstandings are seen most strikingly in music criticism produced by the pens of outstanding composers. As people of acute individuality, they often cannot be reconciled toward the work their no-less-outstanding colleagues. In such situations, alien artistic worlds are rejected and repudiated, often harshly and unconditionally.

Taste, in essence, is comprised of the totality of individual traits of the perceiver, which imply a psychic mechanism already preformed. Taste manifests itself upon the absorption of artistic information, and it embraces all of the aesthetical norms that have coalesced as a result of a purposeful upbringing. To a certain extent, the question here lies in the identification of features of a characteristic social and cultural group to which similar norms of taste are kindred. However, the notion of taste is generally quite individual. And this fact leads us to consider a thing that is very important to artistic perception: *discrimination* of taste. It is possible to observe this discrimination of taste with especial lucidity in the attitudes assumed toward a single artistic phenomenon by people who are close to each other in their upbringing, education, and social milieu. Numerous facts are well known when distinctions of taste can be identified even among people persisting in the same milieu. We can recall, for example, the diametrically opposing attitudes of Robert Schumann and Felix Mendelssohn towards the creative output of Hector Berlioz—a situation that seems quite paradoxical for artists of one epoch and circle, who were like-minded with respect to so many issues and were also friends in life.

We find another interesting in a statement made by Igor Stravinsky. The great master grew up in St. Petersburg and received his musical training under the influence of Rimsky-Korsakov, one of the most important representatives of the famous St. Petersburg group of composers, the "Mighty Handful," which assumed an antagonistic position toward the music of Tchaikovsky. Nonetheless, in his "Dialogues" with Robert Craft, Stravinsky, answering a question about Tchaikovsky, unfolds a whole panorama, the essence of which is a sharp attack against the "Mighty Handful" and their views. "I protested against pictorial qualities in Russian music," Stravinsky asserted, "and stood out against those who did not notice how these pictorial, descriptive qualities are achieved through utilizing a very limited quantity of artful devices. Tchaikovsky was the greatest talent in Russia and—with the exception of Musorgsky—the most truthful."[4]

Taste is a very subtle element of perception. For a composer who has experienced the effects of critical thought on himself, taste turns out to be a filter of sorts, which enables one to develop while simultaneously preserving and even intensifying his individuality. This was the case with the young Sergei Proko-

---

4 Igor Stravinsky, *Dialogi* (Leningrad, 1971), 50.

fiev. To the scandalous reception of his Second Piano Concerto in Pavlovsk and the *Scythian Suite* in Petrograd, the composer reacted with typically shocking behavior and produced a new opera, *The Gambler*. „Emboldened by the interest aroused by the *Scythian Suite*," he wrote in his autobiography, "I chose a musical language for *The Gambler* that was the most radical I could muster."[5] All the more tragic and contrary to the nature of the innovative musician was Prokofiev's psychological breakdown in the last years of his life. After the appearance of the notorious edict of 1948 (of the Central Committee of the Communist Party of the Soviet Union), in which the music of Sergei Prokofiev, Dmitri Shostakovich, Aram Khachaturian, and many other outstanding composers was accused of "formalistic perversities" and "antidemocratic tendencies alien to the Soviet people and its artistic tastes," the composer began deliberately simplifying his musical language. In a brilliant speech about Prokofiev delivered during the 1990 opening festivities of the Prokofiev Museum in Germany, Alfred Schnittke touched upon this problem. "Any adaptation to any supposedly unified taste of a unified nation is a falsehood," Schnittke asserted. "It was merely one step towards the false official concept of a 'people's taste,' but it evoked a number of steps away from the individual taste of one of the greatest composers in Russian music history."[6]

Habits of perception are developed during the process of exposure to a form of art. As the well-known saying goes, "in order to hear, it is necessary to listen." When the question arises about the "prepared" listener, about the responsive, intelligent, "understanding" concert audience, this is precisely what is meant: an audience that possesses the skill to perceive the music presented to us—even when that music is quite complex in its inner organization. Here one must speak of the critic's professional skills. These are developed through frequent exposure to musical phenomena and aesthetical activity, by frequently coming into contact with the sounding musical entities. Among the numerous qualities developed, including a keen ear (in both acoustical and "historical" respects), architectonic sensitivity, and so forth, especially important are the qualities of artistic imagination and associative thinking. The latter refers not so much the concretization of sound or the verbal description of auditory impressions as the capability to "flare up" upon contact with artistic phenomena and to establish contact with them on many levels.

On the other hand, it is important to understand that listening skills are not absolute in their essence. They are developed within a definite artistic milieu and on a definite stylistic basis. They are historically mobile and changeable even within the framework of the life of a single person. Developed in live practice, they are capable of failing upon contact with a new musical system. For instance, the perception of the traditional music of the East may turn out to be in-

---

5   Sergei Prokofiev, *Materialï. Dokumentï. Vospominaniya* (Moscow, 1961), 154.
6   Alfred Schnittke, "Slovo o Prokofieve," *Sovetskaya Muzïka* (1990), no. 11, 3.

accessible even for a developed listener reared in the European tradition, and vice versa. The transfer of listening skills from one musical milieu into another is impossible; what is necessary is the development of a distinct set of skills within each sphere. This is demonstrated by the phenomenon of mass musical culture. For instance, many listeners to rock music, even genuine experts and connoisseurs with considerable auditory and analytic experience, are frequently incapable of perceiving spontaneously music of the Western academic tradition. Similarly, the ear that has been trained within an academic musical environment may turn out to be insensitive toward many aspects of non-traditional musical culture. Naturally, this will be reflected on such a person's critical evaluations.

Artistic attitudes are qualities that are acquired only through the process of education and musical practice. They presume an entire system of aesthetic requirements and expectations exerted on a work of art. It is precisely here that the value criteria of the listener are revealed—namely, the spiritual, aesthetic, social, and cultural needs of a personality. In comparison with personality type and the habits of artistic perception, artistic attitudes present themselves as the most "propitious." Moreover, they operate not on an intuitive level (such as taste or habits of perception) but on a rational level. The listener-critic consciously positions himself within certain artistic frames (such as, "this is art, whereas that is profanity"; or, "this is not a symphony, but merely *music for orchestra*"). The artistic attitudes of an educated music critic constitute his chief means of support during the process of attempting to cast his subjective impressions into an objective guise.

However, the prevalence of the rational principle when approaching an artwork, such that it affects the evaluation process, gives rise not only to value criteria but also *dogmas*. After all, dogmas are a priori value judgments that do not tolerate doubts or proofs. Instead, they must be accepted on faith. It is precisely in this rational part of perception that the danger of losing living, direct contact with art lies, where we risk the emergence of snobbish positions or fanatical adherence to some kind of narrow trend and rejection of musical "dissent." It is also here that that bridge is located upon which perception may suffer the pressure of a "hidden censor"—namely, our perceptions of *Zeitgeist* and other forms of ideology.

As an example, we might examine a critical text concerned with Igor Stravinsky's *Agon*. Its author, Yuri Keldïsh is a scholar and, simultaneously, a music critic of aggressively pro-Soviet ideological views. From the start, he is confined by his dogmatic attitude toward serialism in general, and toward the music of Stravinsky and Anton Webern in particular. The author's position is revealed in his second sentence; it is dogmatic and—as is typical in dogmatic cases—all proof is eschewed in favor of the simple use of harsh, degrading terminology ("degradation," "senile feebleness," "total impoverishment of inventiveness").

Indeed, it is this dogma that determines, in a priori fashion, the conclusions of the critic, which are offered to the reader in the first two sentences of the essay:

> In Stravinsky's *Agon*, only individual sonic curiosities may arouse interest in the listener, whereas in general this composition leaves the listener with the impression of oppressive monotony, inner emptiness and bereavement of any kind of artistic imagination, notwithstanding all the virtuosity of the composer's command of textural means and orchestral writing. Stravinsky's "serial period" bears witness not to enrichment and progress, but, on the other hand, continued artistic degradation, sad and senile feebleness, and a total impoverishment of inventiveness, which he vainly attempts to conceal with the false wisdom of Webern's musical teaching, which received only belated recognition from his side.[7]

The aggregate of all the aforementioned components of perception creates the premises for the individual's original and concrete judgments about art. However, let us not forget that artistic communication is something in which two sides take part: the personality of the perceiver *and* the perceived work of art itself. It is precisely the indivisible unity of these elements, the complex mechanism of interaction between the listener and the musical phenomenon, that determines the final result: the value judgment. Hence, naturally, another set of questions arises. Does the possible variety of approaches and interpretations presume that a work of art does not harbor a unified semantic meaning that the critic aspires to apprehend? Or, does it presume that this meaning exists, but that it is hidden within a multitude of variant readings, approaching or diverging from the inherent, principal meaning? And what, in general, might be regarded as a measure of validity of understanding? As we can see, these kinds of reflections are connected with the search for the *content* of musical works of art, which makes them bearers of spiritual value. Moreover, it is clear that any approach to the semantic meaning of a work of art from the perspective of evaluation is not unequivocal. Rather, it is conditioned by both the definite aim of critical presentation (whether it be informational, educational or analytical) and those evaluating criteria that support that particular aim.

In translation from the Greek, the word *criteria* refers to the measurement for the evaluation of a thing, a means for verifying its value. Value criteria, being imaginary entities, presume the existence of a certain artistic standard, an ideal model of a given type of art. According to Kant, the *ideal* and the *beautiful* are synonyms. Moreover, the concept of the *ideal* is admitted only in art. However, if artistic value has a spiritual character and its measure is beauty, then we might ask the question: What types of criteria can be identified as constituting a

---

[7] Yuri Keldïsh, "Balet 'Agon' i 'novïy etap' Stravinskogo," *Sovetskaya Muzïka* (1960), no. 8, 177.

basis for evaluation in the sphere of art and in the domain of music in particular? And, from what does the *ideal* emerge?

First, criteria for artistic value are historically conditioned, changeable and relative in their truthfulness. They reflect a type of culture of a particular epoch, and each stage of humanity's development—each generation—solves this problem for itself. The evolution of such criteria imprinted in the preserved discourses about art reflects a historical path of development of artistic and critical thought. In ancient cultures, for example, artistic evaluation was generally based upon an applied, practical approach towards art, in which, on the one hand, it was felt that a work of art should be useful, and, on the other, it was held that it should be beautiful. During the middle ages, of course, the *divine* function of music was considered of primary importance; that is, the sacred value of musical art dominated. Incidentally, this latter situation is similar to that which dominated under Soviet totalitarianism, under which official ideology advanced such qualities as "party adherence" and "communist ideals" as value measurements.

In more recent Western European musical cultures, a notion of value coalesced that has remained significant up to the present times. Its most important feature is the priority given to *uniqueness* of artistic creativity. In the ideal case, the author is regarded as a genius, the work of art as a masterpiece, and art in general as an invaluable domain, a complex reflection of humanity's spiritual being. The criterion of uniqueness seems to be the axis around which all individual approaches revolve. It is precisely from such a position, for example, that Igor Stravinsky "made short work" of Richard Strauss when he said: "I would like to administer to all the operas of Strauss any of the chastisements prepared in Purgatory for triumphant banality. Their musical material, which is cheap and poor, cannot be of interest to a musician in our day."[8] And this allows us to come to a very important conclusion: The semantic meaning of a work of art does not exist merely by itself as a constant and unchangeable entity. Moreover, such meaning cannot be regarded as a reflection of the author's desires or intentions, since what is desired and what is actually delivered are not always identical. Rather, the meaning and value of artistic phenomena can be assessed only during the process of perception. Indeed, the former are a result of the latter. That is, they exist only in *comprehension*.

As is well known, culture does exist as a petrified organism. It is heterogeneous and, most importantly, exists in a constant state of development and transformation. The process of music history is reflected not only in the evolution of composers' thoughts, which can be traced through comparison of music of various times and styles, and not only in the evolution of performance practice. It is also reflected in the evolution of ways of comprehending music, of music criticism. Thus, the concept of interpretation takes center stage.

---

8 Igor Stravinsky, *Dialogi*, 115.

In Latin, *Interpretatio* means *explanation* or *commentary*. A performer's interpretation of a musical work is a personal reading of a musical text. When interpreting, the musician embodies the composer's conception in correspondence with this personal understanding of that conception, and with his own artistic conception of that music that he grants a sonic embodiment. The listener perceives and evaluates such interpretation as one of the most important manifestations of performing art. And importantly, the performer-artist is a child of his time. Like any artistic person, he frequently perceives the trends and pulse of his time more acutely than others, but on the other hand he, in turn, also reflects that time period. The evolution of performance styles is not merely the product of the evolution of culture or the effects of new, emerging musical worlds, but also the result of a widely divergent array of individual and inimitable performing personalities.

The perception that is reflected in a critical text can also be revealed by means of interpretation—*the listener's interpretation*. It is realized in verbal images. Although the interpreter draws inspiration from other people's ideas, he endows them with new meanings, corresponding to his own system of conceptions. It is precisely such a complex sort of interpretation that reveals the most important trait of artistic perception—its subjective nature. When interpreting what he hears, each critic aspires to approach the essence of the artistic phenomenon. Moreover, the semantic multiplicity of a work of art or its performance, conditioned by its adherence to living cultural processes, can be understood only through a multiplicity of listeners' interpretations. If, according to Yuri Lotman, "the problem of content always presents itself as a problem of conversion of meaning," then the *perception* of content by the performer or the critic presents itself as a sort of *translation* into its own system of views.[9] Moreover, in the domain of art it never manifests itself as a literal translation, but always as a translation marked by the imprint of a specific personality. This accounts for the variety among assertions made by music critics.

The history of musical culture has seen many examples of changes of attitudes toward various musical phenomena. Such changes emphasize the open, inconclusive character of critical evaluations. One could bring to mind, as an example, the situation with Johann Sebastian Bach, as described by Albert Schweitzer. Two of the most influential music critics of Bach's time, Mattheson and Scheibe, criticized Bach as a composer. "Nobody, even among his many adversaries, could doubt that [Bach] was the prince of harpsichordists and the king of organists," Schweitzer observes. "But nobody, even among his friends, could understand his greatness as a composer."[10]

The interrelations of art with its epoch present a special problem. It is widely known that composers' contemporaries have nearly always found it difficult to

---

9 Yuri Lotman, *Struktura khudozhestvennogo teksta* (Moscow, 1970), 48.
10 Albert Schweitzer, *Johann Sebastian Bach* (Leipzig, 1997), 163-164.

grasp the essence of what those composers created. The genius frequently marches ahead of his contemporaries. When this is observed, it is typically remarked that the artist *surpassed his time*. But this is usually said only when glancing back at the past. Most musicians who have left their traces in history were not understood during their lifetimes. Likewise, not every professional critic has been endowed with the ability of perceiving precisely the scope of an emerging artistic personality, such as, for instance, Schumann. In his very first published article, Schumann greeted the young Chopin with the famous words, "Hats off, gentlemen, there is a genius before you!" And in his final article, he marked, with similar enthusiasm, the debut of young Brahms. On the other hand, Cesar Cui—composer, critic, and member of the "Mighty Handful"—wrote, in his report on Tchaikovsky's final examination at the St. Petersburg Conservatory, that he "does not have a single spark of talent."

Artistic criticism, reflecting as it does the thinking, world-view, and demands of its time and milieu, may indeed overlook or fail to accept a phenomenon for which a great destiny is being prepared in the future. Swiftly moving to greet the new with foresight is a characteristic only of especially gifted personalities, endowed not only with an acute ear but also with imagination and the capacity for nontrivial reaction. Thus, as far back as 1915, the outstanding Russian critic Vyacheslav Karatïgin wrote the following about Prokofiev: "A volcanic temperament, an ability to pour into old sheepskins absolutely new wine or a remarkable harmonic bouquet, the art of combining organically the orderliness of form and texture with content corresponding to the highest degree, and with a contemporary conception of sound—these are the features that distinguish Prokofiev."[11] Here the composer's musical world is disclosed to the reader through the prism of the critic's original interpretation.

Karatïgin's, in addition to their other merits, are of interest because they react to a musical *surprise*. This kind of observation is essential, since criticism presumes either to *evaluate something new* or to *reevaluate what has been heard before*, i.e., to comment from a new vantage point upon something long forgotten or temporarily lost. And a critic's attitude toward innovation gives rise to a very important problem of perception. Contact with the new and unexpected demands a special type of effort in the domain of evaluation. After all, *new texts, as structural poetics emphasizes, are texts that are "irregular" and "incorrect" from the point of view of existing rules*. From a more common cultural perspective, however, they present themselves both as useful and indispensable.[12] In an ideal situation, a critic should at least sense the latter, if not prove it. And he should search for new approaches each time.

Like a litmus test, a critic's reaction to the new shows us what sort of critic he is. In perceiving the new, the listener-critic relies upon ways of hearing that

---

11 Vyacheslav Karatïgin, *Izbrannïe stat'i* (Moscow and Leningrad, 1965), 151.
12 Yuri Lotman, "Fenomen kul'turï," in *Trudï po znakovïm sistemam* (Tartu, 1978), 3.

developed during the process by which he mastered various numerous fields of knowledge. Each time the critic comes in contact with an artistic phenomenon that demands evaluation, he "models" his criteria in a seemingly new way, applying in a unique fashion to every concrete case. This is, indeed, indispensable in all cases. In tune with the spirit of its age, music criticism must always be ready to perceive artistic changes, to interpret and evaluate new phenomena, and to polish and reconsider value judgments pronounced previously. The aforementioned Vyacheslav Karatïgin, reflecting upon the problems posed by all of these activities, emphasized the complex interrelations that comprise critical thought in its encounters with the continuously developing phenomena of artistic sound: "The first fluttering of the musical storm," he wrote in his customarily descriptive manner, "reversed the charge on the compass needle, which itself had only recently been charged; and with this, the previous system of artistic thought and critical views disintegrated."[13]

At the present time, swiftly appearing changes are taking place along the path towards comprehension of new music, giving rise to new trends in musical performance and production. There are changes of *quality*, conditioned by quests in the domains of language, style, and genre undertaken in a deliberately cultivated atmosphere of innovation and novelty. Likewise, there are also changes of *quantity* that are conditioned by the parallel existence of independent and, to a considerable degree, musical spheres that are polar opposites of one another, and which together comprise our image of the world's contemporary musical culture. The perception of these currents poses great difficulties for broad audiences and for professionals alike, with music critics among the latter. It demands constant artistic efforts, since one's approach towards many new musical phenomena requires not so much knowledge as imagination. This is especially true with regard to the music critic, who is frequently compelled to build his own framework for the interpretation of semantics before he can undertake his evaluative task. When enjoying works of art, one must always remember that musical perception constitutes a creative process in its own right, and is also intensive spiritual work.

---

13 Vyacheslav Karatïgin, "O muzikal'noy kritike," in *Kritika i muzïkoznanie* (Leningrad, 1975), 265.

Notes on Contributors

Werner Bachmann studied musicology at Halle University and earned the Ph.D. with a dissertation entitled *Die Anfänge des Streichinstrumentenspiels* (1959)—a study that has since become a standard work of organology, published in both German (Leipzig, 1964) and English (by Oxford University Press as *The Origins of Bowing*, London and New York, 1969). Bachmann served as senior editor at the Deutsche Verlag für Musik from 1956 to 1990. Among the editorial projects he undertook in that capacity was the 22-volume *Musikgeschichte in Bildern* (Leipzig, 1964-88), for which he was granted the Kunstpreis of the City of Leipzig in 1984.

Dagmāra Beitnere is a sociologist and senior researcher in the Department of Sociology and Philosophy of the Latvian Academy of Scinces. From 2005 to 2008 she was Prorector of the Jāzeps Vītols Latvian Academy of Music. She is the author of over forty articles on cultural, religious, and national (primarily Latvian) topics, a frequent lecturer on issues realted to music and sociology, and a regular contributor to *Diena*, *Mūzikas Saule*, and other Latvian periodicals.

Vizbulīte Bērziņa has published widely on Latvian music, authoring monographs on the composers Jānis Ivanovs (Riga, 1964) and Jānis Zālītis (Riga, 1977), and on music criticism in nineteenth-century Latvia (Riga, 1983). From 1964 to 1972 she was head of the music division at the weekly *Literatūra un Māksla* (Literature and Art), and she was a Researcher in the Department of Literature and Art History of the Latvian Academy of Sciences from 1972 to 1985. Her most recent book is a biography of the composer and musicologist Jēkabs Graubiņš (Riga, 2006).

Zdravko Blažeković is director of the Research Center for Music Iconography at the Graduate Center of the City University of New York. He is also executive editor of *Répertoire Internationale de Littérature Musicale* and founding editor of the multidisciplinary journal *Music in Art*. He has published widely on the musics of south-central Europe in the eighteenth and nineteenth centuries. His most recent book is *Glazba osjenjena politikom* (Zagreb, 2002), a social history of Croatian music from the seventeenth through the nineteenth centuries.

Fabio Carboni is professor of Italian philology and paleography at the University of L'Aquila. He has published widely on Italian philology and has produced critical editions of poetic works by Antonio de Thomeis, Simone de Prodenzani, and many others. He is presently editing the sixteen-volume *Incipitario della lirica italiana* (Vatican City, 1977–).

Mikus Čeže lectures on music history at the Jāzeps Vītols Latvian Academy of Music in Riga, where he specializes in nineteenth-century musics of west and central Europe. He has published widely, in German and Latvian, on the history of the Rigaer Stadttheater (1863-1918) and the Latvian National Opera, founded in 1919.

Bathia Churgin is professor emeritus of music at Bar-Ilan University, where she served as founding director of the Department of Musicology from 1970 to 1996. Her research focuses on the Classical symphony, and especially the music of Sammartini, Mozart, and Beethoven. Among her numerous publications are the *Thematic Catalogue of the Works of Giovanni Battista Sammartini* (Cambridge, MA, 1976); and critical editions of Beethoven's Third and Fourth Symphonies, forthcoming in the *Beethoven-Werke Gesamtausgabe* (Munich).

Levon Hakobian (Hakopian, Akopyan) is an Armenian musicologist and professor at the State Institute of Art in Moscow. His varied educational background (in musicology, linguistics, history, philosophy, and theology) is reflected in the breadth of his scholarship; he has published on Armenian sacred music, diverse musics of the Middle Ages, Stravinsky, and Shostakovich. His most recent book is *Music of the Soviet Age, 1917-1987* (Stockholm, 1998).

Myrna Herzog performs on the viola da gamba and is a widely published author on the history of viols, her work appearing in *Early Music*, the *Journal of the Viola da Gamba Society of America*, and other periodicals. As a soloist, she has appeared in recitals and with orchestras throughout Europe, South America, the United States, and Israel. Her recent work as a performer includes appearances with the Israel Philharmonic, where she played in the Israeli premieres of the Passions of Johann Sebastian Bach.

Dagmar Hoffmann-Axthelm is a musicologist and psychotherapist who has taught and researched at the Schola Cantorum Basiliensis since 1971 while working simultaneously as a therapist in private practice. Her research focuses primarily upon the connections between subconscious processes and musical composition. Among her numerous publications in this field is *Robert Schumann: "Glücklichsein und tiefe Einsamkeit"* (Stuttgart, 1994). A revised edition of the latter book is forthcoming in 2010.

Kevin C. Karnes is assistant professor of music history at Emory University (USA) and author of *Music, Crtiticism, and the Challenge of History: Shaping Modern Musical Thought in Late Nineteenth-Century Vienna* (Oxford and New York, 2008). He has co-edited two volumes of essays with Joachim Braun: *Baltic Musics/Baltic Musicologies: The Landscape Since 1991* (London and New York, 2009); and *Post-War Musicology in the Baltic States of Lithuania, Latvia and Estonia: A Reassessment* (Leipzig, 2008).

Alexander Knapp is a musician, musicologist, and ethnomusicologist who has performed and composed, taught and lectured, researched, broadcast, and published on Jewish music for some forty years throughout the United Kingdom, the United States, Europe, Israel, Russia, and China. Prior to his retirement in 2006, he held the post of Joe Loss Lecturer in Jewish Music at the University of London School of Oriental and African Studies.

Rachel Kollender is a musicologist and ethnomusicologist with a particular interest in Jewish music, Karaite music, women and music in Jewish societies, and European musics in the years 1935-1945. Her scholarly essays have appeared in *Asian Music*, *Orbis musicae*, and other periodicals. She is presently a lecturer at Bar-Ilan University and head of the Department of Music at the Jerusalem Girls' Teaching College.

Tatiana Kurysheva is professor of contemporary music history at the Moscow State Pyotr Il'yich Tchaikovsky Conservatory. A widely published writer on Russian music and music criticism, her most recent books are *Dialogi o muzïke pered telekameroy* (Moscow, 2006) and *Slovo o muzïke: O muzïkal'noy kritike i muzïkal'noy zhurnalistike* (Moscow, 1992).

Frans C. Lemaire, a scientist in the Belgian chemical and pharmaceutical industries, has worked as a professional record critic since 1956 and has authored three books on Russian and Jewish music, all published by Fayard in Paris: *La musique du XXe siècle en Russie et dans les anciennes républiques soviétiques* (1994), *Le destin juif et la musique – 3000 ans d'histoire* (2001), and *Le destin russe et la musique, de la Révolution à nos jours* (2005). A fourth book, *La Passion dans l'histoire et la musique. Du drame chrétien au drame juif*, is forthcoming from Fayard in 2010.

Wolfgang Ruf is professor emeritus of musicology at Martin-Luther University in Halle-Wittenberg, where he was founding director of the Musik-Institut. He is the author of *Die Rezeption von Mozarts* Le nozze di Figaro *bei den Zeitgenossen* (Wiesbaden, 1977) and *Wolfgang Amadeus Mozart und seine Zeit* (Laaber, 1995), and editor of *Lexikon Musikinstrumente* (Mannheim, 1999).

Levi Sheptovitsky is a musicologist and philosopher, lutenist and guitarist; holds a doctorate in musicology from the University of Paris-Sorbonne (2003), where he studied with Prof. Louis Jambou, and a Ph.D. from Bar-Ilan University (2004), where he studied with Prof. Joachim Braun. His essays on the history of the lute and on the Cracow Lute Tablature have appeared in *Musica Disciplina* and the *Lute News Quarterly* (UK), *Revue des études slaves* (Paris). He is presently a lecturer at the Department of Music at the Jerusalem Girls' Teaching College and at the Institute of Jewish Studies.

Amnon Shiloah is professor emeritus of musicology at Hebrew University in Jerusalem. A leading expert in Jewish and Arab musics, his many books include *Jewish Musical Traditions* (Detroit, 1992); *Music in the World of Islam* (Detroit, 1995); and *Music and Its Virtues in Islamic and Judaic Writings* (Aldershot and Burlington, VT, 2007). He has also edited *The Theory of Music in Arab Writings (c. 900-1900)* (RISM, ser. B, vol. X) (Munich, 1979; supplement, 2003).

Rūta Stanevičiūtė has been a lecturer at the Lithuanian Academy of Music and Theatre since 1991 and has taught at the Vilnius University of Management and Economics (ISM) in since 2003. She has published widely on twentieth-century music and cultural studies, and she has edited volumes on music semiotics, the phenomenon of nationality in music, and twentieth-century Lithuanian musics. She is presently preparing a collection of essays about the Lithuanian composer Vytautas Bacevičius.

Jan Stęszewski is professor emeritus of musicology at the University of Poznan and the Warsaw Academy of Sciences. His principal research interests are Polish song and Polish national musics. His many co-authored and co-edited publications include the recent volumes *Interdisciplinary Studies in Musicology* (Poznan, 1997); *Witold Lutoslawski: czlowiek i dzielo w perspektywie kultury muzycznej XX wieku* (Poznan, 1999); and *Opera polska w XIII. i XIX. wieka* (Poznan, 2000).

Mira Waner, who specializes in the musical cultures of Hellenistic, Roman, and Byzantine Palestine, received her Ph.D. at Bar-Ilan University in 2007, where she studied with Joachim Braun. Her recent work includes an essay on the musical culture of Roman-Byzantine Sepphoris, published in *Religion, Ethnicity, and Identity in Ancient Galilee*, ed. Jürgen Zangenberg, Harold W. Attridge, and Dale B. Martin (Tübingen, 2007).

Bret Werb, a musicologist, has served as curator of the Music Collection at the United States Holocaust Memorial Museum in Washington, DC, since 1992. The producer of a series of CD recordings for the museum, he also curates the museum's online exhibition "Music of the Holocaust" (http://www.ushmm.org/museum/exhibit/online/music/).

Agostino Ziino is professor of musicology at the University of Rome Tor Vergata and president of the Instituto Italiano per la Storia della Musica. He has published widely on Italian music and its sources from the Middle Ages to the eighteenth century, focusing especially on the *Ars Nova* and other musics of the trecento and early quattrocento.